The Messiahship of Jesus:

What Jews and Jewish Christians Say

N

The Messiahship of Jesus:

What Jews and Jewish Christians Say

compiled by
Arthur W. Kac

author of
The Spiritual Dilemma of the Jewish People
The Rebirth of the State of Israel

MOODY PRESS
CHICAGO

Library of Congress Cataloging in Publication Data

Main entry under title:

The Messiahship of Jesus.

Includes bibliographical references.
1. Jesus Christ—Jewish interpretations—Addresses,
essays, lectures. 2. Jesus Christ—Messiahship—Addresses, essays, lectures. 3. Converts from Judaism—
Addresses, essays, lectures. I. Kac, Arthur W.
BM620.M47   232   80-16018
ISBN 0-8024-5421-6

Printed in the United States of America

Contents

Acknowledgments   9
Introduction   11

Part One—The Changing Jewish Attitude Toward Jesus   17

- **Some Present-Day Jewish Views of Jesus   19**

1. He Became the Light of the World—*Sholem Asch   21*
2. Jesus Is a Genuine Jewish Personality—*Leo Baeck   24*
3. The Image of Jesus in Modern Judaism—
   Shalom Ben-Chorin   25
4. I Seek Him—*Reuben Brainin   27*
5. The Super Jew . . . We Shall Bring Him Back to Us—
   Constantin Brunner   30
6. I Have Found in Jesus My Great Brother—*Martin Buber   31*
7. He Was the Apex and the Acme of Jewish Teaching—
   John Cournos   32
8. The Jewishness of Jesus—*Norman Cousins   34*
9. I Am Enthralled by the Luminous Figure of the Nazarene—
   Albert Einstein   40
10. Who Can Compute All That Jesus Has Meant to Humanity?—
    Hyman G. Enelow   42
11. The Enormity of His Life . . . Speaks to Us Today—
    David Flusser   43
12. Jesus of Nazareth Is the Most Famous Name in the World—
    Solomon B. Freehof   46
13. The Jewish and the Christian Messiah—*Joseph Klausner   48*
14. The Synagogue and the Church—*Kaufmann Kohler   51*
15. The Sinners Drew Near to Him—*Claude Montefiore   53*
16. Sent of God for the Revival of Judaism—
    Isaac Joseph Poysner   55
17. Judaism—the "Eternal Fire"; Christianity—the "Eternal
    Rays"—*Franz Rosenzweig   56*
18. A Jewish Understanding of the New Testament—
    Samuel Sandmel   58
19. A Religious Bridge Between Jew and Christian—
    Hans Joachim Schoeps   60
20. Jesus the Jew—*Geza Vermes   62*

21. Without Jesus or Paul . . . the God of a Handful—
    Harris Weinstock 63
22. He Was the Jew of Jews—*Stephen S. Wise 64*
23. The Figure of Jesus on the Israeli Horizon—
    Ferdynand Zweig 66

Part Two—An Analysis of Present-Day Jewish Views of Jesus 73

- **Some Pertinent Factors in Jewish-Christian
    Understanding 75**

24. No Religion Is an Island—*Ludwig R. Dewitz 77*
25. For More Objectivity in Jewish-Christian Relations—
    Louis Goldberg 80
26. Difficulties in Jewish-Christian Dialogue—*Jakob Jocz 86*
27. Should Christians Propagate the Message of Jesus?—
    Arthur W. Kac 92
28. Bridging the Gulf—*David N. Freedman 98*

- **Anti-Semitism 107**

29. Jews and the Crucifixion: Does the Gospel Story Engender
    Hatred Toward the Jews?—*Morris Zeidman 109*
30. Ten Gentiles and One Jew—*Solomon Birnbaum 112*
31. Jew-Hatred: Its Origin and Cure—*Max I. Reich 116*

- **The Messiahship of Jesus 119**

32. Why Jews Accept Jesus and Reject the "Christ"—
    Dan B. Bravin 121
33. The Founder of Christianity—Jesus or Paul?—
    H. L. Ellison 124
34. The Era of Jewish-Christian Understanding—*Jakob Jocz 131*
35. Who Is a Jew?—*Arthur W. Kac 136*
36. Judaism and Biblical Messianism—*Max I. Reich 143*

- **The Growing Jewish Interest in Jesus 145**

37. The Jewish Quest of Jesus—*Jakob Jocz 146*
38. "The Jewishness of Jesus"—*Arthur W. Kac 152*

Part Three—Statements by Jewish Christians 157

- **The New Testament Is the Completion of the Old
    Testament 159**

39. Monotheism in the Light of the New Testament—
    Nahum Levison 161
40. Law and Grace in Biblical Perspective—*Ludwig R. Dewitz 167*
41. The New Covenant and the House of Judah—
    Heinz David Leuner 172
42. The Unity of the Bible—*David N. Freedman 178*

• **The Old Testament Roots of the Concept of the
    Incarnation 185**

43. The Invisibility of God and the Incarnation—*Jakob Jocz 187*
44. Divine Self-disclosure in the Old Testament—
    Arthur W. Kac 195

• **Messiah's Atoning Death 206**

45. The Death of Jesus—*Arthur W. Kac 207*
46. The Meaning of the Death of Messiah Jesus—
    Mark Malbert 208
47. The Mediator Element in the Messianic Hope—
    Aaron J. Kligerman 213
48. The Cross in Jewish Experience—*Nathan J. Stone 221*

• **Life After Death 227**

49. Was Jesus Raised from the Dead?—*Henry Cooper 228*
50. How People React to Death—*Arthur W. Kac 234*

• **The Mission and Message of Jesus 241**

51. Jesus the Prophet: A Critique—*Emmanuel M. Gitlin 243*
52. Was Jesus the Messiah?—*Nahum Levison 245*
53. Gaal G'ullah—*T. H. Bendor Samuel 252*
54. Bethlehem: Born Under the Law—*Harcourt Samuel 256*
55. Fundamentals of Our Holy Faith—
    Joseph Immanuel Landsman 260
56. Fulfillment in the Messiah—*Bernard B. Gair 264*
57. Jesus of Nazareth . . . the Eternal Glory of the Jewish Race—
    Benjamin Disraeli 268

• **The Return of Jesus 269**

58. The Coming Again of Jesus the Messiah: Why a Second
    Coming?—*Arthur W. Kac 271*

- **The Return of the Jews to the Land of Israel   289**

59. Non-Jewish Pioneers of Zionism—*Elias Newman   291*
60. Zionism and the State of Israel—*Jakob Jocz   303*
61. The Eschatological Significance of the Return of Israel to the Land—*Stephen B. Levinson   309*
62. The Rebuilding of Zion—*Max I. Reich   314*

- **Why Jews Become Followers of Jesus   316**

63. A Polish Talmudical Scholar—*Emmanuel S. Greenbaum   317*
64. A Great-Grandson of a German Rabbi—*Karl Jakob Hirsch   321*
65. A Hungarian Jewess—*Serena Rosengarten Kiss   325*
66. A Hungarian Rabbi—*Isaac Lichtenstein   328*
67. A British Jewess—*Lydia Montefiore   333*
68. An American Rabbi—*Max Wertheimer   336*

Conclusion   341

Awake, My People!—*Emmanuel S. Greenbaum   341*

Index   343

Acknowledgments

Much of the material in Parts Two and Three of this book appeared originally in *The Hebrew Christian* (England) and *The American Hebrew Christian* (USA.). I wish to express appreciation especially to the International Hebrew Christian Alliance (Ramsgate, England) and its American affiliate (Chicago, Illinois) for permission to use the material from their respective official publications.

I also wish to make grateful mention of Dr. George Sweeting, president of the Moody Bible Institute, and the staff of Moody Press for their very helpful cooperation in the task of publishing this work. In addition, I thank all other publishers and owners of copyrighted material for permission to use excerpts from their published works. If any acknowledgment has inadvertently been omitted, apologies are offered.

Introduction

Part One of this work presents selections culled from writings and statements by Jewish authors. Some may object that the statements selected are more or less favorable to the person of Jesus, whereas more negative statements by the same authors have been omitted. In answer, I should point out that to have cited expressions other than positive ones would have defeated the purpose of Part One, reflected in its title "The Changing Jewish Attitude Toward Jesus." That it is not the author's intent to create the false impression of radical and complete change in the Jewish position with reference to Jesus is proved by the voluminous material in Part Two, in which the various facets of the present-day Jewish attitude toward Jesus are examined and critically discussed.

The amazing change in the Jewish attitude toward Jesus that has taken place in the twentieth century may be judged from the fact that until the First World War the bulk of the Jewish people would not even mention the name of Jesus, let alone write about Him. The following statement is attributed to Dr. Isidore Singer, managing editor of the *Jewish Encyclopedia*: "The great change in Jewish thought concerning Jesus of Nazareth I cannot better illustrate than by this fact: When I was a boy, had my father, who was a very pious man, heard the name of Jesus uttered from the pulpit of our synagogue, he and every other man in the congregation would have left the building, and the Rabbi would have been dismissed at once. Now it is not strange, in many synagogues, to hear sermons preached eulogistic of this Jesus, and nobody thinks of protesting—in fact, we are all glad to claim Jesus as one of our people." Dr. Singer said, "I regard Jesus of Nazareth as a Jew of Jews, one whom all Jewish people are learning to love. His teachings have been an immense service to the world in bringing Israel's God to the knowledge of hundreds of millions of mankind."[1]

The deepening Jewish interest in the mission and message of Jesus is reflected in the mounting number of books and articles Jews have written about Him. Since Israel regained statehood, more books have been written about Jesus by Jews in the state of Israel than world Jewry had produced in all the preceding eighteen centuries. Pope Paul's visit to Jerusalem aroused considerable Jewish interest in the subject of Christianity. The New Testament became front-page news in Israel. Within one year of his visit, attendance at the Department of Christian Studies of Hebrew University almost trebled, and three new books on Jesus made their appearance. According to a more recent statement, since the establishment of the state of Israel in 1948, Israeli authors have published in Hebrew 187 books, essays, poems, and articles, and 223 other works—all about Jesus.[2]

More recently a new phenomenon in Jewish-Christian relations has become apparent with the arrangement of dialogues between Jews and Christians. In the fall of 1966, Harvard Divinity School organized a colloquium to which an equal number of Jewish and Christian scholars were invited. An indirect dialogue forms the contents of a book edited by Frank Ephraim Talmage entitled *Disputation and Dialogue,* published in 1975. About half the selections in that book were written by Christian authors.

On August 25, 1975, a dialogue between Pinchas E. Lapide, an orthodox Israeli Jew, and Hans Küng, a Roman Catholic, was broadcast over the German South West Radio. The printed English version of the dialogue appeared in a book entitled *Signposts for the Future.*[3]

December 8-10, 1975, a conference was held in New York City at which evangelical Christians and Jews read papers on various Jewish-Christian subjects. Those papers were published in a book entitled *Evangelicals and Jews in Conversation on Scripture, Theology and History.* The concluding chapter of that book states, "This was the first national conference that brought together evangelical scholars and leaders with their counterparts from the Jewish community."[4] Recommendations were made at that meeting to organize a series of such regional conferences "which would bring evangelical and Jewish leaders together in a cooperative effort to develop new resources for positive teaching and preaching that would lead to improved understanding and mutual respect, interreligious study tours to Israel, and intense dialogue in the area of theology, Scripture and history."[5]

In 1977, *Judaism* invited a number of Jewish and Christian scholars to compose articles on the interfaith movement. Those papers were published in the summer 1978 issue of *Judaism* under the title "Interfaith at Fifty," because it was the fiftieth anniversary of the annual meetings of the National Conference of Christians and Jews, which began in 1928. The participants were asked to write on various aspects of the interfaith movement.

Let us now consider in greater depth the above-mentioned Küng-Lapide dialogue. Hans Küng is professor of dogmatic and ecumenical theology and director of the Institute for Ecumenical Research at the University of Tübingen, Germany. Pinchas E. Lapide emigrated to Palestine in 1938. In World War II he was an officer in the Jewish Brigade of the British army. He served as a diplomat in the Israeli Foreign Office from 1965 to 1971. He holds the B.A. and M.A. degrees from Hebrew University and a Ph.D. degree from the Martin Buber Institute for Judaic Studies at Cologne University.

At the beginning of their dialogue, Professor Küng stated that Christians are exploring at the present time the Jewish roots of Christianity. He asked Dr. Lapide whether Jews, in turn, are seeking to gain a better understanding of the New Testament.* In his reply Dr. Lapide said: "What I find particularly new in our time, in the last ten or fifteen years, is our mutual curiosity. Just as Christianity, or—better—Christendom has never been so inquisitive, so anxious to learn something about its own Jewish roots, so too in the country of Israel there is emerging an almost equal curiosity to learn more about its Christian branches. And the twenty-nine Hebrew books on Jesus published in recent years, which I analyzed in my book *Is This Not Joseph's Son?*, have in common a sympathy and a love for the Nazarene which would have been impossible at any other time during the past eighteen hundred years."[6]

Professor Küng also remarked, "Up to now Christians and Jews have really always talked only about generalities, and in this respect we must simply state that, if we talk merely in a general way about Christians and Jews and not about Jesus of Nazareth, we are overlooking precisely the real point of the controversy. . . . What is it on the whole that distinguishes Christians from Jews, that has distinguished them from the beginning? . . . The distinguishing feature is that Jesus as the Christ [Messiah] is rejected by the Jews and recognized by the Christians."[7]

Dr. Lapide stressed the fact that the real stumbling block as far as the Jews are concerned is the Christian view of the death and resurrection of Jesus. "What really separate us are forty-eight hours from the afternoon of the first Good Friday onward. That means just two days, but they are of course the decisive days on which more or less the whole of Christology rests."[8]

Toward the conclusion of the dialogue, Dr. Lapide made the following deeply significant observations: "Up to a short time ago I thought that anything like a self-abasement of God—*Kenosis*—and incarnation in the Christian sense were alien to Judaism.[9] To my astonishment, I have learned in the meantime that there were germinal traces of both ideas among marginal groups in Judaism as early as the first century before Christ, and still more in the first and second Christian centuries, so that even these things entered later Christianity not from Hellenism, but in fact from certain Jewish circles. With the utmost seriousness, as an orthodox Jew, I must say that I cannot accept what you call resurrection, *kenosis,* and *apokatastasis*[10] since this is not suggested by our Jewish experience of God. But neither can I deny it, for who am I as a devout Jew to define *a priori* God's saving action? . . . I don't *know*. That is all I can say, but unlike the Jewish-Christian controversialists of the last 1800 years, when people turned more and more blatantly from opponents into enemies—I can answer today with a Biblical and humble "I do not know."[11]

"Professor Küng," Dr. Lapide said, "what unites us is everything that can be known and investigated with the tools of scholarship about this Jesus. What divide us are the things that divide not only Jews from Christians, but also knowledge from faith. One thing I know for certain: that faith in this Christ has given millions of Christians a better life and an easier death, and I would be the last [person] to disturb their faith even if I could . . . . What I can and will say is this: you are waiting for the parousia;[12] with you, too, the fullness of redemption is still in the future; I await its coming, but the second coming is also a coming. If the Messiah comes and then turns out to be Jesus of Nazareth, I would say that I do not know of any Jew in this world who would have anything against it."[13]

Concluding the dialogue, Dr. Lapide said this to Professor Küng: "After living and praying *against* one another for nearly 2000 years, let us both [Jews and Christians] study with one another . . . and let us then see where God will further guide us both."[14]

Knowledgeable and fair-minded Jews and Christians have remarked that no faith can be fully understood by any person who is an outsider to that particular faith. That would suggest that, notwithstanding their best intentions, Jews and Christians would find it difficult to gain a fair knowledge of each other's faith. If that is true, then Jewish Christians are uniquely qualified to interpret both the Jewish and the Christian faiths, since they are insiders in both Judaism and Christianity. That is exactly what Jewish Christians are seeking to do in the last two parts of this work.

Notes

1. This statement was contained in a letter to Dr. I. K. Funk, March 25, 1901 and is quoted by E. S. Greenbaum in *The Jewish Attitude Toward Christ* (Philadelphia: Presby. Bd. of Pub., 1920), p. 10.
2. "How Jews See Jesus," *Newsweek*, 18 April 1977, p. 88.
3. Hans Küng, *Signposts for the Future*, trans. Edward Quinn (Garden City, N.Y.: Doubleday 1977, 1978).
4. Mark H. Tanenbaum, Marvin R. Wilson, and A. James Rudin, eds., *Evangelicals and Jews in Conversation on Scripture, Theology and History* (Grand Rapids: Baker, 1977), p. 311.
5. Ibid., p. 313.
6. Küng, p. 71.
7. Ibid., pp. 68-69.
8. Ibid., p. 72.
9. *Kenosis* and *Incarnation*, two New Testament concepts with reference to the Messiah. The term *incarnation* signifies that, in Jesus, God became man in fulfillment of Old Testament ideas culminating in the prophetic statement in Isaiah 7:14, where the Messianic Prince is referred to as *Immanuel* ("God with us"). In the New Testament that concept is expressed in the following statement in the gospel of John: "And the Word became flesh, and dwelt among us" (John 1:14, NASB).

   Kenosis, a Greek word meaning "emptying." That theological truth is presented in the following passage in the apostle Paul's letter to the Philippian believers. "Although He [Messiah Jesus] existed in the form of God, [He] did not regard equality with God a thing to be grasped, but *emptied* Himself, taking the form of a bond-servant, and being made in the likeness of men. And being found in appearance as a man, He humbled Himself by becoming obedient to the point of death, even death on a cross" (Phil. 2:6-8, NASB, italics added).

   The use of the term *kenosis* ("emptying") in that passage teaches that, though the Messiah had a heavenly preexistence, His becoming a human being implied that "He did not regard His being on equal conditions of glory and majesty with God as a prize and treasure to be held fast" (E. H. Gifford, *The Incarnation* [London: Longmans, Green, 1897], p. 71). The phrase "emptied Himself" "indicates a true and complete self-surrender." Paul's statement "is best illuminated when we recognize that *emptied himself . . . . unto death* (verses 7, 8) is a literal rendering of the statement in Isaiah 53:12, that the [Suffering] Servant *poured out his soul to death.*" The term *kenosis* thus signifies "utter self-denial" on the part of Messiah Jesus (H. C. Hewlett, "The Letter to the Philippians," in *A New Testament Commentary*, ed. C. D. Howley, F. F. Bruce, and H. L. Ellison [Grand Rapids: Zondervan, 1969], pp. 474-5.)

   "Incarnation," therefore, tells us what God did—"kenosis," what the Messiah did—for man's salvation.

10. *Apokatastasis,* a Greek word meaning "restitution," is a New Testament concept found in a statement by the apostle Simon Peter in Acts 3:21 to the effect that upon His return Messiah Jesus will "establish a new order free from evil and sin." It will involve the redemption of nature, touched upon by the apostle Paul (Romans 8:18-23), and "the perfecting of human society when God's will is done on earth as it is in heaven" (quotations from Charles F. Pfeiffer and Everett F. Harrison, eds., *The Wycliffe Bible Commentary* [Chicago: Moody, 1962], p. 1130.) There is no doubt that Peter and Paul derived their ideas, in part at least, from *The Old Testament* (e.g., Isaiah 11:6-9).

11. Küng, p. 85.

12. *Parousia,* the second coming of Messiah Jesus.

13. Küng, p. 86.

14. Küng, p. 87.

Part One

The Changing Jewish Attitude Toward Jesus

Some Present-Day Jewish Views of Jesus

*And Jesus went out, along with His disciples, to the villages of
Caesarea Philippi; and on the way He questioned His disciples,
saying to them, "Who do people say that I am?"*

Mark 8:27 (NASB)

He Became the Light of the World—*Sholem Asch*   21
Jesus Is a Genuine Jewish Personality—*Leo Baeck*   24
The Image of Jesus in Modern Judaism—
    Shalom Ben-Chorin   25
I Seek Him—*Reuben Brainin*   27
The Super Jew—We Shall Bring Him Back to Us—
    Constantin Brunner   30
I Have Found in Jesus My Great Brother—*Martin Buber*   31
He Was the Apex and the Acme of Jewish Teaching
    John Cournos   32
The Jewishness of Jesus—*Norman Cousins*   34
I Am Enthralled by the Luminous Figure of the Nazarene—
    Albert Einstein   40
Who Can Compute All That Jesus Has Meant to Humanity?—
    Hyman G. Enelow   42
The Enormity of His Life . . . Speaks to Us Today—
    David Flusser   43
Jesus of Nazareth Is the Most Famous Name in the
    World—*Solomon B. Freehof*   46
The Jewish and the Christian Messiah—*Joseph Klausner*   48
The Synagogue and the Church—*Kaufmann Kohler*   51
The Sinners Drew Near to Him—*Claude Montefiore*   53
Sent of God for the Revival of Judaism—
    Isaac Joseph Poysner   55
Judaism—the "Eternal Fire"; Christianity—the
    "Eternal Rays"—*Franz Rosenzweig*   56
A Jewish Understanding of the New Testament—
    Samuel Sandmel   58
A Religious Bridge Between Jew and Christian—
    Hans Joachim Schoeps   60

Jesus the Jew—*Geza Vermes*   62

Without Jesus or Paul . . . the God of a Handful—
   Harris Weinstock   63

He Was the Jew of Jews—*Stephen S. Wise*   64

The Figure of Jesus on the Israeli Horizon—
   Ferdynand Zweig   66

1 He Became the Light of the World

*Born in Poland in 1880, **Sholem Asch** was one of the best known Jewish writers in his day. He wrote in Yiddish, the language of East European Jewry, which until the Second World War was used by the bulk of the Jewish people. In 1910 he settled in the United States, where he later wrote historical novels dealing with New Testament themes. Asch was catapulted into world prominence with the appearance of his* Nazarene *in 1939. That great novel was followed by several others, each revolving around the person of Jesus of Nazareth and other New Testament characters. His* Apostle *came out in 1943 and* Mary *in 1949. Asch died in England in 1957, having produced more than fifty novels, plays, and short stories. The following excerpts are from his book* One Destiny.*

A little less than two thousand years ago, there came into our world among the Jewish people and to it a personage who gave substance to the illusion perceived by our fathers in their dream. Just as water fills up the hollowness of the ocean, so did he fill the empty world with the spirit of the one living God. No one before him and no one after him has bound our world with the fetters of law, of justice, and of love, and brought it to the feet of the one living Almighty God as effectively as did this personage who came to an Israelite house in Nazareth in Galilee—and this he did, not by the might of the sword, of fire and steel, like the lawgivers of other nations, but by the power of his mighty spirit and of his teachings. He, as no one else before him, raised our world from "the void and nothingness" in which it kept losing its way and bound it with strong ties of faith to the known goal, the predetermined commandment of an almighty throne so as to become a part of the great, complete, everlasting scheme of things. He, as no other, raised man from his probationary state as a beast, from his dumb, blind and senseless existence, gave him a goal and a purpose and made him a part of the divine. He, as no other, works in the human consciousness like a second, higher nature, and leaves man no rest in

*Sholem Asch, *One Destiny* (New York: Putnam's, 1945). The excerpts quoted are reprinted by permission of the Estate of Sholem Asch.

his animal state, wakens him, calls him, raises him, and inspires him to the noblest deeds and sacrifices. He, as no other, stands before our eyes as an example and a warning—both in his divine form and in his human one—and demands of us, harries us, prods us to follow his example and carry out his teachings. . . . No one but he sheds about himself such an aura of moral power, which, with a divine touch, has molded our world and our character: and no one's strength but his own has reached into our own time, being the most potent influence in our everyday lives, inspiring us to goodness and exalted things, being the measure and scale for our deeds at every hour and every minute. . . .[1]

I, as a Jew, whose every move is bound up with the God of Israel, want to know nothing of any other historical wonder, of any other faith, save only the wonder and faith which radiate from the God of Israel. The wonder is revealed to me in two ways: first, the miracle of the preservation of Israel, second, the miracle of the spread of the Judaeo-Christian idea in the pagan world. . . . The preservation of Israel and the preservation of the Nazarene are one phenomenon. They depend on each other. The stream must run dry when the spring becomes clogged, and Christianity would become petrified if the Jews, God forbid, should cease to exist. And just as the spring loses its value, becomes spoiled and moldy when it has lost its mission and does not water the stream, so would Jewry itself become petrified, barren, and dry if there were no Christendom to fructify it. Without Christendom, Jews would become a second tribe of Samaritans. The two are one.[2]

Turning in chapter 5 to events associated with the Nazi period, Asch says:

Quite aside from the fact that of all international movements, including the socialist, Christian faiths of all creeds have best withstood the crucial test of resistance against Hitlerite paganism, Christianity also distinguished itself, in the particular of rescuing Jewish children, by the highest degree of self-sacrifice. It may be stated without exaggeration that almost the entire remnant of Israel which was found in the liberated countries—no matter how small its number—has the Christians to thank for its preservation, Christians who, by performing this action, placed their own lives in danger.[3]

Contrasting the conduct of Christians with that of Muslims in the Nazi period, Asch says:

Note the difference in attitude toward us, in the hour of our greatest trial, between the Christian believers and the Mohammedans. Lulled by the opinion often expressed by learned Jews, who lived in Mohammedan lands, that the Mohammedan religion is nearer to us, through the monotheistic principle which it embraces, than Christianity, many Jews maintain to this day that our people may find a more sympathetic understanding in Mohammedan countries than in Christian lands, and that the Mohammedan is nearer to us because of his Semitic origin. They have entirely forgotten the fact that the lack of the Messianic principle in the Mohammedan makes him an incomprehensible stranger to us. . . .

When Rommel together with his barbarous hordes of Nazis stood at the gates of Alexandria and the danger was great that they might soil the Holy Land with their unclean fingers, the Arabs in Palestine came out of their burrows and openly began to sharpen their knives in preparation for the cutting of Jewish throats as soon as the

Germans should have crossed the borders. They parceled out Jewish lands among themselves ahead of time—those lands which had been recovered by the Jews with the expenditure of so much sweat and toil, and which the Arab representative in Berlin, according to the terms of the agreement with Hitler, was to get in return for Arab aid to the Nazis. Impudently these Arabs appeared in Jewish settlements and worked with chalk the houses, stalls, gardens, and factories which they had betimes distributed among themselves. They also took upon themselves prospectively a little bit of the work of Hitler's bandits—to slaughter Jewish fathers, mothers, children, and to divide up the daughters among their own harems.[4]

In an interview with Frank S. Mead, Asch was asked why he had been writing so much on New Testament themes. He answered:

I couldn't help writing on Jesus. Since I first met Him, He has held my mind and heart. I grew up, you know, on the border of Poland and Russia, which wasn't exactly the finest place in the world for a Jew to sit down and write a life of Jesus Christ; yet even through those years, the hope of doing just that fascinated me. I floundered a bit, at first; I was seeking that something for which so many of us search—that surety, that faith, that spiritual content in my living which would bring me peace and through which I might help bring some peace to others. I found it in the Nazarene.

For Jesus Christ to me is the outstanding personality of all time, all history, both as Son of God and as Son of Man. Everything He ever said or did has value for us today, and that is something you can say of no other man, alive or dead. No other teacher—Jewish, Christian, Buddhist, Mohammedan—is still a teacher whose teaching is such a guidepost for the world we live in. Yes, it is true that Buddha influenced millions, but it is also true that only about—shall we say—five percent of Buddha's teaching has basic value for the twentieth century. One or another of these teachers may have something basic for an Oriental, or an Arab, or an Occidental, depending upon where his teaching is best preserved: but every act and word of Jesus has value for all of us, wherever we are. He became the Light of the world. Why shouldn't I, a Jew, be proud of it?[5]

Notes

1. Ibid., pp. 5-6.
2. Ibid., pp. 8-9.
3. Ibid., p. 77.
4. Ibid., pp. 79, 81.
5. Frank S. Mead, "An Interview with Sholem Asch," *The Christian Herald*, January 1944. Used by permission of *Christian Herald Magazine*.

2 Jesus Is a Genuine Jewish Personality

*Prominent Jewish theologian **Leo Baeck** was born in Germany. He became rabbi in 1897, and was for many years the acknowledged religious leader of German Jewry. During the Nazi period he acted as the representative of German Jews. Baeck was sent to a concentration camp in 1943. He miraculously survived, and in 1946 he settled in England. He is the author of* The Essence of Judaism.

The following statement is from Dr. Baeck's response to Adolf Harnack's work The Essence of Christianity.*

Most portrayers of the life of Jesus neglect to point out that Jesus is in every characteristic a genuinely Jewish character, that a man like him could have grown only in the soil of Judaism, only there and nowhere else. Jesus is a genuine Jewish personality, all his struggles and works, his bearing and feeling, his speech and silence, bear the stamp of a Jewish style, the mark of Jewish idealism, of the best that was and is in Judaism, but which then existed only in Judaism. He was a Jew among Jews; from no other people could a man like him have come forth, and in no other people could a man like him work; in no other people could he have found the apostles who believed in him.[6]

*Leo Baeck, Harnack Vorlesungen über das Wesen des Christentums (Breslau: n.p., 1902). The above excerpt is quoted by Shalom Ben-Chorin in "The Image of Jesus in Modern Judaism," *Journal of Ecumenical Studies* 11, no. 3 (Summer 1974):408.

3 The Image of Jesus in Modern Judaism

Shalom Ben-Chorin was born in Germany and educated in German schools. In 1935 he emigrated to Israel. A well-known journalist and author, he has written in German three books on New Testament themes: Bruder Jesus *(Brother Jesus, 1967);* Paulus *(Paul, 1970); and Mutter Mirjam (Mother Mary, 1971).*

In an article under the above title, Ben-Chorin assembled in condensed form a number of modern Jewish pronouncements on the subject of Jesus. His work is one of the most complete reviews of present-day Jewish writings on the person of Jesus. The following is an introduction to the main body of his article.*

A systematic study of Jewish history has resulted in a renewed interest in the "Jewish Jesus" and in "bringing Jesus home."

Medieval Judaism was generally silent about Jesus due to a fear of introducing heretical ideas into Judaism, and due to possible Christian reprisals. The influential *Toledoth Yeshu,* an anti-Jewish patchwork of stories, was an exception. The *Toledoth* grew out of anti-Jewish persecutions; it represents Jesus as a Jew, although an apostate Jew.

The modern emancipation of the Jews led to a less hostile treatment of Jesus. In their writings Salvador, Hirsch, Geiger, and Graetz chose to situate Jesus in a distinctive Jewish milieu. More recently, Klausner proved that any understanding of Jesus' life demanded a knowledge of Jewish sources. Eisler reintroduced the question of Jesus' role in the anti-Roman movements of his time, a theme reworked by Carmichael. Montefiore, Baeck, Aron, Isaac, Schoeps, Flusser, and, in a special way, Buber all approach Jesus from within the Judaism of his time.

Whether one examines the historians or the representatives of belles lettres, one discovers that the modern Jewish image of Jesus is far more positive than the medieval image. Not only is the historicity of Jesus rarely denied, but much of the gospel material (particularly the synoptics) is readily accepted. Jesus' preaching and

*Shalom Ben-Chorin, "The Image of Jesus in Modern Judaism," *Journal of Ecumenical Studies* 11, no. 3 (Summer 1974):401, 429). This excerpt is reprinted by permission.

parables and prayers, his nationalism, and the tragedy of his life and death are seen to be comprehensible only in a Jewish context. More problematic for Jews are the gospel accounts of Jesus' birth and death and resurrection, as well as the special consciousness and power attributed to him. For the author, Jesus is neither God or Messias, but the prodigal son at last come home to his family.

At the close of his long essay, Ben-Chorin makes the following statement:

This returned Jesus is for us as Buber expressed it, "a great brother": no God and not the Messias. But to the opinion of Maimonides on Jesus, which glowed through dark medieval Judaism, we may assent; "Jesus was a preparer of the way for the King Messias."

4 I Seek Him

Reuben Brainin was born in White Russia and studied in the universities of Vienna and Berlin. He then moved to America where he became editor of the Hebrew journal Hatoren. *An outstanding journalist, Brainin was also a member of the editorial staff of the New York Yiddish daily* Der Tog. *His article "I Seek Him" appeared in* Der Tog *in 1926.* *

Over oceans, over distant lands, in the East and in the West, I wandered and sought Him.

I sought Him with seven lights, the expected-One, the hoped-for, the great Man-Jew, the central personality of our nation. He, the romantic, the mystic, the enchanting personality whom I have sought with life-long intensity of yearning. I sought ceaselessly—and did not find Him.

Again and again I sought: I did not lose my hope, because it surely cannot be that our generation is so orphaned.

I sought the personality who embodies and symbolizes in Himself the universal Jewish soul, the Jewish personality, who embodies in Himself our great past and our yet more glorious future.

I sought Him in the East, and in the West, amongst all parties, amongst the upper as well as the lower stratas, to the right and to the left.

I stretched forth my spirit, the "antenna of my soul," in all directions. But the expected, the central, the redeeming Jewish personality did not reveal itself to me.

Perhaps I am short-sighted; no doubt I sought wrongly; I did not properly conceive. Possibly I brushed past Him—that yearned-for personality, and failed to recognize Him. No doubt the trouble lay in me: too critical, perhaps too analytical, too full of doubt—too great are my demands. . . .

Yet I cease not to ask deep in my soul, "Where art Thou, Thou, the great, the central, the redeeming personality? Thou who hast the God-power to enchant us all and to draw everything which is yet spiritual, ethical, aesthetic, beautiful and good in our nation to Thyself, and to unite us in one great flame, in one great redeeming deed—where art Thou?

Where art Thou, Thou, the noble, the mighty Jewish personality who hast ab-

*Reuben Brainin, "I Seek Him," *Der Tog, 23 December 1926. The above English translation by Henry Einspruch was published in *The Mediator* 1, no. 2 (March 1928):2-3 and is used by permission of The Lederer Foundation.

sorbed into Thyself the eternal light hidden in our spirit-treasures, those bright sparks of the universal soul? Thou from whom streams forth wisdom, comfort and hope, goodness and exaltation—where art Thou, great Brother, where art Thou, great Teacher, Leader and Fulfiller—Thou whom I have sought all my life long?

Ordinary and intelligent Jews, clever, and overly-clever Jews—of these we have enough, yea, more than enough: I came across them in all countries. We are also well represented by Jews of genius in the scientific, artistic and literary domains, Jews who have brought about revolutions, who have left their mark on world-politics, science and the arts—I met all these in my wanderings through the world.

But where is the central Jewish figure, *the* Jewish greatness? Where is the prophetic, the guiding, the redeeming Jewish personality? That personality who absorbed in Himself the thirst, the urge for redemption of the whole creation, of all generations?

Where is that personality who symbolizes the historic conscience of our people? I seek Him still.

I seek the great Jewish personality, the eagle-nature, free of every vestige of prejudice, not bound to any temporary party or social wing, the cosmological Jewish personality who is full of righteousness. I seek the highest righteousness, filled with truth, to whom every Jewish soul is more precious than His own life.

I seek not the superman, the Nietzschean superman—not him do I seek. Him we do not need. He cannot be the redeeming spirit for us. The superman, if such there be, can also be a Lucifer, a Mephistophiles, a catastrophe for us.

I seek that great Jew who grew out of the people and with the people, suffered with it, and for it—grew up with the people—and above it. Is great, and knows not that He is great. Is radiant, and knows not that He is full of light and illuminating power. I seek to discover Him who has not discovered Himself.

I seek not the *Nazir*, the sanctimonious, the solitary, the exclusive: I seek not the holy, the living-dead man, I seek the Man-Jew, Him, who can tell the truth, the whole truth, the purest truth: tell the truth to right and left, the truth to those who sit above and to those who sit below—even the deepest depths.

I seek Him who can liberate us from our littleness and from narrow politics, who can, with one sweep, lift us and tear us free of the shocking, impure social atmosphere, from spirit-deadening party machinations and the tyranny which lowers and demoralizes.

I keep on seeking the great Jewish prophetic personality, who is able to draw to Himself the Jewish youth, light in their young hearts a holy flame, vivify their fantasy, their vision-treasures . . .

We all seek, we all expect this Jewish personality.

Our hope is not yet lost.

The Hebrew Christian Semitic scholar Paul Levertoff states that he had been in correspondence with Mr. Brainin for a couple of years. Dr. Levertoff asserts that one can hardly doubt that the person Brainin was writing about was Jesus.[1]

Notes

1. Paul Levertoff, "Jewish Opinions About Jesus," *Der Weg* (Warsaw) 7, no. 1 (January-February 1933):8.

5 The Super-Jew. . . . We Shall Bring Him Back to Us

Constantin Brunner (1862-1937) was a German Jewish philosopher whose thought is related to Spinoza's philosophical system. He looked upon Jesus as the representative of pure Judaism. Brunner is the author of several books, including Der Judenhass und Die Juden *from which the following excerpt is taken.**

It is amazing how many Jews write about Jews and Judaism while ignoring the super-Jew and super-Judaism. I refer to Jesus the Messiah and to Christianity. . . . What happened here? Is it only the Jew who is incapable of seeing and hearing all that others see and hear? Are the Jews stricken with blindness and deafness as regards Messiah Jesus, so that to them alone he has nothing to say? . . . Understand, then, what we shall do: We shall bring him back to us. Messiah Jesus is not dead for us—for us he has not yet lived: and he will not slay us, he will make us alive again. His profound and holy words, and all that is true and heart-appealing in the New Testament, must from now on be heard in our synagogues and taught to our children, in order that the wrong we had committed may be made good, the curse turned into a blessing, and that he at last may find us who has always been seeking after us.

*Constantin Brunner, *Der Judenhass und Die Juden* (Berlin: Oesterheld, 1918), p. *34*. The above quotation, translated by J. I. Landsman, appeared in *Der Weg* 3, no. 1 (January-February 1929):7.

6 I Have Found in Jesus My Great Brother

Martin Buber (1878-1965) was born in Vienna and educated in German universities. He was professor of social philosophy at the Hebrew University from 1938 to 1951. Buber wrote several books. The following are excerpts from two of his writings.*

It is a peculiar manifestation of our exile-psychology that we permitted, and even aided in, the deletion of New Testament Messianism, that meaningful offshoot of our spiritual history. It was in a Jewish land, that this spiritual revolution was kindled; and Jews were those who had spread it all over the land. . . . We must overcome the superstitious fear which we harbor about the Messianic movement of Jesus, and we must place this movement where it belongs, namely, in the spiritual history of Judaism.

From my youth onwards I have found in Jesus my great brother. That Christianity has regarded and does regard him as God and Savior has always appeared to me a fact of the highest importance which, for his sake and my own, I must endeavor to understand. . . . My own fraternally open relationship to him has grown ever stronger and clearer, and today I see him more strongly and clearly than ever before. I am more than ever certain that a great place belongs to him in Israel's history of faith and that this place cannot be described by any of the usual categories.

*The first paragraph, from "Three Talks on Judaism," is translated by Paul Levertoff in "Jewish Opinions About Jesus," *Der Weg* 7, no. 1 (January-February 1933):8. The second paragraph is excerpted from Martin Buber, *Two Types of Faith*, trans. Norman P. Goldhawk (Macmillan, 1940; reprint, Harper Torchbook ed., New York: Harper, 1961), pp. 12-13, and is reprinted with permission of Macmillan Publishing Co., Inc. from *Two Types of Faith* by Martin Buber. Copyright 1952 by Macmillan Co., Inc.

7 He Was the Apex and the Acme of Jewish Teaching

John Cournos (1881-1966) was born in Russia. He was ten years old when he came to America. In 1912 he settled in London, where he became a free-lance writer for English periodicals. Cournos wrote novels and translated Russian writings into English.* He regarded Jesus as the leading Jewish prophet.

The age we live in is perhaps more conducive to a Jewish acceptance of Jesus than any previous age. And more than in any previous age is there a need for a recognition of Jesus and of all those fundamental values of which Jesus is a symbol. . . . The evils of our time, the evils attendant upon our post-war world, of which indeed the War [World War I] itself was symptomatic, have been—it cannot be denied—directly due to Christendom's failure to live up to the religion it has been professing.

Yet, to be fair, it must be admitted that Christianity, or the measure that Christianity still retained of the spirit of Jesus, has acted as the only check on what might have otherwise been a wholly unrestrained barbarism.

If there were no Jesus . . . Jesus would have to be invented. Without him, without all he stands for, Western humanity would be wholly bankrupt. The spirit of Jesus needs greater diffusion today than ever before: it is the only dyke against the tides of the Antichrist trinity of Hitler, Stalin, and Mussolini. . . .

As far as the Jew is concerned, a little reason should counsel the most recalcitrant Israelite that at the worst Christianity is a Jewish heresy, and that a Jewish heresy is better than a deliberately anti-Jewish Satanism.

There is a more fundamental, a more dignified reason for the Jewish reclamation of Jesus. A very simple, a very honest reason. And that is that Jesus was a Jew—the best of Jews. . . .

Jesus was not only a Jew. He was the apex and the acme of Jewish teaching, which began with Moses and ran the entire evolving gamut of kings, teachers, prophets, and rabbis—David and Isaiah and Daniel and Hillel—until their pith and essence was crystallized in this greatest of all Jews. . . .

For a Jew, therefore, to forget that Jesus was a Jew, and to deny him, is to forget

*The quoted extract is from John Cournos, *An Open Letter to Jews and Christians* (New York: Oxford U. Press, 1938), pp. 10-13, 25, 31.

and to deny all the Jewish teaching that was before Jesus: it is to reject the Jewish heritage, to betray what was best in Israel. For a Christian to forget that Jesus was a Jew is to deny Christianity itself. . . .

It may seem an even greater wonder that now, after a lapse of nearly fifty years, I should feel the strongest compulsion to step boldly out into the open and affirm with a deep conviction which has been slowly and inevitably growing upon me—until silence is out of the question—that the time has come, is indeed ripe, for the Jews to reclaim Jesus. . . .

I am not alone, however, in arriving at the inevitable conclusion voiced throughout this book. For I know a number of Jews who believe as I do, who believe it is time that the Jews reclaimed Jesus, and that it is desirable that they should do so. Some of them hesitate to speak, lest their own people disclaim them. A great Jewish novelist, whose name for a similar reason I cannot divulge, said to me a year or two ago: "The Jews should come to terms with Christianity." These persons, it will be said, are intellectuals and do not represent Jewry. I reject this notion, because, to take three examples among them, one is a novelist, whose books are about Jews and read by Jews; one is an educator, whose work is among Jews and who knows Jews exceptionally well; and one is a scholar interested in Jewish Sunday schools—if he were permitted by the elders he would include among his readings of "gems" of Jewish literature the Sermon on the Mount.

8 The Jewishness of Jesus

*Norman Cousins (b. 1912) is a graduate of Teachers
College of Columbia University. He held the position of
executive editor of the Saturday Review from 1940 to 1942,
and the position of editor from 1942 to 1971, and from 1973
to 1977. He has been the recipient of numerous awards,
including the United Nations Peace Medal, and has written
many articles and books.**

Christianity and Judaism share one of the great reluctances of history. Both are reluctant to live openly and fully with the fact that Jesus was a Jew. Christian theology is incomplete; it has never been able to explain to itself why Jesus should have come out of Judaism. And Judaism has tended to dwell outside the full significance of the Jewishness of Jesus and his vast spiritual role in human history.

The reasons behind the reluctance are, of course, different. So are the effects. In any case, it seems reasonable to suggest that the reluctance be reexamined and restudied. For if the question is subjected to the full play of creative inquiry, it is conceivable that a new relationship between Christian and Jew could emerge. Not a common faith, but an important new amity and concurrence; possibly even a sense of spiritual community.

We proceed, therefore, to the reexamination.

The earliest Christians knew neither awkwardness nor reticence over the fact that Jesus was a Jew. Most, if not all, were Jews themselves. Christianity to them was not a faith apart from Judaism but an assertion of it. They never claimed to be the originators of a new religion; they were summoning men to Jesus' vision of moral excellence. They called for a return to the great simplicities of essential Judaism, for an awareness of the reality of Biblical prophecy, and for a response to the sense of God that lay deep within man. They were critical of the nature of the existing Temple and of temple worship. They turned away from sacrifice and from the exercise of the religious spirit through elaborate ritual. And they reaffirmed the fundamentals of Judaism: the oneness of God, the omniscience of God, the justness of God, and the reality of God's total command of the universe and history, now and forevermore. The purpose they saw in Jesus was to reawaken and strengthen this faith and not to replace it.

*Norman Cousin's article "The Jewishness of Jesus" appeared in *American Judaism* (Rosh Ha-Shono issue) 10, no. 1 (1960):8-9, 35-36, and is reprinted by permission of Mr. Cousins and the publisher, the Union of American Hebrew Congregations.

To these Jews, the Jewishness of Jesus was not incidental or extraneous but inevitable. His coming, they believed, had been foretold in the Hebrew Scriptures; it awakened the dictates of faith that were natural to the Prophecy. Messianism was in the air; the idea of salvation was powerful and dominant.

The Jews who carried this message of Jesus carried it primarily to their own people, for it was only natural that the fulfilment of Hebrew prophecy should be recognized by members of the Hebrew faith. Moreover, the idea of Messianism was an important article of faith among Jews at the time; almost all expected salvation in one form or another. Even so, the actual confrontation in living history with the fact of a Messiah found many Jews resistant. The idea that the greatest of all religious prophecies could occur during one's own lifetime was as difficult then to accept for many people, however religiously impelled, as it would be now. If, for example, there would appear in our own time a figure of the same character and dimensions as Jesus, would it be easy to find a church that would accept him? Events of this magnitude do not easily fit into a contemporary frame.

The Apostles were Jewish. The historical record is skimpy on this subject but there has been speculation that the first Pope may also have been Jewish. And the religious ideas in the New Testament are preponderantly and authentically Jewish in accent and outlook. Indeed, there is a consistent progression from the Torah, with its revelation of the word of God, and its spiritual poetry, to the New Testament which is based not alone on the reality of the fulfilment, but on the nature of God—His presence, His words, His acts on earth, and His direct teachings for man. These were the Witness Chronicles; they told and retold the signs of the birth and the story of the birth, the growing up and the coming of age, the natural wisdom and the natural power, and the circumstances of death and resurrection. The narrative is not of a piece with what Christians call the Old Testament; neither, for that matter, are the books of the Old Testament themselves of a single piece. But the line of development between Old and New is visible and real; there is a direct kinship in purpose and values.

If the impact of Jesus' followers on their fellow Jews was not immediate and sweeping, it must be recalled that Judaism at the time was subject to many calls for reassertion and renewal and to the cross-currents and impulses for change. There was no paucity of proclaimers about the imminent end of the world and the doom of man. Jesus' own vision about world's end was viewed by many against this general background.

Still another barrier to the recognition of Jesus as Messiah was the view held by some religious scholars at the time that Jesus was born in Nazareth of Galilee, and grew up in Galilee. The New Testament is specific on the point that Jesus was a Galilean. Yet the Biblical prophecy had clearly stated that the Messiah would be born in Bethlehem. Was it unreasonable to raise the question of a disparity in what was literally the most important matter in the history of man? In any case, Jesus grew up in Galilee; the difference between the religious environments of Galilee and Bethlehem had considerable importance. Bethlehem was traditional, Orthodox, secure. Galilee was deeply religious, too, but it was surrounded by non-believers and Gentiles. The contrasting winds were many; they produced a gale of ideas.

People were in a mood for reappraisal and self-examination. The atmosphere, if not cosmopolitan, was at least mixed.

The spread of the Christian Gospel by Gentiles created something of a paradox when they attempted to convert Jews. It seemed strange that non-Jews should have to tell Jews what their own Bible meant, and to pass judgments concerning the fulfilment of Hebrew prophecy.

The response of non-Jewish Christians—and also of what might be called "Jewish Christians"—to this argument was that while God revealed Himself to the Jews He was a universal God, as Judaism itself declared. "God is One." Therefore, the Old Testament was not the book of Judaism alone but the spiritual fund of all mankind. Anyone who felt its truth should feel free to listen to the voice of the Deity through it and also to speak to the Deity through it in prayer. Moreover, the early Christians reiterated they were not trying to start a new religion but to act on the new revelations that Judaism had been awaiting for many centuries. In this sense, what they were espousing was a "reformed" or a "Christian" Judaism. In any event, a branch was breaking away and was finding its deep and powerful root.

The most dramatic and significant aspect of the break, of course, was represented by the crucifixion. Though the Romans sentenced and nailed Jesus to the cross, the Jews had rejected him and had entered the complaint. The Christians' cry, "They killed our Lord!" has no historical substance but in back of it was their conviction that if the Jews had accepted Jesus as their king, Jesus would not have been killed.

And here we come to what is perhaps the greatest single paradox in the history of Western religion. Christianity could not exist without the crucifixion. That one event and the witnessed resurrection that proceeded out of it form the specific and vital crystallizing element of Christian faith. The virgin birth and the miracles lead in a straight line to the culminating symbol of Christ on the cross. "He died for our sins" is the cry that keeps the cross alive in the Christian soul, and makes the resurrection possible. The suffering gives depth to the identification.

Yet these two cries—"They killed our Lord!" and "He died for our sins!"—are basically at war with each other. The first assumes an act of human free will. The second assumes an act of divine determination. If Jesus died on the cross in order to purge man, then every act that leads up to it is essential, explicable, predetermined. In the same sense, if Christianity could not have come about without the Crucifixion, and if it was the will of God that Christianity should have been born in this way, then all the circumstances of the Crucifixion are part of a design, and the people who figured in the event, whatever their role, were carrying out the parts divinely assigned to them. The idea of the all-powerful God makes explicit the fact that God cannot be killed. Therefore, the incident of Calvary takes on a symbolism independent of those who were essential to it.

Can Christians believe that God had no power or purpose in the circumstances attending the death on the cross?

Is it reasonable for Christians to believe that God, who arranged a virgin birth for His manifestation on earth, did not also have a divine plan for His departure? And if divine determinism did exist, is it not sacrilegious to assail anyone who belonged to that final Plan? Can Jews or Romans be condemned for the cross without bringing into question the divinity of Jesus?

Christianity has not fully faced up to these questions or the paradox involved in the accusation that though Jesus died in order to make people aware of their sins, Jews are to be held responsible for his death.

The world, two thousand years ago, like the world of today, was a world of many peoples. There were Chinese, Japanese, Africans, fair-skinned northern Europeans, dark-skinned Near Easterners, red-skinned Westerners (later known as American Indians), Eskimos, and Icelanders—many of them with their own gods and religions. The contacts among these people were either slight or incomplete, yet they were all God's children. Why did God choose to be born a Jew? The "Christian" Jews said that this was the way God wanted it, or He would not have revealed His coming to them in the Holy Scriptures. Other Jews, with a feeling perhaps for a universal design, wondered why He would have appeared on earth as a member of a particular sect.

But the essence of faith is the appearance of truth to the individual, whatever its form, whatever its circumstances, whatever the challenge, whatever the array of contrasting evidence. And Christians rest their faith on the reality of Old Testament prophecy and its fulfilment in Jesus. And they therefore do not question the fact that Jesus chose to be born a Jew. Yet should it not also follow, in the same terms, that Christians must not allow themselves to become separated from Jesus' own religion? There is not a single word in John or Mark or Matthew or Luke in which Jesus repudiates Judaism. He practiced Judaism scrupulously. He gave constant expression to the religious and ethical requirements of Judaism. He observed all the Jewish Holy Days. It is widely believed that the Last Supper was a Passover ceremony.

The question growing out of all this for Christians is whether they can detach themselves from the allegiances and observances of Jesus. Can a Christian, believing in revelation through Jesus, accept him as Messiah but reject his own religion? And if it is contended that Jesus did not believe in Judaism, why did he choose to be born a Jew? In the same sense, are not acts against Jews, solely because they are Jews, a direct repudiation of Jesus? Should not the fact of Jesus as Jew serve as the holiest of bonds between Christian and Jew? Should not Christianity regard itself actually as a kind of "Christian" Judaism—that is, a religion accepting the mission of Jesus as he himself defined it—namely, to simplify, purify, and rekindle the Hebrew faith into which he was born? So long as the New Testament rests on the base of the Old Testament, so long as it stands as fulfilment of Biblical prophecy, the essentials of the Old Testament that Jesus himself held sacred cannot be set aside by Christians. For the reforms of Jesus were not directed to the elimination of the essentials but to the recognition of their full significance. These essentials most assuredly embraced moral excellence, restraint, and humility in the daily affairs of men. The statement of these ethics, magnificent though they were, did not burst upon Judaism as totally new concepts; the strain of gentleness, purity, charity, simplicity, and selflessness had been present in the works of Hillel and other Jewish moralists who were influential only a few decades before Christ.

Moreover, terms like "The Kingdom of God," "Messiah," "salvation," "Judgment Day," "repentance," and "blessed"—important words in the vocabulary of Jesus—were in the mainstream of the Jewish tradition.

If all this be true, how and why did Christianity veer away from Judaism? How account for the substantial differences that were to give Christianity its distinct character? The historical answer is that though Christianity is Jewish in origin, it is Greek and Roman in its principal early influences. The need to define and codify, the sense of eternal mystery, the mythological habit—all these inevitably helped to mold the emergent new faith. What was most interesting about the total mixture, Jewish, Greek, and Roman, was that it was to bring together the worlds of East and West. Jesus was not European but Asian, yet Christianity took its strongest root not in Palestine but in Greece and Rome, with a consequent change in accent.

This turning to the West was an important factor in the subordination of the fact of the Jewishness of Jesus. The Jewishness of Jesus was explicable, in the light of Biblical prophecy, but it was not a congenial fact to Christians. Indeed, it could be an uncomfortable fact. It created connections and obligations many Christians were to find awkward to recognize or even acknowledge. But recognized or not, it is the presiding fact; Christian theology, worship, and practice can never be whole until it accepts it and acts on it, not out of reluctance, but out of genuine and essential conviction.

Is it extreme to suggest that it might be salutary if the members of the first Christian family were referred to in terms of their origins, i.e., "The Jewess, Mary," or "Joseph, the Jew," or "Jesus, the Jew"? Isn't it likely that the absurdity of anti-Semitism might become more visible and audible through such reminders? This emphasis might now be necessary were it not for the fact for two thousand years it has been subdued or overlooked or its implications shunned.

It is by setting aside the reluctance to see Jesus as a Jew that a creative and compassionate basis can be found for Christianity's new approach to Judaism.

The same is equally true of Judaism in its approach to Christianity.

Judaism's reluctance has been fortified by long centuries of adverse symbolism. The cross for millions of Jews has been identified with cruelty, heartbreak, prejudice, The cross to them has not become a sign of mercy or peace or charity or justice. Christians spoke and acted in the name of Christ; it was difficult to separate their acts from their faith. A new image of Jesus took shape for Jews, one that had no sanction either in the reality of Jesus or the ideas of Jesus. The image was not spiritually fulfilling; the new image meant pain and despair; the new image was resisted.

Over the centuries, this resistance has hardened to the point where the name Jesus almost produces a conditioned reflex among Jews. If Jesus' name is invoked in a company of Jews, the effect on many of them is one of profound uneasiness, as though their inner citadels were suddenly being challenged. Their reaction makes it seem as though a social contract were being violated. This condition has been more severe among the Orthodox than the other branches of the Jewish faith, but even among many Reform Jews a reticence exists toward the fact of Jesus. Most of the Reform congregations will discuss, occasionally, aspects of Jesus in pulpit or Sunday School, but most of the members themselves seem possessed by the historical rigidity. The New Testament as such is not studied in most Reform schools. However, Hebrew Union College now has a chair in New Testament studies so that graduating Reform rabbis may be in a position to institute the new studies.

There is every reason for Judaism to lose its reluctance toward Jesus. His own towering spiritual presence is a projection of Judaism, not a repudiation of it. Jesus is not to be taxed for the un-Christian ideas and acts of those who have spoken in his name. Jesus never repudiated Judaism. He was proud to be a Jew, yet he did not confine himself to Judaism. He did not believe in spiritual exclusivity for either Jew or Gentile. He asserted the Jewish heritage and sought to preserve and exalt its values, but he did it within a universal context. No other figure—spiritual, philosophical, political or intellectual—has had a greater impact on human history. To belong to a people that produced Jesus is to share in a distinction of vast dimension and meaning.

Jesus' own teachings are a high point in the Jewish tradition. A sense of inspired recognition must run through the Jew who knows his Torah, the poetry of the Psalms, or the gentle aphorisms of great Jewish teachers and philosophers like Hillel. Jewish teachings are based on the idea of a natural goodness in man; it is to this • goodness that Jesus the Jew has spoken.

The modern synagogue can live openly and fully with Jesus. It can do more than take pride in the fact of his being and in his existence and his ideas and his claim on history. And the rediscovery of Jesus can help Jews in the most vital respect of all; he can help them to forgive their tormentors—including those who have done evil to them in Jesus' name.

If it will help the Christian to come to terms with the fact of Jesus as Jew, so it may help Judaism to give weight to the same fact of Jesus' Jewishness—openly, fully, freely, proudly.

For twenty centuries two branches of the same religion have lived without harmony and understanding. Both have a common origin and can come together in a new attitude toward the figure of Jesus, the Jew. The common reluctances can give way to common knowledge and respect based on the reality of the connecting figure of Jesus. Such an amity speaks to the spiritual condition of both Christian and Jew. And out of this amity can come the nourishment of reconciliation.

9 I Am Enthralled by the Luminous Figure of the Nazarene

*World-renowned scientist **Albert Einstein** (1879-1955) was born in Germany and educated in German schools. He was awarded the Nobel prize for physics in 1922. Einstein served as professor of mathematics and theoretical science at the Institute for Advanced Study, Princeton University, 1933 to 1945.*

The following is part of an interview printed years ago in the Saturday Evening Post.*

"To what extent are you influenced by Christianity?"

"As a child I received instruction both in the Bible and in the Talmud. I am a Jew, but I am enthralled by the luminous figure of the Nazarene."

"Have you read Emil Ludwig's book on Jesus?"

"Emil Ludwig's Jesus is shallow. Jesus is too colossal for the pen of phrase-mongers, however artful. No man can dispose of Christianity with a *bon mot.*"

"You accept the historical existence of Jesus?"

"Unquestionably! No one can read the Gospels without feeling the actual presence of Jesus. His personality pulsates in every word. No myth is filled with such life."

The next paragraph is excerpted from Einstein's letter to the Episcopal bishop Edward R. Welles in 1945 concerning the behavior of the church during the Holocaust.†

Being a lover of freedom . . . I looked to the universities to defend it, knowing that they had always boasted of their devotion to the cause of truth; but, no, the universities immediately were silenced. Then I looked to the great editors of the newspapers whose flaming editorials in days gone by had proclaimed their love of freedom; but they, like the universities, were silenced in a few short weeks. Only the

---

*George Sylvester Viereck, "What Life Means to Einstein," *The Saturday Evening Post,* 26 October 1929. Reprinted from THE SATURDAY EVENING POST © 1929 The Curtis Publishing Company. Used by permission.

†Reprinted by permission from Joseph Gallagher, "I Have Set Before You Life and Death . . . Choose Life," *The Evening Sun* (Baltimore), 13 April 1979.

church stood squarely across the path of Hitler's campaign for suppressing the truth. I never had any special interest in the church before, but now I feel a great affection and admiration because the church alone has had the courage and persistence to stand for intellectual truth and moral freedom. I am forced to confess that what I once despised I now praise unreservedly.

10 Who Can Compute All That Jesus Has Meant to Humanity?

*In 1900 **Hyman G. Enelow** received the Doctor of Divinity degree from Hebrew Union College. He became president of the Central Conference of American Rabbis (1927-1929) and served as rabbi of Temple Emanuel in New York. Enelow was the author of several books.**

Jesus has become the most popular, the most studied, the most influential figure in the religious history of mankind. There may be more Mohammedans and Hindus in the world than Christians and Jews. But no Mohammedan prophet nor Hindu saint has exercised the same sway on the heart and imagination of the world as Jesus. Whether we like it or no, Jesus has fascinated mankind. Even in circles which have discarded Christian dogmas and creeds, Jesus has preserved his influence. . . . No sensible Jew can be indifferent to the fact that a Jew should have had such a tremendous part in the religious education and direction of the human race. . . .

Who can compute all that Jesus has meant to humanity? The love he has inspired, the solace he has given, the good he has engendered, the hope and joy he has kindled—all that is unequaled in human history. Among the great and the good that the human race has produced, none has even approached Jesus in universality of appeal and sway. He has become the most fascinating figure in history. In him is combined what is best and most mysterious and most enchanting in Israel—the eternal people whose child he was. The Jew cannot help glorying in what Jesus thus has meant to the world; nor can he help hoping that Jesus may yet serve as a bond of union between Jew and Christian, once his teaching is better known and the bane of misunderstanding at last is removed from his words and his ideal.''

*This excerpt is from Hyman G. Enelow, *A Jewish View of Jesus* (New York: Macmillan, 1920) pp. 4-5, 9, 181, and is reprinted by permission of Bloch Publishing Company.

11 The Enormity of His Life . . . Speaks to Us Today

*Born in Vienna, **David Flusser** studied Judaistics and New Testament at Prague University. In 1939 he emigrated to Palestine and there continued his studies of Jewish history and the early church. After the discovery in 1947 of the Dead Sea Scrolls, Flusser became one of the leading students of those documents. In 1956 he was appointed head of the department of New Testament at the Hebrew University in Jerusalem. The following excerpts are from Flusser's book* Jesus.*

The present age seems specially well disposed to understand Jesus and his interests. A new sensitivity has been awakened in us by profound fear of the future, and of the present. Today we are receptive to Jesus' reappraisal of all our usual values and many of us have become aware of the questioning of the moral norm, which is his starting point too. Like Jesus, we feel drawn to the social pariahs, to the sinners. . . . If we free ourselves from the chains of dead prejudice we are able to appreciate his demand for undivided love, not as philanthropic weakness, but as true psychological consequence.

The enormity of his life, too, speaks to us today: the call of his baptism, the severing of ties with his estranged family and his discovery of a new, sublime sonship, the pandemonium of the sick and possessed, and his death on the cross. Therefore, the words which Matthew (28:20) puts into the mouth of the risen Lord take on for us a new, non-ecclesiastical meaning: "Lo, I am with you always, to the close of the age."[1]

Dr. Flusser has an interesting discussion of the so-called Golden Rule enunciated by Jesus and its bearing on the Old Testament commandment "You shall love your neighbor as yourself" (Lev. 19:18 [RSV]). The Golden Rule laid down by Jesus reads:

> *"So whatever you wish that men would do to you, do so to them: for this is the law [of Moses] and the prophets"*
>
> Matthew 7:12 [RSV]

*David Flusser, Jesus, trans. Ronald Walls (New York: Herder & Herder, 1969), pp. 12, 69-70, 96-97, 122. Reprinted by permission of Rowohlt Taschenbuch Verlag, Hamburg, Germany.

An old Aramaic translation of this Biblical precept [of Leviticus 19:18] runs like this: "Love your neighbor, for whatever displeases you, do not do to him!" This paraphrastic translation turns the phrase "as yourself" into the negative style of the Golden Rule. . . . You are not to treat your neighbor with hatred, because you would not like him to treat you in that way. . . . Rabbi Hanina, who lived approximately one generation after Jesus, explicitly taught that this commandment to love one's neighbor is: "A saying upon which the whole world hangs, a mighty oath from Mount Sinai. If you hate your neighbor whose deeds are wicked like your own, I, the Lord, will punish you as your judge: and if you love your neighbor whose deeds are good like your own, I the Lord, will be faithful to you and have mercy on you" (*Aboth de R. Nathan* second version, p. 53). . . . This is not far from Jesus' commandment to love; but Jesus went further and broke the last fetters still restricting the ancient Jewish commandment to love one's neighbor. Rabbi Hanina believed that one ought to love the righteous and not to hate the sinner, but Jesus said: "I say to you, Love your enemies and pray for those who persecute you" (Mt. 5:44 [RSV]).[2]

As far as I can gather, Dr. Flusser accepts the New Testament account of the transfiguration as an authentic vision. The following is his discussion of that event.

According to the gospels, Jesus was addressed by the heavenly voice as "Son" as early as his baptism: but the presumption is justified that at that time he was simply described as the chosen servant. Not until the voice at the Transfiguration was he truly named "Son." Jesus took Peter, and John, and James, and climbed with them up to a mountain: his face became different, and his clothes became shining white: Moses and Elijah spoke to him. When they departed, Peter said to Jesus: Rabbi, it is good for us to be here: let us make three huts, one for you, one for Moses, and one for Elijah: Then a cloud came and overshadowed them and a voice out of the cloud said: "This is my [only] Son: hear him" (Luke 9:28-36). . . .

The heavenly voice is significant. The words "hear him" are made intelligible by the prophecy of Moses: 'The Lord your God will raise up for you a prophet like me from among you, from your brethren—him you shall heed' (Dt. 18:15 [RSV]). The fact that there appeared two great prophets of old, Moses and Elijah, underlined the meaning of the voice: Jesus is the prophetic preacher to whom the Old Testament had pointed. The voice designated Jesus "only Son,"[3] as God had said to Abraham: "Take your son, your only son Isaac, whom you love . . . and offer him there as a burnt offering" (Gen. 22:2 [RSV]). This alludes to the coming martyrdom of Jesus. Luke (9:31) says, in fact, that on the occasion of the Transfiguration, Moses and Elijah spoke with Jesus about his imminent departure in Jerusalem.[4]

Finally, it appears that David Flusser accepts as valid the New Testament record of the appearances of Jesus after the crucifixion.

There can be no doubt that the Crucified "appeared to [Peter], then to the twelve. Then he appeared to more than five hundred brethren at one time. . . . Then he appeared to James, then to all the apostles." Last of all, he appeared to Paul on the road to Damascus" (1 Cor. 15:3-8 [RSV]).[5]

Concerning Flusser, Pinchas E. Lapide declared: "The uniqueness of Jesus in the history of Jewish thought, the supremacy of his message of love and the rele-

vance of that message for our nuclear age constitutes the triple concern of David Flusser." He also stated that impromptu interfaith symposia took place, presided over by Dr. Flusser and attended by clergymen from various denominations, Dominican friars, and visiting rabbis from Europe and America. At one of these informal "agapes," Flusser made the following observation:

Jesus asked us to repent and to return to God. If for a Jew it is not difficult to understand Jesus' message, it is imperative for Christians today to accept it. . . . If Jewish scholarship could only rediscover Jesus for the Jew, as well as for our Christian brethren, our work will not be in vain.[6]

In an interview of Professor David Flusser by Pastor Fritz May of Wetzlar, West Germany, Dr. Flusser made the following observations:

I don't think there are many Jews—fanatics and ill-informed excepted—who are not fascinated by the Person and Teaching of Jesus. Perhaps much more so than many Gentiles and so-called 'Christians.' I might add that the approach of Jews to Christianity can only be made via the Message of Jesus. . . . There is now a growing sense of inquiry here [in Israel], concerning the things of Jesus and Christianity. The reasons being that prejudices are dying down."

Professor Flusser stressed the need to study what the Bible teaches with reference to the end time of history, the "aharith ha-yamim" (the last days).

Personally speaking, I believe the end of the age is very near. Why? Not because of pollution and its grave consequences, but because of the Churches' apostasy. Not only do many fall from the faith, but there is a growing tendency within Christendom to make room for the rise of the Antichrist. He will be an imitator of Christ, of Jesus, whose teachings he will twist and pervert.[7]

Notes

1. Flusser, *Jesus*, p. 12.
2. Ibid., pp. 69-70.
3. In note 164, Flusser indicates that the phrase "beloved Son" in the New Testament is the Greek translation of the Hebrew "only Son."
4. Ibid, pp. 96-97.
5. Ibid., p. 122.
6. Pinchas E. Lapide, "Jesus in Israeli Literature," *The Christian Century,* 21 October 1970.
7. Interview of David Flusser by Fritz May, *The Messianic Witness* (Summer 1975). Reprinted by permission of Fritz May.

12 Jesus of Nazareth Is the Most Famous Name in the World

Solomon B. Freehof (b. 1892) was London born. He came to America in 1903. He received his rabbinical diploma and the Doctor of Divinity degree from the Hebrew Union College in Cincinnati. From 1915 to 1924 he was assistant professor of medieval liturgy and rabbinics at Hebrew Union College. He is editor of the department of liturgy for the Universal Jewish Encyclopedia and has written several books.*

'Jesus of Nazareth' is the most famous name in the world. The Galilean teacher looms as large today as he did centuries ago. His words are still on the tongues of men, and his parables are as fresh as when he first uttered them. Artists are as eager to paint him as they were in the Middle Ages. Scholars study him as much as ever. Prayers are addressed to him with unabated fervor. . . . . Millions praise him, but for widely differing reasons. To some he is divine, the veritable Son of God, foretold by inspired prophecy, born miraculously, who lived and died in order to fulfill his Father's plan of salvation, and after death was resurrected from the tomb, and enthroned in heaven as part of the three-fold Godhead. To others he is a man— human, but exceptional; the highest of all the prophets, the grandest moral teacher, the gentlest spirit that ever lived on earth.

Some emphasize the importance of the miracles which the Gospels ascribe to him . . . . Still others speak of him as a literary genius. They find his power explained by the magnificent expressions which he gave to his ideas. His brilliant parables, his striking contrasts, his thrilling declarations have made his words unforgettable. . . .

All this vast diversity of opinion has not lessened the vividness of the personality of Jesus. The opposite opinions have not balanced each other into immobility. All the opinions are still staunchly held and ardently defended. The years have not diminished the urgency of the question: "What do you think of Jesus?"

His career is known to every child in the western world. It is not necessary to retell the familiar story, from his birth in Bethlehem to his crucifixion on Golgotha. His sayings and parables are constantly quoted. They have become part of the daily speech of men. . . .

*The following excerpt is from Solomon B. Freehof, *Stormers of Heaven* (New York: Harper and Row, 1931), pp. 205-10. Copyright, 1931, by Harper & Brothers. Reprinted by permission of Harper & Row, Publishers, Inc.

Although the meaning of his career is subject to endless debate, there can be no dispute as to his importance. . . . The secret of the influence of Jesus will perhaps always remain a mystery. After painstaking scholarship has explained all that is explicable, the secret of his power remains unsolved. . . .

The personality of Jesus was such that his sonship to God was magnificently evident. The divine spirit seemed manifest in his words and deeds. He impressed himself upon the world, perhaps more so than other prophets and saints, as a "child of the living God." It may be that historical circumstances conspired to perpetuate the magic of his personality. The world was ripe for the adoration of just such a teacher of prophetic morality. . . . Be that as it may, the consciousness of the presence of God has come to millions of men and women through Jesus.

That it is his personality which is the essence of his power should be evident to every objective student of Christian literature. It is not merely that legends have been woven around his name. Every great religious genius has been en-haloed with loving legend. The significant fact is that time has not faded the vividness of his image. Poetry still sings his praise. He is still the living comrade of countless lives. No Moslem ever sings, "Mohammed, lover of my soul," nor does any Jew say of Moses, the teacher, "I need thee every hour."

13 The Jewish and the Christian Messiah

*Born in czarist Russia, **Joseph Klausner** received his Ph.D. degree from Heidelberg University in Germany. He was professor of modern Hebrew literature at the Hebrew University, 1925-1949; professor of Jewish history of the Second Temple era, 1944-1949; and author of several scholarly books.*

The essay under the above title forms an appendix to Dr. Joseph Klausner's book The Messianic Idea in Israel.* *The three parts of that book were written during various periods of the author's life. In this essay the author makes concluding observations on the "Jewish Messiah" and the "Christian Messiah." Finally he places the Jewish and Christian concepts side by side, in order to pinpoint the differences between them. The following is a reproduction of the last part.*

The Christian Messiah is in essence only a further development of the Jewish Messiah. For from Judaism Christianity received the ideas of redemption, the redeemer-Messiah, the Day of Judgment, and the kingdom of heaven. And much of what was common to Judaism and Christianity with respect to Messianic thinking remained even after estrangement and separation between them took place. Nevertheless, the difference between the Jewish and the Christian Messiah is very great.

First of all, Jewish redemption can be conceived without any individual Messiah at all—something which is absolutely impossible in Christianity. Also, "the Redeemer of Israel" for Judaism can mean God alone; in Christianity the Redeemer is Jesus only. Without the Jewish Messiah, Judaism is defective; without the Christian Messiah Christianity does not exist at all.

Second, there is an irrational side even in the Jewish Messianic conception: where there is not mysticism at all, there is no faith. But the irrational and mystical element in the Jewish Messiah is only unnatural, but not anti-natural, not opposed to nature. The unity of God is not affected in any essential way by the Jewish Messiah.

*This excerpt is reprinted with permission of Macmillan Publishing Co., Inc. from *The Messianic Idea in Israel* by Joseph Klausner, trans. W.F.F. Stinespring. Copyright 1955 by Macmillan Publishing Co., Inc.

In the last analysis, the Jewish Messiah is only, as said above, the instrument of deity—although of course a choice and superb instrument. But in Christianity monotheism is obscured by the Messiah, who is "Son of God," the "Logos," the "Lord," a "God-man," and "one person with two natures." And from this spring the rest of the marked differences between the Jewish and Christian Messiahs: one cannot pray to the Jewish Messiah, he is not a mediator between God and man, he is not a "Paraclete" for man, and so on.

Third, the Jewish Messiah is the redeemer of his people and the redeemer of mankind. But he does not redeem them by his blood; instead, he lends aid to their redemption by his great abilities and deeds. Even Messiah ben Joseph, who is slain, affords no atonement by his blood and his sufferings are not vicarious. Judaism is familiar with "the sin of Adam," but the Jewish Messiah does not with his blood redeem from "original sin," nor from death, nor from Satan. To be sure, Satan will be vanquished in the Messianic age—not by the Messiah, but by God. Man must redeem himself from sin not by faith alone, but by repentance and good works; then God will redeem him from death and Satan. (Generally speaking, Satan does not occupy in Judaism the central place that he takes in Christianity; Satan in Christianity is almost like the God of Evil of the Persians.) Each man is responsible for himself, and through his good deeds he must find atonement for his sins. He cannot lean upon the Messiah or upon the Messiah's suffering and death.

Fourth and finally, since the Jewish Messiah is only "a righteous man ruling in the fear of God," and since he brings only ethical perfection to the world, the progress of humanity does not depend on him, but on humanity itself. Numberless times the Talmud returns to the idea that redemption depends on repentance and good works; well known is the interpretation of the verse "I the LORD will hasten it in its time" (Isa. 60:22 [RV]): "If they are worthy, I will hasten it [the redemption]; if not, it will come in its [own good] time." And the Hebrew people, who were the first to acknowledge faith in One God, the God of goodness, and to whom came prophets of truth and righteousness, can and will be the first to "hasten the redemption" by repentance and good works. In other words, the Jews can and must march at the head of humanity on the road of personal and social progress, on the road to ethical perfection. This will be possible only when they have returned to their own land, have gathered in their exiles, have reestablished their own state, and are no longer under the oppression of foreigners; but the "kingdom of heaven" is their goal and their highest aspiration, and without this goal Israel would never be freed from "bondage to foreign powers" cessations of which will be the obvious external sign that the Days of the Messiah are near.

Therefore, we can say, without being suspected of undue bias toward Judaism, that the Jewish Messianic faith is the seed of progress, which has been planted by Judaism throughout the whole world.[1]

In another of his books Klausner makes the following observation†:

Jesus of Nazareth . . . was a product of Palestine alone, a product of Judaism

†The following excerpt is reprinted with permission of Macmillan Publishing Co., Inc. from *Jesus of Nazareth* by Joseph Klausner, trans. Herbert Danby. Copyright 1925 by Macmillan Publishing Co., Inc., renewed 1953 by Herbert Danby.

unaffected by any foreign admixture. There were many Gentiles in Galilee, but Jesus was in no way influenced by them. In his days Galilee was the stronghold of the most enthusiastic Jewish patriotism. . . . Without any exception he is wholly explainable by the Scriptural and Pharisaic Judaism of his time. . . .[2]

Jesus was a Jew and a Jew he remained till his last breath. His one idea was to implant within his nation the idea of the coming of the Messiah and, by repentance and good works, hasten the "end". . . .

In all this Jesus is the most Jewish of Jews . . . more Jewish even than Hillel. . . .

From the standpoint of general humanity, he is, indeed, "a light to the Gentiles." His disciples have raised the lighted torch of the Law of Israel . . . among the heathen of the four quarters of the world. No Jew can, therefore, overlook the value of Jesus and his teaching from the point of view of universal history. This was a fact that neither Maimonides nor Yehuda ha-Levi [medieval Jewish scholars] ignored.[3]

Notes

1. Joseph G. Klausner, *The Messianic Idea in Israel,* trans. W. F. F. Stinespring (New York: Macmillan, 1955), pp. 529-31.
2. A number of the statements in the above dissertation are not borne out by the teachings of the Old Testament. Dr. Klausner himself admits that the Jewish Messianic concept in Jewish extrabiblical writings is not the same as the Messianic concept in the Old Testament. As to Klausner's statement that "the Jewish Messianic faith is the seed of progress which has been planted by Judaism throughout the whole world," we need to point out that it is the Messianism of the Bible, Old and New Testament, rather than the Messianism of rabbinic Judaism, that has been the seed of progress, and that biblical Messianism has been planted not by Judaism but by Jewish and Gentile followers of Jesus.—EDITOR
3. Joseph Klausner, *Jesus of Nazareth* (New York: Macmillan, 1925), pp. 363, 368, 374, 413.

14 The Synagogue and the Church

*Rabbi and educator **Kaufmann Kohler** (1843-1926) was born and educated in Germany. In 1869 he emigrated to America and served in synagogues in Chicago, Detroit, and New York. In 1885 he convened the "Pittsburgh Platform," which became the foundation of Reform Judaism in America. In 1903 he became president of Hebrew Union College in Cincinnati. He was the author of a number of books.*

The religious congress that was held in connection with the Chicago Fair in 1893 brought together representatives of various religious persuasions from many parts of the world, including many rabbis from Europe and America. The congress was addressed by Rabbi Kohler, regarded at that time the foremost exponent of Reform Judaism. The subject of his address was "The Synagogue and the Church," in which he sought to prove how close Judaism and Christianity stood to each other. The following is that portion of Dr. Kohler's address in which he dealt with the person of Jesus.*

Jewish scholars are making a great mistake when they compare Jesus of Nazareth with Hillel the Elder, the tolerant Tanna, or Philo, the Jewish philosopher from Alexandria. Jesus did not belong to any party. He was a man of the people. In him the Essene ideal of love and fellowship assume a new and grand expression.[1] In contrast to John the Immerser, Jesus felt himself drawn with the power of divine love to the lowest of his fellow men. Being filled with true greatness he communed with shepherds. publicans and sinners, the very people whom the Essenes had regarded as headed for hell, with whom they had no dealings for fear of becoming tainted by contact with them. He ate and drank with them, saying: "I came to save the lost sheep of the house of Israel; not those who are well, but who are sick, need the physician. . . . The heart which is filled with impure thoughts is unclean. . . . Woe to you Pharisees, you clean the outside, but the inside you leave uncleansed and filled with evil. To you, hypocrites, are applicable the words of Isaiah: 'They approach me only with their mouth, and honor me with their lips, but their heart is

*See Union of American Hebrew Congregations, *Judaism at the World's Parliament of Religions* (Cincinnati: Clarke, 1894), pp. 118-20, 122-23.

far from me:' " These are the words of a prophet, of a fearless reformer. . . .

With the same courage of genuine love with which he converted sinners, Jesus also defended the woman in whom the Essenes only saw an instrument in the hands of Satan to entice men to sin, and he shattered the forces making the woman's lot lonely.

With the same freedom of his spirit, he broke the chains of the "Sabbath laws." "The Sabbath," he said, "was made for man and not man for the Sabbath." We have here before us a great and profound thinker, a tremendous personality, a religious genius. . . . The Jewish people in general, and its leader in particular, have had no cause to hate the most noble and most exalted of all the teachers of Israel.

It cannot be denied that the ideal of human life as set up by the Church is unequaled in greatness and loftiness. Back of all the teachings and dogmas of the Church stands the enchanting figure of human goodness and love: a more lovely and more exalted figure than that of Jesus mankind was not given to honor. All features of the Greek philosopher and of the saintly Jew are harmoniously blended in the man who died on Calvary. No ethical system, no textbook on religion, are capable of exerting such a deep impression on us as that great personality of Jesus, standing, as none other, midway between heaven and earth, equally near to God as to man.

He was the ideal representative of the Essene brotherhood, no, he was the embodiment of brotherliness of all mankind. . . . Jesus, the helper of needy, the friend of sinners, the brother of all sufferers, the comforter of the unfortunate, the lover of mankind, the liberator of the woman, he won and conquered the human heart.

Of what possible use was the proud philosophy of the wise men, and the corrupt religion of the priests, to a world which hungered for God and thirsted for redemption from sin and cruelty. The times of Jesus were ripe for a social upheaval, for the Messianic Age, when the proud will be brought low, and the humble will be lifted up. Jesus, the most lowly of all men, the despised, beyond comparison, of the despised Jewish nation, has ascended the world's throne to become the Great King of the whole earth.

Notes

1. Essenes—community of Jews in the neighborhood of the Dead Sea, who did not marry, lived solely from the work of their hands, and aspired to a life of holiness and moral perfection.

15 The Sinners Drew Near to Him

Claude G. Montefiore (1858-1938) was one of the most scholarly theologians of Reform Judaism. He was born in London and educated at Oxford University. He wrote on biblical subjects of both Old and New Testaments and championed the cause of liberal (Reform) Judaism in England.

Here in the Gospels we have religion and morality joined together at a white heat of intensity. The teaching often glows with light and fire. Nothing is to interfere with the pursuit of the highest moral and religious ideal; nothing is to come before it.[1]

Observing that the idea of the fatherhood of God is a characteristically Jewish doctrine that finds expression in the Old Testament and rabbinic writings, Montefiore stresses that in those works the concept lacks the prominence given to it in the New Testament.

We certainly do not get in the Hebrew Bible any teacher speaking of God and to God as "Father," "my Father," "your Father," and "our Father," like the Jesus of Matthew. And this habitual and concentrated use rightly produces upon us an impression. . . we are moved by it to wish that we too could feel that doctrine, even as Jesus teaches that we ought to feel; and that we, too, could order our lives in its light and by its strength.[2]

The following are Montefiore's comments on the stress laid in the New Testament on the idea that "God is love." Passing from the fourth chapter of the gospel of John, where that divine attribute is proclaimed, to the doctrine of "God is love" as taught in the first epistle of John, Montefiore declares:

Nothing can be more striking or more noble than the ethical use to which the doctrine is put, or the argument which leads up to it. It is an appeal to the disciples and believers, but it could be equally an appeal to all our fellow-men. "Let us love one another, for love is of God: and every one that loves is begotten of God, and knows God. He that loves not knows not God: for God is love." It is idle to attempt to minimize or to pare away the greatness of these moving and wonderful words. And it would be foolish to argue that goodness and righteousness could be put equally well in the place of love. . . . The Hebrew word for righteousness does not mean and imply all that the Christian means by love, and it is doubtful how far the Hebrew word Chesed[3] . . . means quite the same as the Christian means by love, or as the author of the Epistle meant by Agape.[4] The Christian and the author of the

53

Epistle mean something more forthgoing, more passionate, more venturous, more self-sacrificing, more eager, more giving, than can honestly be said to be connoted by righteousness or goodness. It is the virtue which, as the author of the Gospel says, does in its height "cause a man to lay down his life for his friend." It is the virtue which drives a man forth to save, to redeem, and to forgive. *That* virtue is more than "goodness" and more than "righteousness." It is charged with emotion. It is filled with longing and yearning. It is, in short, "love," and love, being all that, is more than goodness and more than righteousness, and we dare not forego the word, lest we do not practice or adore the thing. Moreover, the saying in the Epistle lays down the one great "proof" to the believer of the existence of God. Love calls out to love. Human love recognizes divine love. We are unable to believe that man's love has not a superhuman source and a superhuman guarantee. And only through love can we, in spite of evil, believe in God's love or in God. From the visible to the invisible. The author is justified in arguing: "He that does not love his brother whom he has seen, cannot love God whom he has not seen" [1 John 4:20, RSV]. . . . Jews, as well as Christians, can be grateful for it: they, too, can believe that "God is love."[5]

Commenting on the parables of the lost sheep and the lost coin as recorded in Luke 15, which begins with the statement "Then drew near unto him all the tax collectors and sinners for to hear him," Montefiore says:

This verse sums up one of the specific characteristics of Jesus and one of the new excellences of the Gospel. "The sinners drew near to him." Surely this is a new note, something which we have not yet heard in the Old Testament or of *its* heroes, something which we do not hear in the Talmud of its heroes. "The sinners drew near to him"; his teaching did not repel them. It did not palter with or make light of sin, but yet it gave comfort to the sinner. The virtues of repentance are gloriously praised in the Rabbinical literature, but this direct search for, and appeal to, the sinner, are new and moving notes of high import and significance. The good shepherd who searches for the lost sheep, and reclaims it and rejoices over it, is a new figure, which has never ceased to play its great part in the moral and religious development of the world.[6]

Notes

1. Claude G. Montefiore, "The Synoptic Gospels and The Jewish Consciousness," *The Hibbert Journal* 3 (1904-5):660.
2. Claude G. Montefiore, *The Old Testament and After* (London: Macmillan, 1923) pp. 205-6. Reprinted by permission.
3. Usually translated "loving-kindness" or "steadfast love."
4. A Greek word that came to express God's love for man reflected in the sacrificial death of Jesus.
5. Montefiore, *The Old Testament and After*, pp. 208-10. Reprinted by permission.
6. Montefiore, *The Synoptic Gospels*, 3 vols. (Macmillan, 1927; reprint ed., New York: Ktav, 1968) 2:520-21. Used by permission of Ktav Publishing House, Incorporated.

16 Sent of God
for the Revival of Judaism

Little is known of **Isaac Joseph Poysner.** *His book* The
Kingdom of the Messiah *was written in Yiddish and was
published in Warsaw, Poland, in 1925.**

A change of attitude must take place between the Jew and Christianity. I
have no desire to discuss here our sins against the first Christians, for which we have
paid so dearly, and which served as a pretext in the hands of our persecutors. Such
victims of the dominant power and order every other nation has . . . on its conscience, and the same Christians have suffered much more from others [than from
us]. A whole people, however, is not responsible for the actions of a certain clique,
or even of a mob. The nation condemns them later, and the victims are rehabilitated
and honored, and this is their vindication. The nation is the supreme court and
judge, where the victims [ultimately] obtain justice and fatherly love.

The mutual prejudice between Judaism and Christianity must cease and Judaism
must take the first step in this direction. Christianity is bone of our bones, and flesh
of our flesh. The bearers of the Christian message were Jews, and they hailed from
Judaism. Christianity was a Jewish movement. We may oppose it on ideological
grounds, but we cannot exclude it from Judaism.

Judaism's prejudice against Christianity must end, and then Judaism will perceive Christianity's true meaning and significance, namely, that it was sent of God
for the revival of Judaism, and that Christianity truly fulfills Judaism's mission, and
that it is part and parcel of the salvation of Israel.

The controversy between Judaism and Christianity belongs more to the past, to
history. The recognition of Christianity by its [Jewish] people means the recognition
of [its] role in history, and the assigning to it and to its bearers a proper place in the
pantheon of Judaism's creative achievements, historic treasures and heroes, and its
welcome into Judaism's paternal bosom and heart.

**I am indebted to the Yivo Institute for Jewish Research for making available to me the Yiddish text of
the above excerpts (pp. 235-36, 238). The translation is my own.—*ED.

17 Judaism—the "Eternal Fire"; Christianity—the "Eternal Rays"

Philosopher-theologian **Franz Rosenzweig,** the son of a well-to-do Jewish family, was born in Cassel, Germany, in 1886. He spent two years in the study of medicine, then switched to modern history and philosophy. He became deeply interested in Hegel's philosophic idealism. However, while attending a Day of Atonement service in a traditional synagogue in Berlin in 1913, Rosenzweig experienced a "closeness to God," and that experience became the turning point in his life. He gained a conviction of the impotence of Hegel's idealism when confronted with existential problems of human life and life's ultimate question: Who am I and what is the purpose of my existence?

While in the Balkan foxholes with the German army in the First World War, he began to compose *The Star of Redemption,* which became his *magnum opus* (1921). He wrote it on army postal cards, which he sent on to his mother. During the postwar period, he and Dr. Martin Buber collaborated in a new German translation of the Hebrew Bible, which is said to be the finest since Martin Luther's translation.

Rosenzweig is considered to have been the "single greatest influence on the religious thought of North American Jewry."[1] At one time he came very close to embracing the Messianic faith of Jesus. He carried on an extensive correspondence with knowledgeable Christians, some of whom were his own kinsmen, and gained a sympathetic understanding of the Christian faith.

According to Rosenzweig, Judaism and Christianity possess equal religious validity and represent complementary aspects of God's revealed truth. Judaism is "the eternal fire"—Christianity, "the eternal rays." Judaism is "the eternal life" with God, Christianity is "the eternal way" to God. Judaism is oriented inward to the Jews, whereas Christianity is facing outward to the Gentiles. In fact, Christianity is "Judaism for the Gentiles." Israel stays with God, Christianity goes out into the world to bring the unredeemed peoples to the God of Israel. Christianity's function is well symbolized by the cross, the vertical beam of which looks heavenward to God and the horizontal beam is outstretched towards mankind. Only in the endtime, when the task of mankind's redemption will have been completed, will Judaism and Christianity fuse into one faith.[2]

Notes

1. Milton Himmelfarb, "The State of Jewish Belief," *Commentary* 42, no. 2 (August 1966), p. 71.
2. Franz Rosenzweig, *The Star of Redemption* (New York: Holt, Rinehart and Winston, 1971), pp. 336-79; see also Will Herberg, "Rosenzweig's 'Judaism of Personal Existence,' " *Commentary,* December 1950; F. E. Talmage, *Disputation and Dialogue* (New York: Ktav, 1975), pp. 243-45.

18 A Jewish Understanding of the New Testament

Ordained rabbi by the Hebrew Union College in 1937,
Samuel Sandmel *became professor of biblical and*
Hellenistic literature at Hebrew Union College. He is the
author of several scholarly works. *

When Judaism and Christianity are compared with each other, the sense of their diversity from each other is a natural conclusion. It is as if they were on opposite sides of a fence. Yet when they are seen in the light of a third element, such as Nazism or Communism, the impression changes quickly, and Judaism and Christianity are seen rather as being on the same side of the fence.

How Judaism and Christianity can live together in the fullest amity, but with dignity and adherence to principle, is a quest imposed by modern democracy. It needs to be recognized that the wish for them to live amicably contradicts what was their history for almost seventeen hundred years. I have mentioned several times the anti-Jewish sentiments found in the New Testament. Jewish life in the Middle Ages was largely one persecution after another. Yet it would be unreasonable for modern American Jews to regard our American Christian neighbors as the perpetrators of those medieval misfortunes. The sad history of the Jews in Europe makes it difficult still today in America to steer a middle course between condescension and obsequiousness. Yet it must be recalled that Nazism was virtually as hostile to Christianity as to Judaism. The course of harmony based on deep understanding must steer carefully past the perpetuation of old grievances, however justified in the past, and the partial perception of modern difficulties. It will need more than simply good intentions. It will need also comprehension and wider horizons.

For American Jews to understand the New Testament as scholars do is only the beginning of understanding. A further step is to learn what one's usual Christian neighbor or friend sees in it. Much of what is distinctive in the religious observances of the Christians comes from a period after the New Testament. This is the case, for example, with the observance of Christmas and with the office of the Pope. Understanding the New Testament sympathetically falls short of understanding Christianity.

*This article is excerpted from Samuel Sandmel, *A Jewish Understanding of the New Testament* (Cincinnati: Heb. Union Coll., 1956), pp. 320-21, and is reprinted by permission of the author.

For Jews, the New Testament is not and cannot be a literature sacred to us. But the sacred literatures of others can be enlightening and broadening to us, even giving us fresh perspectives on our own belief, if we try to understand sympathetically the profound perplexities and deep aspirations which human beings have been inspired to express, and how the lives of our contemporaries are moved by those ideals and institutions which embody them.

The New Testament, although it is not ours, is closer to us than any other sacred literature which is not our own. It shares in a legacy which is eternally precious to us. For American Jews it is the Scripture of our neighbors—and, happily, of fellow citizens and friends.

19 A Religious Bridge Between Jew and Christian

Professor **Hans Joachim Schoeps** *is an eminent German Jewish theologian. He was born in Berlin and educated in German schools, including the universities of Heidelberg, Marburg, and Leipzig. At the time the article under the above title appeared in* Commentary, *Professor Schoeps was teaching at the University of Marburg. He is the author of a number of works in German.**

With Franz Rosenzweig, I would even go so far as to declare that perhaps no Gentile can come to God the Father otherwise than through Jesus Christ. In thus recognizing that the revelation of the church of Jesus Christ has its sphere of validity from which only Israel is excepted by virtue of its direct election by the Father, I do not believe that I offend against Jewish tradition. For even if we go to great lengths in recognizing covenants of God with non-Israelitic mankind, the absolute validity of the revelation of the Torah to Israel remains unimpaired.

According to Jewish tradition of the centuries, Israel was chosen, however undeserving, to be the bearer of God's covenant. The covenant concluded with the patriarch Abraham was sealed on Mount Sinai by the promulgation of the Torah, and confirmed through the mouths of the Prophets. This covenant, concluded with the seed of Abraham and extended to cover the *ger tzedek* (full proselytes) who joined with Israel, by no means excludes the possibility that outside Israel's sacred sphere God may have concluded other covenants beyond the scope of Jewish knowledge and judgment. In any event, the modern Jew need face no fundamental contradiction in regarding the "new covenant" professed by the Christian church as in no way prejudicial to him and his own certitude of salvation. The Christian who, according to his belief, comes to the Father through Jesus Christ—or who, through the church in which Jesus Christ lives, participates by belief in the coming-to-the Father of Jesus Christ—stands before the same God in whom we Jews believe, the God of Abraham, of Isaac, and of Jacob, the God of Moses our teacher, to whom Jesus also said "Father."

*This article is reprinted from Hans Joachim Schoeps, "A Religious Bridge Between Jew and Christian," trans. Ralph Manheim *Commentary* (February 1950). Reprinted from *Commentary,* February 1950, by permission; all rights reserved.

This fundamental fact, which we can acknowledge at all times, guarantees Judaism's inner bond with Christianity and opens up the possibility of a Jewish-Christian rapprochement. The limit to such an understanding is that we cannot recognize Yeshuah ha-Nozri [Jesus of Nazareth] as the Christ, i.e., as the Messiah for Israel. We are, however, prepared to recognize that, in some way which we do not understand, a Messianic significance for non-Jewish mankind is attached to the figure of this man. . . .

For the God who named himself to Moses as "I will be who I will be" is in all the diversity of his revelations and covenants the eternally same God; he is absolute for the Jews as the God who is and will be, just as, by a different form of mediation, he has become God for the Christians. Hence Jews and Christians cannot and must not deviate from the absoluteness of their different testimonies of truth. And, consequently, they will go their separate ways through history according to the will of providence, up to that point in the future where the parallels intersect.

The end of the two covenants will come to pass in the days of the Messiah, when "old" and "new" covenants become *one* covenant, when all mankind assembles under a single covenant to worship only God. The Messianism of Israel aims at that which is to come, the eschatology of the Gentile church at the return of him who has come. Both elective covenants confront the ebb and flow of the finite world in the shared expectation that the decisive event is still to come—the goal of the ways of God that he travels with mankind in Israel and in the Church.

The church of Jesus Christ has preserved no portrait of its lord and saviour. If Jesus were to come again tomorrow, no Christian would know his face. But it might well be that he who is coming at the end of days, he who is awaited by the synagogue as by the church, is one, with one and the same face.

20 Jesus the Jew

Educator and author **Geza Vermes** *was born in Hungary. In 1957 he was appointed lecturer in biblical studies at the University of Newcastle upon Tyne. In 1965 he was elected to the Readership in Jewish Studies at Oxford University. In 1971 he became chairman of the Curators of the Oriental Institute. In 1971 he was appointed Visiting Professor in Judaica at Brown University.*

Having devoted in his work Jesus the Jew *a whole chapter to the subject of the close relationship of Jesus to the miracle-working holy men in Palestine in the first century B.C., the author makes the following concluding observations*:*

The discovery of resemblances between the work and words of Jesus and those of the Hasidim, Honi and Hanina ben Doza, is however by no means intended to imply that he was simply one of them and nothing more. Although no systematic attempt is made here to distinguish Jesus' authentic teaching. . .it is nevertheless still possible to say. . .that no objective and enlightened student of the Gospels can help but be struck by the incomparable superiority of Jesus. . . . Second to none in profundity of insight and grandeur of character, he is in particular an unsurpassed master of the art of laying bare the inmost core of spiritual truth and of bringing every issue back to the essence of religion, the existential relationship of man and man, and man and God.

It should be added that in one respect more than any other he differed from both his contemporaries and even his prophetic predecessors. The prophets spoke on behalf of the honest poor, and defended the widows and fatherless, those oppressed and exploited by the wicked, rich and powerful. Jesus went further. In addition to proclaiming these blessed, he actually took his stand among the pariahs of this world, those despised by the respectable. Sinners were his table-companions and the ostracised tax-collectors and prostitutes his friends.

*Geza Germes, Jesus the Jew (London: Collins, 1973), pp. 223-24. The quoted sentences are used by permission of the publisher.

21 Without Jesus or Paul . . . the God of a Handful

*London-born **Harris Weinstock** eventually settled in California where he built up a successful business. He was president and director of several companies and banks. In 1913 President Woodrow Wilson appointed him a member of the Industrial Relations Committee.**

Had there been no Abraham, there would have been no Moses. Had there been no Moses, there would have been no Jesus. Had there been no Jesus, there would have been no Paul. Had there been no Paul, there would have been no Christianity. Had there been no Christianity, there would have been no Luther. Had there been no Luther, there would have been no Pilgrim fathers to land on these shores with the Jewish Bibles under their arms. Had there been no Pilgrim fathers, there would have been no civil or religious liberty. . . .

Without Jesus or Paul, the God of Israel would still have been the God of a handful, the God of a petty, obscure, and insignificant tribe; the magnificent moral teachings of Moses would still have been confined to the thinly scattered believers in Judaism, and the great world of men and women would have been left so much the poorer because of their ignorance of these benign teachings.

Let the Jew, despite persecution and suffering, be thankful that there was a Jesus and a Paul. Let him more fully appreciate that, through the wonderful influence of these heroic characters, the mission of the Jew is being better fulfilled, and his teachings are being spread to the remotest nooks and corners of the world by Christianity, "a religion by which millions have been, and still are, quickened and inspired." Let the Jew not forget that, through the influence of Jesus and Paul, the Ten Commandments of Moses, the sublime utterances of Isaiah, of Micah, of Jeremiah, the proverbs of Solomon, and the psalms of David, have brought, and are bringing, and will continue to bring, balm and comfort, joy and happiness, spiritual bliss and moral sunshine, into untold homes. Thus is the Christian, through Jesus and Paul, deeply indebted to the Jew; and thus is the Jew also, through Jesus and Paul, deeply indebted to the Christian.

*Harris Weinstock's article is from Harris Weinstock, Jesus the Jew (New York: Funk & Wagnalls, 1902), pp. 28-29.

22 He Was the Jew of Jews

*American Reform rabbi as well as communal and Zionist leader, **Stephen S. Wise** (1874-1949) founded the Free Synagogue in New York in 1907 and served as rabbi there the rest of his life. In 1922 he founded the Jewish Institute of Religion. He was editor of* Opinion *and author of several books.* **

It is a sign of the times that it is possible for a Jewish teacher to speak frankly and forthrightly about the life and teaching of Jesus the Jew, and that, save for a handful of bigots within or without Israel, few will take exception to the honest utterance of a Jew respecting Jesus. Through the centuries it has been almost impossible for a Jew to bring himself calmly and judicially to consider anything connected with the life and teachings of Jesus, whose name had been made one of terror to his people because of the cruelly unjust attitude of Christendom towards Israel for nearly nineteen hundred years. Moreover, the Jew almost scrupled to plumb the depths of his own appreciation of Jesus, lest such appreciation token disloyalty to his deeply wronged people. During the centuries that have passed an ofttimes Christless Christendom has made it impossible for the Jew to look upon Jesus as a Jewish teacher or as a Jewish prophet, for to the Jews he could be little more than the founder of a "Jewish heresy," which resulted in infinite disaster to his own people.

Even if Jesus had not been born unto Israel, even if he had borne no relation to the people of Israel, it becomes of importance for Israel to determine for itself what shall be its relation to the man who has touched the world for nearly two thousand years as has no other single figure in history.

What we think of Jesus we must say, not only because of his position in the world of religion, but because he was a Jew, because Christianity is an offshoot of Judaism. The eternal paradox of the Jew, giver of everything, keeper of little or nothing, once the giver of the gift of Jesus' life and teachings to the world, and now under the need of declaring what is his attitude toward him, who was not only flesh of his flesh but very soul of his soul!

Neither Christian protest nor Jewish lamentation can annul the fact that Jesus was a Jew, an Hebrew of the Hebrews.

*This article by Stephen S. Wise appeared as "The Life and Teaching of Jesus the Jew," in *The Outlook*, June 7, 1913, and is reprinted from *The Dawn*.

Surely it is not wholly unfit that Jesus be reclaimed by those who have never unitedly or organizedly denied him, though oft denied by his followers; that Jesus should not so much be *appropriated* by us as *assigned* to the place in Jewish life and Jewish history which is rightfully his own. Jesus was not only *a* Jew but he was *the* Jew, the Jew of Jews, and it is little less than tragic that, with respect to Jesus, the world imagines that his life belongs to Christianity even as his death was due to Israel. That Jesus was a Jew is only half admitted, when not wholly denied; but that Judas was a Jew is always affirmed without doubt or hesitation. Whatever the death of Jesus may have been, we believe that his life was Jewish, and we devoutly affirm that Jewish was his teaching. In that day when history shall be written in the light of truth, the people of Israel will be known not as Christ-killers, but as the Christ-bearers; not as the God-slayers, but as the God-bringers to the world.

23 The Figure of Jesus on the Israeli Horizon

*Ferdynand Zweig is a well-known English scholar. He served several years as Visiting Professor in Sociology and Labor Relations at the Hebrew and Tel Aviv Universities.**

The figure of Jesus, the Jew from Nazareth, looms large on the Israeli horizon, although not much is said about him openly and most Jews cautiously refrain from mentioning his name in public. Still he is very much in the mind of the Israeli Jews, more now than ever, and the awareness of his shadow in Israel is constantly growing.

In the Galilee, the most beautiful and inspiring part of Israel, he is the dominating figure. Every site of antiquity and every beauty spot in Galilee bears his footprints. He is still "walking by the sea of Galilee" (Matthew IV, 18), "on the Sabbath day he enters into the synagogue in Capernaum" (Kfar Nahum) (Mark I, 21), in Tabgha close to Capernaum he performs the miracle of the loaves and fishes (Luke IX, 17). On the Mount of Beatitudes which overlooks the waters of the Lake, he utters his immortal Sermon on the Mount. Of course, Nazareth is the centre of his life, and Jerusalem the scene of his last ministry. Much of the charm and magnetism of the holy land is due, not only to echoes of the Bible, but also to the echoes of Jesus' life.

Being confronted with Jesus in this way is a new experience to the Jew. In the Diaspora Jesus looked alien to the Jew, an outsider, an interloper. But in Israel he is seen as the Jew from Nazareth, a native of this country, a Sabra, with claims to the land as strong as any. He cannot be brushed aside as a foreign influence.

How to deal with him? Of course he is a valuable asset to his country. He is a big "dollar earner," as a first-class tourist attraction. The tourist posters of the Israel government, of El Al and of all Israeli shipping lines proclaim, "Come to the Holy Land, see all of the Holy Places," meaning not only those holy for Jews but also for Christians. The tourist guides are full of descriptions of sites venerated by Christians.[1]

When the Jews left their land two thousand years ago, the land was holy for them alone; when they returned, the land was holy also to more than half of the world.

*The article here reprinted is from Ferdynand Zweig, *Israel: The Sword and the Harp* (Cranbury, N.J.: Associated U. Presses, 1969), 219-29, Used by permission of Associated University Presses. All numbered footnotes are Zweig's.

The land had become sanctified in the meantime to millions and millions of non-Jews. The same applies to the Bible which had been a book holy to the Jews alone and which has become a holy book for millions of non-Jews. Both the Book and the Land have become sanctified to the world and this was not the work of the Diaspora Jews who, in spite of the injunction, did not become "a light to the Gentiles," but was the work rather of a single Jew and his band of Jewish followers, all of them Sabras. They were all born and bred in the Land, which is in this sense the most fruitful land on earth.

Shall the Israelis disclaim and brush aside this work with an allegation that it was all heresy, an allegation which sounds hollow to a secular Jew in the twentieth century (and most European Jews in Israel are secular Jews), or shall they claim back their natural inheritance, the fruit of the Land to which they have returned?

The Israelis cannot forget that in a way Jesus was also instrumental in their return to the Holy Land. Have they reconquered the Land all by themselves? Were they not helped by the British at first, then by the Americans and the United Nations? Were they not assisted by all the Christian Zionists, including Churchill, Roosevelt, Truman? Was not the vision of the Holy Land, restored to the People of the Holy Book, instrumental in obtaining this help? The wish to fulfil the Divine Promise and the Holy Prophecy for an ingathering of the scattered Tribes, and for the resurrection of the Dry Bones of Israel, was consciously and even more sub-consciously a driving power towards the assistance which has been forthcoming from the Christian countries under many forms, such as political support in the United Naitons, armaments, and finance. Suffice to say that, without Jesus, the Holy Book would have remained for the non-Jew and obscure Book, and the Holy Land an exotic small country with no greater significance than Tripoli or Sudan. Actually the Jewish reconquest of the Holy Land may be considered as an heir to the Crusades, strange as this may sound. One could class the reconquest of the Holy Land by the Jews as the last and the most successful Crusade, undertaken this time by the Jews but not without considerable help, especially initial help, from the Christian powers, without which the Crusade could not have started and gained its initial impetus.

When the Jews returned to Israel, they had to re-define their historical identity, which is now centred and pivoted on the Land of Israel, and they had to make a long journey backwards in time, in fact two thousand years back. The Third Commonwealth, the present-day Israel, had to be linked with the end of the Second Commonwealth. And that was the time of Jesus' ministry. The exile from the Land coincided in time with the spread of Jesus' message. And when the Israeli Jew starts to ponder over the annals of the end of the Second Commonwealth, he has first of all to ask the fateful question: Were his forefathers right in rejecting Jesus? Why is it that more than half of the world have accepted Jesus as God (Christians), or as a Prophet (Moslems), or as The Ideal Man (Humanists), while the Jews of his own kith and kin have rejected him? And his answer must be that after all and in spite of everything, from the point of view of the preservation of a distinct body of Jewry, the ancestors were right in rejecting Jesus, when they lost their land and began their pilgrimage. They had really no alternative but to reject this universalistic interpretation of the Jewish Faith if they wanted to preserve a distinct body of Jewish people, once they had lost their land, their State and their language. If the Jews had accepted Jesus, the Jews would have been dissolved in the sea of Christianity and that would have been the end of their road. Diaspora Jewry was forced to close its ranks, erecting the Ritual Law which enclosed the Jewish community of the Ghetto. Any universalistic interpretation of the Judaic creed was out of the question if the Jews wanted to survive as Jews.

But how is it now? Do the Jews who have returned to their land need the props of the Ritual Law to retain their identity, now that they have their own Land, State, language and culture? What is the reason now for rejecting Jesus who was the fulfillment of Jewish dreams for greatness and importance in the world, the fulfillment of their dreams to be a light unto the nations? Can Jesus the Jew be taken back to the fold where he belongs, can he be incorporated in the body of Judaism, as a genuine Israeli product?

Of course one does not refer here to the doctrines of Christianity which grew on, and from, Jesus' teaching, which in essence are and must remain foreign to the Jew; here one refers only to the teaching of and personality of Jesus the Jew, as presented by his Jewish disciples in the Synoptic Gospels. They show Jesus as a Prophet in Israel, a major product, an heir of Isaiah and Jeremiah.

Was he then a prophet in Israel? Secular Jews are often inclined to answer this question in the affirmative, and religious Jews answer, of course, in the negative. The main argument against Jesus' status as a prophet in Israel is based on the contention that he, in his message, lacked a national and political awareness or a concern about the fate of Israel. This view is for instance expressed by Joseph Klausner, the author of *Jesus of Nazareth*, who writes that "he lacks the prophet's political perception and the prophet's spirit of national consolation in the political-national sense."[2] Such a view seems to be devoid of both meaning and substance. Firstly, because the prophet's spiritual and religious perception was always superior to his national and political perception, and secondly, because Jesus' message was highly relevant to the political and national issues of his time. His injunction "Love thine enemy" was not only the greatest and noblest of personal messages but also and highly significant national-political implications. It had a great functional value in the time directly preceding the destruction of the Second Temple, and might have saved Jerusalem and the Temple from total destruction, had the Jews followed the precepts and attempted to "love" the Romans, or at least to be friendly with them and understand their point of view, understand the great values of the Greek-Roman civilization without imitating or following them. After all Rome and Athens were great centres of civilization and culture. Jesus sensed the coming disaster, the greatest disaster in the history of the Second Commonwealth, which sealed its fate. Hence his messages: "Resist no evil" and "Render unto Caesar what is Caesar's," which if followed could have saved Israel from the impending disaster.

Martin Buber has interpreted the message of Jesus: "Resist no evil" in a not dissimilar way, linking it directly with the age-long teaching of Judaism, writing inter alia:

> The other message of Jesus: "Resist no evil" means: resist the evil by
> doing good, do not attack directly The Realm of Evil, but join forces to

attain the Kingdom of Goodness—then the time will come, when the Evil will not be able to harm you, not because you have redeemed it. Jesus wanted to build out of Jewry a Temple of True Community, which could bring down by its mere appearance the walls of the state governed by force. However, the future generations have not understood him in this way.[3]

If Israel is the heir to the Second Commonwealth, is she not heir also to the most significant spiritual message of that Commonwealth? Rabbinical Judaism was the Judaism of the Diaspora. What is the Judaism of the Third Commonwealth to be? Should it not incorporate the most important message of the preceding Commonwealth?

The mystery of this simple Jew from Nazareth, who managed to conquer almost the whole world and whose spiritual power was stronger than that of the whole of Jewry is simply puzzling to the Israeli Jew. Who was he? Where lies the secret and mystery of his power? How did this Jew manage to attract the immense love and adoration of the world, while the Jews attracted only hatred and contempt? How did he manage to fulfil the task set in the Bible for the Jews to serve as "a light unto nations," while Jewry failed? Why was it that only he managed to shape and mould the world, while the Jews played a losing game, rolling in the dust? Why has the genius of Jesus never been repeated within the Jewish gates? And will it ever be repeated?

A hope is often expressed in many quarters, both Jewish and non-Jewish, that the Third Commonwealth will bring forth a new felicitous and forceful message, a good tiding similar to the message brought forth by the Second Commonwealth. Louis Finkelstein, chancellor of the Jewish theological seminary in the United States, speaking about Israel as a spiritual force, expressed this hope in the following way: "It may seem arrogant to suggest that the State of Israel, recognizing the severe limitations of the temporal world, and associating itself with Jewry in other lands, may yet beget such an idea, a concept so forceful that it may itself redeem mankind; yet the world's need for such an idea can scarcely be questioned."[4] He seems to have forgotten that the most forceful and significant idea begotten by the Second Commonwealth still remains rejected up to the present and is left outside the gates of the Third Commonwealth. How can the Third Commonwealth beget "a new forceful and significant idea," if the forceful and significant idea of the Second Commonwealth is expelled from its precincts?

A similar hope was expressed by the greatest Israeli poet, Chaim Nachman Bialik.

> Not in vain has the hand of God led this people through the straits of Hell, only to restore it to its home for the third time. The book of Chronicles, last in the Canon, is not the final record of Israel's career. To its two sections shall be added a third. If the beginning of Chronicles is "Adam, Seth, Enosh," and its end the Cyrus Proclamation which after six hundred years resulted in tidings of salvation for the ancient pagans, so shall the beginning of its third division be the Balfour Declaration and its end—the new tidings of salvation for humanity[5]. . . .

Israel gathers in its land for the third time. Why cannot the miracle occur again?[6]

Other Israeli poets, novelists and writers have speculated also on the same theme of Jesus and new tidings, such as the novelist A. A. Kabak and the poet Avigdor Ha'Meiri. The great Israeli writer Y. C. H. Brenner said,

> The same importance which I recognize in the Bible in remnants of memories from distant days and in the development of the spirit of our people and the humanistic spirit within us over many generations and ages—such importance I also feel in the books of the New Testament. . . . The New Testament is also our book, bone of our bone and flesh of our flesh.[7]

The American Rabbi, David Polish, writes about Israel's interest in Jesus:

> Ever since the new Yishuv began, a special interest in Jesus has been manifested. This does not indicate, as some theologians have wishfully stated, a turning toward Christianity. It does, however, show that in the free atmosphere of Israel, a new approach towards Jesus, removed from the realm of polemics or vituperation common to medieval Judaism, is taking place. It is to be expected that in the land where Jesus lived and from which the Christian message went forth, a deep interest should be stirred among Jews.[8]

And Rabbi Polish expresses again the same hope and expectation as that quoted earlier,

> The view of the State as an instrument of higher purpose is very old in Judaism, but it can be given a special and an urgently needed application now. The reconstruction of the Jewish Commonwealth was only a road towards a messianic goal. It was to be the source from which the universal concepts of peace and world unity were to emanate. Unless Israel addresses itself to this task, even now, amidst its travail and its jeopardy, it will fail in its chief justification.[9]

We can find a very strong contrast to those millennial hopes and expectations in the present moral and religious atmosphere of Israel, which can be best described as one of alienation from its deeper self. I believe it was Hegel who first coined this term: The alienation of society from its deeper self. This term has nowhere fuller application than in Israel. It is a new society but with very old values which are rapidly being totally discarded, while equivalent new values are not forthcoming, hence the general feeling of a spiritual vacuum. The tragedy of Israel is that the old religion, practised only by the orthodox, is ritualistic, petrified and ossified, and deprived of its vivifying, life-enhancing and tender forces, while the rest of society, the majority, is atheistic, agnostic, or religiously indifferent, disinterested or unconcerned. So religion in Israel is hardly alive in any direction. This situation was tolerable so long as socialism and social humanism were the living creeds of the elite. The pioneers in Israel were either socialists or Humanists, who believed in man and his progress, and substituted Man for the Godhead. This creed no longer holds the allegiance of the elite, let alone the masses of Israel. Consequently, we are witnessing a very general aridity of the spirit. Generally speaking ideals are at present out of fashion everywhere, not only in Israel, and Israel is not unique in this situation. But it is worse for these reasons:

Firstly, the Jews are a spiritual nation with spiritual needs and aspirations. The Jew needs a creed for his very existence as much as anyone else needs air and water; secondly, Israel is a new society which has to be built on new foundations, and these must have roots in spiritual values of a more permanent nature. Thirdly, Israel is ingathering her Tribes which need a common creed as a cementing factor.

Emil Durkheim, himself a son of a French Rabbi, in a lecture to the International Congress of Philosophy at Bologna in 1911, speaking about value judgements and judgements of reality, referred to spells of collective enthusiasm and creative synthesis which take place at crucial moments of historical development. 'At such movements this higher form of life is lived with such intensity and exclusiveness that it monopolizes all minds to the more or less complete exclusion of egoism and the commonplace.'[10] Such a creative synthesis, and such higher forms of life have not occurred in "Israel" up to now. The creation of the State of Israel, a unique historical moment, has not been accompanied by a supreme and unique creative intensity of social and spiritual life, out of which great symbols or great ideals could emerge to provide a frame for social integration, identification and aspiration, for the society as a whole. The supreme creative synthesis which should have accompanied the supreme event in Jewish history, really the two supreme events, the Holocaust on one hand and the creation of the Jewish State on the other, has up to now failed to materialize. The culminating point in the development of the Jewish identity has not been accompanied by the creation of culminating creed or renewal of creed or the emergence of an ideal-synthesis of Jewish existence. There is no "purified reflection of the unique historical movement," to use Durkheim's phrase, there is no all embracing dynamic ideal to act as a catalyst of emotion, as a focus of national communal interest, as a spur for a dynamic drive towards the fulfilment of the age-long aspirations of Jewry.

The Jewish religion seems to be at present to the large mass of Israeli Jews uninspiring and uninspired. Could it be that Jesus could give it a new lease of life? Could a new, Israeli stage of Jewish religion escape from the Ghetto wall made up of 613 bricks, and instead incorporate the personality and message of Jesus, the Jew from Nazareth, as a major prophet for Israel, of course excluding all Christianized stylization of Jesus as Christ? These are perhaps the most exciting, the most portentous questions, most pregnant with potentialities, affecting not only the people of Israel, but also those of the world at large. The Tribes of Israel parted with what the world regards as the best and the finest they have produced so far when they left the Ancient Land, no doubt for good reasons, if one looks back from the vantage point of history. But now, coming back to their Land, will they be able to claim back also their spiritual inheritance which was nurtured in their Land, the child of their spirit and body? Accepting this inheritance and nourishing it in their own spirit, reinterpreting it in the spirit of Judaism, might make all the difference in the fight for survival by the Israeli Jews, in their development as a nation, and as a spiritual force in the world, as well as in the peaceful settlement of their conflict with the Arab nations.

Notes

1. The El Al advertisements in the British Press read: 'Come to Israel to see the Room of the Last Supper, Via Dolorosa, Bethlehem and Nazareth, where Jesus spent his boyhood and his youth, the Kfar Cana of the Gospels where Jesus performed his first miracles,' etc.
2. *Jesus of Nazareth,* p. 144. Jerusalem, 1922.
3. Martin Buber, *Der Heilige Weg. Ein Wort an die Juden und an die Völker,* p. 44. Frankfurt, 1920.
4. Moshe Davis, *Israel: Its Role in Civilization,* p. 14. Harper Bros. New York, 1956
5. Bialik, *Devarim Sheb' al Peh,* p. 55, Vol. I. Tel Aviv, 1935.
6. Op. cit., p. 54.
7. Brenner, *Kol Kitve, Ha-Poel Ha-Mizrachi,* pp. 103-4, Vol. VI. Dvir, Tel Aviv, 1927.
8. David Polish, *The Internal Dissent: A Search for Meaning in Jewish History,* p. 207. Abelard-Schuman. New York, 1961.
9. Op. cit., p. 210.
10. Durkheim's *Sociology and Philosophy,* p. 93. Cohen and West, London, 1953.

Part Two
An Analysis of Present-Day Jewish Views of Jesus

Some Pertinent Factors in Jewish-Christian Understanding

And do not suppose that you can say to yourselves, "We have Abraham for our father"; for I say to you, that God is able from these stones to raise up children to Abraham.

Matt. 3:9 (NASB)

There is neither Jew nor Greek, there is neither slave nor free man, there is neither male nor female; for you are all one in [Messiah] Jesus.

Gal. 3:28 (NASB)

Or is God the God of Jews only? Is He not the God of Gentiles also? Yes, of Gentiles also.

Rom. 3:29 (NASB)

And Jacob called his sons, and said, Gather yourselves together that I may tell you what shall befall you in the lat er days. . . . The scepter shall not depart from Judah, nor the ruler's staff from between his feet, till Shiloh* come and to him the nations will render willing obedience.

Gen. 49:1, 10 (author's trans.)

And there shall come forth a shoot out of the stump of Jesse, and a twig shall grow forth out of his roots. . . . And it shall come to pass on that day, that the root of Jesse, which stands as banner of the peoples, him shall the nations seek, and his dwelling-place shall be glorious.

Isa. 11:1, 10 (author's trans.)†

Behold my servant, whom I uphold; mine elect, in whom my soul delights; I have put my Spirit upon him; he will bring forth justice to the nations. . . . He will not fail or become broken till he has established justice in the earth; and the isles shall wait for his teaching.

Isa. 42:1, 4 (author's trans.)†

---

*Traditional Jewish Bible expositors interpret "Shiloh" to mean King Messiah, probably on the basis of the Ezekiel passage 21:25-27 (21:30-32 Heb.). See *Ezekiel* (London: Soncino, 1950), p. 141.

†Traditional Jewish Bible expositors apply both of these passages to the Messiah.

No Religion Is an Island—*Ludwig R. Dewitz* 77
For More Objectivity in Jewish-Christian Relations—
   Louis Goldberg 80
Difficulties in Jewish-Christian Dialogue—
   Jakob Jocz 86
Should Christians Propagate the Message of Jesus?—
   Arthur W. Kac 92
Bridging the Gulf—*David N. Freedman* 98

24 No Religion Is an Island

*When not quite seventeen, **Lüdwig R. Dewitz** attended a Christian youth camp in his native Germany and there gained the conviction that Jesus is the culmination and finality of biblical truth as revealed in the Hebrew Scriptures. He then took up studies at two theological schools, but the Nazi Gestapo made continued attendance impossible. Through the kindness of a British Christian group, Dewitz was able to emigrate to England. There in 1945 he received his B.D. degree from University of London. Later, he studied under Dr. F. W. Albright at Johns Hopkins University and in 1960 received his Ph.D. degree in the field of Near Eastern studies. During the last twenty years Dr. Dewitz has been professor of Old Testament languages, literature, and exegesis at Columbia Theological Seminary, Decatur, Georgia.*

"No Religion Is an Island" is the title of an article by Abraham Joshua Heschel, which appeared in the *Union Theological Quarterly Review* 21 (January 1966):117-34.

"No Religion Is an Island" is an observation that seems to state the obvious. The intent of Heschel's article is, however, not to state the mere historical facts that illustrate positively or negatively the way in which various religions have lived in proximity with each other, but his concern is more restricted. Heschel does not deal with the religions of the world at large; but his concern is confined practically to the relationship obtaining between Judaism and Christianity, with an occasional aside to Islam. The purpose of it all is to make a fervent plea for interreligious cooperation, which, in Heschel's words, would mean "to help one another; to share in sight and learning. . . .to cooperate in trying to bring about a resurrection of sensitivity, a revival of conscience . . . to nurture openness to the spirit of the Psalms, reverence for the words of the prophets, and faithfulness to the living God."

These words are understandable in view of the fact that the author of the article is a Jew who is pleading for openness and understanding throughout. The question arises, however, whether Christians, for instance, have not already nurtured in common with the Jews a proper and right understanding of the Psalms and prophets and have not striven to exhibit "faithfulness to the living God." Should there not be opportunity given for Christians to present a call to nurture openness to the spirit of the gospels, reverence for the words of the apostles, and, thus, faithfulness to the living God?

Of course, everybody would agree with Heschel that we ought to unite our religious forces in combating a worldwide encroaching nihilism, that a "holier than thou" attitude with overtones of arrogance and contempt is unworthy of the spirit of true religion, and that a sympathetic understanding of another's religion is an essential premise in any dialogue between people of differing creeds. We can gladly echo his penetrating statement: "The human is a disclosure of the divine, and all men are in God's care for man. Many things on earth are precious, some are holy, humanity is holy of holies."

In discussion among Jews, Muslims, and Christians, the fact that theologically their religious outlook is determined by strict monotheism, and historically by having its *Sitz im Leben* in God's revelation to Moses, provides a broad base for mutual understanding; the question is whether co-existence is all that we must emphasize.

Heschel seems to argue very much along that line, and he seems to be saying more or less what Rabbi Seymour Siegel has expressed in these words: "If Christians have a sincere devotion to the cause of the Jews, let them assist Jews to remain Jews." It is significant that Heschel avoids meticulously any quote from the New Testament. The thrust of his article is that Christians be conceded a role in the salvation of the world as long as they refrain from seeking to propagate the gospel to Jews: "A Christian ought to realize that a world without Israel will be a world without the God of Israel. A Jew, on the other hand, ought to acknowledge the eminent role and part of Christianity in God's design for the redemption of all men."

In other words, Heschel acknowledges that the gospel contains a redemptive message for the world at large, but implies that for the Jews there is a separate, special way of redemption available, different from that of the gospel. At the same time, he emphasizes the necessity for Christians to realize that theirs is a "Jewish religion": "Judaism is the mother of the Christian faith. It has a stake in the destiny of Christianity. Should a mother ignore her child, even a wayward, rebellious one? On the other hand, the Church should acknowledge that we Jews in loyalty to our tradition have a stake in its faith, recognize our vocation to preserve and to teach the legacy of the Hebrew Scripture, accept our aid in fighting anti-Marcionite trends as an act of love."

For Heschel, Christianity is a child of Judaism, but it is a wayward child. Now, any Jew has the right to have his personal opinion about Christianity, but he cannot demand that the essential message of the gospel be changed to suit his preferences. In fact, Heschel demands that the New Testament not be the New Testament. If there be gospel contained in it, it ought to be for Gentiles only, but the fact is that the New Testament clearly states that the gospel "is the power of God for salvation to every one who believes, to the Jew first and also to the [Gentile]" (Rom. 1:16, NASB).

It is true that the Christian church would do well to realize that it has framed its message too much in a Greek rather than a Jewish garb, and Heschel is right to draw our attention to this. Yet, he also admits that the Christian church has brought the knowledge of the God of Israel and the Holy Scriptures to the world at large.

One might argue that much of modern Christendom has deviated too much from its Jewish moorings, but a case could equally be built to show that modern rabbinical Judaism has moved a long way from its biblical foundation.

Vital to the whole discussion is ascertaining how biblical tradition views the role of Israel in its relationship to the world at large. Obviously the emergence of Abraham after humanity's precarious adventures outlined in Genesis 1-11 and climaxing in the "Tower of Babel" incident is of importance here. After the united attempt to provide security and fulfillment for humanity ended in utter failure, Abraham was called to become a blessing to all the nations of the world. Obviously that blessing is connected intimately with the unique revelation and knowledge of God. Contrary to all prevailing religious conceptions of deity bound to nature, the Bible emphasizes the transcendent and immanent character of God, working in history in such a way that ultimately no comparison with other deities is possible. Heschel admits that the knowledge of the God of Israel has become disseminated through Christians who believed that Jesus was the Messiah, but that movement was started by Jews who believed that Jesus was the Messiah.

To make Christianity consonant with "Gentile" religion, which should exist alongside Judaism pure and simple, is too superficial a view of the historical and theological factors that bind the message and content of the Old and New Testaments together. To relegate Jesus simply to the Christians, implying that He does not present a challenge to the Jews, is too facile a solution in view of what the New Testament claims for itself.

If there is a Messianic message in the Old Testament, then it can hardly be maintained that that Messiah would be one for the Gentiles only and that He would have no impact on Israel herself. Heschel's weakness is that he does not really come to grips with the question of the Messiah as He is represented in the New Testament. Whether he will come to the conclusion that Jesus of Nazareth is the Messiah according to the Old Testament or whether he will arrive at a different interpretation, the fact is that, assuming religions are not islands anymore, the issue of the Messiah must be faced squarely by Jews as well as by Christians, and it is not enough to tell Christians: Proclaim the Messiah to the world, but leave us Jews alone."

25 For More Objectivity in Jewish-Christian Relations

Louis Goldberg is professor of theology and Jewish studies at the Moody Bible Institute of Chicago. He has been a member of Old Testament committees on translation and review of translation for the New King James Version. He has also served on several Old Testament committees on translation for the New International Version. *Dr. Goldberg is a contributor to:* The Wycliffe Bible Encyclopedia; Old Testament Theological Word Studies; Tyndale Family Bible Encyclopedia; Thomas Nelson Bible Almanac; *and the* Bible Expositor Sunday School Quarterly.

The late 1960s and early 1970s were a turbulent period in recent American history. They were years in which the advocates of the counter-culture (including many Jewish young people) filled the air with far-left rhetoric concerning revolution. Their message was anti-Israel, antiestablishment, anti————, anti————, anti————.

There were also those who issued theological pronouncements concerning the religious establishment. They disseminated their "God is dead" theology and declared that we are entering the post-Christian era. There has been much conjecture as to the kind of world we shall have without the political, social, and theological influence of the church.

As we look back upon that agitated period from the current position of Christianity's increasing influence with young people, Jewish as well as Gentile, some of the "post-Christian era" pronouncements appear empty of meaningful content. One statement in particular dealt with the position Judaism should take in the new "post-Christian era" and became the subject of an article entitled "Judaism in the Post-Christian Era" by Eliezer Berkovits.[1]

The purpose of this essay is to show (1) that in his studied consideration of Christianity and the church, Berkovits was certainly not objective, and (2) that there is, at this juncture of history, a necessity for Christians and Jews to take a good look at their common history and the Scriptures which both of them affirm.

WE NEED TO DIFFERENTIATE BETWEEN GENUINE CHRISTIANS AND PSEUDO-CHRISTIANS

It soon becomes apparent from a perusal of Berkovits's article that when he uses the term *church*, he has in mind the medieval church. It is also apparent that in his use of the term *Christian* he makes no distinction between genuine believers and pseudo-Christians. In general, Jews apply the word *Christian* to any Gentile in the countries of Christendom. But a Gentile living in a "Christian" country may be an agnostic, a theist, a secularist, or a Communist. There is a vast difference between a pseudo-Christian and a genuine Christian, just as there is a great difference between a secularist Jew and a genuine orthodox Jew.

In the New Testament, the word *church* is derived from a Greek word that means "the called out ones" and is equivalent to the Hebrew word *kehilah* (a calling together, an assembly). In the New Testament the church consists of people, Jews and Gentiles, whom God has "called out" to be His people, who—as Jesus said to Nicodemus—have experienced a spiritual rebirth ("born anew," "born from above"), whose mission in the world is to be witnesses of God's saving grace made possible through the atoning death and resurrection of Messiah Jesus. Those, and those only, are "Christians" in the New Testament sense of the word. All those who speak of themselves as Christians but who have never experienced that spiritual, regenerating change of their lives are pseudo-Christians.

When Constantine the Great joined the church, Christianity became a state religion, and it began to absorb many pagan ideas. In his book *The Anguish of the Jews,* published in 1965,[2] Edward H. Flannery, an outspoken friend of the Jewish people, carefully points out that with the Hellenistic institutionalization of Christianity, which came about following the Nicean Council, Christendom became flooded with people who had never experienced a real change of heart—people who remained pseudo-Christians. The expulsion of the Jews from Spain, the Chmielnicki massacres in Eastern Europe, the pogroms in Tsarist Russia—all these and other crimes perpetrated on Jewish people were the work of pseudo-Christians. On the great day of judgment they will find themselves among those to whom Jesus will say: "I never knew you: depart from me, [you evildoers]" (Matt. 7:23).

Even in the dark Middle Ages, the light of the gospel was burning, however dimly, and in every age there have been genuine Christians who treated Jews with Christian love. Yet how seldom are those true Christians mentioned in Jewish pronouncements on the subject of Jewish-Christian relations.

Berkovits claims that the Nazis were children of "Christians," and he therefore blames their "Christian" background for what the Nazis did to the Jewish people. But Berkovits is silent about the millions of Poles and Russians who also were murdered by the Nazis. He says nothing about the hundreds of genuine Christians, Catholics and Protestants, who perished in concentration camps because they opposed the Nazi philosophy.

One can be certain that most Nazis were not children of Christian parents. It was in Germany that, in the nineteenth century, a movement sprang up aiming to destroy the biblical faith. Theologians by undermining the Old Testament, believing quite rightly that if the Old Testament can be proved to be based on fables rather than facts, the New Testament will fall apart. The Nazis were filled with that anti-Christian poison, and there is evidence that had the Nazis won the war they would have sought to uproot Christianity.

Whereas Berkovits blames "Christians" for what the Nazis did to the Jews, he says nothing about what Christians did to save Jews during the Nazi period, often at the risk of their own lives. Not a word is said about that Christian minister who headed a rescue mission that secretly transported practically all Danish Jews to Sweden. Nothing is mentioned by Berkovits of the activities of the Catholic cardinal (who later became Pope John XXIII) and the Swedish mission in Budapest that saved many Hungarian Jews from certain death. Not a word is heard from Berkovits about the many silent, genuine Christians who furnished food and hiding places to individual Jews and whole families, at a time when to do so was risking capital punishment.

How are we to account for the failure by Berkovits to mention that anti-Semitism was practiced by the heathen world in the long centuries prior to the rise of Christianity? Pagan Egypt made the first attempt to exterminate the Jews. In heathen Persia another such an attempt was unsuccessfully tried in the days of Mordecai and Esther. Jews were intensely hated by pagan Greeks and Romans. And the Second Jewish Commonwealth, including the second Temple, was destroyed by pagan, not Christian, Rome.

Berkovits also strangely omits saying anything about the anti-Semitism of atheistic Communism or that at this juncture of history atheistic, communist Russia is the world center of intense anti-Semitism and hostility to the state of Israel.

THE CHRISTIAN OUTREACH

Berkovits attributes the spread of Christianity in Asia and Africa to colonial rule by those Western nations that had conquered those continents. The truth of the matter is that the only assistance that Christian missionaries received from colonial governments was permission to enter the countries under their rule and engage in Christian activities there. On the other hand, it is established fact that those Christian missionaries often denounced the immoral practices of unscrupulous Western traders and some unjust policies of colonial governments. Also, Christian missionaries often fought to eliminate child marriage and the heartless exploitation of women, which were normal features of certain cultures. Not only so. Christian missionaries often planted in the hearts of the nationals a desire for individual and collective freedom that eventually led to the liberation of the colonial peoples.

We would also like to know how Berkovits accounts for the powerful Christian movement surging ahead at the present time in many parts of Africa and Asia among peoples that now are ruled by their own native governments.

As to Christian missionary activities aimed at Jewish people, it is the religious duty of genuine Christians to make the gospel available to all peoples, Jews and Gentiles. If unethical methods have been used at times in propagating the message, we deplore and condemn such things. But is it not true that certain Jewish leaders in America are seeking to make it impossible for Jews to hear the gospel? Did not one of the prominent and genuinely religious Jews in America declare some time ago that certain Jewish groups are seeking to silence the gospel in America, not because it is Christian but because it is a religious message and it takes seriously the Bible as the Word of God? And did not the former rabbi of the Fifth Avenue Synagogue in New York City (who subsequently became chief rabbi of Britain) state that American Jews want to eradicate religion from American public life because, compared to the active interest in Christianity manifested by Christians, Jewish religious indifference makes Jews look bad?

The New Testament gives indirect evidence that in the first century Jews carried on intensive missionary propaganda among the Gentile people in the Roman empire. The "God-fearers" attached to many synagogues were Gentiles who were sympathetic to the message of Judaism. With the rise of the Messianic movement of Jesus, His Jewish followers merely continued that Jewish practice of missionary activities.

WHY DOES ISRAEL SUFFER?

Berkovits stresses the point that man rather than God was responsible for the suffering of the Jewish people. He points particularly to the statements made by the church from the days of Chrysostom through the Middle Ages. It was Augustine who posited two points for a proper understanding of the position of the Jewish people since the coming of Jesus: first, Christians ought to have a special love for Jewish people because they are loved by God for the sake of their fathers; second, the Jewish people have become a sign and a warning to others of what happens when a people forsakes God's truth. Unfortunately, pseudo-Christians often disregarded Augustine's first point, and dwelt on the second. But genuine Christians have never ceased to thank God and the Jewish people for their biblical faith. Genuine Christians have always acknowledged that they owe their spiritual heritage to the Jewish people. For centuries, genuine Christians have prayed for the restoration of the Jewish people to their ancient land. And since the present state of Israel came into existence in 1948, genuine Christians have underscored their pro-Israel position and have toured Israel every year in large numbers.

But there is something about Augustine's second thesis that compels us to plumb deeply its meaning. Setting aside for the moment a specific people, is there not a basic biblical truth in what Augustine formulated? Did not Moses, our teacher, indicate what would happen to the Jewish people when they set aside God's truth (Leviticus 26, Deuteronomy 28)? Did not the prophets warn Israel that if they turned away from God's revealed truth they would suffer the consequences? And does not the Prayer Book affirm the reason for Israel's sufferings in the following passage, based in part on Isaiah 53, and recited on the Day of Atonement?

> We are ever threatened by destruction because of our evil deeds, and God does not draw nigh us—He, our only refuge. Our righteous Messiah has departed from us. We are horror-stricken, and have none to justify us. Our iniquities and the yoke of our transgressions He carries, and He is wounded because of our transgressions. He bears on His shoulder the burden of our sins, to find pardon for all our iniquities. By His stripes we shall be healed. O, Eternal One, it is time that Thou shouldst create Him anew! O, bring Him up from the land of Seir, to anounce salvation to us from Mount Lebanon, once again through the hand of [Messiah] Yinnon.

What has happened to ancient Israel happened also to many Christian communities in Asia Minor and North Africa, which disappeared when they became unfaithful to the Word of God. The same fate has overtaken apostate Christendom in Europe. Shall we say, as implied in the words of Berkovits, that the sufferings inflicted on European nations in two world wars are purely the works of man? Can we not see the providential discipline of the hand of God in the fate of the European nations that once had the truth of the Word of God and then turned against it?

AN INTERCHANGE BETWEEN JEWISH PEOPLE AND GENUINE CHRISTIANS

Berkovits insists that it is useless from emotional, philosophical, theological, and ethical points of view for Christians and Jewish people to even discuss the Scriptures that the two peoples have in common (pp. 290 ff.). In his opinion, the Christian view of the Old Testament and the Jewish person's view of the Old Testament are so diametrically opposed and there is such a dichotomy between the two faiths that discussion is useless.

Although it is true that each people comes to the Old Testament from a different vantage point, nevertheless there are many areas that both groups do hold in common, for example, the basic necessity for a moral view of man in society, the place of prophecy in Scripture, the correct attitude toward Zion, and so on. In those and other areas, both faiths can certainly find points of agreement and share with one another wholeheartedly.

Can Berkovits honestly say that the relation of Jewish people and genuine Christians is the same as in the Middle Ages? Does he really think that we are living in a day when both faiths are still in their retrenched positions and where nothing can be said between them? Indeed, have we not reached the day when both faiths need to discuss common interests?

The existence of a new relationship and the necessity for interchange is put into sharp focus by what one Dominican priest of the St. Isaiah House in Jerusalem said recently during a radio interview at Moody Bible Institute. He had been asked, "What can Christians learn today from a willingness to search the Scriptures with Jewish people?"

He said, "I think we are rediscovering a continuity between Jewish and Christian peoples. We are reaching the point where we can talk to each other clearly, loyal to ourselves, but without hatred indeed. We do agree to disagree on key issues. It is clear that Jesus Christ is between Jews and Christians a stumbling block. It is awfully painful to see that. We are separated by the person of Christ. But, having said that, we can rediscover, at least on the Christian side, the lines of continuity between our two faiths. Jesus the Messiah, the Jew, appears now as the one who separates us, but yet at the same time, He unites us. In other words, we were victims during almost two thousand years of a family quarrel, and, as you know, the quarrels in the family are the most bitter quarrels. . . . Too many in the church insisted too much on the quarrel, but we are now rediscovering that it is really a *family* quarrel. My conviction is, at least in some milieu in Jerusalem, that the new way of discussion between Jewish people and Christians is possible between people of good will."

But on what basis shall there be interchange? Berkovits admires Socrates (p. 289). But although the pagan philosopher has some good things to say, where do we go for ultimate authority? For a Jew, that place can be none other than the written Law (the Word of God)!

However, we see two problems in a Jewish approach to the understanding of the Scriptures. Reform Judaism has all but given up on the Hebrew Scriptures as an authoritative source from God. By means of humanism, utterly devoid of biblical authority, theologically liberal Judaism has sought to face the problems of the past hundred years, and we now realize how bankrupt is such an approach. Berkovits insists that a Christian point of view is bankrupt today (pseudo-Christianity always was), but the genuine Christian at least does take the Bible at face value. Is that approach bankrupt? With divinely revealed principles one has a proper view of anthropology and a means by which man's basic nature can be changed. Anything apart from the divinely revealed Scriptures will only lead down a road with no signposts or guide marks. In fact, that road leads absolutely nowhere except into confusion. Many young people today have seen the results of that approach and have come back to a more biblical point of view.

There is also a specific problem concerning rabbinical Judaism as it was restructured after the destruction of the second Temple. Part of its intent was to discredit the Jewish believers in Jesus the Messiah, particularly, and a belief in Jesus in general by all peoples. Now without the testimony of the exchange of life principle in substitutionary atonement in the Temple format, in the place of Temple sacrifices rabbinical Judaism substituted its great triad: repentance, prayer, and good works. That leaves atonement on the basis of law and good works and completely shuts out grace, which one sees in both the Hebrew Scriptures and New Testament. God becomes impersonal and a nagging question persists as to where one finds Him.

Certainly, both Christians and Jewish people are entitled to their views and interpretation regarding the Old and New Testaments. Nevertheless, if both peoples claim to be peoples of the Book, then certainly the Book should be preeminent in the thinking of both.

Long ago, the prophet Isaiah wrote:

> The grass withers, the flower fades,
> But the word of our God stands forever.
> [Isa. 40:8]

Can there be any other word for personal fulfillment and atonement for sin in the vertical relation with God? Can there be any other word by which society can govern itself? Is there any other word that tells us of the return of the Messiah, who alone will bring in the Messianic kingdom for which men have longed?

Notes

1. Eliezer Berkovits, "Judaism in the Post-Christian Era," *Judaism,* Winter 1966, pp. 284-95.
2. Edward H. Flannery, *The Anguish of the Jews* (New York: Macmillan, 1965), pp. 45-63.

26 Difficulties in Jewish-Christian Dialogue

Jakob Jocz is a third-generation Hebrew Christian.
Born in Lithuania, he was educated in Poland, Germany,
England, and Scotland. He received from Edinburgh
University his Doctor of Philosophy and Doctor of Letters
degrees. Dr. Jocz is a past president of the International
Hebrew Christian Alliance. He is the author of several
books on theological subjects. He is professor emeritus of
systematic theology at Wycliffe Seminary, University of
Toronto and is a regular contributor to the national
Anglican journal, The Canadian Churchman.

Traditionally the church has stood over against Jewry in a missionizing attitude. But in recent years there has been a transition from mission to dialogue. The change has accelerated since the end of World War II and even more so as a result of Vatican II.

In the past, the two faiths met in hostility. There was nothing to dialogue about. Either the church was right or the synagogue was right; there was no neutral ground. But in our syncretistic age and multi-cultural situation that either-or attitude has given way to greater tolerance on both sides. It has appeared more reasonable in view of changed circumstances to meet in conversation. On the Jewish side, the church is expected to abandon her missionary effort and to agree to meet on equal terms. There must be no sense of superiority on either side. The difficulty about dialogue lies in the fact that once both parties have taken their position on neutral ground, there is little to dialogue about except generalities. That is recognized by some Jews, especially the orthodox, who see no merit in a dialogical encounter.

Reformed Jews, whose universalism tends towards a syncretistic attitude, are more open and willing for conversation with Christians. There is precedence for such meeting between Christians and Jews beginning with Justin Martyr and the Jew Trypho in the second century. More recently such exchange of views has taken place in Europe between a number of outstanding Jews and Christians.

Martin Buber has laid down rules that, if observed, should make genuine dialogue possible. First, both parties must take each other seriously; they must be able to listen to each other without suspicion or prejudice. There must be no hidden or ulterior motives in the encounter. Because of the subjective nature of faith, both sides must recognize that the ultimate secret of either partner is impenetrable from the outside. In Buber's words, "We are not capable of judging its meaning, because we do not know it from within as we know ourselves from within." That is now an accepted rule frequently stated by Jewish writers.[1]

In view of the subjective limitation accepted by both parties, it is difficult to see the rationale of the enterprise. Because the partners speak from entirely different points of view, dialogue can only result in incoherence. At the same time, Jewish scholars who engage in dialogue frequently stress that discussion can only be successful if both sides place themselves on neutral ground. But if that be the case, in what sense can the exchange be a discussion between Jews and Christians?

Walter Jacob is aware of the difficulty and readily admits that an encounter between Jews and Christians must not take place in an "aseptic atmosphere" as if it were a matter of an autopsy and did not concern living beings. He recognizes that "emotion is necessary in dialogue" and that "one must have strong commitment, otherwise the enterprise loses its value."[2]

That creates a difficult situation because neutrality and commitment are contradictory. One cannot maintain such a position without tension. There seems to be no escape from impasse. As a result, the dialogue, at any rate in written form, tends to take a nontheological position and avoids dealing with matters of faith. Instead, it concentrates on history and ethics. The latter subject is especially close to the Jewish mind, both because Jews are a suffering minority and because they strongly emphasize moral values.

The "Quest for Common Ground" (the subtitle of Jacob's book) is hardly supported by the subject matter the author presents. Beginning with Moses Mendelssohn (d. 1786), who is described as a pioneer, and ending with contemporary efforts on the part of Jewish scholars, the book presents an overview of Jewish attempts to assess the significance of Christianity in history.

Such assessment is not an easy task for Jewish writers who, on the one hand, have to acknowledge the Christian affinity with Judaism, but, on the other hand, have to stress Christianity's alienation from the "mother" religion. In the past, and by tradition, Jews have always maintained that Jesus and Paul were renegade Jews who had nothing in common with the Jewish people. But as a result of intensive studies in more recent years, that attitude has changed to a more cautious rejection. It has become fashionable, especially since Joseph Klausner, Martin Buber, and Leo Baeck, to claim Jesus as a Jew who "exaggerated" Judaism without realizing the consequences and to speak of Christianity as a "daughter religion." Jews have persuaded Christian writers of two things: first, that there is a direct and unbroken line of development between the Old Testament and later rabbinism; and, second, that Pharisaic Judaism was the religion in which Jesus was reared and which prevailed at the time of the New Testament. Seen in that perspective, Christianity is the wayward daughter of the synagogue and ought to be led back to its source. Granted that understanding, there can be no "common ground." On the contrary, most of the writers in Jacob's book look forward to the day when Christianity will disappear and will be replaced either by Judaism or a religion akin to it. As Jacob puts it: "All paths lead to Judaism, which represents the hope of mankind."[3]

Naturally enough, in the center of Jewish attention are the two outstanding figures of the New Testament—Jesus and Paul. In view of the widely divergent views among Gentile scholars, it is not to be wondered at that Jews are equally divided.

Jesus represents a puzzle that cannot easily be resolved: Did he claim to be the Messiah? Did he intend to initiate a new religion? What was his attitude to Judaism? Was his hostility to the Pharisees, as claimed by the gospels, true to fact? Was he a nationalist, a fanatic, a religious genius, or a man suffering from delusions? Those and many other questions occupy Jewish writers as they approach the New Testament.

An equally contentious figure is Saul of Tarsus. Traditionally, there was greater hostility towards Paul than towards Jesus. Most Jews hold that the real founder of Christianity was Paul and not Jesus. He is presented as the archenemy of the Law and the destroyer of Judaism. Only recently has a more positive note crept into the discussion concerning Paul. Writers like Max Brod, Richard Rubinstein, and Hans Joachim Schoeps have refused to assign to Paul a purely Hellenizing role. But that is a novel attitude as far as Jews are concerned. Samuel Sandmel has no difficulty in presenting Paul as a Hellenistic Jew who abandoned Judaism from a sense of discontent. But even he mitigates his position by contending that Paul's pre-Christian Judaism was the Judaism of the Diaspora and therefore not a different Judaism but only shot through with Hellenistic ideas. The same position is taken by Klausner. It is noteworthy that Walter Jacob has limited his book to so-called "scholarly" effort and has left out the work of Sholem Asch, who in his book *The Apostle* presents a more positive and thoroughly Jewish attempt to understand Saul of Tarsus.

The dialogue between Jews and Christians in personal encounter now taking place in different countries, especially in Europe, and the increasing number of articles and books produced by Jewish scholars indicate a spirit of good-will that is reciprocal. On the Jewish side, there is an obvious desire to avoid denigration and to find positive features common to both Judaism and Christianity. To Franz Rosenzweig, Christianity is God's way with the Gentile world; it contains divine truth directed towards non-Jews. Jacob remarks: "Rosenzweig was the first Jew to grant Christianity such recognition."[4] Schoeps, under Rosenzweig's influence, goes so far as to allow the possibility of a new revelation outside the covenant, for Christians in Jesus and for Muslims in Mohammed.[5]

Perhaps the most positive stance thus far is taken by Rabbi Hershel Matt. In an article "How Shall a Believing Jew View Christianity?"[6] Matt makes allowances seldom dared by a Jewish critic. Instead of taking the usual route of historic analysis from a partisan position, Matt approaches the subject theologically. He sees Christianity and Judaism as two *vehicles* of revelation that are closely related: "the *People* Israel, bearers of the Torah: in the other case, the *Person* of Christ, one-man embodiment of Israel and the Torah."[7] Those two "vehicles," Judaism and Christianity, serve the same end—to make known God's Word and will and to affirm His indwelling presence. The Jewish community does that on an ethnic basis, the church on a universal scale. Regarding "moral law," both faiths agree that an essential mark is a life of holiness.

In view of Leo Baeck's criticism that Christianity is a "romantic religion," lacking "truthfulness," and is passive in regard to ethics, Matt's admission is a great step forward. Matt is even prepared to admit that Judaism by reason of its "greater *resort* to law" runs "greater *risk* that law may degenerate into legalism." To this writer's knowledge, only Claude Montefiore dared to go that far. It is almost a rule among Jewish scholars to deny any proneness to legalism in the observance of Torah.

But Rabbi Matt goes beyond Montefiore, who, as the father of liberalism in Great Britain, could not admit miracles in either Testament. Allowing for the fact that no Jew can accept the characteristic Christian doctrines (such as the virgin birth, the incarnation, the resurrection, Christ as Savior, and the Trinity) and remain a Jew, Matt asks: "But need he deny them?" His answer is that Jewish nonaffirmation of Christian truth is not tantamount to the affirmation of its falsehood. Even the miracles "performed by Jesus *need* not be *denied* by a believing Jew." In respect to the resurrection, Matt points to Scripture and Talmud as an article of faith: "He who says that the resurrection of the dead is not derived from the Torah has no share in the world to come" (Sanhedrin X1:1-2).

Rabbi Matt is not prepared to answer the question regarding a dual form of covenant, nor is he able as a Jew to answer the question regarding the Trinity either "affirmatively or negatively." The "most" he can do is to acknowledge the fact "that in the lives of countless men and women who profess Christ the power and presence of God appear to be evident." Many Jews would privately make a similar admission, but few would have the courage to say it publicly. Sholem Asch, to the end of his life, lived under the shadow of suspicion of crypto-Christianity for expressing similar views.

That is not to say that "Christianity" as known in history is beyond criticism. There is much that the church has reason to be ashamed of. But aberrations are the result of human limitation and are common to all men, Jews included. It was Claude Montefiore who maintained that fairness would require that we look at each faith at its best and not at its worst.

Jewish criticism of "Christianity" suffers from the false presupposition that it can be abstracted from the people who profess it as if it were an entity existing in space and time. As there is no "Judaism" apart from Jews, so there is no "Christianity" apart from Christians. Viewed concretely, there are only people who are either labeled or label themselves in one way or another.

Another fallacy underlying the Jewish effort is to make a radical division between Jews and Christians as if they belonged to two different species of humanity. Jews, Christians, Muslims, Hindus all share a common humanity. Race, color, and culture do not make so radical a difference as to destroy the common tie that binds all human beings. There is a Jewish proverb that in translation runs something like this: "As it happens with Christians, so it happens with Jews." In the last resort, underneath all the differences acquired as a result of historical vicissitudes, there is a core of solid humanity that indwells us all. Before a person is a Jew, a Christian, or whatever, he is a human being with all the frailties that adhere to human nature.

Related to that is the other mistake of taking man as a completed entity. No Jew is a perfect Jew, and no Christian is a perfect Christian. In the flux of historical existence, that is, existence in space and time, man is always in the process of becoming. The Greek poet Pindar (fifth century B.C.) wisely said, "Labour to become what you are." Goethe paraphrased the saying: *"Werde was du bist"* — become what you are. Every human being is an heir of the past, but the past only becomes our possession by an effort of intellect and will. To quote Goethe again:

> *Was du ererbt von deinen Vätern hast*
> *Erwirb es, um es zu besitzen . . .*

"What you have inherited from your forebears, labour to make it your possession." Even the covenant with Israel, though offered freely by a gracious God, can be spurned by the individual and the nation.

Rosenzweig's greatest mistake is that he gives to Israel a purely ethnic interpretation. He makes blood relationship the guarantee of Israel's election. To be born a Jew means, for him, to be already a son of God. Though he distinguishes between the individual and the nation, the distinction is only an artificial one. The non-Jew is always a stranger—where as the Jew belongs to God by reason of birth: "We possess what the Christian will one day experience; we have it from the time of our birth and through our birth it is in our blood."

Walter Jacob tries to exonerate "this emphasis on genetic heritage" as "an element of early-twentieth-century German thought."[8] But that is not entirely fair, for the medieval poet Judah Halevi in his *Kuzari* had already interpreted Jewish election in purely racial terms.[9] For that reason, Jewish writers find the New Testament concept of *metanoia* ("inward change," "conversion") as described in John 3 difficult to understand. For them, conversion always means change of religion, usually from the God of Israel to an alien god. The Jew therefore requires no conversion in the Christian sense; in Rosenzweig's words: he "need no longer come to the Father" for he is already with Him by reason of his birth.

Another peculiarity of the Jewish approach to Christianity concerns the preoccupation with what Jesus taught, as if Christ's teaching were the essence of the Christian faith. Only seldom do Jewish writers grasp the fact that the essence of the Christian faith is not the teaching of Jesus, but Jesus Himself. His "teaching" derives from the authority of His Person and not the other way around. The result is that much Jewish scholarship is expended upon comparisons between Jesus and Moses, the prophets, the rabbis, the Talmud, and so on. Whereas *torah* as "teaching" is an essential feature of Judaism, it is not so in Christianity. The teaching that Jesus is the "teacher," the preacher, the storyteller may be the mark of some liberal Christians tainted with Unitarianism, but it is not the quintessence of the Christian faith. And is that not what Jeremiah had in mind when he told the people of his generation that God will some day conclude with Israel a new covenant that will not be like the Sinai covenant? "But this is the covenant which I will make with the house of Israel after those days, says the LORD: I will put my law within them, and I will write it upon their hearts; and I will be their God, and they shall be my people. And no longer shall each man teach his neighbor and each his brother, saying, 'Know the Lord,' for they shall all know me, from the least of them to the greatest, says the LORD; for I will forgive their iniquity, and I will remember their sin no more" (Jeremiah 31:33-34; 31:32-33, Heb.)

In the center of the church is not the Book but the Person, the risen Christ. The Book bears witness to Him, hence the Christian's loyalty to the Scriptures. All Christian doctrine is formulated with a view to Him whom the church calls Savior and Lord. Church discipline has meaning only if it is an aid to discipleship. For the Christian therefore the problem is not how to comply to church rules but how to express one's loyalty to the Master. That shift from impersonal obedience to *mizvot* ("precepts") to a personal relationship to the Savior is the ultimate secret of the Christian believer.

Real dialogue therefore will only be possible when the believing Christian in an encounter with the believing Jew will be allowed to tell his brother the innermost secret of his faith in God. The Jew on his part will exercise the same freedom in his dealing with the Christian. Dialogue can take place only in an honest and respectful meeting of people in true intimacy and not in books or articles. However, books and articles are useful means in preparation for dialogue.

Notes

1. Cf. Walter Jacob, *Christianity Through Jewish Eyes: Quest for Common Ground* (Cincinnati; Hebrew Union College, 1974), pp. 95, 125, 173, etc.
2. Ibid., p. 6.
3. Ibid., pp. 60, 82, 135, 171, etc.
4. Ibid., p. 126.
5. Ibid., p. 190.
6. Hershel Matt, "How Shall a Believing Jew View Christianity?" *Judaism,* Fall 1975, pp. 391 ff.
7. Italics here and hereafter are those of Rabbi Hershel Matt himself.
8. Matt, p. 128.
9. Cf. Jakob Jocz, *The Jewish People and Jesus Christ* (C.P. C.K.: London, 1949), pp. 310-11 (see Judah Halevi, Al Khazari I, p. 115).

27 Should Christians Propagate the Message of Jesus?

Arthur W. Kac grew up in Warsaw, Poland, where he was educated in the Hebrew and Talmudical schools, and came to the United States in 1927. He holds the B.A. and M.D. degrees from the University of Minnesota.

A certified roentgenologist, Dr. Kac is a member of several scientific societies. He is an author, is editor of The Interpreter, *and has been a lifelong student of the Hebrew Bible.**

Some time ago there was a discussion in certain Christian quarters concerning whether it is right or proper for Christians to include Jews in their evangelistic outreach. Because no Christian standing on biblical ground can take the position that Christianity is meant for some and not for others, what really mattered in that discussion was the Jewish side of, and Jewish reaction to, the question. The Jewish point of view was set forth by Rabbi Arthur Hertzberg in an article in *The Christian Century*.[1] In the present article we wish to discuss the subject from the Jewish and Hebrew Christian viewpoint. Thousands of Jews in America are affiliated with Christian churches. Some of them are pastors, although the vast majority hail from all walks of life. The Jewish people are our people; the Jewish hope is our hope; the Jewish destiny is our destiny. We are followers of Jesus because we believe Him to be Israel's Messiah and also because in Him we, together with millions of other Christians all over the world, find life's meaning and ultimate purpose. In certain respects our position is that of a bridge between the synagogue and the church, or between the Jewish people and Jesus Christ. In the light of that relationship, we believe we can make a valuable contribution to the subject under consideration by, first, analyzing the Jewish position and, second, defining the Hebrew Christian position.

THE PRESENT JEWISH POSITION

1. Evangelistic activities among the Jews may open old scars.
   (a) Memories of the horrors of Nazism
While admitting that there were Christians in Germany who stood for decency,

---

*Arthur W. Kac's article, here reprinted with stylistic changes, appeared under the title "Are Jews Entitled to Know The Christian Message?" in *The American Hebrew Christian* 46, no. 1 (Summer 1960):106. Used by permission.

the presence of Christian chaplains with the Nazi armies proves—according to Rabbi Hertzberg—that other Christians in Germany supported the Nazi regime. It is somewhat difficult to see why the presence of Christian chaplains with the Nazi armies should indicate Christian support for the Nazi regime. There are Catholic chaplains in the Polish army in spite of the mutual antipathy that exists between the communist government and the Catholic church of Poland. We have chaplains in the American army even though in America religion and state are separated. The chief, if not the only, function of any chaplain in any army is not to demonstrate his denomination's attitude to a particular regime, but to care for the spiritual needs of those soldiers who might wish to avail themselves of his services. As a matter of fact, Christians were probably the only people in Germany who dared to denounce publicly the Nazi excesses against the Jews. During World War II thousands of Jews in Nazi-occupied Europe were saved by Christians, some of whom paid with their lives for their activities on behalf of the Jews.

(b) The Christian attitude to the state of Israel

The Christian attitude toward Israel is another sore point   Jewish-Christian relations, which Rabbi Hertzberg thought may become aggravated by evangelistic activities among the Jews. "Jews," Rabbi Hertzberg maintained, "will contemplate the pronounced anti-Zionism of many church circles and note that every single state that has arisen in Africa and Asia since World War II . . . has found almost unqualified support in organized Christianity, except Israel." It is regrettably true that certain Christian circles have manifested a negative approach to the reborn state of Israel. However, that has probably been counterbalanced by the genuine and helpful interest in Zionism shown by other Christian groups and individuals, both in the past and present. In 1891 William E. Blackstone, a devout Christian and Bible scholar, presented to President Harrison a memorandum signed by over five hundred prominent clergymen and Christian business and professional men. The petitioners of that memorandum asked the President to convene a conference of the European powers including Turkey, to consider the question of returning Palestine to the Jews. Chaim Weizmann, the great Zionist leader who became first president of the state of Israel, states in his autobiography that men like Arthur James Balfour, David Lloyd George, Winston Churchill, Alfred Milner, General Jan Christaan Smuts and many others were Bible-believing Christians to whom Zionism represented a great tradition that they held in enormous respect. Of Orde Wingate of World War II fame, who trained Palestine Jews in self-defense methods, Weizmann said that he was an ardent Zionist whose Zionism stemmed from his lifelong study of the Bible.[2] In America, many of us are acquainted with the American Christian Palestine Committee and the American-Israel Society, which number among their members outstanding American Christians and which have been laboring for a better American appreciation of Israel's position in the world.

The Jerusalem Post reported the presentation by Dr. W. A. Criswell to the Israel Ambassador Simcha Dinitz of a scroll "proclaiming Evangelical Christian solidarity with the State of Israel." The presentation ceremony was attended by some twenty other prominent evangelical Christian clergy. Dr. Criswell is the pastor of the largest single Southern Baptist congregation in America, numbering thousands of members. In presenting the scroll, Dr. Criswell declared his community's "total support for Israel, 'with all our heart and soul.' " *The Jerusalem Post* called that event "an extraordinary outpouring of support for Israel" by the leadership of the evangelical Christian community in America numbering about forty million evangelical Christians.[3]

2. Evangelistic activities endanger America's position in the world.

Opposition to Christian evangelism in the modern world, Rabbi Hertzberg stated, is not confined to the Jews. Increasing resistance to those activities is displayed by the non-Christian nations of Asia and Africa. A continuation of those activities "will not only embarrass America before the world, but lend new fuel to the appeal of communism in the East." It is quite true that present-day Christian activities in Asia and Africa are encountering serious obstacles, but for reasons that are the very opposite of those suggested or implied by Rabbi Hertzberg. Many, if not all, of the nations that gained political independence since World War I received a helping hand from the Christian church. Christian missionaries in the foreign field were often the first to plant in the hearts of subjected peoples the seeds of political and civil liberties. Not only is that true of the Arab Middle East,[4] but also of the nations of the Far East.

In his discussion of the causes underlying the stirring in the backward regions of the world, Frank Laubach stated that the teachings of Jesus were the first factor responsible for the tremendous change of the mood of those peoples from one of sullen hopelessness to grim resolve. The multitude of Christians who distributed Bibles never realized what new hope and determination the poor and oppressed derived from the words of Jesus, from His compassionate deeds, and from His death. " 'Blessed are you, poor, blessed are you that hunger now, for you shall be satisfied. Woe to you that are rich, woe to you that are full now, for you shall hunger . . .' Here was good news for the poor, release to the captives, liberty to the oppressed, sight to the blind—these words were dynamite, for the Bible is dynamite."[5]

The peoples of Asia and Africa will not so soon forget those who brought that message to them, the many splendid men and women who left the comforts of their home surroundings and went to faraway primitive places to establish medical schools, to open hospitals, and to teach the nationals a more decent way of life. Contrary to Rabbi Hertzberg's statement, it is not the American government, or any other government of the West, that stands to be embarrassed by Christian activities in Asia and Africa. It is the Christian Church that has at times been embarrassed by some colonialist practices of certain Western governments.

3. The world will respond to American leadership if religion is kept out of it.

African and Asian peoples, we are told, will respond to American leadership only if what we propose as a counter faith to Communism is not Christianity (or even Judeo-Christianity) but rather that greatest of all American values: "the vision of a world order in which all men serve side by side and help each other to be true to themselves, to their own hopes and aspirations." Those words from the lips of a religious leader will probably come as a shock to many religious hearts; they will not surprise those of us who are acquainted with the secularism of many present-day

Jewish religious leaders.

That the non-Christian world of today (and for that matter the "Christian" world, too) needs first and foremost a spiritual rebirth may be seen from the following statement by an Asian intellectual: "To my mind, the first component of the malaise from which the Indian intellectual suffers is utter uncertainty and instability. Political independence has been achieved in an age when the forces of communism and democracy are drawn up against each other in preparation for a mighty war of extermination, and in between the two there are any number of warring groups owing allegiance to an infinite variety of shades of pink faith. . . . What makes our burden appear so heavy is that we are not spiritually equipped to bear it. There is no faith and no object of faith."[6] No, "man does not live by bread alone, but by every word that proceeds out of the mouth of Jehovah does man live" (Deut. 8:3, author's trans.). In fairness to Rabbi Hertzberg we should mention that when writing to Jews he strikes a different note, as seen from the following passage: "The present condition of the Jew clearly demands a new spiritual impulse. . . . There is no escape from dealing with our time as it really is. It is an age to which the Word has not yet been spoken, but which, in its deepest soul, is waiting for it."[7]

THE HEBREW CHRISTIAN POSITION

"Let us stand separately for our various truths. Let us stand together for the peace of society. Let us not do to one another that which is hateful to any of us." In those concluding words Rabbi Hertzberg strikes at the heart of the matter. Christian evangelistic activities, which to the Christian are an expression of his concern for the spiritual welfare of others, are hateful to Jewish religious leaders. The underlying cause for that Jewish reaction is the concern of the Jews for their national survival in countries of their residence outside the state of Israel. That concern is greater now than years ago, inasmuch as the destruction of East European Jewry cut off the human replenishments that weak Jewries of the West were receiving from Eastern Europe. American Jews are apprehensive about their ability to maintain indefinitely their national identity. Christian conversions, intermarriages, religious indifference, and the inexorable leveling process of the American melting pot are making deep inroads into the Jewish community of America.

However, the real issue between Judaism and Christianity is theological in character. If Judaism is right, Christianity is wrong, and vice versa. In the first century Judaism took the position that Jesus of Nazareth is not the true Messiah. That fateful step had a powerful effect on the development of Judaism in the following centuries. Judaism was forced to relegate the Old Testament to the periphery of Jewish life for a variety of reasons, not the least of which was the fact that the Old Testament contains the seeds of New Testament truth, and the New Testament revelation appears to be the logical completion of the revelation of the Old Testament. Thus the study of the Talmud took precedence over that of the Old Testament. Any unusual interest manifested by a Jew in the prophetic writings made him at times suspect of heretical leanings.

The determination to seal off the Jew from the influence of Jesus led Judaism to adopt a severe attitude to the Hebrew Christian. As early as the end of the first century, when Christians—not Jews—were experiencing severe persecution at the hands of the Roman government, Jewish religious leadership set out to separate the Hebrew Christian from his Jewish brethren. A series of oppressive measures was introduced, the worst of which was the so-called Birkat Ha'Minim. That was a petition, composed at the end of the first century, which subsequently found its way into the Prayer Book, and which pronounced a curse upon the Jewish followers of Jesus. That prayer, or curse, gradually raised a wall of separation between Jew and Hebrew Christian. The Hebrew Christian who till then lived in peace and friendship in the midst of the Jewish people found it increasingly unpleasant to continue the same friendly relations in that sort of atmosphere. Thus an estrangement set in between Jew and Hebrew Christian that deepened with the passage of time. And that is exactly the way the synagogue intended it to be.

In the nineteenth century alone about a quarter of a million Jews joined the Christian church. Among them were eminent men of science, literature, art, and politics. We will mention only a few of the more generally known: Benjamin Disraeli, Queen Victoria's Prime Minister; Alfred Edersheim, known for his classic work *The Life and Times of Jesus the Messiah*; Johann Neander, the great church historian in Germany; Karl Paul Caspari of Norway; a number of Moses Mendelssohn's descendants, the best known of whom is the famous composer Felix Mendelssohn-Bartholdy; Daniel Chwolson, professor of Oriental languages in St. Petersburg, Czarist Russia; Bishop Schereschevsky from Poland, who labored in China, where he translated the Bible into one of the Chinese dialects; Izaak Da Costa, the great Dutch poet. Had Hebrew Christians been encouraged to remain within the Jewish community and form their own religious group, as was the case with the Hassidic sect, which came into existence in the eighteenth century, Hebrew Christianity would have in time evolved a distinctive Jewish Christian movement and exerted a powerful spiritual influence upon its own people and upon the world at large. As things stand now, the Jewish convert to the Christian faith finds it increasingly difficult to remain indefinitely in the Jewish community. Looked upon as a traitor, rebuffed and repelled, his ties with his people became gradually dissolved. Many of us still remember the unhappy experiences of the late Sholem Asch, who found himself persona non grata in the Jewish community for writing and speaking lovingly about the "Nazarene."

Should Christians include Jews in their evangelistic activities? Dr. George E. Sweazey gave the only consistent Christian answer in his article in *The Christian Century*, 29 April 1959: "For Christianity to do otherwise would mean to be unfaithful to its nature and mission." But the problem has implications above and beyond its mere theological connotation. Are Jews (or anyone else for that matter) entitled to hear the Christian message? Should Christians engage in religious discussions with non-Christians, whether Jews or Gentiles? Is it desirable for people of different religious beliefs to exchange their religious views with one another? There can be no true freedom of religion unless it includes the liberty to propagate one's religious convictions, even as there can be no true political freedom without the liberty of free political discussions. Conditions in countries under Communism bear out the validity of this principle.

Notes

1. Arthur Hertzberg, "To Believe and to Wait," *The Christian Century,* 16 September 1959, pp. 1051-56.
2. Chaim Weizmann, *Trial and Error* (Philadelphia: Jewish Publication Soc. of Amer., 1949), 1:157; 2:398.
3. *The Jerusalem Post International Edition,* 2 November 1976.
4. George Antonius, *The Arab Awakening* (New York: Putnam's) 1965.
5. Frank Laubach, *Wake Up Or Blow Up* (Westwood, N.J.: Revell, 1951), pp. 30-32.
6. Quoted by M. R. Masani in "The Mind of Asia," *Foreign Affairs,* July 1955.
7. Arthur Hertzberg, "Jewish Education Must Be Religious Education," *Commentary,* May 1953.

28 Bridging the Gulf

David N. Freedman is professor of biblical studies and director of the Program on Studies in Religion at the University of Michigan. He is past-president of the American Society of Biblical Literature, and former director of the Albright Institute for Archaeological Research, in Jerusalem. In 1939, while traveling in the Orient with his older brother, he became interested in Christianity. The two brothers began to read the Bible, and David became impressed with the Book's spiritual meaning. He enrolled at Princeton Theological Seminary and in 1944 was ordained as a Presbyterian minister. *

The tragedy of the Christian era has been the gulf between Christian and Jew. It is inconceivable that the wise and loving Father of both Christian and Jew should desire or intend that this gulf persist forever, or even any more. Is the solemn assertion of Saint Paul and his earnest longing for the reunion of Jew and Gentile in the Kingdom of Christ to be written off as the impossible dream of a fool? This is an apostolic and prophetic burden that the Christian dare not abandon.

The subject of this discussion is the issue between Jew and Christian and a possible approach to its solution. And since the religious question is both the basic one and the only valid one between Christian and Jew, we begin by a careful definition of the terms, "Jew" and "Christian."

We shall use the term "Jew" to designate one who is religiously a Jew, one whose ultimate faith rests upon the books of Moses, the Prophets, and the Writings, or the Old Testament, though never so designated by Jews, of course, who use either the abbreviation TNK or Miqra. In like manner, we may define a "Christian" as one for whom the ultimate ground of faith is the Bible, including both Old and New Testaments.

We do not mean to say, of course, with regard to both definitions that Jews and Christians have faith in a book, or that the heart of their religions is belief in words. Obviously the central thing is for the Jew the relationship to the God of Abraham, Isaac, and Jacob—the God of Israel; to which the Christian would attach, at the beginning, that this God is also the Father of our Lord Jesus Christ, in whom faith becomes real.

*This article by Dr. David N. Freedman appeared in *Western Watch* 6, no. 4 (15 December 1955):9-17, and is reprinted by permission of the author.

But again, the sole source for the God of Israel is the Old Testament: it alone describes this person and his activity, his purpose and his will; likewise there is no source for the life and career of Jesus other than the New Testament.

Thus the distinctive feature of these ethical monotheistic faiths is the Old Testament for Judaism and the Bible for Christianity; and it becomes immediately clear that there is a close interrelationship between these two. Essentially, and we emphasize the word, there is nothing in Judaism, as we define it, that Christianity does not affirm.

Now it must be granted that Judaism in its present modern form is incompatible with New Testament Christianity, but there are certain modern forms of Christianity that probably are too. Certainly, different modern forms of Christianity are incompatible with each other.

If we are able to speak of Christianity in generic terms, we must reduce it to certain common, but essential, characteristics; and Judaism must be treated in similar fashion. When we take Christianity and Judaism in their different modern forms, their most significant common element is the Old Testament.

Hence, as a Jew becomes a Christian he need not renounce anything of his previous faith to the extent that this involves the Old Testament.

Judaism, in other words, is compatible with Christianity, though both Christians and Jews have endeavored over the centuries to prove that this is just an illusion.

Thus the Church of the Middle Ages compelled all converts from Judaism to renounce and denounce Judaism on the ground that there was nothing in common between Christianity and Judaism. But actually the mediaeval Church was taking the Bible away from the Jew with one hand, and giving it back to him, wrapped as a Christmas gift, with the other.

In the same way Jewish attempts to misconstrue the Gospel as violating fundamental precepts of the Old Testament, or to regard Christianity as a pagan polytheism, have proved fallacious.

We are not suggesting, of course, that Judaism and Christianity are identical. But they do have a common literary foundation, upwards of seventy-five percent of the total by volume.

This means that a Jew who becomes a Christian is not converted in the ordinary sense of the term. He does not turn around, or change direction. On the contrary, he proceeds in the same direction; he advances in faith from the Old Testament to the New Testament.

To put it another way, a Jew remains a Jew when he becomes a Christian; or to revise our statement, a Christian is partly a Jew.

By our definition, then, there are more Jews than Christians in the world: that is, the Old Testament is the foundation upon which belief in Jesus Christ properly is built.

But the main issue between Jew and Christian is the matter of Jesus Christ. A Jew as we define him is one, who, while accepting the Old Testament, does not yet accept Jesus Christ or the New Testament; the Christian, on the other hand, is essentially a Jew who does.

Before this major issue can be met in a reasonably satisfactory way, it is necessary to clear away some of the peripheral debris which has piled up during the centuries of conflict.

On his side, the Jew has charges to make against the Church which, if sustained, would make a dialogue of any kind impossible; and until they are swept away, the main issues cannot be tackled.

Always overshadowing any discussion of the claims of Jesus Christ, or of the Church for Him, is the record of the suffering of the Jews at the hands of the Christian. It was no ordinary torment; bad enough to be persecuted, but to recognize as the chief weapon of condemnation in the enemy's arsenal your own sacred scripture, analyzed with a malevolent acumen that assigned all the curses to the Jews and all the blessings to the Church—that made an ineradicable impression of evil. It led Jews to the conviction that at best the Church was the "rod of divine anger" like Assyria, and at worst an instrument of Asmodeus and his cohorts.

In its apologetic, Judaism emphasized the more obviously pagan characteristics of the Church; ultimately it set the Church down as violating almost, if not all, the Ten Commandments at once. Roman Catholicism was an easy mark for charges of idolatry, blasphemy, apostasy, Sabbath-breaking, and so on. Since the Reformers made many of the same charges against a corrupt Church, this tended to confirm the Jews in their views; the counter-charges levelled by Rome against all non-Romans strengthened this conviction.

An excellent case in point is the doctrine of transubstantiation. Aside from the questionable theology of the doctrine, the incredible superstition which accompanied its promulgation throughout Europe, resulting in the fantastic charges against Jews of desecrating the host by stabbing it repeatedly until it bled to death, was clear proof to Jews (as it must also be to many others) that there was something fundamentally wrong with such a religion.

At worst, therefore, Christianity to Jews was a congeries of pagan superstitions, magical and absurd beliefs and practices, and abominable behavior, all stemming from belief in a three-headed God (or three Gods, one of whom was a renegade Jew). At best it could be regarded as a dilute form of Judaism, tricked out with ornamental features to attract the mobs, especially with an easy promise of salvation, and with the consequent tendencies and results. A friend of mine, a devout Jew, put it in almost precisely those terms: Christianity is the socially acceptable form of Judaism.

We need not long delay with a refutation of these charges. At most, they are only true of part of Christianity part of the time.

Essential Christianity cannot be dismissed as a pagan religion. Since it cannot be divorced from its Old Testament background, any basic charge against Christianity becomes a basic charge against Judaism. They have the same God and many of the same rules. The Ten Commandments have always occupied a basic position in both faiths, whatever the theological framework in which they are placed.

This applies in reverse as well. Many of the Christian charges against Judaism are equally trivial. Both are ethical monotheistic religions of the highest order. Both Christianity and Judaism exhibit the prophetic spirit of self-criticism, so that both are constantly in the process of reform and restoration on the basis of the biblical revelation. Each such reform brings them closer to each other.

Now the basic Christian charge against Judaism needs to be dealt with more carefully. This is not really a charge, but a dismissal of the whole case. The argument is that Judaism has been swallowed up and superseded by Christianity, so that there really is no reason for Judaism at all.

That argument naturally makes Judaism's survival somewhat of a problem for the Church. Historically the solution was found in the idea that the Jews were suffering punishment for their rejection of Jesus Christ—and the Church was not always averse to demonstrating the validity of this doctrine by encouraging the local authorities to carry out the manifest will of God!

We may well think it true that the destruction of Jerusalem and the Temple in 70 A.D. was a judgment on Israel and confirmed the prediction made by Jesus as to the consequences of rejecting him. But to suppose that God persists in punishing his recalcitrant people for a period of 1000 years seems rather difficult and finds no parallel anywhere in Scripture.

On the other hand, the survival of the Jews can hardly be explained on the grounds that they are examples of what happens to those who reject Jesus Christ. It is an inescapable conclusion that God has preserved unbelieving Israel in as miraculous, or even more miraculous fashion than is recorded in the Bible, and that he has done so for a definite purpose.

This preservation of Israel, as well as its suffering, is not only an embarrassment to the Church, but a judgment on her as well. Surely it was God's intention that the Church should carry on where the old Israel left off, and that the essential life and being of Israel should continue in the Church of Christ along with the ingathering of the Gentiles. There is little reason to doubt that had the Church sufficiently fulfilled this purpose, the Jews who did not come along would gradually have merged into the surrounding populations and Judaism would have vanished.

But this did not happen; and the destruction of the Temple was a final judgment. Logically the nation should have perished and its people with her. Yet the Jews survived. This fact alone would prove to the biblical eye that the God who had judged his people nevertheless had once more saved them, as he did through Moses, and then again after the destruction of the first Temple.

But why? The answer, if it is to be biblical or religiously oriented, must suggest that Judaism had a service to perform for the Church, or rather for the Kingdom, one which the Church had either neglected or bungled.

Now it is apparent that the only area in which Judaism could perform a service decisive for the kingdom of God would be in connection with the Old Testament. Revelation and inspiration ceased in Israel with the closing of the canon of the Old Testament, just as they did in the Church with the New Testament. But it is precisely in this area that Judaism rendered a decisive service.

It is perhaps a little known fact that with very few exceptions the Church preserved no copies of the Old Testament in the original language. There was no Hebrew scholarship in the Church to speak of until the Reformation.

While it is perhaps too small a point to labor, the implication would seem to be that had the Jews disappeared, the Hebrew Old Testament would have disappeared with them. A comparison of the Hebrew with the Greek Old Testament will confirm the magnitude of this loss; it would be as if only a Vulgate of the New Testament survived, instead of the original Greek, only worse.

More significant is the matter of the canon of Old Testament books. The Reformation canon is identical with the Jewish canon. Thus not only did Judaism preserve the original text of the Old Testament, but likewise the true canon.

The confirmatory evidence is found in the New Testament itself, where practically all of the canonical books of the Old Testament are quoted and assigned the status of scripture, but where there are practically no quotations from or allusions to non-canonical books. The canon of Jesus and the Apostles was the canon of Judaism, and came to be the canon of the Church by way of the Reformers.

The role of the Reformers in the history of the Church is very instructive from this point of view. In dealing with the Old Testament, both Calvin and Luther were greatly aided by Jews and Jewish Christians in their study of Hebrew and exegesis. Reformation exegesis, aside from Christological interpretations, was based largely on the sound, relatively rational exegesis not of the Church Fathers but of rabbis like Rashi and Ibn Ezra.

With the rise of Protestantism and the recovery of the Bible in its original languages, with the vast advances in scholarship and understanding of the Scripture, the question now comes with renewed vigor as to whether Judaism still has an independent purpose or function in the providence of God, or whether the time has not arrived in the divine plan for Jews and Christians to bridge the abyss between them.

The question gains increased significance when we observe that Judaism never found its way after the break with Christianity. Nothing has happened since to build on to the Old Testament, to complete and fulfill the work which is clearly a work of hope and expectation if it is anything.

Judaism has turned to one thing after another as a possible fulfillment and found them all wanting. It is indicative that the Old Testament itself cannot sustain a people; something more is needed.

Rabbinic Judaism, for example, is essentially a system for holding a people together, in which the Old Testament is embalmed, much as the Bible is treated in the Roman Church. And a reform movement of Judaism in the 8th century, known as "the Karaite," which among other things was essentially a return to the Old Testament and a rejection of the Talmud and the tradition, ultimately failed.

The modern Reform Movement has had a checkered history, but it will probably fail in the long run. There is a tendency already to drift back in the direction of orthodoxy. For some Jews it is a short step into the void of secularism, and for others there is an inevitable movement toward some liberal form of Christianity.

Old Testament religion, unprotected by the hedge of Orthodox Judaism is actually helpless in the face of Christianity. The tremendous power of Jesus' personality working on the Old Testament believer is hard to resist today even as it was a long time ago. All Jesus required was that a man break loose from the tradition of the elders and scribes, and beginning with Moses and the Prophets, he would show him the truth of Scriptures concerning himself.

It is time once again to initiate conversation with the Jews on the subject of Jesus Christ. Just as it is the business of the Church to prepare itself to present the case for Jesus to the Jew, so it will be the final service of Judaism to the Church to ask the key question, to set the issue of Jesus in its proper context.

That key question is the one voiced by John the Baptist when he sent his disciples to inquire of Jesus: "Are you he who is to come, or shall we look for another?" (Matthew 11:2 ff., Luke 7:22 [RSV]).

This in its simplest terms is the issue between Judaism and Christianity. It is not technical nor theological nor metaphysical. It does not require a Nicene formula. The answer may not be orthodox at first or even later. All the Church must do is give a reasonable answer to the question.

We cannot answer the question completely here. But the first part of our answer must be a sound, a careful exegesis of the Old Testament expectation.

What gives rise to this question at all? What sort of person is it that is to come?

While the phrasing is indefinite, the word "He who is to come"—in Hebrew, habba—is full of implications and connotations. And since this is exegesis of the Old Testament, a creative interchange with Jews is necessary. The Old Testament is one book and there can be only one meaning. One cannot impose an artificial meaning on a passage simply because it fits better with Christians predilections, or because tradition has labelled it messianic, or the like. Some general agreement may be attained.

A note of caution: Christians are accustomed to reading the Old Testament through the eyes of the New Testament. In fact, this has become so much a dogma of Christian exegesis that the new procedure may not be easy: that is, to read the Old Testament from the beginning.

But why should it be necessary for us today to impose a specifically Christian interpretation on the Old Testament in order to make it fit with the New? The first disciples, all ordinary readers of the Old Testament, had no insuperable difficulty in responding to the message and person of Jesus.

The Church defeats its own purpose in dealing with Jews by reading into the Old Testament what is thought to be in the New Testament, or reading out of it what is thought to be incompatible with the New Testament. The Christian case must stand on sound historical and linguistic methods, on the basis of scholarly standards acceptable to honest men, Jew and Christian alike, or it will not stand at all.

A second part of the answer must deal with the second clause: ". . . shall we look for another?"

By all means let Jew and Christian search the pages of history for another. But surely it is a telling argument that there is no serious contestant apart from Jesus Christ. At least it will be agreed that there is no other claimant worthy of the name. The Jews tried but .ouldn't make one; only God can.

And after 1800 years since the last serious claimant, and over 2000 years since Daniel and the close of the Old Testament canon, the conclusion based upon the biblical time-table would have to be that either the Messiah has already come, or there simply isn't going to be any. In fact, many Jews are turning to that idea: that God will bring in a messianic age but no messiah.

Thus the field for the presentation of Jesus will be cleared. No man certainly has a better claim than he; all other possibilities have been found wanting. And it is most unlikely that anyone appearing in the future will be able to make even as strong a claim as the already defeated candidates.

Now in arguing that Jesus is the Messiah sent by God, the evidence must be gathered carefully. We must begin with self-supporting or automatically acceptable material, and then proceed to the factually probable, to the possible, and finally to articles of faith.

Remembering always Abraham's admonition in the parable of the rich man and Lazarus, that the resurrection itself will not be convincing, it is better for us to begin with the teaching of Jesus. The first fruit of the laborious study of the Old Testament will be a comparison of the lessons of Jesus with those of Moses and the Prophets. It becomes imperative, first, to show that Jesus stands in the line of these, even as he claimed.

Then there is a strong case to the effect that Jesus was a true prophet. Although it is questioned by some, it seems inescapable that he foretold the destruction of Jerusalem. Fulfillment of a similar prophecy is what confirmed Jeremiah to an otherwise hostile audience.

Agreement on the prophetic character of Jesus would be a good start and might be sufficient to establish communion, certainly a creative communication between Christian and Jew.

There would remain the thorny problem as to whether Jesus were a prophet in the order of Prophets, expecting and preparing the way for the messiah, or the messiah himself. Maimonides, the great Jewish theologian of the 12th century, thought that Jesus was certainly to be regarded as a forerunner. A good deal of orthodox Christian theology runs parallel to this: emphasis on the second coming of Christ usually centers on the unfulfilled prophecies of the Old Testament regarding the kingly functions of the messiah, as well as on similar passages in the Gospels and Revelation.

Jesus himself, however, was willing to answer the question of John the Baptist on the basis of the evidence to hand, which includes very little of the evidence normally available to the Christian. Nevertheless it is his answer that is most important: a basic response to a basic question.

Like the questioner, Jesus avoids technical language. The evidence he presents is all in terms of actions, not of claims or assertions which cannot be checked, but of evidence available to the skeptical, or at least to the honest inquirer.

And this is a hint to the Church. When the Church deals with the question asked by John the Baptist, which is ultimately the question of the Old Testament Jew, the answer must be like Jesus' answer:

"Go and tell John what you [have seen and heard]: The blind receive their sight, and the lame walk, lepers are cleansed and the deaf hear, and the dead are raised up, and the poor have good news preached to them." (Matthew 11:2 ff., Luke 7:22 [RSV]) This is evidence that the kingdom has come, which is proof that the king has also come.

Now when the Church has presented its case soberly and honestly, it will have demonstrated a vital connection between the Old Testament and the New Testament. It is too much to hope that the Jews will be immediately convinced—they will continue to ask the question, and other questions; and so the debate will continue and the dialogue go on.

But this itself will be a great gain. For the more insistent the question, the better will be the answer . . . and in the interchange the Church will recover the Old Testament and the Jew will discover the New Testament.

But the final act will not take place in an exegetical discussion. It is not only the answer that Jesus made, recorded in the Gospels, that supplies evidence that he is indeed the one who should come. It is also the answer along the same lines that the church has made throughout the centuries, and that it makes even now, that clinches the case.

If Jesus is Lord and the Church is the instrument by which his kingdom comes, then the Church can report with equal fidelity: "The blind receive their sight, the lame walk, lepers are cleansed. . ."

When the Church exhibits in its life the Messiahship of Jesus and his Lordship over its life, then the world, and the Jews especially, will take notice. Then the Church will answer the question of John and of the Jews, and more than answer it: that Jesus is not only the one who should come, but also the Son of God and Saviour.

Anti-Semitism

But it shall come to pass, if you will not obey the voice of the Lord your God to observe and to do all his commandments and his statutes which I command you this day, then all these curses shall come upon you and overtake you. . . . And you shall become an astonishment, a proverb, and a byword, among all the peoples where the Lord shall lead you.

Deut. 28:15,37 (author's trans.)

And I scattered them among the nations, and they were dispersed through the countries; according to their way and according to their doings I judged them. And when they came among the nations whither they went, they profaned my holy name in that men said of them: These are the people of the Lord, and yet they had to go out of his land.

Ezek. 36:19-20 (author's trans.)

Who gave Jacob for a spoil, and Israel to the robbers? Was it not the Lord? He against whom we have sinned, and in whose ways they would not walk, neither were they obedient to his law.

Isa. 42:24 (author's trans.)

Jews and the Crucifixion—*Morris Zeidman*   109
Ten Gentiles and One Jew—*Solomon Birnbaum*   112
Jew-Hatred: Its Origin and Cure—*Max I. Reich*   116

29 Jews and the Crucifixion: Does the Gospel Story Engender Hatred Toward the Jews?

Morris Zeidman was reared by devout parents in an orthodox Jewish home in Poland. He received the usual Jewish schooling available at that time. When he came to Canada, he attended night school and worked during the day. He enrolled at the University of Toronto from which he was graduated. In the meantime he was led to faith in the Messiahship of Jesus. He then entered Knox Presbyterian College in Toronto where he received the Bachelor of Divinity degree.

From 1941 until his death, Dr. Zeidman directed the Scott Mission in Toronto, which under his leadership engaged in religious activities and the rendering of a variety of social services to many segments of society. *

Books are being written and sermons preached with a view to alter the story of the Crucifixion in its relation to the Jews. The purpose is to remove the perpetration of Calvary from the shoulders of the Jewish people. It is said that the story of the Cross causes Christians to hate the Jews, and if the story were obliterated from the curriculum of Christian Sunday Schools friendship would take the place of hatred. The inference, naturally, is that before the Crucifixion took place, the Jewish people lived in safety, peace and contentment.

That is interesting! It deserves historical analysis.

What does history say to that? The exact contrary! History shows that our people suffered much more in the thousand years before the Crucifixion than it did after it, that it began to drink the "bitter cup" even before we were organized as a people.

1. In Egypt we find the Hebrews as slaves, persecuted and oppressed, and their children thrown into the waters of the Nile.

2. The Amalekites were Israel's arch-enemies. "Remember what Amalek did unto thee by the way, when ye were come forth out of Egypt"—Deuteronomy 25:17.

*The original source of this article is unknown. It is reprinted by permission of Annie A. Zeidman.

3. The Canaanites and Philistines were constantly warring with Israel.

4. The Assyrians, too, contributed to the woes of our people. In the time of King Hezekiah, the Assyrian Sennacherib systematically destroyed the land of Israel and took over 200,000 captives.

5. The Chaldeans, under Nebuchadnezzar, managed to take away from the Hebrews the final vestige of their political sovereignty. They mercilessly tortured the Hebrew King by removing his eyes, but not before they had killed his children in his presence.

6. Haman's plans to destroy the Jews of Persia are equally well known.

7. We next come to the "cultured" Greeks, and find that they were not immune to the ghastly poison of Jew-baiting. The blood-libel, generally accepted as the invention of Roman Catholicism, finds its origin among the Greeks. We read of Apion being charged with accusing the Jews of annually fattening a Greek in the Temple, killing him, offering his body as a sacrifice, eating his internal organs and swearing an oath of enmity against all Greeks (See Contra Apion ii. 8/95, by Josephus). And what shall be said of the numerous pogroms perpetrated by the Greeks long before the story of the Crucifixion came into being?

8. The Syrian King, Antiochus Epiphanes, added his share to Jewish suffering, as the story of the heroic Maccabees fully illustrates.

9. And Rome! Was it not Tiberius Caesar who expelled the Jews from Rome? And how about Tessius Florus who encouraged his troops to pillage the homes of the Jews in Jerusalem. About 3,000 innocent men, women and children were butchered on that occasion. Three outstanding massacres followed in this period before the final destruction of Jerusalem under Titus, when about 1,100,000 were killed and 97,000 taken captive. And Titus was not a Christian!

10. The Persians were no different. The Sussanians destroyed the Jewish synagogues and forbade Jews the free observance of their religion. Bodies buried in the Jewish cemetery were exhumed and given to the dogs, because the Parsee religion forbade the pollution of the earth with corpses.

These historic references to Jewish suffering and bitter persecution are not complete, but we have attempted to present the outstanding instances as briefly as possible to prove that our people suffered in every age and in every land wherever they settled in considerable numbers, and that such persecutions were in vogue long before there was the story of the Crucifixion.

In fairness to the subject, we must remind our readers that religious bigotry is not to be ascribed to Gentiles only. Our people are not altogether immune to it. History which records the infamous deeds of Gentile nations also relates of instances when Jews used the sword to propagate their religion and to further their interests. Here is what we read in the Book of Esther on Purim:

"But the other Jews that were in the King's provinces gathered themselves together, and stood for their lives, and had rest from their enemies, and slew of them that hated them seventy and five thousand—but on the spoil they laid not their hand—on the thirteenth day of the month of Adar, and on the fourteenth day of the same they rested, and made it a day of feasting and gladness" (Esther ix. 16-17 [KJV and author's trans.]).

Hyracanus I compelled the Idumeans to be circumcised and accept the Jewish religion, and those who refused were hewn down with the sword. He also destroyed the Samaritan temple on Mt. Gerizim and coerced the Samaritans to attend the Temple of Jerusalem.

Dhu Nowar, Jewish King of Temen, not only persecuted the Christ ans, but forced them to renounce their belief in the Trinity and in "A Crucified God, ' as he termed it. When Christians refused to deny Christ, many were killed and others sold into slavery. The body of a Christian bishop was exhumed and burned; monks perished, nuns were martyred, men and women were put to death for their faith when they refused to accept Judaism.

But, let us forget the ghastly past! Let us return to the question: Does the narrative of the Crucifixion, as recorded in the Gospels, provoke Christians to hate the Jews? I have not taken a "straw-vote" on the subject, but have interviewed Christians of Protestant denominations and all expressed themselves that had they been at the Crucifixion, they might have followed the mob and been just as guilty as those who nailed Jesus the Messiah to the Cross. Among the many frank answers that I received, none showed any hatred for the Jews.

If the narrative of the Crucifixion has been used by Jew-baiters to stir up the passions of the ignorant mob, genuine Christians condemn it quite as vigorously as do Jews.

It is not the Crucifixion story, but ignorance of the true meaning of the Calvary episode that has been responsible for all the woes of Jew and Gentile. The inner meaning of that awe-inspiring occurrence is still hidden from many eyes. Let us behold the beauty of Him who hung on the Cross and take Him to our hearts, and there will be less Calvaries in our lives.

30 Ten Gentiles and One Jew

Solomon Birnbaum was born into an orthodox Jewish home in Chernovitz, Austria-Hungary, before World War I. After having become a follower of Jesus, he entered King's College in London from which he received the Bachelor of Divinity degree. For seventeen years he directed the Jewish Studies Department at the Moody Bible Institute in Chicago. From 1959 to 1970 he was director of the Bethel Children's Home in Haifa, Israel. *

Twenty-five centuries ago a Jewish prophet drew the following picture of the Jews among the nations:

"In those days shall ten men of all the languages of the Gentiles take hold of the skirt of him that is a Jew. . ." (Zech. 8:23).

Gentiles taking hold of Jews to curse and maltreat them is a familiar picture, and from time immemorial this seems to have been the lot of Jews everywhere. Some of us have been the victims or the witnesses of such experiences. To the Pharaohs, the Hamans, the Inquisitors—to the Hitlers of all times and places—a proportion of ten Gentiles to one Jew conjures up problems which cause them unspeakable torments. They begin to see visions of terror as to what one Jew might do to ten Gentiles. In order to avert such dreaded calamities, the ten rush upon the Jew and take hold of him . . .

Ten Gentiles to one Jew appears to be the danger signal!

Long before the arrival of Hitler this phobia seems to have been the concern of many people with regard to the Jews of Poland. "Three and a half million Jews in Poland," they said, "among a Polish population of barely thirty million—more than ten percent! This is a frightening situation. Something terrible is bound to happen. At least one million Jews must emigrate!"

In this manner even some of the best friends of the Jews argued. One Jew among ten Gentiles is too much! I felt suspicious of those arguments. They sounded like anti-Semites. What could happen to the Jews in Poland that had not happened to them already, I wondered. As it turned out, however, no one, even in his wildest dreams, could have imagined the catastrophe which was so soon to overtake them.

Anti-Semitism in its many forms and disguises is still pouring forth an unending

*"Ten Gentiles and One Jew" by Solomon Birnbaum appeared in *The American Hebrew Christian* 55, no. 3 (Summer 1970):4-6, and is reprinted by permission.

stream of hatred and prejudice to poison the soul of mankind. It is not satisfied with the six million victims it has recently claimed. It is hungry for more. Even today it is making headway. Ten Gentiles are ready to take hold of the skirt of him that is a Jew, and with curses and beatings shout, "Get out, you————Jew, get out."

Up to this point however, we have seen only one part of the prophetic picture— that part which is exemplified in our experiences.

But the prophet has a different ending to this story. The Gentiles, indeed, still take hold of the Jew, but not to shout at him, "Get out you————Jew," but to entreat him, "We want to go with you."

In this picture, the prophet, as a matter of fact, does not intend to depict the tragedy of anti-Semitism; his purpose, on the contrary, is to point out the sure remedy for this plague. He wants to show what can be done in order to eradicate for ever this frightful disease. A great many have given up hope that anything can be done. The plague has endured so long and is so widespread that even the most expert physicians have despaired of ever finding a cure. But the prophet of God assures us that the cure is here! We need only open our eyes to see it. We need only the will and the courage to apply it.

What is the cure?

It is shown clearly in the prophetic word which we have quoted in part at the beginning of this article and which we are now quoting in full:

"Thus saith the Lord of hosts; in those days it shall come to pass, that ten men shall take hold out of all languages of the [Gentiles], even shall take hold of the skirt of him that is a Jew, saying, We will go with you: for we have heard that God is with you" (Zech. 8:23).

What an amazing and miraculous contrast between this kind of taking hold of the Jew and the one we have been used to! The ten Gentiles no longer shout, "Get out!" but plead, "We want to go with you." Something extraordinary must have happened to bring this about.

The ten Gentiles answer: "We have heard that God is with you." Nothing spectacular happened; only the Gentiles, in some way, became convinced that the Jews were the people of God, and that God was with them. It is this conviction that has made all the difference! It has turned the enemies of the Jews into friends; out of persecutors it has made disciples and followers. In short, it has stopped absolutely the plague of anti-Semitism!

Someone might now ask: But how shall we go about convincing the Gentiles that we, Jews, are the people of God and that God is with us? Shall we now become more orthodox than even the orthodox Jews of the Polish ghettos which have disappeared? Shall we become more strict about eating Kosher, and order our lives more rigidly, according to the minute rules and regulations of the Schulchan Aruch? Shall we also more assiduously give ourselves over to the study of the Talmud? Will that convince them?

No, that kind of orthodoxy never brought such conviction to the Gentiles in the past, and will never do so in the future. On the contrary, the more we practiced that kind of piety, the less we and our way of life were respected by them.

But again someone may ask, Why should we at all bother about the opinions of the Gentiles? Shall we, Jews, learn from them in order to find out whether or not we are on the right track? What do the Gentiles know about our Jewish religion?

Nevertheless, Moses himself told us that we should look to the Gentiles. God has placed them before us as a mirror into which we are to look in order to examine ourselves as to whether or not we, and our way of life, are as God wanted them to be. Here is what we read:

"Now therefore, hearken, O Israel, unto the statutes and unto the judgments, which I teach you. . . . Ye shall not add unto the word which I command you, neither shall ye diminish ought from it. . . Keep therefore and do them; for this is your wisdom and your understanding in the sight of the nations [Gentiles], which shall hear all these statutes, and say, Surely this great nation is a wise and understanding people" (Deut. 4:1, 2, 6).

These words make it perfectly clear that it would be to our advantage to look to the Gentiles and take notice of their opinions regarding us and our conduct. The same words also declare that the Gentiles will treat us with respect and admiration only on condition that we obey and observe the commandments of God solely, and not the additions and traditions of the rabbis. We are urgently warned against adding to, or taking away from, the word of God as commanded us through Moses. The rabbinical additions and traditions have put us to shame before the Gentile world. The unfavorable attitude of the Gentiles toward us should have long ago acted as a danger signal warning us that there must be something wrong with our orthodoxy, and that we must change our ways.

Now this picture painted for us by the prophet Zechariah reveals a different kind of orthodoxy, one that has at last succeeded in convincing the Gentiles that we are truly the people of God and that God is with us.

What is this different, this new, orthodoxy?

It is summed up in the four words which we used above, and which in Hebrew spell just one word. That Hebrew word is Immanuel, which translated into English means "God is with us."

Now Immanuel is a name of the Messiah, and refers to none other than the Lord Jesus of the New Testament.

God is with us, Immanuel, the Messiah is the cure and remedy for anti-Semitism! He is the new orthodoxy which possesses the power finally to convince the Gentiles that we are a people who may sincerely claim that God is with us. Messiah-Immanuel in the heart of the Jew will change the heart of the Gentile in such a manner that instead of shouting, "Get out!" he will say, "We will come with you."

This is not anything imaginary, something that is supposed to take place in the distant future. The evidences of this fact are around us today, and they are innumerable. Whenever a Jew accepts Immanuel—the Messiah—invariably a group of Gentiles gather around him and are willing to go with him and help him. Jews may reject him, call such a one Meshummed [Traitor] or other similar names, but the Gentiles will say to him: "We will go with you because we have heard that God is with you."

This does not mean that the Jew ceases to be a Jew, or that he abandons his Jewish heritage, but rather, through accepting the Messiah, he fully enters upon his heritage and glorifies the name "Jew" in the sight of the Gentiles.

The Messiah-Immanuel has the power to accomplish this miraculous change because He has the power to change man's heart from self-love and sin to the love and service of the living God. Sin is the cause of all hatred, misery and evil. The Lord Jesus, the Messiah, died upon the Cross to save us from sin. Through faith in Him we obtain forgiveness and cleansing.

The Messiah-Immanuel has the power to change man's nature and bring about the New Birth. Things of this earth become secondary, and though we live in this world our treasure is in heaven.

Any person who has had this experience, be he Jew or Gentile, will not hate or fight or curse; he will bless. His sole purpose will be to live to the glory of God, and for the service of his fellow-men.

All these blessings flow from the Messiah-Immanuel. Let us yield ourselves to Him. And then not only ten Gentiles but all the peoples of the world according to the vision of the prophet Isaiah, will flow to Mount Zion, the capital of the Jewish nation, and say:

"Come, let us go up to the mountain of the LORD, to the house of the God of Jacob; and he will teach us of his ways, and we will walk in his paths; for out of Zion shall go forth the law, and the word of the LORD from Jerusalem" (Isaiah 2:3).

31 Jew Hatred: Its Origin and Cure

At the age of nine, **Max Reich** *was brought from Germany to England and there grew up in the strict atmosphere of orthodox Judaism. John Crane, foreman of the London printing shop where Max was an apprentice, by his life revealed to the young orthodox Jew the saving power of Jesus. When one evening the youth timidly asked Crane to tell him his life's secret the foreman answered: "Jesus."*

After deep and painful spiritual struggles Max Reich surrendered his life to Jesus. He did not consider himself to have left his religion. Rather he was convinced he had rediscovered its true meaning.

Max Reich became a gifted speaker and writer of religious prose and poetry. But the happiest part of his life was his last fifteen years, spent in the ministry of Chicago's Moody Bible Institute.*

I have chosen to use in this essay the term *Jew-hatred,* for that wide-spread mental disease with which so many non-Jews are afflicted, rather than the more familiar *anti-semitism.* The latter is hardly a correct definition for that hostile feeling, or attitude of mind. towards the Jewish people. The Jews form but a small part of the family of Semitic peoples, and Jew-hatred is as marked a feature of the Semitic as of the non-Semitic world.

In seeking for the causes of the universal feeling of hostility toward the Jewish people, we have to go far back in human history, even prior to the existence of the Jews themselves. In the Garden of Eden, before fallen man's expulsion therefrom, mention was made of enmity between the seed of the serpent and the seed of the woman. The Deliverer of mankind was to come through the woman, and the serpent who had beguiled her would hate the seed that sprang from her. Thus back of Abel's martyrdom was the serpent, anxious to get rid of the coming conquering seed. When Seth took the place of the slain Abel, the serpent changed tactics and began to corrupt the seed he could not destroy, so that only one man, Noah, remained uncorrupted in his generation, with whom God then made a new start.

After the Flood, the serpent's work was seen in the seduction of the descendants

*Max I. Reich's article "Jew Hatred: Its Origin and Cure" was published in The Hebrew Christian Alliance Quarterly *20, no. 4 (Winter 1936):7-9.*

of Noah into idolatry, which necessitated the call of Abram the Hebrew, to whom was made the promise that the Messianic seed would spring out of his loins. The enmity against that seed was soon manifest even in his own household. Ishmael persecuted Isaac, because divine election had made Isaac the seed of Abraham instead of the son of the Egyptian bondwoman. Again, Esau hated Jacob, who had supplanted him by divine decree in the matter of the birthright. The old animosity against the people of God's choice on the part of Ishmael and Esau has not died out yet. The so-called "Arabs," their descendants, even though Semites, are the bitterest opponents of the Jewish people now returning to their God-convenanted patrimony.

The ancient Gentile world hated the people sprung from the patriarchs, because of the enmity of the serpent in their hearts, even when the Hebrews bore hardly any marks of being God's chosen people. During their sojourn in Egypt, the Hebrews had sunk very low indeed. Having adopted Egyptian polytheism (see Ezek. 20:5-9), they were no credit to Jehovah, the God of their fathers. They had no altar, no priesthood, no public witness to the divine unity and holiness. Pharaoh no doubt could make out a good case against the Hebrews in his policy of oppression and extermination. Yet he was but the unconscious instrument of the serpent who wanted to prevent the seed of the woman's being brought forth.

Hence Moses, when he identified himself at no small sacrifice with that downtrodden people, acted "by faith" (Heb. 11:24-25). He knew they were, in spite of appearances to the contrary, "the people of God." Doubtless he had secretly kept up relations with his godly mother, his reputed nurse. She must have told him of the promise made to the fathers concerning the Messiah and of the vocation and destiny of the people whose son he was. His father's name, Amram—"The people is high"—and his mother's name, Jochebed—"Jehovah is exalted"—must have taught him much. For "faith cometh by hearing, and hearing by the word of God" (Rom. 10:17). Thus, I believe, faith, leading to a life of sacrificial service on behalf of the Hebrews, was begotten in Moses.

It is evident that although Israel was often subject to the chastening hand of God on account of her sins, she was also the object of satanic hatred on account of her association "according to the flesh" with Him who is Christ—our most blessed Redeemer. Either the enemy sought to prevent His appearing or, when he could not do so, raged against the people who gave Him to the world. The many odious charges made against the Jews have been merely excuses for and not causes of their persecution. For instance, it was charged that they poisoned wells in the Middle Ages and brought on the black plague; that they used Christian blood at the Passover; that they secretly plotted against Christian nations, as alleged in the infamous Protocols. Communists blame Jews for being the pillars of capitalism! Capitalists charge them with being the cause of Communism. Israel's sins merited the rod of divine displeasure, but behind all the malicious accusations is the enmity of the serpent who hates the people of divine choice.

Revelation 12 gives the key to the problem. The travailing woman bringing forth the Man-child is the ideal Israel. The Man-child is the seed of the woman, the Messiah. The dragon is the old serpent, the devil. He was foiled in his attempt to devour the Man-child at His birth. After the Man-child was "caught up to God, and to His throne," the dragon "persecuted the woman which brought forth the man-child" (Rev. 12:5, 13). He cannot touch Christ in glory, but he pours out his rage on the people of whom He came.

That is the way history has developed, and will develop, in spite of the lulls that divine providence compels from time to time in the story of Jewish suffering, until the glorified Man, hidden in heaven, returns with the iron rod of imperial dominion and casts the dragon into the abyss.† As the earth will help the persecuted woman in the hour of her supreme peril (Rev. 12:16), so the earth has often done in centuries past. When the Crusaders drove the Jews out of their homes in central Europe, Poland received them. When Spain expelled them, Holland welcomed them. Russian pogroms drove many of them to America, and Hitler's oppressive measures have won the Jews of Germany back to Israel and back to Israel's forgotten land. As we review the past, we can say truly, whatever be the still future application: "The earth helped the woman—and swallowed up the flood which the dragon cast out of his mouth" (Rev. 12:16). Satan can only go the length of his permit; God will never allow him to ultimately succeed in his machinations, and "the gifts and callings of God are without revocation" (author's trans.)

In the meantime, the poison of the serpent finds its antidote in the love of God, poured into Jewish and Gentile hearts by the Holy Spirit. The mutual "enmity" is slain by the cross in the hearts of those who are reconciled in one body, whether Jews or Gentiles, now "one new man" in Christ Jesus.

The best way to combat the insidious disease of Jew-hatred is to bring men into the experience of the love of God. Any other method is only daubing the wall with untempered mortar and crying, "Peace, peace," when there is no peace.

†A reference to the return of Messiah Jesus.—ED.

The Messiahship of Jesus

*And I heard the voice of the Lord, saying: 'Whom shall I
send, and who will go for us?' Then I said: 'Here am I, send
me!' And he said: 'Go, and tell this people: Hear you indeed, but understand not; and see you indeed, but perceive
not. Make the heart of this people fat, and make their ears
heavy, and shut their eyes; lest they, seeing with their eyes,
and hearing with their ears, and understanding with their
heart, repent, and be healed.'*

Isa. 6:8-10 (author's trans.)

*A remnant shall return, even the remnant of Jacob, to
God the Mighty. For even if your people Israel will be as the
sand of the sea, only a remnant of them shall return.*

Isa. 10:21-22a (author's trans.)

*Who has believed our preaching, and over whom has the
arm of the LORD been revealed? For he sprang up like a
sapling before him, and like a root out of a dry ground. He
had no form nor comeliness that we should look upon him;
nor beauty that we should delight in him. He was despised
and forsaken by men; a man of pains and well acquainted
with disease; and like one from whom men hide their face;
despised, and we esteemed him not. Surely our diseases he
did bear, and our pains he carried; but we regarded him as
one stricken, smitten of God and afflicted. Whereas he was
pierced for our sins, bruised for our iniquities; and the
chastisement for our welfare was upon him, and through his
stripes we were healed. All we like sheep went astray; we
had turned every one to his own way; and the Lord caused
the iniquity of us all to fall on him.*

Isa. 53:1-6 (author's trans.)

Why Jews Accept Jesus And Reject the 'Christ'—
   Dan B. Bravin   121
The Founder of Christianity—Jesus or Paul?—
   H. L. Ellison   124
The Era of Jewish-Christian Understanding—
   Jakob Jocz   131
Who Is a Jew?—*Arthur W. Kac*   136
Judaism and Biblical Messianism—*Max I. Reich*   143

32 Why Jews Accept Jesus and Reject the "Christ"

*The father of **Dan Bravin** was an official of the largest of the eight synagogues in his native town of Kreitzburg, Russia, but Dan, the youngest of four sons, became a follower of Jesus the Messiah. Eventually he became an ordained minister of the Lutheran church and for many years was the spiritual leader of a Hebrew Christian congregation in Pittsburgh, Pennsylvania.**

Some time ago, a Pittsburgh rabbi preached a sermon from his pulpit on the above theme. He said that he did it "in the spirit of deep respectful group-understanding."

"Neither the mass of the Jews of his time nor the historic religion of Judaism down through the centuries has ever had any reason whatsoever to reject Jesus the man, his life, or his teachings," said the Rabbi. "Nor, for that matter, does Judaism deny or shy away from that part of Jesus' preaching which had to do with his claim of being the long-awaited and eagerly sought-for Messiah.

"On the other hand," said the Rabbi, "Judaism flatly rejects as thoroughly un-Jewish Paul's alien concept of Jesus as the mystical, supernatural, mass-atoning and intermediating Christ."

The Rabbi said that the religion *of* Jesus was Jewish, but that the religion *about* Jesus was not. And who changed the religion *of* to the religion *about* Jesus? Paul, of course! It was Paul, he says, who first referred to Jesus as "The Messiah."

Now, we all know that there is no reliable information about Jesus or Paul outside of the Bible. The Rabbi avails himself of this source of information only where he thinks it will suit his purpose, like the Jewishness of Jesus for instance. But a little knowledge is a dangerous thing! If the Rabbi knew where in the Bible to look for it, he would have discovered that it was not Paul who first claimed that Jesus was the Messiah; it was Simon bar Jonah (Peter). *Vayomer elov, atah hu hamoshiach—* "And he said unto Him, Thou art the Messiah" (Gospel of Mark 8:29).

But Paul was the one who made the Jewish Messiah and Saviour known outside of Judaism. In doing this, he also made the God of Judaism, and Moses, and the Prophets, and the Old Testament, known to the people outside of Judaism. But the rabbis cannot forgive Paul for having shared the light of life with other nations.

*This article is reprinted from *The Dawn* 27, no. 4 (September-October [no year]):6-8.

G. K. Chesterton, in a Foreword to his book, *Francis of Assisi,* tells how unequal he felt of writing this book, by saying: "It would really require a saint to write the life of a saint." This might be paraphrased by saying that it would require a devout Christian to give an appraisal of the life and work of Christ.

Granted that the teaching of Jesus was Jewish. Why did the ancient rabbis reject Him? Wherein did His teaching differ from theirs? That they did reject Him is beyond doubt. And Jews still reject Jesus—whether man or Christ. The Rabbi should not have been unaware of this.

In discussing the Jewishness of Jesus, the Rabbi would have done well had he have learned from his mentor, Dr. Solomon B. Freehof, who said: "Wellhausen and those Jewish scholars who find a parallel to every one of the sayings of Jesus in Talmud literature must see that Jesus was an extraordinary man, since it was his version of Jewish ethical idealism which conquered the western world and changed human history.

"The secret of the influence of Jesus will perhaps always remain a mystery. After painstaking scholarship has explained all that is explicable, the secret of his power remains unsolved. Scores of men have believed themselves to be the Messiah and have convinced many of their contemporaries, but those who believed Jesus to be the Messiah have built a great church upon the rock of their belief."[1]

Wherein was Jesus "extraordinary," and what was the "secret" of His influence? Was it not in this that His Personality, though human, was equally divine? Let us not enter here into theological polemics; let us but say that anyone who claims to be scholar enough to discuss the Personality and teaching of Jesus has to be able to give an account of the "secret" of this "extraordinary" Man. To say merely that He was a Jew does not answer the question. Millions of Jews have lived and died but did not accomplish what Jesus did! Dr. Freehof . . . does answer the question. In the same book, page 209, he says: "The personality of Jesus was such that His sonship to God was magnificently evident. The divine spirit seemed manifest in his words and deeds. He impressed himself upon the world, perhaps more so than other prophets and saints, as a 'child of the Living God.' "

Here we are getting nearer to an appraisal of Jesus the Christ-Messiah. Nor is this far from Paul's estimate of Him, when he states that in Jesus "dwells all the fulness of God bodily" (Colossians 2:9). Not that Jesus the Man became a god— Christianity does not teach this—but that God dwelt in all His fullness in the Man Jesus; that in Him divinity and humanity blended beautifully and uniquely. If this is the teaching of Paul, for which the Rabbi would condemn him, it is also the teaching of the Hebrew Prophet Isaiah, who speaks of a certain Child coming into the world whose characteristic quality is that of Almighty God (see in the Old Testament, Isaiah 9:6). It is also the teaching of the Prophet Jeremiah who tells of God raising up a Righteous Branch from the seed of David, whose characteristic quality is Yehovah Tzidkenu—God our Righteousness (see Jeremiah 23:5, 6).

Yet the Rabbi criticizes Paul for calling Jesus Lord. "We Jews apply the name Lord to the one and only Father which art in Heaven," he says. That is exactly what is wrong with us! Why doesn't the Rabbi criticize Isaiah, Jeremiah or the other Prophets who credit divinity to the Messiah?

And, now, an interesting question: Where did the Rabbi get the idea that the teaching of Jesus was different from that of Paul? Not from the New Testament, surely! Yet the Rabbi admits that "the only available sources of Paul's life are those written by the New Testament writers." The same, of course, must be said concerning the life and teaching of Jesus. Is the New Testament true or false? Is it reliable or unreliable? If it is the former, why does not the Rabbi believe it. If it is the latter, why does he quote from it to support his private opinions? "Consistency, thou art a jewel!"

Nay, what the Rabbi attempts to do is to detach Jesus from Christianity. He would have it that Jesus was all right, but that it was that "rascal" Paul who was all wrong; and that Paul was the real founder of Christianity, therefore Christianity is all wrong. The Rabbi is not original in this; it is an old "trick of the trade."

C. S. Lewis, in his Introduction to J. B. Phillips' translation of the Letters of Paul, deals with this matter. Quote:

"In the earlier history of every rebellion there is a stage at which you do not attack the King in person. You say, 'The King is all right. It is His Ministers who are wrong. They misrepresent Him and corrupt all His plans—which, I am sure, are good plans if only the Ministers would let them take effect.' And the first victory consists in beheading a few ministers; only at a later stage do you go on and behead the King Himself" (*Letters to Young Churches,* page x.)

For the Rabbi to say that Jews accept Jesus the Man but not the Christ is preposterous! Jesus cannot be severed from Christ, and He cannot be dissociated from Christianity. A discussion on the Lord Jesus is essentially a discussion on Christianity.

We, too, are interested in the promotion of "deep respectful group-understanding," but we differ with the Rabbi in method. Not by befogging the issues can clarity emerge but by clarifying the issues will the fog be dispersed.

Notes

1. Solomon B. Freehof, *Stormers of Heaven* (New York: Harper, 1931), p. 208. Copyright, 1931, by Harper & Brothers. Reprinted by permission of Harper & Row, Publishers, Inc.

33 The Founder of Christianity—Jesus or Paul?

H. L. Ellison is a second generation Hebrew Christian. He has held the following positions: lecturer at London College of Divinity, London Bible College, and Moorlands Bible College; visiting lecturer at Spurgeon's College, London, and Birmingham Bible Institute; and supervisor in Old Testament at Cambridge. Author of a number of scholarly works in the field of biblical literature, Dr. Ellison has contributed to the New Bible Commentary, Baker Dictionary of Theology, The New Bible Dictionary, New International Dictionary of the Christian Church, *and* The Zondervan Picture Encyclopedia of the Bible.

The apostle Paul went out of his way to insist that, though he had grown up in Tarsus, his surroundings had been those of Palestinian orthodoxy (Philippians 3:5) and that his education had found its climax in the school of Rabban Gamaliel (Gamaliel I), the greatest teacher of his time (Acts 22:3). Although he insisted on equal standing as an apostle with the original twelve, he made no claim for originality in his preaching of the gospel beyond his understanding of the position of the non-Jew in the church (Ephesians 3:4-6).

Paul's assertion was seldom challenged until last century. The rise of the Tübingen school under the leadership of F. C. Baur (about 1830) led to an effort to drive a wedge between Paul as a Hellenistic Jew and Peter as the representative of the Palestinian Jews who had joined the church. That involved the driving of a wedge also between Jesus and Paul. Thus a religious movement, which was ,by origin one of the many divisions in first-century Palestinian Judaism, became, according to that view, an essentially Hellenistic religion with a greater appeal to the Gentile than to the Jew.

About the same time an increasingly close study of the gospels was leading to a drastic separation of the synoptic gospels (Matthew, Mark, Luke) from that by John, which by many was dated as late as A.D. 150. The former were looked on as depicting a simple Galilean teacher standing in the general stream of Pharisaic Judaism, even though He fell out with many of its representatives because He regarded them as being unduly strict. It was repeatedly claimed, especially by Jewish writers, that there was little or nothing in His teaching that could not be paralleled in the teaching of the Tannaitic rabbis. John's gospel was dismissed as having no historical value. Its author was thought to have been strongly influenced by Philo of Alexandria (d. about A.D. 50). In addition, he was regarded as the logical heir of Paul's thought and the completer of the process of separating the early church from its roots in Palestinian Jewry. It further became fashionable to interpret Pauline thought in terms of the mystery religions so popular in the eastern Mediterranean world in the first century.

Broadly speaking, that has been the position taken up by those Jewish scholars who have seriously approached the New Testament and early Christianity. Martin Buber may be allowed to serve as an example. He had a deep veneration for Jesus, but could hardly bring himself to deal objectively with Paul. In *Two Types of Faith*, Buber seriously propounded that faith (*Emunah*) meant radically different things for Jesus and Paul; for the former it meant a deep personal trust in and commitment to God, as it had for leading characters in the Old Testament, but for the latter it implied believing that certain things were true. In mitigation it should be said that the meaning of faith he attributes to the apostle was the official one of the Roman and Greek churches through much of their history, and it is one not unknown in Judaism (cf. *The Thirteen Principles of Faith* by Maimonides). Even C. G. Montefiore, in spite of his much fairer concept of Paul, could write, "No one misunderstood Judaism more profoundly than Paul."[1]

One of the few adequate Jewish studies of Paul in recent years is *Paulus* by Hans Joachim Schoeps. Yet he can bring himself to say, "Whence comes Paul's belief in the Son of God, if it cannot be traced to Jewish sources? The answer is: We see in the belief in the Son of God, and only in it, the only, but for all that decisive, pagan premise in Paul's thinking. All that is connected with it, or may be deduced from it, e.g. the coming down of the heavenly man in *Philippians,* dying with Christ, the giving of positive value to the sacraments, etc., is not Jewish and leads us close to the pagan concepts of the time."[2] It is not surprising that he minimizes the influence of Gamaliel on Paul's education.

It is no chance that the most appreciative Jewish study of Paul has been *The Apostle* by Sholem Asch, in which Asch shows a deep appreciation of primitive Christianity and sees Paul in his essential Jewishness.

Though the concepts of Jesus as the Pharisaic Jew and of Paul as the Hellenist have become part and parcel of more liberal Judaism, their foundation stones have become gradually eroded.

Today the views of the Tübingen school are regarded as mainly a historical curiosity, even though it is recognized that some of its insights have some value. There was a time when some elements of Palestinian Jewish Christianity launched a fierce attack on Paul, making Peter their spokesman, but that was in the early second century, when both apostles were long dead, as has been shown especially by Schoeps.[3] He later argued cogently that that was probably due to the remnants of the Qumran community coming into the Palestinian church after the destruction of the Temple in A.D. 70 had shown them that the great revolt against Rome was not the final war between good and evil, as they seem to have thought.[4]

True enough, there was conflict between Paul and many Palestinian Jewish Christians, as is abundantly reflected in his letters. But this was caused by Paul's attitude towards the Torah, especially as it affected Gentile converts, not by his views on the church or the nature and work of Jesus. As W. D. Davies wrote, "Between Paul and extreme Judaizers in the early Church, of a Pharisaic orgin, there was an unbridgeable cleavage. But neither James nor Peter belonged to these."[5] It is significant that Paul's main opponents are consistently depicted as being "Hellenistic" Jews (e.g. Acts 13:45, 50; 14:2, 19; 17:5, 13; 18:12; 20:3). In a moment of crisis, Pharisaic leaders were even willing to defend him (Acts 23:6-9).

Then, in spite of the arguments of Montefiore[6] and Schoeps,[7] the differences between the Jews of Palestine and Mesopotamia and those of the Western Diaspora have been steadily eroded by modern research. S. Safrai in *The Jewish People in the First Century* (vol. 1, ch. 4) stresses how close the links were between the Diaspora and the Land of Israel. Also the works of W. D. Davies have familiarized us with the extent to which much in Paul's writings that was confidently regarded as Hellenistic is actually to be linked with Palestinian rabbinic thought and speculation.[8]

The discoveries at Qumran throw light not only on Paul's thought but also (and to even a greater extent) on some aspects of John's teaching, which was taken for granted by so many to be Hellenistic. In addition, there has been a growing belief among New Testament scholars that we are dealing here with a gospel that was originally written in Aramaic, or by a man whose mother-tongue was Aramaic, who had access to authentic material concerning Jesus. We now have sustained argument by J. A. T. Robinson, no conservative writer, that the gospel received its final form before A.D. 70,[9] even as he dates the other gospels before that date.

Once we separate John from a late date and a Hellenistic origin, the absurdity of Schoeps's argument that the Pauline teaching on Jesus as the Son of God was derived from pagan sources and thinking becomes obvious. If it had been so derived, it is impossible to believe that the opposition to him in the church would have been confined to the Judaizers, and that they would have been apparently concerned only with his attitude towards the Torah. They would have rejected his teaching root and branch.

All these lines of evidence taken together show that no real cultural and theological wedge can be driven between Jesus on the one hand and Paul and John on the other. But that does not dispose of the argument that Jesus did not make the claims for Himself that Paul and John did. Here the argument centers mainly on whether Jesus claimed to be the Messiah.

That he claimed a unique position for Himself is clear from the synoptic gospels and can be denied only by denying the truth of the records. That is done by many, who suggest that the synoptic gospels show a gradual reframing of the disciples' memories in the light of the developing church. Quite apart from the fact that such a process demands a much later date for the gospels than we can allow on other grounds, it is hard to see where the ideas would have come from if Jesus had not made the claims attributed to Him.

Jesus' claim to uniqueness is perhaps clearest in Matthew 11:27-30. Here He not only calls men to Him to find rest for their souls, as they bow to His authority by taking His yoke on them—compare the frequent rabbinic mention of taking the yoke of the Torah upon oneself—but He also claims a unique relationship to the Father, with His unique nature known only to Him (cf. Luke 10:22). In addition, He claimed authority to forgive sins, which the scribes rightly claimed was a divine prerogative, and showed His right to do so by healing the paralyzed man (Matt. 9:2-6; Mark 2:5-12; Luke 5:20-25).

This is not the place to discuss the enigmatic title Jesus chose to use for Himself, 'the son of man,' suggestive of Daniel 7:13. The problem becomes clear when we try to translate the Greek of the gospels into the Aramaic or Hebrew term used by Jesus. In spite of the claim of some scholars that it meant no more in its original form than "man," as great a scholar as Franz Delitzsch rendered it *ben ha-'adam* in his translation of the New Testament into Hebrew, and he has been followed in the latest translation issued by the United Bible Societies. In any case, it was not Paul who does not use the term, but the earliest Greek speaking Christians who put it in a form suggesting that Jesus was more than just "a man." In fact, whatever the reason, the title does not form part of the Pauline vocabulary, though he does speak of Jesus as "the second man," that is, the only true man since the fall of Adam.

As the shadow of the cross fell over Jesus, He said, "The Son of man came . . . to give his life a ransom for many" (Matt. 20:28; Mark 10:45) and in so doing claimed to be the fulfillment of the prophecy of the servant of the Lord (Isa. 52:13-53:12). "Many," as in Isaiah 53:12, means "all"—for all are "many." The word does not imply exceptions.

The only time that Jesus openly claimed the title Messiah was when in the narrow circle of His disciples at Caesarea Philippi, the modern Banias. There He commended Simon Peter for recognizing Him as such (Matt. 16:15-17, Mark 8:29-30, Luke 9:20), and in all three narratives the declaration is confirmed shortly afterwards by the record of the transfiguration, the shining out of His inward glory (Matt. 17:1-8; Mark 9:2-8; Luke 9:28-36). At other times He returned what is claimed to be an ambiguous answer (e.g., to Caiaphas and Pilate, cf. Matt. 26:63-64; Luke 22:66-70 with Mark 14:61-62; also Matt. 27:11; Luke 23:9). It should not be overlooked, however, that Jesus never disclaimed the Messianic titles "son of David" and "son of God" (Psalm 2:7), though He did not use them Himself. His refusal to reject them tacitly implied acceptance.

How are we to explain this? We must first of all remember that the Messiah's task was to introduce "the kingdom of God," or "the kingdom of heaven"—*malkut shammayim* as the rabbis preferred to call it, that is, God's sovereign rule. For Jesus' contemporaries that involved, in the first place, not teaching but the defeat and destruction of Israel's enemies. The only proof of Messiahship was that one had done the work of the Messiah. That helps to explain Rabbi Johanan ben Torta's bitter reaction to Rabbi Aqiba's recognition of Bar Kochba as Messiah. He said to him, "Aqiba, grass will sprout through your cheeks ere the son of David comes." The same attitude lies behind the answer attributed to a number of leading rabbis in more recent times. When some enthusiastic Christian put forward the claim of Jesus to be the Messiah, one is said to have gone to his study window, to have watched the busy life outside, and to have said to his visitor, "I am sorry, but I cannot accept your claim, for nothing has changed."

Accordingly, if Jesus had made a public claim to be the Messiah, He would immediately have been under extreme pressure to justify His claim and to justify it in the way in which His hearers expected Him to act. In fact, in John 6:15 we find such an effort, which was frustrated only by Jesus' withdrawal. The demonstration in Jerusalem on Palm Sunday was also intended to have such an effect.

That principle lies behind Paul's statement that the foundation of the Christian faith was "the gospel concerning [God's] Son, who was descended from David according to the flesh and designated Son of God [i.e., Messiah] in power according to the Spirit of holiness by his resurrection from the dead, Jesus [the Messiah] our Lord" (Romans 4:4 [RSV]). Paul meant that by His death Jesus had been doing the Messiah's work and that His resurrection proved His victory and God's acceptance of it. Clearly enough, there is no gap here between Paul and Peter, for from the first the latter stressed the resurrection as the proof of Jesus' Messiahship.

The critic, however, both Jewish and Gentile, will retort that there is nothing of all this in Jesus' public ministry, and they suggest that the stress on Jesus' Messiahship was a later creation by the church as it tried to come to terms with His apparent failure. Such a view in fact denies the whole stress of the New Testament documents. It claims that Jesus was first and foremost a teacher, or more convincingly, a charismatic prophet.[10] But in none of the strands of the New Testament is His teaching stressed, neither in James or Peter, John or Paul. Even in the gospels, the main stress is not on His teaching; in Mark, almost universally regarded as the earliest of them, there is virtually no reference to it. Peter, in speaking to a Roman centurion, summed up Jesus' activity by saying, "He . . . went about doing good and healing all that were oppressed by the devil" (Acts 10:38, RSV).

The main stress in the gospels is on the way in which Jesus by His actions was making the Kingdom of God a reality. It is striking how often His teaching, even in John, is related to a context of action. If that is not so obvious in Matthew, it is because there the teaching is grouped in sections for convenience. When John the Baptizer wished to know if Jesus was the Messiah, Jesus' answer laid chief stress on what He was doing (Matt. 11:2-6; Luke 7:18-23). Similarly, both when the twelve and the seventy were sent out, their main task was to show by their actions that the Kingdom of God had come in power (Matt. 10:5-15; Luke 10:1-12).

We need not quarrel with Jewish writers who claim that all Jesus' teaching can be paralleled in the teaching of the Tannaitic rabbis, though this is not the whole truth, as C. G. Montefiore[11] and Joseph Klausner[12] in different ways make clear. Jesus proclaimed that He was the bringer in of the Kingdom of God, not the teacher of a new doctrine. It was not by chance that when Scribes and Pharisees demanded that He authenticate His authority by a sign from heaven (Matt. 12:38; 16:1), they did so in the context of miracles. The only sign He offered them was "the sign of the prophet Jonah," that is, His resurrection. Virtually always, when we turn to the writings of those, Jews and non-Jews, who reject the Pauline presentation of Jesus as Messiah and Son of God, we find them also rejecting the reality of His physical resurrection, though more and more there is a willingness even of Jewish writers to grant a spiritual reality to the Christian claim. "It is impossible to suppose that there was any conscious deception: the nineteen hundred years' faith of millions is not founded on deception. There can be no question but that some of the ardent Galileans saw their lord and Messiah in a vision."[13] We can compare that statement with this: "That there was some kind of experience of seeing Jesus after his death, an appearance or appearances which came to be known as his resurrection, seems virtually certain in view of the survival and growth of the tiny original Jesus movement. . . . But we cannot ascertain today in what this resurrection-event consisted."[14] Such is the voice of scepticism.

Once Jesus' disciples knew that their Lord was alive forever and seated at God's right hand, waiting until His enemies were made His footstool, and that He would return in glory with all the angels (Matt. 25:31), then the significance of the title "Son of the living God," which had meant no more than Messianic King on Peter's lips (Matt. 16:16), was bound to widen and deepen. There is nothing in Paul's teaching for which we need seek pagan or Hellenistic roots. He may have dressed his proclamation of Jesus as Messiah and Lord in terms more easily understood in Corinth than in Jerusalem—for this was an adaptation to his listeners that every preacher and missionary must learn—but no contradiction between it and the teaching of the Old Testament or of Jesus can be established. Jesus by His resurrection and exaltation to God's right hand demonstrated that He was the fulfillment of all the promises made by God and that in Him God had come down to men and dwelt among them.[15]

The founder of Christianity—Jesus or Paul? It is probable that such a question would never have been put had the day not come when the decaying and declining Roman empire realized that the only moral and cohesive force left in it was Christianity and so adopted it as a means of self-preservation. That meant that Christianity became a theological system that was forced on men, sometimes at the point of the sword, and the teaching of Jesus (and of Paul) was subordinated to national interest. The Jew became hated and persecuted in the name of the Jewish Savior, and those who held the highest office in the church denied its Lord by their behavior and life-style. But at all times there were those whose spiritual eyes had been opened and who were prepared to give up all for Him who had given up all for them. Both then and now they have tried to live as Jesus taught, but they have known that they needed to begin anew and that in themselves they had no strength to reach the goal. Thanks to them the light has been kept burning until the knowledge of Jesus has been carried to the ends of the earth.

Although man's judgment on the church over its history may be deservedly severe, none will doubt that the message of Jesus has brought untold blessing with it. But that message has been in the form that Paul gave it. Are we really to believe that a belief in a resurrection that never took place and an interpretation of Jesus' death based on pagan ideas would have been the most potent power for good that mankind has known? Is our God one who uses falsehood to achieve His ends?

Wise men and scholars, Jewish and non-Jewish alike, may see the "foolishness" of Christian preaching and contradictions in the Christian Scriptures, but they have been able to do no more than proclaim what they think should be. At all times they have lamentably failed to produce what they have longed for.

Notes

1. C. G. Montefiore and H. Loewe, eds. *A Rabbinic Anthology* (New York: Schocken, 1970), p. xiii.
2. Tübingen: J. C. B. Mohr, 1959. My translation is from p. 163 of the German original, where everything from "We see in the belief . . . " is in italics.
3. Hans Joachim Schoeps, *Theologie and Geschichte des Judenchristentums* (Tübingen: n.p., 1949).
4. Hans Joachim Schoeps, *Urgemeinde, Judenchristentum, Gnosis* (n.p., 1956).
5. W. D. Davies, *The Setting of the Sermon on the Mount* (n.p., n.d.), p. 339.
6. C. G. Montefiore, *Judaism and St. Paul* (n.p., n.d.).
7. Schoeps, *Paulus,* pp. 12-28.
8. S. Safrai, *The Jewish People in the First Century* (n.p., n.d.) 1:86-99; *Paul and Rabbinic Judaism;* Davies, *The Setting of the Sermon on the Mount;* W. D. Davies, *Christian Origins and Judaism* (n.p.:n.d.)
9. J. A. T. Robinson, *Redating the New Testament* (Philadelphia: Westminster, 1976), chap. 14. It is worth adding that all theories that John had been written in the mid-second century were finally buried by the discovery of a papyrus fragment of the gospel dating from near the beginning of the second century!
10. So Geza Vermes, *Jesus the Jew* (London: Collins, 1973), 86-99.
11. C. G. Montefiore, *Rabbinic Literature and Gospel Teaching.* Rev. ed. (New York: Ktav, 1970), pp. 47, 52, 85, 221, 254, 299, 325, 344, 365, 372.
12. Joseph Klausner, *Jesus of Nazareth* (New York: Macmillan, 1925), p. 390, "Thus his ethical teaching apparently goes beyond that of *Pirke Aboth* and of other Talmudic and Midrashic literature."
13. Ibid., p. 359.
14. John Hick, ed. *The Myth of God Incarnate* (Philadelphia: Westminster, 1978). p. 170.
15. Recently C. F. Moule in *The Origin of Christology* (New York: Cambridge U. Press, 1978) has strongly defended the view that the apostolic language, including Paul's about Jesus, was the natural development from what He had said about Himself, and that there was nothing necessarily Hellenistic about it. A more popular treatment of the subject is given by F. F. Bruce in his work *Paul and Jesus* (Grand Rapids: Baker, 1974).

34 The Era of Jewish-Christian Understanding

Jakob Jocz

Whatever else the Second World War may have accomplished, it certainly brought about a remarkable change in Jewish-Christian relationships. It is a tragedy that such change for the better had to be bought at the price of millions of lives and untold human suffering. Only after the starkness of anti-Semitism was laid bare by the cruel and premeditated destruction of European Jewry was the Christian conscience stirred. Among many Christians today there is a genuine sense of shame for past failure. Officially, on both the Roman Catholic and Protestant sides the Church has declared herself unequivocally against anti-Semitism in any form. In Germany, the classical seat of this vile disease, there are Protestant and Roman Catholic groups active in the interest of Jewish-Christian understanding. We will only mention the influential part played by the Marienschwesternschaft in Darmstadt-Eberstadt, the Roman Catholic circles connected with the Freilburger Rundbrief.

The most recent statement as far as the Church is concerned comes from the World Council of Churches in New Delhi, 1961, where anti-Semitism was denounced unanimously as a "sin against God and man." The *Jewish Chronicle*, commenting editorially on the resolution, called it "a hopeful sign" and added: "It is hoped that this pronouncement will turn out to have been the first step in a practical programme to undo the harm of centuries."[1] This is too cautious a statement, for, as a matter of fact, many efforts have already been made by the churches on a wide front to combat the evil with every possible means.

The change of atmosphere in Jewish-Christian relations is reflected in the daily press, in Christian publications, in the pulpit, in the Sunday school, and generally on the level of parochial life. But this very fact raises the problem of meaningful encounter.

I

THE PROBLEM OF CO-EXISTENCE

Eclecticism and syncretism, or by whatever other term we may choose to describe the levelling tendency of our civilization, can make little difference. It is a fact that

"The Era of Jewish-Christian Understanding" was published in *The Hebrew Christian* 35, no. 1 (Spring, 1962):4-8, and is reprinted by permission. The numbered footnotes are Jocz's.

in a civilization which becomes top-heavy, as was the case in the Roman empire on its way to decline, a standardization of life takes place, pressing towards sameness not only outwardly in custom and convention, but also inwardly in thought and values. The result is that today there is culturally little difference between Jew and Gentile. Both live the same kind of lives and pursue similar goals. This is the burden of Will Herberg's book *Protestant, Catholic, Jew.* Martin E. Marty, in his book *The New Shape of American Religion,* has shown what happens when the edge of peculiarity has been rubbed off and religion becomes standardized.

The desire for co-existence, especially in the United States, is working itself out in a peculiar fashion. Christian ministers, not to offend their Jewish neighbours, drop the name of Jesus Christ at joint meetings, and when invited to Jewish pulpits speak in terms of religious generalities to avoid offence. Naturally the Rabbis do the same. The result is that neither of them speak sincerely out of the depth of their convictions, but remain on the superficial level of convention. Ordinary people, both Jews and Christians, receive the impression that the common denominator is religion and that the rest does not matter. It is therefore important to both sides to realize that co-operation between Jews and Christians has its definite limitations. Francis H. House, in an article in *Common Ground* rightly observed: "Religious cooperation between Christians and Jews cannot go far without coming up against the scandal of the Cross." He proceeds to explain: "No amount of good feeling, no degree of 'liberalization' consistent with the integrity of the Christian and Jewish faiths, and no penitence, however deeply felt, by Christians for their treatment of the Jewish people in the past, can remove our basic differences of belief or should be allowed to obscure them."[2]

There are, however, large areas of endeavour where Christians and Jews can and should co-operate. W. W. Simpson has carefully outlined these areas in the symposium *The Church and the Jewish People.* Such co-operation need not imply a compromise on either side. It is only when these spheres of cultural and social endeavour become ends in themselves that the danger arises. Unfortunately, most encounter between Jews and Christians remains on this superficial level. In such circumstances it is easy to forget that "neither tolerance, mutual respect, good will, nor even brotherhood, are ultimate goals of human existence."[3]

This is no problem for secularized nominal "Jews" and "Christians," but it is a real problem for believers, and the problem is this: how is our co-existence to be made meaningful? This brings us to the thorny question of Jewish missions.

II

MISSIONS TO JEWS

Jewry regards the missionary effort of the Church as an insult and an imposition. Jewish writers, by constant propaganda, have succeeded in convincing even leading Christian theologians of the harmful effect of missions. Reinhold Niebuhr has written against the missionary effort on the grounds that "the two faiths despite differences are sufficiently alike for the Jew to find God more easily in terms of his own religious heritage. . . ."[4] Paul Tillich in a more reserved fashion, though against active missionary work, admits a "passive mission" ("Aufnehmende Judenmission").[5] He explains: *"Daruber hinaus wurde ich nicht gehen,"* i.e. he would not go beyond a willingness to accept a Jew into the Church at the Jew's request(!). A much more militant antagonist against Jewish missions is James Parkes. Though an historian and not a theologian, Parkes has tried to evolve a theological basis for Judaism which would exempt it from the missionary obligation of the Church.

Among Jews there is a well-established legend about the cunning and the cant of missionaries, especially Hebrew Christians. It is taken as a matter of fact that the missionaries only succeed in their task by means of bribery and corruption. In fact most Jews deny the possibility of a sincere conversion. Max Eisen, in his account of *Christian Missions to Jews in North America and Great Britain,* accepts the testimony of the twice-renegade Samuel Freuder that Jewish missions are "reeking with insincerity and dishonesty."[6]

We will not deny that sometimes missionaries in their eagerness and zeal, have gone beyond the bounds of propriety and have exposed themselves to deserved criticism. But there is also the other fact, the deliberate misconstruction on the part of Jewish critics. This became only too apparent in the hue and cry raised by the organizers of the Keren Yaldenu "to buy back Jewish children from the missions." Such and similar accusations were flatly denied by Professor R. J. Zwi Werblowsky, who made a personal investigation into the matter.[7] The fact is that informed Jews know only too well of the evergrowing array of outstanding Jewish men and women who accept the Messiahship of Jesus not because they are bribed by missionaries but from personal conviction.

III

THE BASIS OF ENCOUNTER

The question of missions raises a major issue. Secularized Jews and secularized Gentiles have no problem: they meet on common ground of disbelief. The problem arises when believers of heterogeneous faiths are to meet not only as neighbours but on a deeper level. The problem was raised by the late Leo Baeck in a lecture on "The Scope and Limitations of Co-operation between Christians and Jews." Baeck sees the answer to this problem in a recognition on the part of believers on both sides of the mystery of the neighbour's faith: "The Church is a Church and the synagogue is a synagogue. Christianity is Christianity by the grace of God, by virtue of the mystery; and Judaism is Judaism by the grace of God, by virtue of the mystery. Not in spite of that, but through that, and on the strength of that, they will really co-exist; and they will co-operate."[8]

Thus in spite of the fact that Christianity and Judaism are different they remain "interrelated" by the mystery of faith and therefore must take no offence "at the other's missionary work on purpose."[9] In the sphere of spiritual contest Rabbi Baeck acknowledges "no monopolies or reserved regions."

Zwi Werblowsky, though holding quite different views from those of Rabbi Baeck, is looking forward to the time when "the activity of the Christian missions in Israel, instead of being the occasion of conflict and mutual recrimination, will develop into a genuine spiritual contest.''[10] Such a change in attitude will require greater respect and sincerity on both sides.

IV

THE CHALLENGE TO HEBREW CHRISTIANS

An editorial in *Christianity Today* on Jewish-Christian understanding (10th November, 1961) poses the questions: "Can Jews and Christians now transcend their ugly recent past?" and "Can new respect for religious freedom launch them toward mutual understanding without surrendering a vigorous Judeo-Christian dialogue?"

The first question especially may come as a surprise to Jews who have been reared in a tradition that all the "transcending" is the responsibility of the Christian majority. It is only seldom that Jews allow their own prejudices to come into the open; in fact, they are hardly conscious that such exist. Yet there is a deep-seated hostility as a result of the "wounds of centuries which do not heal in a day," to quote Professor Werblowsky again. Here lies a fundamental obstacle to a genuine Jewish-Christian encounter. The question is, can Jews transcend their bitterness and meet their Christian fellow men without prejudice? Such an attitude will require both discipline and good will. Those who read the symposium of the thirty-one Jewish intellectuals in *Commentary* will appreciate the problem. We quote Philip Roth for his blunt outspokenness. In connection with the question of Jewish coherence he remarks: "There does not seem to me a complex of values or aspirations or beliefs that continue to connect one Jew to another in our country (i.e., the U.S.A.), but rather an ancient and powerful disbelief which it is not fashionable or wise to assert in public, but is no less powerful for being underground: that is the rejection of the myth of Jesus as Christ.''[11] Roth continues to explain that the Jewish rejection, their "abhorrence" of the "Christian fantasy," separates the Jewish community not only from their Christian neighbours, but even from those Gentiles who have a nominal affiliation with Christianity.

The blame for that "abhorrence" falls not upon the Jews but upon Christians. It is a frightening indictment of the Church for a Jewish writer to assert that the main evil Jews had committed was to invent Christianity.[12] It is an undeniable fact that only secularized society has produced a social environment "conducive to the welfare of religious minorities.''[13] It is here that the Hebrew Christian faces his greatest challenger.

In some Hebrew Christian circles, especially in Israel, there is an obvious tendency to denigrate Gentile Christianity as an abysmal failure. Behind this attitude is a lack of theological insight. It would go beyond the scope of this short article to enumerate a catena of faulty premises. Suffice it to be reminded of the Pauline words: "For God has consigned all men to disobedience, that he may have mercy upon all" (Romans 11:32 [RSV]). Put in the original context this means that the Church is not the Church, as Israel is not Israel, because of merit or desert, but by reason of God's grace. Man always fails: this is his tragedy.

The challenge to Hebrew Christians is not to exonerate the Church and not to dissociate ourselves from her, but to share her guilt, to acknowledge her failure and to stand in the breach. Only thus will we help our people to "transcend the ugly and recent past" and help to bring about a "mutual understanding without surrendering a vigorous Judeo-Christian dialogue," for dialogue there must be if the encounter between Jews and Christians is to be more than mere social convention.

Notes

1. *The Jewish Chronicle* (London), December 8, 1961.
2. Francis H. House, *Common Ground* (London), November-December 1954.
3. W. W. Simpson, *The Church and the Jewish People,* edited by Gote Hedenquist (Edinburgh House Press: London, 1954), p. 140.
4. Cf. *Christianity Today,* December 8, 1958.
5. Cf. Die Judenfrage, ein christliches und ein deutsches Problem (Berlin, 1953), p. 15.
6. Mac Eisen, *Christian Mission to Jews in North America and Great Britain,* 1948, p. 32 f.
7. Cf. *The Jewish Chronicle,* December 30, 1960 and March 3, 1961.
8. Leo Baeck, "The Scope and Limitations of Cooperation between Christians and Jews," in *Common Ground,* November-December 1954, p. 11.
9. Leo Baeck, in *The Church and the Jewish People,* pp. 102, 108.
10. *The Hibbert Journal,* vol. LVI (1958), pp. 273 ff.
11. *Commentary* (New York), April 1961.
12. Ibid., p. 346.
13. David Danzig, in *Commentary,* September 1961, p. 226; cf. also, Gregory Baum, *The Jews and the Gospel,* 1961, p. 12.

35 Who Is a Jew?

Arthur W. Kac

Oswald Rufeisen, a Polish Jew, saved many Jewish lives in his native Poland during the Nazi occupation. Through the friendship shown to him by certain Roman Catholics he became interested in the message of the New Testament. In the course of time he accepted the Christian faith and joined one of the Catholic monastic orders. In 1959, under the name Brother Daniel, he went to Israel as a member of the Carmelite Monastery.

In Israel, Brother Daniel petitioned the government to grant him Israeli citizenship on the basis of the Law of Return. This law, passed by the Israeli Parliament in 1950, permits every Jew to settle in Israel. Approval of Brother Daniel's petition would have amounted to a recognition by the Israeli government that Brother Daniel is a Jew. The Government, however, refused to grant Brother Daniel citizenship status on the basis of the Law of Return, but offered him citizenship on the basis of a non-Jewish immigrant. Brother Daniel took his case to the courts, and on December 6, 1962, the majority of the judges of the Supreme Court upheld the action of the government.

It is the sovereign right of any country to determine what type of immigrants shall be admitted into its territory and what kind of aliens should be granted citizenship status. The obvious aim of the Law of Return was to assure a Jewish majority in the newly established state of Israel. Here is where the problem began: Who is a Jew? When in 1958 the government made up its own definition of who is a Jew for the purpose of registering its population, the religious parties precipitated a cabinet crisis, and the government had to seek guidance in that matter among the various Jewish communities in countries outside of Israel. The question, Who is a Jew? has troubled the Jewish people at least from the time of their political emancipation in western Europe at the beginning of the nineteenth century. With the establishment of the state of Israel, that question assumed urgent and practical importance, and Jews admit today that they are still unable to provide an answer to the question, What or who is a Jew?

I

THE JEWISH ATTITUDE TO THE HEBREW CHRISTIAN

In defending the government's refusal to recognize Brother Daniel as a Jew, the

This article by Arthur W. Kac appeared originally under the title "The Daniel Case: An Evaluation" in *The American Hebrew Christian* 49, no. 2 (Fall 1963): 3-11. It is reprinted with some stylistic changes and by permission.

attorney for the state admitted that a Jew who forsakes the Jewish religion is still a Jew, as long as he does not accept another religion. By another religion—it will be shown further in this article—he meant Christianity. Why is a Hebrew Christian not considered a Jew, whereas the Jewishness of Jewish atheists and Jewish Communists is not questioned, not even for the purpose of synagogue affiliation? The answer lies in the Jewish attitude to the Hebrew Christian. That attitude forms a tragic chapter in the annals of the Jewish history of the last nineteen centuries. Past mistreatment of Jews in Christendom undoubtedly has much to do with the Jewish attitude to the Hebrew Christian, but it does not offer a satisfactory explanation. Jewish hostility to the Hebrew Christian dates back to the first century when the Messianic movement of Jesus was still strongly Jewish. The so-called Birkat Ha-Minim prayer of hate was composed before the end of the first century and was designed to separate the Hebrew Christian from his Jewish brethren. There is no country in the world where Jews have been treated with more kindness and consideration than in this blessed country of America. And can that kind of treatment of Jews in America be fully accounted for apart from America's Christian heritage? In spite of that, the American Jews are not willing to practice tolerance in relation to the Hebrew Christians.

In an attempt to justify the verdict of the Israeli Supreme Court that a Christian Jew is not a Jew, Chief Justice Silberg declared that Christian Jews "inevitably are cut off from our national family tree, for the simple reason that their children marry into other nations."[1] That statement is not fully accurate, for many Hebrew Christians, including this writer, have Jewish wives. On one hand, Jewish leadership does all in its power to keep Hebrew Christians and Jews apart; and when, as a result, Hebrew Christians marry Gentile Christians, they are accused of cutting themselves off from their national family tree.

II

AT THE HEART OF THE DANIEL CASE IS THE JEWISH ATTITUDE TO JESUS CHRIST

The Jewish attitude to Jesus Christ, not to the Hebrew Christian, is at the heart of the matter. The state attorney who argued the Daniel case before the Supreme Court declared: "We cannot come and tell the Jews in all the lands of their dispersion, to fathers and mothers, that a man can become a Christian and remain a Jew."[2] That means that a Jew may deny the divine origin of the Scriptures, as the majority of Jews do now, that a Jew may even be an avowed atheist, and still be considered a Jew. But once a Jew voices his conviction that the writings of the New Testament are as much the Word of God as those of the Old Testament and that the Christ of the New Testament is the Messiah of the Old Testament, he ceases to be a Jew.

The Daniel case was not merely a controversy between an Israeli law and a Christian Jew but also was an issue of vital importance for all Jews. In dealing with that case, the Israeli Supreme Court, strictly speaking, acted on behalf of the state of Israel, but in reality it spoke for all Jews. The Jews of the whole world had a stake in that issue. What the stake is may be seen from the following statement by the Chief Justice: "For all the admiration and gratitude we as Jews owe to Oswald Rufeisen . . . for having risked his life many times to save fellow Jews from the

Nazis . . . we dare not allow this to serve as grounds to empty the name and content of the term Jew.''[3]

To acknowledge, then, that a Christian Jew is a Jew is to empty the word *Jew* of its content. Why? Because under the influence of Rabbinic Judaism the word *Jew* has, among other things, come to mean opposition to Jesus Christ. Actually, since the first century much of Judaism developed as a reaction against Christianity. In the first century the apostle John stated that "the law was given by Moses, but grace and truth came by Jesus Christ" (John 1:17): two revelations, one through Moses, and the second through Jesus Christ. In opposition, the Midrash declares that the Torah is unchangeable. No other Moses will come to bring another Torah, for there is no other Torah left in heaven (Midrash Dt.R. 8:6). The same idea is set down in the Maimonides Creed, which Jews have for centuries recited in their daily prayers: "I believe with perfect faith that the whole Torah, now in our possession, was given to Moses our teacher, peace be unto him. I believe with perfect faith that the Torah will not be changed, and that there will never be another Torah from the Creator, blessed be his name."

One of the participants in the symposium published in *Commentary* in 1961 said that it is the rejection of Jesus as Christ that binds American Jews together. It is by the rejection of the Messiahship of Jesus—he declared—that we proclaim to the world that we are still Jews. But what message, he asked, do we Jews have for ourselves?

In the light of the above considerations, to have granted Brother Daniel's request that he be recognized as a Jew would have meant in effect a recognition on the part of the state of Israel that the centuries-old Jewish struggle against Christianity was a grievous error, and it would have amounted to a declaration by the state of Israel that Christianity is true. "If a Jew accepts such a convert [to Christianity] as good a Jew as himself," declared Dr. David Flusser of the Hebrew University of Jerusalem, "then he automatically goes halfway along the road to Christianity. He endangers the entire Raison d' être of the existence of the Jewish people."[4] And the editor of a Tel Aviv paper is said to have stated that"if the court decides he [Brother Daniel] is a Jew, it will be a catastrophe for world Judaism."[5]

III

MANY JEWS DISAPPROVE OF THE SUPREME COURT DECISION

The verdict of the Israeli Supreme Court caused a number of eminent Jews in Israel to speak up in defense of Hebrew Christians. The following are a few examples.

One Israeli journalist declared it is high time that Jews rid themselves of certain fixed ideas acquired in the centuries of the exile. Brother Daniel, he said, accepted his religion from inner conviction; he has not changed his nationality.

"The decision of the High Court in the case of Daniel Rufeisen has brought a tragic blow upon the principles of freedom of conscience and the separation of religion from the State of Israel. It established [a precedent] that a person has to be judged according to his thoughts and not according to his deeds, and gave the right

138

to the State to watch over the relations of man with God in order to decide whether he deserves first class citizenship. . . . The claim by Judge Silberg, Chief Justice, that a decision granted in favor of Daniel Rufeisen would 'deny all the spiritual values for which we were massacred during various periods of our long exile' has the smell of negativism. One should not impose on Rufeisen [Brother Daniel] the responsibility for the sins of the Roman Catholic Church, even as we have no right to accuse a just religious Jew for the acts of extremist religious Jewish clericals in Israel. Judge Silberg casts stones from a glass house, for though we never approved the ways of Torquemada [of the Spanish Inquisition] who wanted to gain souls through affliction and fire, we have not risen above our own religious and social pressure in mixed marriages."[6]

"The question whether Christ was the Messiah was debated at the time [of the first century], as we see in Chapter V of The Acts. The grand counsellor, Rabbi Gamaliel the Pharisee, told the people in the council to have nothing to do with Jesus. He pointed out that other individuals had claimed to be the Messiah, mentioning Theudas and Judas of Galilee, the Zealot. All those who supported these pseudo-Messiahs came to grief in finding out their claims were invalid. So, argued Gamaliel, if Jesus was a false Messiah, his followers would be overwhelmed with disaster, while, if his work really was of God, they could not overthrow him, as it was impossible to fight against God. This reasoning convinced the council.

"In the result, can we say whether Rabbi Gamaliel was right? The Christians claim that the success of Christianity proves that Jesus was the Messiah, but the Jews answer that Christianity succeeded only among the Gentiles, and never became the religion of the Jews. . .

"With regard to the question of an atheist Jew who maintains that there is no God at all, the common opinion among Jews is that such a Jew is more Jewish than one converted to Christianity. Mind you, one Rabbi in the Middle Ages said that a believing Christian is nearer to him than an atheist Jew, and I am not so far off from his opinion.

"I know less about Islam than about Christianity, but it is true that the Moslems believe in one God, and that Mohammed only claims to be the prophet of Allah, never more than a man. . . . I would say that the tension between Islam and Judaism is less than that between Christianity and Judaism, but Christianity is nevertheless much closer to Judaism and considers itself an offshoot of it. Christianity and Judaism come from the same olive tree . . . The Jewish Christian movements have been going on for 100 years, and some of them have been more sympathetic to Zionism than many movements which remained Jewish."[7]

IV

Hebrew Christians in Israel State Their Case

For many years Jews have attributed to Hebrew Christians ulterior motives. Jews who embraced the Christian faith were supposed to do this out of a desire for material gains, or because they wanted to detach themselves from their people and become submerged in their Gentile environment. Brother Daniel's struggle for recognition of his Jewish identity shattered those fixed Jewish ideas. *The Jerusalem Post* offered an opportunity to three Hebrew Christians in Israel to state their cases.

The first statement is by Tereska Levin, the wife of writer and novelist Meyer Levin. She is the daughter of the eminent French sculptor, the late Marek Szwarc. Mrs. Levin is an author in her own right, having written seven books in French, several of which have been translated into English by her husband. This is her story:

"I want to emphasize at the outset that Meyer is vigorously Jewish and so are my sons . . . I was born Jewish and Catholic at the same time. My parents became converted before my birth and kept their conversion secret for several years, so as not to upset their families—my father's father was an extremely orthodox Jew and my father had had a very orthodox upbringing. Ever since I was a tiny child my father told me that I was a Jew of Catholic religion, but he did not make his conversion public until I was 11. When he did so, my grandfather tore his clothing and put ashes on his head. Jews threw stones at our house and called my father a traitor. But he was a very serene man and told me not to worry; he said it would pass. And it did. He and my grandfather were reconciled eventually.

"I was brought up in a convent school in Paris, where everybody knew that I was Jewish and Catholic, and accepted this as very natural. If anything, I was considered by the pupils and nuns to be somebody somehow superior to other Catholic girls, precisely because I was Jewish—they felt that I was a sort of cousin of Jesus Christ! Throughout my childhood I was surrounded by converted Jews, many of whom became priests and nuns without denying their Jewishness—there was a Father Cohen, and Abbe Glasberg.

"I resent very much an allegation which is sometimes made that converted Jews want to escape from Judaism and the burdens of being Jewish. This may have been true in the old days, but it certainly was not true in western countries during the last 30 years. These converted Jews, like my father, were proud of their Jewishness, loved the Bible, studied it, spoke Hebrew and were devoted Zionists.

"My father knew all about Judaism; he studied it both before and after his conversion. Almost all his sculptures were devoted to Jewish themes. He was a very mystical man, and his conversion was emotional; he believed that Jesus was the Messiah. He once explained to me that the only difference between Catholic Jews and other Jews was that we believed that salvation had been achieved, while they did not. . .

"The real question is one of freedom of religion. I do not think that in the modern world of today we can have tyranny of one religion over another. It is entirely a personal question for each man or woman to decide whether he believes in Jesus Christ or Mohammed or anything else. The Jews of Israel should be entitled to the same freedom of worship as any other people. As a matter of fact, there are hundreds of Jews converted to Catholicism who believed passionately in the State of Israel, and who live here, but are frightened to admit their Catholicism openly, because they are worried about their children being made to suffer. My own conviction is that we should be building bridges between Christians and Jews, not trying to tear them down. We Jews of all people should be the most tolerant.

"I would like to say in conclusion that I have always found this tolerance among the sabras [native or young Israeli Jews], who understand my position very clearly, and do not find it in any way paradoxical. It is the Jews from Eastern Europe who resist the idea of real freedom of conscience most vigorously. The sabras see it as being a part of our being a normal people to allow people like me to believe whatever we like without accusing us of betraying our Jewishness."[8]

The two Hebrew Christians whose stories follow are not Roman Catholics. They are not formally affiliated with any particular church. They profess and practice the faith of the New Testament much the same as did the Hebrew Christians of the first century of whom we read in the book of Acts. There are hundreds like them in Israel today.

One of those, Dr. Lilly Wreschner of Tiberias, is a doctor of psychology. "I was born and brought up by Jewish parents in Switzerland," she says. "I feel Jewish, am proud of being Jewish and look Jewish. From early childhood I passionately searched for a satisfying content to this my Judaism. I found it after agonizing struggles 23 years ago in the greatest Jew: Jesus the Messiah. Like Paul, I had the wonderful experience of being grafted into my own olive tree. I became a true daughter of Abraham, full of faith, and love for the God of Israel, the Messiah of Israel, the people of Israel and also the Land of Israel. I became a true Zionist and came to Israel 20 years ago. I have not accepted another religion. I have accepted the Messiah of Israel . . . In the eyes of God I am a Jewess. In the eyes of Gentiles I am a Jewess. In my own conviction I am a Jewess. And what is my identity in Israel?"[9]

Marion Eigeles came to Israel from one of the lands under Communism. In Israel he received the Master of Science degree. This is what he writes:

"Eight years ago, in a country behind the Iron Curtain, I found in Jesus Christ my personal Savior. My first prayer was made in Hebrew. I asked Him to take me and my people into our country, Eretz Israel, and protect us from our enemies. My prayers were answered. The authorities of that country opened the door for us to Israel, and so I came to my country. The fact is that Jesus did not estrange me from my people, but rather He gave me a deeper understanding of my Jewish destiny: we are the chosen people of God, a Messianic people. The waters of baptism meant for me not the severing of my bonds to Judaism, but rather the putting off of my godless nature ('Yetzer ha'ra'), thus making me able to enter into the promises made by God to our forefather Abraham. . . . Pastor Isaac Feinstein died (Al Kiddush Ha-Shem) in the pogrom of 1941 in Jassy, Rumania. He could have been saved but preferred to die with his own people. There were Hebrew Christians who died in Bessarabia and those in Theresienstadt who died together with their compatriots in Auschwitz. They did not use their Christian faith in order to save their lives. They died as Jews. The fact is that the Hebrew Christian wants to find a place in Israeli society and to make his contribution to the building up of the State without renouncing the worship of God according to his conscience."[10]

Notes

1. *The Jerusalem Post,* 7 December, 1962.
2. "Daniel in the Den of Judgment," *Maariv,* 5 December, 1962.
3. *The Jerusalem Post,* 7 December, 1962.
4. Philip Gillon, "Jews of Christian Faith Defining Their Position," *The Jerusalem Post,* 8 February, 1963. Used by permission.
5. Herzl Rosenblum, editor of *Yediot Aharonot,* Tel Aviv, quoted in *Time,* 7 December, 1962.
6. Dr. Harshaft, "Request of Rufeisen," *Ha'aretz* (Tel Aviv), 17 December, 1962.
7. Philip Gillon, ibid.
8. Ibid.
9. Ibid.
10. Ibid.

36 Judaism and Biblical Messianism

Max I. Reich

Both Jews and Christians confess before the world their faith in one God. He is to them one Creator, Preserver and final judge of men. Moreover, both Jews and Christians confess the ethical quality of the divine nature. He is righteous and loveth righteousness. He expects His people to pattern their lives on His attitude towards good and evil; to love the good and hate the evil. However, modern Jews and Christians tread different paths as to some important aspects of this great theme. To the Judaism of today, God is largely a proposition, a point of metaphysical speculation. Hence Jews are fond of speaking of their God-idea as that of an "ethical monotheism." There is no warmth, no tenderness, no heart, in this form of speech. When we turn to the Old Testament we find something very different. Men were enthusiasts for Jehovah. He is over and over again presented in anthropomorphic terms. He feels and acts like man; in all our afflictions He is afflicted; He shares our joys and our sorrows; He walks with us in sympathetic love. No wonder that He becomes the fountain of "exceeding joy" to His worshippers! To see His countenance is to them the acme of blessedness; His frown spells unhappiness and wretchedness. In His favor alone is true life.

Moreover, instead of philosophical unicity, the Old Testament indicates that there is in God a richer inner self-consciousness, making room for the more developed doctrine of the Tri-unity of the New Testament. Thus the triune divine blessing Jacob invokes on the sons of Joseph (Genesis 48:15,16); the triune benediction of the priests in Numbers 6:22-27; the Trisagion of the seraphim (Isaiah 6:3); and the wonderful tri-unity in the mission of the Messiah: "I," "the Lord God" and "His Spirit," in Isaiah 48:16. The God of modern Judaism remains ever lonely in His unapproachable spirituality and super-worldly majesty. If the sum of the self-revelation of God in the Old Testament is "Love" as "Love" is the summing up of the Law and the Prophets, then there must have been in the Godhead One Beloved before ever a creature existed, and a spirit of love between both, in other words, a trinity. Judaism is blind to this. But to a Christian it is the light of divine revelation in which he walks by faith, till faith is merged into sight at last.

If we inquire into the causes of this divergence from the original God-concept in Israel on the part of modern, so-called "liberal" Judaism, we must take into account the influence of two Jewish philosophers, Spinoza and Mendelssohn.

"Judaism and Biblical Messianism" appeared as "Judaism and Christianity" in *The Hebrew Christian* 35, no. 2 (Summer 1962):65-66, and is reprinted by permission.

Spinoza has given to modern Judaism its pantheistic tendency and Mendelssohn its deism. The Sh'ma, "Hear, O Israel, Jehovah thy God is one Jehovah," is interpreted by the disciples of Spinoza to mean that "The Being," i.e., the universal life force, is Israel's God. The disciples of Mendelssohn, on the other hand, emphasize the divine transcendence, God being the unapproachable, the exalted One, far above the world. The well-known Cincinnati Rabbi Kohler endeavored to combine both concepts in his doctrine of God: "For the modern seeker in the sphere of religion, the emphasis of religion lies in the doctrine of man—in anthropology. Man with his homesickness for heaven, with his highest urge, beholds with Isaiah the fringe of the divine glory. He seeks and finds that God is above him while he is aware of Him as within. He must, of course, pass through all the steps between, till through self-knowledge he arrives at the knowledge of God!"

Is this the God of Abraham, Isaac, and Jacob? Or are not these words mere phrases tinged with religious philosophy, but devoid of power and life, such as a bruised and broken human heart seeking reality cries out for?

The New Testament God-idea is rooted in the revelation which was granted to ancient Israel. Modern Judaism is a departure therefrom. It is in the face of Jesus Christ we see the effulgence of the glory of God. He is the goal of the divine outshining when the God of glory appeared to Abraham.

As it has been aptly said: "In the Old Testament we see God in profile. In the New Testament, in the person of the incarnate Son, we see God face to face."

The Growing Jewish Interest in Jesus

And as they approached Jerusalem, at Bethphage and Bethany, near the Mount of Olives, He sent two of His disciples, and said to them, "Go into the village opposite you, and immediately as you enter it, you will find a cólt tied there, on which no one yet has ever sat; untie it and bring it here. . . ." And they brought the colt to Jesus and put their garments on it; and He sat upon it. And many spread their garments in the road, and others spread leafy branches which they had cut from the fields. And those who went before, and those who followed after, were crying out, "Hosanna! Blessed is He who comes in the name of the Lord. Blessed is the coming kingdom of our father David; Hosanna in the highest. . . ." And some of the Pharisees in the multitude said to Him, "Teacher, rebuke Your disciples." And He answered and said, "I tell you, if these become silent, the stones will cry out."
Mark 11:1-2, 7-10; Luke 19:39-40 (NASB)

For the people of Israel shall abide many days without king and without prince, without sacrifice and without pillar, without ephod and without teraphim. Afterward shall the people of Israel return, and seek the Lord their God and David their king*; and shall come trembling to the Lord and to his goodness in the latter days.
Hos. 3:4-5 (author's trans.)

The Jewish Quest of Jesus—*Jakob Jocz*   146
"The Jewishness of Jesus"—*Arthur W. Kac*   152

---

*"David their king" is rendered in the Targum as "Messiah the Son of David their king."

37 The Jewish Quest of Jesus

Jakob Jocz

There was a time when the name of Jesus was never mentioned by Jews except in derision. One who wanted to refer to Him used circumlocution, such as *oto ish* ("this man") or *ish ploni* ("the unnamed one"). It became customary to alter His name by omitting one Hebrew letter. Thus the name *Yeshua* became Yeshu, which was meant to represent an anagram for a malediction.[1]

According to a scurrilous parody of Jesus' life, a medieval tale fabricated to dishonor the mother of Jesus and to declare Him a bastard, His real name was Yehoshua, but when His origin became known it was altered to Yeshu: "This boy is indeed a bastard and the son of an adulteress. They then published him as such by the blowing of 300 trumpets, declaring him not fit to come into the congregation, and called his name Yeshu, signifying that his name and memory deserved to perish."[2]

Joseph Klausner tried to justify the spelling of Yeshu by suggesting that it was an abbreviated form of Yehoshua, and he himself used that spelling in the Hebrew edition of his *Life of Jesus*. But his argument is not convincing.[3] More recently Jews have felt uncomfortable with the spelling of Yeshu, which traditionally carried a defamatory implication of his birth. *The Encyclopedia of the Jewish Religion*[4] frankly admits that the *Toledot Yeshu* offers a "scurrilous account" and that it contains "the most ignoble interpretations" of the details relating to the life of Jesus. That change of attitude is an indication of an effort on the part of Jewish writers to find a more positive approach to the Man of Nazareth.

Educated Jews feel ill-at-ease with the fact that the Man whom the rest of the world admires, and whom many regard as Savior and Lord, should be regarded so utterly a stranger by His own kith and kin.

Let it be said at once that Jewish hostility towards Jesus has been largely due to the persecution Jews suffered at the hands of so-called Christians. But there is yet another reason that must not be overlooked, for it is of a profoundly theological nature. The importance Christians ascribe to Jesus as Messiah is such that Jews have no alternative left. In the Jewish view no such homage can be paid to any man, no matter how great. In a sense, therefore, hostility towards Jesus has been in reality an expression of opposition to the faith of the church.

In modern times, when studies of the life and teaching of Jesus are taken up seriously, there is a consistent effort made to separate the Christ of the church from the historic Man of Nazareth. In a sense, Jewish scholarship has taken over the position of nineteenth century German liberalism and is trying to blame Paul for Gentile Christianity while claiming Jesus as the most essential Jew. Martin Buber described Him as the "central Jew."

Among Jewish writers it is now regarded as an established fact that "Paul was responsible for the new religion," while the real Jesus was and remained a Jew to the very end.[5] Even Hans-Joachim Schoeps, who allows for a connection between the historic Jesus and the heavenly Christ and who goes out of his way to show his appreciation of Paul's great achievements, calls the apostle the "first Christian."[6] The Karaite Rabbi Isaac of Troki (1533-94) strained to show that Jesus, keeping the Law and praying to God, never claimed to be more than human; yet, the rabbi failed to appreciate His Jewishness and the attractiveness of His character.[7] Those two characteristics were left to be discovered by contemporary Jewish writers. It was under the influence of liberal Judaism that the change of attitude began to take shape.

The extent of Jewish occupation with the Man of Nazareth was conveyed in a recent article by the Israeli scholar Shalom Ben-Chorin.[8] That comprehensive study provides a bird's-eye view of the interest shown by Jewish writers on the wide canvas of Jewish life, from historic research, to apologetic writings, to novels, to drama, to lyrics, to painting. Some of those efforts are trivial, such as Hugh J. Schonfield's *The Passover Plot*, which Ben-Chorin justly describes as "a Jewish *speculation* versus the Christian *faith*."[9] Other efforts, such as Buber's, are profoundly moving and full of nostalgia. Here is a passage that deserves to be quoted in full: "From my youth onwards I have found in Jesus my great brother. That Christianity has regarded and still does regard him as God and Saviour has always appeared to me a fact of the highest importance which, for his sake and my own, I must endeavour to understand . . . My own fraternally open relationship to him has grown ever stronger and clearer, and today I see him more strongly and clearly than ever before." He continues: "I am more than ever certain that a great place belongs to him in Israel's history of faith and that this place cannot be described by any of the usual categories."[10] But Buber failed to elucidate what role Jesus is meant to play in "Israel's history of faith." A special case is Sholem Asch with his trilogy, *The Nazarene, The Apostle* and *Mary*. These historic novels not only attempt to recreate the genuine Jewish background against which the drama of the early Hebrew Christians was played out, but also try to convey the spiritual qualities that gave life to the primitive church. No wonder that Sholem Asch was bitterly attacked by Jewish orthodoxy.

Of more recent vintage, the studies by the Jewish scholars David Flusser and Geza Vermes, both of international fame, merely reiterate what has been already said many times over: Jesus was and remained in all respects a Jew. All they purport to do is to correct the distorted image imposed upon the historic Jesus both by Jews and Christians. The true Jesus was neither a god nor a villain but a God-fearing and law-abiding Jew. The anonymous author of *The Disputation* is concerned with attacking Christianity and not Jesus. As far as the early Christians are concerned, they "were just another sect, keeping the Jewish Sabbath and Festivals, praying in the Temple and synagogues and keeping even the dietary laws." It was only when the message reached the Gentiles that its paganization set in. It is only, says the writer, when the New Testament is read with an open and unbiased mind that "the humbug and propaganda fall away, and the whole pagan idiocy is revealed."[11] The anonymous Rabbi, however, finds himself in a twofold contradiction; first he uses the New Testament as a source and then decries it as inadequate. But he is also for and against Jesus at the same time: Jesus is the pious Jew who keeps the Law, and Jesus is the illegitimate fool, mentally unbalanced, whom his mother and family regard as a crackpot.[12] A similar contradiction underlies much of Jewish endeavor in the effort to come to terms with Jesus of Nazareth. There is the desire, especially on the part of liberal Jews, to rehabilitate Jesus, but on the other hand, His is not easily placed alongside Jewish tradition. Vermes readily concedes the "incomparable superiority of Jesus" when measured against some of the saintly Rabbis. But wherein His superiority lies is not easily evident. What is evident to Jewish writers is that Jesus "was *in fact* neither the Christ of the Church, nor the apostate and bogey-man of Jewish popular tradition."[13] Who was He?

The main tendency among Jewish writers is to establish Jesus' Jewishness. But by doing that, the significance of Jesus is by no means clarified. Ben-Chorin falls back upon Maimonides' position: "Jesus was the preparer of the way for the King Messiah." But that hardly justifies Jewish attention in view of the fact that "Messiah" is not even a vague hope for the majority of contemporary Jews.

The question is raised all over again by Ferdynand Zweig's chapter in his *Israel: the Sword and the Harp: The Figure of Jesus on the Israeli Horizon.*

Ferdynand Zweig, an English Jew, who was visiting professor of sociology and labor relations at the Hebrew and Tel Aviv Universities and spent five years in Israel, was struck by the inevitability of an encounter between Jesus of Nazareth and the Israeli Jews. He writes: "The figure of Jesus, the Jew from Nazareth, looms large on the Israeli horizon, although not much is said about him openly and most Jews cautiously refrain from mentioning his name in public."[14] As Zweig sees it, the Israeli Jew finds himself in a different situation from that of the Jews in the Diaspora. There Jews are confronted with the church and Christianity, but in the land of Israel, it is the pilgrims, the tourists, and the holy places that serve as constant reminders of the presence of the Man of Nazareth. "How to deal with Him?" is the crucial question he asks. It seems to Zweig that there is no escape from that question. That leads him to yet another question on behalf of the Israeli Jew, even more insistent than the first: "Were his forefathers right in rejecting Jesus?"[15] Once those questions are raised, inevitably other questions follow: "Why is it that more than half the world has accepted Jesus as God (Christians), or as a Prophet (Muslims), or as the Ideal Man (Humanists), whereas Jews of His own kith and kin have rejected Him?" Zweig allows that for Jews in the Diaspora the rejection of Jesus was a necessity if they were to survive without being "dissolved in the sea of Christianity." He asks, however: "But how is it now?" Can an Israeli today avoid Jesus and His teaching? The writer is not concerned with the doctrines of Christianity but with the Man Jesus, the Jew "as presented by his Jewish disciples in the Synoptic Gospels." Jesus' teaching, especially the injunction to love one's enemies, Zweig regards as most relevant for the situation in Israel today.

He thinks that had Jews heeded Jesus' words two thousand years ago, they would have defeated Rome by love instead of perishing by the sword of their enemies.

Any informed reader of that fascinating chapter, which breathes deep earnestness and moral concern, is forced to ask the inevitable question: Why attach all that importance to Jesus as if Jewry is lacking teachers, sages and prophets? Zweig himself is groping for an answer.

First, Zweig disagrees with Klausner, who refuses to regard Jesus as a major prophet, the heir of Isaiah and Jeremiah. To Zweig, Jesus occupies a superior position of spiritual and religious perception which singles Him out as a prophet of the first order. As prophet, He could provide inspiration and guidance of which contemporary Jewry is in great need. Second, Jesus' injunction to love the enemy still has for Jewry "highly significant national-political implications." For that reason, He cannot be ignored.

Third, Zweig wants to know how Jesus "managed to conquer the whole world" by his spiritual power. That is a puzzle both to him and to the Israeli Jew. They therefore ask: "Who is he? Wherein lies the secret of his power? How did this Jew manage to attract the immense love and adoration of the world while Jews attract only hatred and contempt? How did he manage to fulfill the task set in the Bible for the Jews to serve as 'a light to the nations,' while Jewry failed? Why is it that only he managed to shape and mold the world, while Jews played a losing game, rolling in the dust?"[16]

Such are the searching questions that puzzle Zweig and, according to him, many an Israeli Jew.

Is there an answer to those questions? It seems that on Zweig's terms not only can there be no answer but the questions themselves are inappropriate. Such importance attaching to a man leads to hero-worship and pagan mythology. Zweig raises those questions because he is profoundly aware of the bankruptcy of traditional Judaism. He writes: "The tragedy of Israel is that the old religion, practised only by the orthodox, is ritualistic, petrified, and ossified, and deprived of its vivifying, life-enhancing and tender forces, while the rest of society, the majority, is atheistic, agnostic or religiously indifferent, disinterested or unconcerned."[17] What Zweig is saying of rabbinic Judaism has been an open secret for a long time, though fervently denied by propagandists. He makes the point that rabbinic Judaism was suited for the Diaspora but is inadequate for the new situation in Israel. He therefore asks the inevitable question: "What is the Judaism of the Third Commonwealth to be?" It is at that point that Zweig advocates a return to the message of Jesus, which would thus connect the preceding Commonwealth with the new State of Israel. Israeli Jewry, according to the author, is in need of a creed that would synthesize Jewish existence. Such a creed would break through the "Ghetto wall" and remove the 613 "bricks" of which it is composed.[18] He therefore asks the last and ultimate question: "Could it be that Jesus could give it [i.e., Israeli Jewry] a new lease of life?"

That places the author in a difficult dilemma: Can one have the message of Jesus without the Man? Though he attempts to exclude "all Christianized stylization of Jesus as Christ," he realizes that the person of Jesus and His message are of one piece. At that point he goes beyond the traditional attitude of Judaism, no matter of what brand. In his most daring sentence, he is prepared to replace the 613 precepts as defined by rabbinic Judaism with "the personality and message of Jesus, the Jew from Nazareth." There can be no other way; the two are inseparable.

To a Jewish believer in Jesus as Savior and Lord, Zweig's concern strikes a deep and sympathetic cord. However, his emphasis upon the "message" reveals the typical naive Jewish optimism, which can have no place after the Holocaust. Any good rabbi will tell him that nothing Jesus preached is new to Judaism. It is all there; all a Jew needs is to practice it.

No one has ever been radically helped by a lofty message. The difference between a believing Christian and a pious Jew is not ethics against ethics, doctrine against doctrine, torah against torah. The difference lies in the personal relationship between Jesus as Savior and man as sinner. The path to the new life Zweig is seeking for his people is the one that leads through the atoning death and resurrection of Jesus. Here lies the secret of power on the part of the Man of Nazareth. Questions about Jesus can only be asked existentially. The questioner must first answer them personally before they are addressed to others. It is only in personal confrontation with Jesus that the human condition appears in its true light. In the last resort, there is no difference between Israel and the nations. The spiritual lethargy, the inner void, and the voice of despair are the universal mark of our age.

Dr. Abraham L. Feinberg, rabbi-emeritus of Holy Blossom Temple in Toronto, in an article in the daily press, called Jesus his "brother." "Not," Feinberg explained, "because he was a Jew who loved his Hebraic heritage and people," but because He desired "to share, however inadequately, his courage and compassion."[19] That is a noble sentiment that must be respected. But Jesus is too demanding a figure to be satisfied with compliments. For in reality, it is not we who are doing the questioning; it is He who is questioning us: "Who do you say I am?"

Our eternal destiny is determined by the kind of answer that we are prepared to give to His question.

Notes

1. "Yeshu" was supposed to stand for "his name and memory be blotted out."
2. It is not known at what point in time the Jews began to interpret the name of Jesus in that manner. According to some scholars the tradition goes back to at least the fifth century (c.f. Jakob Jocz, *The Jewish People and Jesus Christ* [London: S.P.C.K., 1949], pp. 60 ff.; 338 ff.; fns. 299 ff.
3. Cf. Joseph Klausner, *Jesus of Nazareth: His Life, Times and Teaching* (New York: Macmillan, 1925), p. 299 and fn.
4. "Toledot Yeshu," in R.J. Werblowsky and Geoffrey Wigoder, eds., *The Encyclopedia of Jewish Religion* (New York: Holt, Rinehart, Winston, 1966), p. 386.
5. *The Disputation* (London: Scholarly Publications, 1972), p. 115.
6. Hans Joachim Schoeps, *Paulus* (Tübingen: J. C. B. Mohr, 1959), p. 127.
7. Cf. H. D. Leuner, "Faith Strengthened," *The Hebrew Christian* 14, no. 2 (Summer 1971):80.
8. Shalom Ben-Chorin, "The Image of Jesus in Modern Judaism," *Journal of Ecumenical Studies* 11, no. 3 (Summer 1974):401-29.
9. His italics.
10. Martin Buber, *Two Types of Faith*, trans. Norman P. Goldhawk (Macmillan, 1940; reprint, Harper Torchbook ed., New York: Harper, 1961), pp. 12 ff.
11. Ibid., p. 115.
12. Ibid., pp. 61, 208.
13. Geza Vermes, *Jesus the Jew* (London: Collins, 1973), p. 17.
14. Ferdynand Zweig, *Israel: The Sword and the Harp* (Cranbury, N.J.: Associated U. Presses, 1969), p. 219.
15. bid., p. 221.
16. Ibid., p. 226.
17. Ibid., p. 228.
18. Ibid., p. 229.
19. Abraham Feinberg, "I Call Jesus My Brother and Want to Share His Compassion," *Toronto Daily Star,* 28 March, 1970.

38 "The Jewishness of Jesus"

Arthur W. Kac

Some time ago *American Judaism* published an article by Norman Cousins, editor of *Saturday Review,* entitled "The Jewishness of Jesus." The writer appealed to both Christians and Jews for a re-examination of the fact of the Jewishness of Jesus, in the hope that recognition of the significance of that fact would create a new basis for a better understanding between Jews and Christians. The article evoked considerable interest among the readers of that publication.

A subsequent issue of *American Judaism* printed a reply by Rabbi Roland B. Gittelsohn to Mr. Cousin's plea. Rabbi Gittelsohn agreed wholeheartedly with that portion of Mr. Cousin's article that called on Christians to accept the fact of the Jewishness of Jesus with all its implications. But when Mr. Cousins asked Jews that they open their hearts and minds to Jesus, Rabbi Gittelsohn apparently began to feel quite uncomfortable. Which Jesus, the rabbi asked, did Mr. Cousins have in mind? For there was one Jesus, the Jewish Jesus, who taught nothing that He did not learn from Judaism of His day. There was also a second Jesus, the rabbi assured us. That second Jesus, he declared, recommended that people should lead a single, unmarried life. He castigated the rich for no other reason than that they happened to be rich. He taught that morality had nothing to do with politics. Such teachings, the rabbi stated, were contrary to the spirit of Judaism. Then there was a third Jesus—the Christ. That Jesus formed the core of Christianity and constituted an insurmountable obstacle to a real understanding between Jews and Christians.[1]

We can be thankful for the increasing number of fair-minded Jews who use a more objective approach to the subject of Jesus Christ than does Rabbi Gittelsohn. Unfortunately, we still too often encounter among Jews an unwillingness to gain a true knowledge of what the New Testament really teaches and a tendency to lift certain things in the New Testament out of their context and read into them ideas that are not there. If some teachings of the New Testament appear to be in conflict with those of Judaism, it is because Judaism has moved away from the Old Testament. That thought may be imbedded in the conclusion of the parable of Lazarus and the rich man: "If they hear not Moses and the prophets, neither will they be persuaded, if one rise from the dead" (Luke 16:31 (RV)).

The above article is reprinted by permission, with stylistic changes, from *The American Hebrew Christian* 48, no. 3 (Winter 1963):3-7.

I have selected for discussion three of Rabbi Gittelsohn's statements about Jesus in the New Testament.

"THE TEACHINGS OF THE JEWISH JESUS ARE AT BEST A CARBON COPY OF JUDAISM."

The ethical imperatives of the Jewish Jesus, we are told by the rabbi, were Jewish in origin. The God of love whom Jesus preached was recognized eight hundred years earlier by the prophet Hosea. The plea for Jews to accept that Jesus amounts to urging that Jews accept a carbon copy of Judaism.

Does Hosea's teaching about the love of God, centuries before Jesus, necessarily mean that Jesus could not make some new contribution to the subject? If we take that position, then Hosea repeated what someone else had said centuries before him. For even in the Pentateuch (Chumesh) we meet with the concept of the love of God, as seen from the following passages: "And the LORD said, I have surely seen the affliction of my people which are in Egypt, and have heard their cry by reason of their taskmasters; for I know their sorrows; and I am come down to deliver them out of the hand of the Egyptians" (Exodus 3:7-8); "Ye have seen what I did unto the Egyptians, and how I bare you on eagles' wings, and brought you unto myself" (Exodus 19:4).

When we turn to the writings of Hosea, we meet with a different concept of divine love. Hosea arrived at that concept, partly at least, through a tragic experience in his family life. His wife whom he loved dearly committed adultery, but God told Hosea to take back his wife and restore her to his love. From that experience Hosea gained new insight into the nature of God's love for Israel. In Exodus, Israel is God's people, in Hosea, God is Israel's husband (Hosea 2:19). Israel's transgression against God is therefore spiritual adultery, but God's love for Israel is so great that, though He must punish her, in time He will restore her to Himself.

If we pursue further the subject of divine love in the Bible we find it often likened to the love of a shepherd for his flock. A classical example is Psalm 23, from which I will quote a few sentences: "The LORD is my shepherd; I shall not want. He maketh me to lie down in green pastures: he leadeth me beside the still waters . . . Yea, though I walk through the valley of the shadow of death, I will fear no evil: for thou art with me; thy rod and thy staff they comfort me" (Psalm 23:1-2,4).

Ezekiel presents another aspect of God's shepherd love. In the passage cited below, Israel becomes scattered sheep and exposed to danger. God, Israel's shepherd, goes out to search for His sheep: "As a shepherd seeketh out his flock in the day that he is among his sheep that are scattered; so will I seek out my sheep, and will deliver them out of all places where they have been scattered in the cloudy and dark day" (Ezekiel 34:12).

Jesus advanced the idea of divine love one step higher. He was once criticized for associating with "publicans" (the despised Jewish tax collectors working for the Roman government) and "sinners" and eating in their homes. He answered His critics with the following parable: "What man of you, having an hundred sheep, if he lose one of them, doth not leave the ninety and nine in the wilderness, and go after that which is lost, until he find it? And when he hath found it, he layeth it on his shoulders, rejoicing. And when he cometh home, he calleth together his friends and neighbours, saying unto them, Rejoice with me; for I have found my sheep which was lost. I say unto you, that likewise joy shall be in heaven over one sinner that repenteth, more than over ninety and nine just persons, which need no repentance" (Luke 15:4-7). That the shepherd was ready to give his life in the process of rescuing the lost sheep may be seen from this additional statement: "The good shepherd giveth his life for the sheep" (John 10:11). In the above parable Jesus teaches that God's love for lost mankind is of such a character that through the Messiah He is willing to pay a price in order to recover even the worst moral and social outcasts. With that, all that biblical revelation could say about the love of God had been said. The meaning of the above parable of the lost sheep is well expressed in the following hymn:

> But none of the ransomed ever knew
> How deep were the waters crossed;
> Nor how dark was the night that the Lord passed thro'
> Ere He found His sheep that was lost.
>
> "Lord, whence are those blood-drops all the way,
> That mark out the mountain's track?"
> "They were shed for one who had gone astray
> Ere the Shepherd could bring him back."
>
> ELIZABETH C. CLEPHANE

DID JESUS TEACH THAT MORALITY HAS NOTHING TO DO WITH POLITICS?

We are told by the rabbi that Jesus taught that morality had nothing to do with politics, and the two are placed in two separate categories of experience. As proof, the rabbi quotes the following statement by Jesus: "Give unto Caesar what is Caesar's, and unto God what is God's." Judaism, we are told, insists that morality enters into every area of life including politics.

Some Jews, the extreme nationalists, in the days of Jesus were opposed to paying taxes to heathen Rome. A group of those who were ill-disposed toward Jesus asked Him one day whether He thought that it was religiously lawful to pay taxes to the Roman government. If His answer had been in the affirmative, His popularity among Jews, or certain Jews, would have suffered. If He had answered in the negative, He would have gotten Himself in trouble with the Roman officials. In reply, Jesus asked the questioner to show him a Roman coin, for taxes had to be paid in Roman currency. Then He asked, "Whose image is on this coin?" "Caesar's," was the reply. Then Jesus said, "Give to Caesar what is Caesar's, and to God what is God's" (NIV). From the above we can see it is not quite fair to say that Jesus taught that morality and politics had nothing to do with each other. The unbiased observer of the political life of the various nations will admit that political morality is considerably higher in countries under the influence of biblical Christianity. The above statement by Jesus merely acknowledges that the child of God has an obligation to the state, and until the kingdoms of men become the Kingdom of God, religion and the affairs of state, or sacred and secular life, will move in two areas. Furthermore, that statement by Jesus is supported by the rabbinic dictum that in

154

certain areas of life "the law of the state is law."

But another aspect of the great principle "Give to Caesar what is Caesar's, and to God what is God's," must be pointed out here, and its relevance to human freedom and happiness has never been more clear than at the present juncture of human history. Almost from the beginning of the Messianic movement of Jesus, His followers have recognized that human government, however bad, is ordained of God as long as it maintains law and order and affords protection to human life. But once human government leaves its specific area and invades the area of human conscience and the religious convictions of its citizens, such government is not ordained of God. It is on the basis of that principle that the Jewish followers of Jesus insisted on their right to propagate their religious views (see Acts 4:19). It was also on the basis of that principle that Jewish and Gentile followers of Jesus defied the might of Rome when it sought to force them to give up their religious convictions. Every totalitarian system, whether secular or religious, no matter how it begins, sooner or later attempts to violate the principle "Give to Caesar what is Caesar's and to God what is God's." American democracy, with its insistence on separation of state and established religion, adheres to the same principle.

Jesus Urged His Followers to Love Their Enemies."

"Judaism," the rabbi declares," is far too realistic and sober a faith to endorse so psychologically impossible a precept as that. Judaism orders its adherents to help their enemies when they are in trouble, to rescue the animal of an enemy when it lies helplessly under a heavy burden. . . . But Judaism," the rabbi states, "would never torture its adherents with guilt by expecting them to love their enemies."

I assume that when the rabbi refers to Judaism he includes the Hebrew Bible. If so, I must ask, since when has biblical revelation proclaimed truths and precepts that are psychologically possible? Was it psychologically realistic for God to tell Abraham when he was seventy-five years old to cut himself loose from his past, to leave home, kin, and country, and to proceed to a foreign land? Was it psychologically realistic for the Sinai revelation to speak out against swearing falsely, stealing, and adultery, which practices are deep-seated tendencies of human nature? The whole religion of the Bible is a struggle against certain inclinations of man's nature? "For my thoughts are not your thoughts, neither are your ways my ways, saith the LORD. For as the heavens are higher than the earth, so are my ways higher than your ways, and my thoughts than your thoughts" (Isa. 55:8-9).

That the precept to love our enemies is not un-Jewish may be seen from the following passages in Jewish post-biblical writings:

"And if any one seeketh to do evil unto you, do well unto him, and pray for him, and ye shall be redeemed by the Lord from all evil."[2]

"He who returns evil for good, evil shall not depart from this house; even he who returns evil for evil, evil shall not depart from his house."[3]

"Our rabbis taught: Those who are insulted but do not insult, hear themselves reviled without answering, act through love and rejoice in suffering, of them Scripture saith, 'But they who love Him are as the sun when he goeth forth in his might.' "[4]

"R. Abbahu said: 'A man should always strive to be rather of the persecuted than of the persecutors, as there is none among the birds more persecuted than doves and pigeons, yet Scripture made them alone eligible for the altar.' "[5]

"O my God guard my tongue from evil and my lips from speaking guile; and to such as curse me let my soul be dumb, yea, let my soul be unto all as the dust."[6]

Life magazine, March 31, 1961, related in its editorial section the following incident: In 1958, a twenty-six-year-old Korean boy, a student at the University of Pennsylvania, left his uncle's home in West Philadelphia to mail a letter. A few minutes later he was brutally beaten to death by ten juvenile delinquents. People in Philadelphia were shaken. The mayor wept at the funeral.

Then came a letter from Pusan from the boy's parents, who are devout Christians. "We are sad," the parents wrote, "not only because of our son's unachieved future, but also because of the unsaved souls and paralyzed nature of the murderers. We are grateful to God for giving us a plan by which our sorrow may be turned into a Christian purpose. Our family has met together and decided to ask that the criminals be given the most generous treatment possible under the laws of your government." In addition to the letter, they sent $500 as a contribution to the work of juvenile crime prevention. That sum was five times the per capita yearly income of Koreans.

That "Epistle from the Koreans" is said to have profoundly stirred the conscience of the people of Philadelphia to a new concern for the inter-racial problem of their city. The Presbyterians raised $1.6 million dollars for social work. The city established a scholarship fund to bring other Korean students to the university. A film entitled *An Epistle from the Koreans* was produced, and in the first year alone it was shown in 5,000 churches. Thus "one pebble of Christian forgiveness is sending its ripples still."

I have known Christians whose love for Jesus knew no limit. I know many Christians who pray for Israel and for the peace of Jerusalem, and who praise God for the way He used the Jewish people to give them their Christian faith. I am grateful for articles such as that by Norman Cousins. I pray that the Judaeo-Christian dialogue may continue to be conducted in a spirit of good will.

Notes

1. Roland B. Gittelsohn, "Not so Simple, Mr. Cousins.' ", *American Judaism* 10, no. 4 (Passover 1961):7, 32-34.
2. Testaments of the Twelve Patriarchs, Joseph 18.2.
3. Genesis R. 38.3.
4. Shabbath 88*b*.
5. Baba Kamma 93*a*.
6. Morning prayer as found in the Daily Prayer Book.

Part Three

Statements by Jewish Christians

The New Testament
Is the Completion of the Old Testament

Do not think that I came to abolish the Law or the Prophets; I did not come to abolish, but to fulfill.

Matt. 5:17 (NASB)

And beginning with Moses and with all the prophets, He explained to them the things concerning Himself in all the scriptures.

Luke 24:27 (NASB)

Monotheism in the Light of the New Testament
    Nahum Levison   161
Law and Grace in Biblical Perspective
    Ludwig R. Dewitz   167
The New Covenant and the House of Judah—
    Heinz David Leuner   172
The Unity of the Bible—*David N. Freedman*   178

39 Monotheism in the Light of the New Testament

Nahum Levison was the youngest son of Rabbi Nahum Levison of Safad, Israel. His father was not a local rabbi, but a Sheliach Tsibor, that is, an emissary, for various purposes, of the Jews in Palestine to various Jewish communities elsewhere. Young Nahum received a Talmudic education first in Safad, and later in Jerusalem, but he was allowed to go for two hours each week to the German-Jewish school in Jerusalem to learn German, French, and modern Hebrew. A friend there gave him a New Testament, and as a result of reading it Nahum became a believer in the Messiahship of Jesus.

In 1912 Dr. Levison enrolled at McCormick Theological Seminary in Chicago where he received his Bachelor of Divinity degree. In 1922 he returned to Scotland where he held several pastorates. During that period he wrote scholarly works on biblical subjects.*

The greatest difficulty which confronts a Jew when he considers Christianity is the belief that Christianity teaches that there is more than one God. Of course Christianity teaches nothing of the kind when properly understood, but this the Jew does not realize till he has learned the full and clear teaching of the New Testament. I have seen it stated by Unitarian and even Christian scholars that the first three Gospels do not teach the deity of Jesus. If these scholars want to put their theory to the test let them give the New Testament, the first three Gospels or any of them, to a pious Jew who has never before read them, nor read any theories about them, and they will find that their interpretation of the facts is not correct. I was given before my conversion the Gospel of Matthew to read, and could make no advance with it, because it seemed to me to violate the principle of monotheism. I only came back to the Gospels after reading St. Paul's epistles. I found I could read these, especially Romans and Galatians (not that these were less Christian), because

*This article is an adaptation of Nahum Levison, "What Christ Did for Me and What He Means to Me," *The Hebrew Christian* 2, no. 3 (October 1929):102-105; Nahum Levison, "Monotheism and Christianity, *The Hebrew Christian* 3, no. 1 (April 1930):31-36. Used by permission of The International Hebrew Christian Alliance (London).

they were more Jewish, and their Jewish mentality attracted me, and I could pass over any passages which spoke of Jesus as God.

> Thou shalt not make unto thyself any image nor any likeness from the sky above, the earth beneath, nor the waters below the earth.
>
> [Exodus 20:4]

> I believe with a perfect faith, that God is not corporeal, nor is he in any way touched with material properties, nor has He any form or substance of any kind.
>
> [The Third Article of Faith by Maimonides]

These two expressions of faith or articles of belief haunt the unsophisticated Jew and reduce God to nothingness. The pious Jew lives in constant terror lest he should be guilty of transgression of the commandment by making an image of God in his thoughts; he must avoid thinking of either the essence or substance of God, and thus even the idea of God exists in an impenetrable cloud. In Old Testament times the prophets, seers, and teachers had to resort to anthropomorphisms, which had very unfortunate results. The people argued, if God can speak, can use His hands, feet, etc., He must be like man, and they would not and could not be dissuaded from making themselves images of Jehovah, and the inevitable result was idolatry of a very vicious type. The modern Jew who does not come into contact with Western philosophy lives in a world of attributes, which he does not dare to examine or reduce, and his theism, or monotheism, is a string of attributes lacking in reality. The Jewish philosopher Spinoza could not tolerate that state of unreality, and proceeded on the lines of some of the more courageous Rabbis, and like them, landed in crass pantheism. If God has no substance or form and yet exists, Spinoza and the Rabbis argued, He must exist in the creature, and in that form alone can He have existence or reality. I am sure that this school, of which Spinoza was the outstanding figure, deserves our sympathy, for no other means of believing in God was left for them, save that of atheism, and Jews by nature and breeding are not atheistical.

Christian readers will no doubt be surprised at the above statement, but they need only project themselves into the place of the Jew when he has to begin to extricate the *Memra* (the Word of God or Logos), the *Shekinah* (God's Presence), the *Malach Adonai* (the Angel of Jehovah), and many other presentations from the God idea itself, to realize the difficulty that the Jew is faced with. Modern Judaism has borrowed such terms as "personality" and "individuality" from Western philosophy, and now uses these vague terms to express their conception of God. The orthodox Jew, however, does not know these new attributes, and they convey nothing to him.

We must examine this doctrine of monotheism in the light of the Old Testament. There is a passage which is of great significance in the consideration of our subject, and it reads as follows:

> Hear, O Israel, Jehovah [is] our God, Jehovah [is] one [or sole].
>
> [Deuteronomy 6:4-5]

This passage is known as the "Shema." Every Jew, no matter how ignorant he may be of the rest of the Law and Prophets, knows the "Shema," that is, the verse quoted from Deuteronomy. The pious Jew repeats it thrice daily, and with these words every Jew commits his soul to God. The words of the "Shema" are ingrained in the conscience of the Jew as no other words in any other religion.

In the Exodus passage cited previously the word "Elohim" (i.e., gods) is used in the Hebrew text, and in the Deuteronomy passage, Jehovah, and Eloheynu (our God) are the two words used. The word Elohim (gods) is the plural, and is used in the Old Testament to designate the God in whom the Jews believed. Now, the fact that the word Elohim is a plural is quite evident to any one who has even a very slight knowledge of Hebrew, and many pages have been filled to explain this apparent difficulty. While one must be very careful not to jump to conclusions in matters of such importance, but must follow by careful study, and step by step, the development of the idea underlying the words, it is safe to say that Elohim means Godhead in a generic sense, just as the word "man" includes many men and women in a generic sense, i.e., mankind, and it further follows that the old Testament writers use it consciously in that sense.

The following passage will illustrate this claim.

> And Elohim said, Let us make man in our image, after our likeness.
>
> [Genesis 1:26]

The verb, "let us make," and the nouns, "our image," and "our likeness," occur in the plural in the Hebrew text. If literally translated into English the sentence should read "And Elohim said, Let us make man in our images and our likenesses." Now, it is extraordinary that up to this point in the Genesis account of creation Elohim alone is the Creator, but in the story of the creation of man a double plural appears. The answer given is that God was speaking to the angels, and other commentators say it is Wisdom to whom God is speaking, and still others that it was the *Memra*, that is to say the personified Word of God (the Logos of the New Testament). All these explanations may pass muster for theories, but cannot be accepted as fact. The entire use of the word argues against such explanations, unless the angels are associated with God in the creation of man, or that the *Memra* and *Wisdom* have an individuality of a personal nature. If the latter is accepted, we have no further problem with monotheism; it is plain that there were other individualities apart from God in the act of creation, and from the beginning. The author of the Proverbs does not hesitate to express the idea that God had the aid of *Wisdom* in the creation of the world, and there can be no doubt about the writer of Proverbs's presentation of *Wisdom* as a personal individuality (Proverbs 3:19).

Apart from the foregoing we have the *Spirit of Jehovah* given a distinct personal individuality.

> There fell [rested] upon me the Spirit of Jehovah, and he said unto me, "Speak, 'Thus says Jehovah:' "
>
> [Ezekiel 11:5]

Could there be anything plainer in definition of two individualities? Were that the only passage, no weight could be laid upon it, but the Ru-ach (i.e., the Spirit) plays a great part in the prophetic office and claim. We are told in Scripture that man cannot see Jehovah and remain alive. Even the ingenuity of Jewish commentators cannot reconcile such two statements as the following. To Moses' request that God show him His glory, God said:

> "You cannot see my face; no human being can see me and remain alive."
>
> [Exodus 33:20]

> In the year that King Uzziah died I saw the Lord sitting upon a throne, high and exalted, and his train filled the temple.
>
> [Isaiah 6:1]

Can Jewish theophanism satisfy either monotheism or the human yearning for communion with God?

Monotheism is a reality only so long as it remains undefined; when we try to define it, it resolves itself either into pantheism or atheism. Christians who have inherited a rich conception of God through the teachings of Jesus, and the New Testament in general, cannot very well realize how very difficult the Jewish position is without these enlightening sources. Even the idea of God as Spirit might add much to the Jewish conception, but then the Jews do not have the Gospel of John.[1] The Jew reiterates the formula, "Hear, O Israel, Jehovah our God, Jehovah is one," much in the same way as the Muhammadan repeats his favorite saying, "There is no God but God!" but neither dares investigate or define his formula. Both Jew and Moslem live in dread of arriving at a false conception of God. His nature and being therefore ever remain a shadowy and ethereal concept.

On turning to the New Testament the shadow is changed into substance, and the vague ideas of Judaism are clarified in a creed about which there can be no mistake. It is true that at first sight this creed disquiets the Jewish mind. For a considerable time after I became a follower of Jesus I could not bring myself to speak or sing of Jesus in terms which refer to His deity. I used to substitute the name God in the hymns for the name Jesus. The orthodox Jew honestly believes that a Jew cannot become a Christian because he knows how very difficult it is to think of Jesus as God, but then he never gets beyond the first stage of the new experience. I found that as time went on and I learned to know Jesus, all that both heart and mind desired to know of God was manifested in Him. All attributes became realities, all vagueness about the essence and being of God were swept away. I realized the Fatherhood of God in the Sonship of Jesus. Let it not be forgotten that the idea of the Fatherhood of God was deeply imbedded in the conscience of the Jew prior to the advent of Jesus. In the pre-Christian prayer known as the "Ahavah" (Love), God is addressed twice in the most tender and reverent way as Father. In the Old Testament the love of God is emphasized with all prophetic power, but here again—with certain few exceptio .—these things are attributes and not realities. God's love and Fatherhood, like human love and fatherhood, cannot be understood in abstracts. In the Sonship of Jesus, God's Fatherhood becomes a reality, at

164

Calvary God's love becomes manifest. I might go on to speak of all the other things which the heart and mind require of knowledge of God, that they might be able to render that service and love which are due to the object of worship and adoration, but to go on would serve no useful purpose. God has become a reality to me only since I have seen and known Him through Jesus. Jesus reveals the only God I can know and love, and in turn know that I am loved by. If the Godhead is not manifested in Jesus then it is incapable of manifestation; if Jesus is not God then God, whatever He is, ought to be like Jesus, for only as He is like Jesus can I serve and love Him, know Him, and be known of Him.

Christians do not realize how much they owe to Paul's self-manifestation and self-expression in his Epistles, and especially in his Epistle to the Romans. The heart-breaking struggle of the Jew towards the attainment of righteousness and justification can hardly be set forth, yet Paul does give a very clear insight into them. The demands of the Law and the Rabbis, upon those who set in quest of these are numerous and difficult. From earliest childhood we are told that we consist of a dual personality. Within us are the good persuader, or the good nature (Yetser Hara) and the evil persuader, or evil nature (Yetser Hatov). These two selves fight the battle of existence among themselves, and the real ego is left to the tender mercies of this dualism. This ego can do but little in the struggle, and thus the result is often stark fatalism. The only result of a scrupulous life is to find out how impossible it is to attain to the ideal. The law and the precepts of the Rabbis only increase the tendency to fatalism, for the more one tries to realize them, the more conscious he becomes of the impossibility of doing so. Life is peopled with angels and demons, who are invoked for good or evil. All this leads in one direction, viz., despair. There is no possibility of fulfilling the Law and the teaching of the sages, and there is no escape from their demands. With these conceptions of life, the coming of Jesus into it cannot be fully estimated nor indeed expressed. Through Jesus the Messiah it is realized that the struggle is not a hopeless one, that God is very near, and that He is actively interested in life. He is always by one's side, ready to aid in the conflict and to make life victorious. Life ceases to be evil in itself, and escape from it is no longer desired, for it is realized that with the Messiah there is nothing common or unclean about life save what we ourselves make common and unclean. It must be admitted at first the teaching of Jesus frightens. The shifting of the struggle from the material to the spiritual makes it appear even more difficult. Love thy enemy. Do not allow the mind to covet or possess that which is not thine—this is much harder than, Thou shalt not steal or commit adultery. But when one turns from the teaching to the Teacher, to that pure, sinless and blameless life, one realizes that these are the things that make life's warfare a joy and life itself worthwhile. The coming of Jesus into the life of the Jew means that the Law and precepts, which only say to you, "You cannot realize us, we are too high and lofty for human attainment," are swept away, and a higher and nobler conception and ideal come in their place with the blessed assurance that through Jesus the Messiah we can attain, we can realize them, and we can be victorious. The life of defeat with which the Law confronts you is exchanged for a life of victory through Jesus the Messiah, the Lord of life.[1]

Notes

1. Among the passages in the gospel of John that the writer of this essay probably had in mind are the following: "And I will pray the Father, and he will give you another Counselor, to be with you for ever, even the Spirit of truth, whom the world cannot receive, because it neither sees him nor knows him; you know him, for he dwells with you, and will be in you. But the Counselor, the Holy Spirit, whom the Father will send in my name, he will teach you all things, and bring to your remembrance all that I have said to you" (John 14:16-17, 26, RSV).—ED.

40 Law and Grace in Biblical Perspective

Ludwig R. Dewitz

From a biblical standpoint, the order of the words in the title of this article should not be "law and grace," but "grace and law," because in matters of primacy grace comes first. Furthermore, it should be pointed out before we go any further that the word *and* carries great weight. Popular theologizing may go to the extreme of creating an artificial anthithesis between the Old Testament as a book of law and the New Testament as a book of grace, and presenting the God of Israel as a kind of legalistic judge opposite the Father of Jesus Christ as a gracious redeemer. On the contrary, any cursory reading of the Bible as a whole will show that grace and law are two abiding factors essential to the dynamics of life as purposed by God.

Somehow or other, "grace" seems to come to us as a great, positive quality for life whereas "law" sounds restrictive and negative. Yet, the writer of Deuteronomy and worshipers reciting Psalm 1 or 119 would go contrary to that opinion, saying: "His delight is in the law of the Lord" (Psalm 1:2) "Oh, how I love thy law!" (Psalm 119:97, RSV). The whole book of Deuteronomy is a burst of joyful exclamation in praise of God's law, which is not seen as something difficult at all, but as something to be enjoyed while it is done; "But the word is very near you, in your mouth and in your heart, that you may observe it" (Deut. 30:14, NASB).

Even Paul, from whom unconsciously, and often uncritically, we derive our antithesis of law contra grace, is quite in line with the Old Testament writers when he affirms: "So then, the Law is holy, and the commandment is holy and righteous and good" (Rom. 7:12, NASB). Problems arise in the realms of law and grace when we fail to keep them in proper balance and try to utilize those factors in improper ways.

Let us now have a closer look at the relationship of grace and law in the Old Testament. Without going into details as to various expressions used for statements of law, such as precepts, judgments, and statutes, we might subsume them all under the general term *Torah*. We know that the rabbis found 613 commandments in the Old Testament and yet, when we look at the bulk of the books of which the Old Testament consists, we are struck by what little space, comparatively speaking, is really allotted to "the Law." Even if we take just the five books of Moses, which technically are known as the Torah, we notice that the actual legal statements are only part of a bigger story. As a matter of fact, the introductory book, Genesis, does not contain any legal material at all in the sense of what we call law.

One way to refer to the Bible is to speak of the books of the Old and the New Covenant. That is a good designation, for it goes to the heart of biblical concern. From beginning to end, the Scriptures are concerned with the relationship of God to man. We are not presented with a compendium of religious truth consisting of abiding eternal ideas and concepts regarding God's essential nature and attitude to man and vice versa, but we are confronted with a series of historical events in which God's unique nature and will is revealed. Those decisive episodes involved the people of Israel in a special way, but always so that they became a means to God's ultimate ends.

Let us take a quick bird's eye view of the biblical panorama. Creation is introduced as God's first work in a series of happenings. The first eleven chapters of the book of Genesis are concerned with mankind's exhibiting the theme of sin and salvation, with God's final word always being a word that lets life go on. God's answer to the universal folly of man's building the Tower of Babel is the call of Abram into which is built a promise of universal blessings: "In [you] shall all families of the earth be blessed" (Gen. 12:3). The patriarchs function as bearers of God's promise to become a nation, which takes place in Egypt, and to inherit a land, which is climaxed by David's establishing the united Kingdom of Judah and Israel. God's purpose for Israel goes on, however, in a series of events exhibiting judgment and salvation in the destruction of the Temple, the Exile, the restoration, the rebuilding of the Temple, and the formation of Israel as a community under the Word of Yahweh and Ezra. His purpose finds its climax in the appearance of Jesus of Nazareth among the Jews. With that Messianic event, Israel becomes the means of bearing the good news of salvation to the world at large. The God of Israel is now revealed to be the Savior of the world, and in His church a people is gathered from Jews and Gentiles to be His witnesses until this age will be consummated in a new heaven and a new earth.

Throughout that history grace and law were at work. A few incidents will illustrate that truth. The work of creation is seen as an act of free will on God's part by which He fashioned the universe out of chaos and nothingness. Man, created in God's image, was given a specially privileged position in that world as God's representative. He was meant to cooperate with God, and as a sign of the fact that God was creator and man His creation, man was endowed with a commandment that involved moral decision. The injunction not to eat from one tree, while there were a multitude from which he might have eaten, was given for the good of man, that is, for the protection of his life lest he die (Gen. 2:17). So, let us mark well, the law here was a good law, meant for man's life. It was the transgression of it, the breaking of it, that spelled man's doom. The law was clearly an expression of God's grace, which man, however, spurned, because he thought mistakenly that he could live independently, apart from God's grace and law.

We have said already that, in spite of what man does, life goes on by the grace of God. A case in point is the story of the Flood: "But Noah found grace in the eyes of the LORD" (Gen. 6:8). It was after the Flood, when life was spreading again over the earth, that the decisive word "covenant" appeared, for God expressed His relationship to man by a gracious word of promise that no flood should ever destroy man's life on earth again (Gen. 9:11). It is interesting to note that in that context a warning was given that sounds like a law: "Whoever sheds the blood of man, by man shall his blood be shed; for God made man in his own image" (Gen. 9:6, RSV). Obviously, that law was meant to protect man's life; it was a gracious provision for man to exercise the freedom of his life.

The next time we come across the establishment of God's special relationship to man is in the case of Abram. Chapters 15 and 17 of Genesis both tell of a covenant of promise and fulfillment and that circumcision was to be a sign of that covenant between God and His chosen people. Indeed, disregard of circumcision was to be tantamount to breaking the covenant. Election certainly was by grace, but those who were elected would show that fact by the ritual of circumcision. The observance of the law, if we wish to call it that, was simply here the acknowledgment of grace. It would be fatal to see it in any other way. Circumcision as such could never guarantee election, and Paul argues that point cogently in Romans 2:25-29.

Of course, when we are thinking of the giving of the law, the events connected with Israel's Sinai experience come to mind. Two things must be remembered; the first of which is that Sinai was a sequel to the Exodus experience. In other words, the fact of redemption did not depend on the giving of the law on Sinai; yet, the Exodus event necessarily led to Sinai. Religious freedom does not exist in a vacuum, but is spelled out in rules of life. One could also put it this way: the gift of life is an unmerited gift, but growth is vouchsafed by the gracious provision of regulations.

Second, when we come to what is generally believed to be the core of the Sinai legislation, namely the Ten Commandments (they are never referred to in the Old Testament as the Ten Commandments, but rather as the "ten words"), the form in which they are presented is that of a covenant, in which the stipulations spelled out are based on the gracious act of God's redemption, introduced thus: "I am the LORD, your God, who brought you out of the land of Egypt, out of the house of bondage" (Exod. 20:2, RSV). So we see clearly that grace and law form an inseparable unit. The same truth is expressed in Deuteronomy 27:9-10, which reads as follows: "This day you have become the people of the LORD your God. You shall therefore obey the voice of the LORD your God, keeping his commandments and his statutes, which I command you this day" (RSV).

Anyone who reads attentively all the books of the Old Testament must realize that the burden throughout, and especially in the prophetical oracles, is that the separation of grace and law lies at the bottom of Israel's tragic experience of God's judgment. The easy cry "This is the temple of the LORD, the temple of the LORD, the temple of the LORD " (Jer. 7:4, RSV) shows a hollow "believism" in cheap grace. Just believe that Israel is God's chosen people, and all will be well. To that Jeremiah rightly replied: "Behold, you trust in deceptive words to no avail. Will you steal, murder, commit adultery, swear falsely, burn incense to Baal, and go after other gods that you have not known, and then come and stand before me in this house, which is called by my name, and say, 'We are delivered!'—only to go on doing all these abominations?" (Jer. 7:8-10, RSV). Here we have the kind of religion that will acknowledge God as the giver of all good gifts, but will do nothing in response to grace received. It is all a matter of creed, but with no deed.

A different situation is depicted in the first chapter of Isaiah, as well as in the books of Amos and Hosea. Here we have a kind of legalistic observance, at least, of the ceremonial laws: "What to me is the multitude of your sacrifices? says the LORD; I have had enough of burnt offerings of rams and the fat of fed beasts; I do not delight in the blood of bulls, or of lambs, or of he-goats" (Isa. 1:11, RSV). In that case we have an outward performance of certain laws as if religious observance could be a substitute for genuine faith, not to mention the one-sided observance of the law that pays no regard to the ethical demands of God relating to the social organism of Israel.

Torah, which is often translated as "law," has, of course, a far greater compass than the sum of certain rules or regulations. The verbal root from which the noun is formed means "to shoot," that is, to mark the direction pointed out by an arrow. Torah thus combines elements of revelation and teaching of which legislation forms only a part. Torah means the total directive will of God as exhibited in creation, history, redemption, and the uttered word of judgment and salvation. It includes grace and law.

Just as Paul would recognize that the vitiating factor in the relationship between God and man is sin, a fact the law made clear, Jeremiah realized that the existing provisions of the old covenant were insufficient to maintain the proper relationship between God and His people. He envisioned the future when the Lord would make a new covenant with the house of Israel and the house of Judah (Jer. 31:31). A new act of grace would establish that new covenant, the content of which he described in this manner: "I will put My law within them, and on their heart I will write it; and I will be their God, and they shall be My people" (Jer. 31:33, NASB). Let it be noted again that the combination grace and law still obtains, the difference lying in the fact of a new dimension in which that grace is revealed and through which the law becomes operative.

It is, of course, in the new covenant, centered in the person and work of Jesus Christ, that grace and law find their fruitful relationship. It is in the light of the foregoing that we must read John's words: "For the law was given through Moses; grace and truth came through Jesus Christ" (John 1:17, RSV). That does not mean the law is of no value now that Jesus Christ has come, but that only through Him can it be properly evaluated, as Paul puts it so well in Rom. 10:4: "For Christ is the end of the law, that every one who has faith may be justified" (RSV). "End" is here to be understood not in the sense of ceasing to be but in the sense of achieving the goal, attaining the purpose, very much in the sense of Christ's own words, recorded in Matthew 5:17: "Think not that I have come to abolish the law and the prophets; I have come not to abolish them but to fulfill them" (RSV).

Just as the old covenant was based on grace and law, so is the new covenant, although with this great difference: the new covenant lays a basis for forgiveness and renewal of life, which the old covenant with its historical restrictions could not do. The personal bond that establishes Jesus of Nazareth as God's Anointed in His work as prophet, priest, and king, thereby reconciling the world unto God, lays the new ground on which grace and law will bear living fruit. That "new," which here carries the idea of renewal, comes out well in the first letter of John when, dealing with the demands of love, the author writes: "Beloved, I am not writing a new commandment to you, but an old commandment which you have had from the beginning; the old commandment is the word which you have heard. On the other hand, I am writing a new commandment to you, which is true in Him and in you" (1 John 2:7-8, NASB).

The Sermon on the Mount in Matthew, John's stress on the relationship of loving Christ and keeping his commandments (John 14:15-21), and the moral injunctions in the final chapters of most of Paul's letters all indicate clearly that life under the new covenant is also a matter of grace and law. The gift of salvation is indeed apart from the law, but the living out of that new life is related to the law of love: YOU SHALL LOVE THE LORD YOUR GOD WITH ALL YOUR HEART, AND WITH ALL YOUR SOUL, AND WITH ALL YOUR MIND. This is the great and foremost commandment. And a second is like it, "YOU SHALL LOVE YOUR NEIGHBOR AS YOURSELF" (Matt. 22:37-38, NASB).

In Christ, the two dimensions of service (to God and to man) become accentuated on the basis of His incarnation, crucifixion, and resurrection. The New Covenant does not prescribe precise commandments in a legalistic sense, but does demand service involving sacrifice. It is clear from the way in which the prophets spoke and in the way in which Christ observed the law that the law was not meant to become a burden in a legalistic sense, but that it was to be a way of life for God's children. The law was intended to bring out all that is best in man for giving value to life. Law is always to be seen within the compass of grace, never to be isolated from it as an independent factor, just as grace must be seen as the enabling power to execute the will of God within the compass of the commandment of love.

41 The New Covenant and the House of Judah

Heinz David Leuner was born in Breslau; his parents were conservative Jews. He obtained his secular education in a classical high school (equivalent to high school and two years of college in the United States). His religious training he received in Jewish afternoon schools ("heder"). In 1932 he entered the field of journalism. In 1933, haunted by the Nazis, he left Germany and settled in Prague. There he became absorbed in Bible studies that resulted in his acceptance of the Messiahship of Jesus.

When the Germans occupied Prague, the Leuners emigrated to England where Mr. Leuner studied at the University of Glasgow and at Trinity College. He became ordained in the Church of Scotland.

In 1950 Mr. Leuner was appointed Secretary for Europe by the International Hebrew Christian Alliance, a world Fellowship of Hebrew Christians with headquarters in London. He is the author of When Compassion Was a Crime *(London, 1966).**

When the Hebrew people established under Saul a state of their own, the name Israel as a soteriological term was in danger of becoming secularized. The secularization became real with the division into the kingdoms of Israel and Judah in 930 B.C. It is well to remember that Amos took the task of "prophesying against Israel" so literally that he left his home in Judah and directed his ministry almost entirely to the inhabitants of the northern kingdom (Amos 7:15). There was a time when the name "Israel" was in jeopardy of being lost through the disappearance of the unified state. It was the prophet Isaiah who not merely regained the divinely ordained significance of Israel but made it clear beyond doubt that "Israel as a soteriological term comprised the two kingdoms, and applied to both of them. At a time when the northern kingdom still existed he deliberately spoke of "both the houses of Israel" (8:14). Ezekiel, delivering his message in captivity prior to the fall of Jerusalem, goes even farther by speaking of "the house of Israel and Judah,"

*"The New Covenant and the House of Judah" is reprinted from *The Hebrew Christian* 39, no. 1 (Spring 1966):10-15, and is used by permission of *The International Hebrew Christian Alliance* (London).

using the singular *beth Yisrael vi-Yehudah* (9:9). Later on, in that most graphic chapter on the resuscitation of the dry bones, he employs the picture of the two sticks to drive home the truth that there can only be one whole, consisting of Ephraim and Judah, when the chosen people ultimately return to their homeland (37:15-28). And, accepting the early date of Zechariah (chapters 1-8), we find the prophet envisaging the union of the houses of Israel and Judah at a time when only a proportion of Judah had returned (8:8). A distinction between the two houses seems, therefore, untenable whenever the covenant relationship between God and His people is under discussion.

In saying that, we do not deny the historical fact that there always was bitter rivalry and at times violent hatred between Israel and Judah such as is frequently found between close relatives. The Old Testament echoes this hostility again and again. Only Judah could talk of Israel in the venomous manner shown, e.g., in Psalm 78:67 or Amos 9:7. Jeremiah is perhaps the only prophet equally fair to, and critical of, both houses; the other prophets have usually, though not invariably, a more severe condemnation for those tribes to which they do not belong. In comparison with the northern kingdom, a definite distinctiveness attaches to Judah, and at least some marks deserve to be mentioned.

There can be little doubt that from the days of David and Solomon Judah was the predominant tribe, and retained on the whole a purer religious faith than did the north, though for that very reason her apostasy came in for even stronger judgment in the prophetical utterances. It was Judah that kept up the Davidic line of succession, and this Davidic dynasty of Judah seems repeatedly legitimated and justified in the sayings of the prophets without thereby being magically protected against failure. Her name was frequently linked with Jerusalem and all the spiritual and covenanting connotations embodied in the place where the temple stood. Judah produced the three greatest of all prophets and seems to be conditioned of God for the task of producing the very climate and atmosphere required for the first indication of the new covenant and the ultimate appearance of Him in whom the new covenant will be vested, revealed and take shape, Jesus of Nazareth, the Lion of the tribe of Judah.

While Israel apparently disintegrated in Assyria, Judah gained the chance of returning from Babylon, for her people had clung to Yahweh and observed the law. In fact, we may take it that her faith had deepened and become cleansed during the banishment. The exiles held on to their ethnical, linguistic and religious peculiarities; they had tended affectionately whatever they possessed in the way of literature, not least the poetry so reminiscent of their link with the Davidic kingdom. It was Judah in Babylon that began to take seriously the teaching of the prophets, their call to righteousness as much as their denouncement of the failure both of individuals and whole nations. It was in their Babylonian exile that they discovered a new way of serving, and communicating with, Yahweh by means of prayer, for sacrifices could no longer be offered, as there was no temple. But let it be repeated that, speaking theologically, Judah was part and parcel of Israel's covenant relation to Yahweh. Hence the post-exilic writers insist on speaking of "all Israel," "the children of Israel" and similar names, although they never attempt to conceal the fact that only the people of Judah had availed themselves of the opportunity to return. But, whereas the post-exilic historians consider the renewal of the cultic heritage as a sign of Yahweh's continued guidance, it becomes obvious from the study of the prophetical writings, especially Isaiah, Jeremiah and Ezekiel, that the prophets realized a complete breach in the divine history and proclaimed a new beginning. A marriage relationship has existed between Yahweh and His people, thus the people's apostasy was equal to whoredom which could not be erased. Yahweh would have to provide a new exodus, a new covenant and a new Moses, its analogy being founded on God's unchanging faithfulness. If he had done great things in the past he could and would do even greater things in the future.

When the prophets use the term covenant they refer to Sinai. There is little mention of it to be found in the older prophets. The idea the covenant expresses is certainly present, but the explicit word rarely occurs. With Jeremiah the term covenant becomes very prominent, serving as a distinctive expression of Yahweh's relationship to Israel, the reason being that doom was approaching fast and revealed the purpose and provisions as much as the failure of the Sinaitic covenant. Thus it is Jeremiah to whom we must turn for further elucidation of the term.

According to Jeremiah, Yahweh demands purity within, a circumcision of ear and heart, the removal of the carnal disposition which prevents God's voice from being heard and His will from being accepted (4:4; 4:14; 6:10). He goes as far as to say that the outward forms of the cult had not been ordained by God. "Jeremiah enunciates the principle that all outward helps to religion have purely a symbolic, not an objective, value."[1] Other prophets may have prepared the way, but Jeremiah openly declares the emancipation of religion from the state and the cult. While Isaiah (in chapters 55 and 56) still sees the remedy in the law, in the keeping of the commandments, Jeremiah looks forward to a new regime based entirely on Yahweh's love, which is to take the place of the old relation (31:31ff.). For him *ahavah* and *chesed,* love and covenant grace, coalesce as do the conceptions of election and covenant. He may not have risen to the insight that Yahweh is the universal ruler of all nations, but he knows that no man can escape from Him (23:23f.) and that He is just in all His dealings with the nations. Israel has broken the marriage vows made to Yahweh and forfeited its rights. Nevertheless, "God does not abolish physical Israel, but in saving it transcends it, just as He does not scrap this earth but renews it."[2] The prophet realizes that written law can never accomplish all that man needed, nor is this the only point to bring him very close to the Messiah, for he prays for his enemies, who are his own people, from whom he cannot and will not dissociate himself. Most important, he draws, 500 years before Jesus, a picture of God going out into the wilderness to bring His people rest (31:1-3), portraying the Father's initiative as we have come to know it from Jesus in the stories of Luke 15. T. H. Robinson is right when he calls Jeremiah "the father of all the saints."[3]

Before coming to the prophet's central message about the new covenant as contained in chapter 31, we must once more emphasize that though Jeremiah is essentially a prophet out of Judah his concern is with both houses, for the simple reason that the oneness of Yahweh demands the oneness of His people. Chapter 31 may well be called the connecting piece between the Old and New Testaments, for it is here that the new covenant is first mentioned and God's gracious promise of continuation and fulfillment is brought out. Here we read for the first time about the great change in human hearts and learn that to hear God's voice and to obey the covenant really are two sides of the same coin. Here begins the gospel of Messiah Jesus, here is the first reference to the good news, but also the clear statement that God has not cast away His people; for the whole universe is pledged as a token of God's faithfulness to Israel (vv. 35-37). When the prophet uses his favourite expression "the seed of Israel" both houses are meant. They have rebelled against God, have betrayed Him, but He is and remains the faithful Lord whose gifts are without repentance. Nobody else but *He Himself* will make a new covenant with Israel and Judah, not with a new or a spiritual Israel but with His chosen people. No longer will He be their *baal,* their taskmaster. It is interesting to note in this connection that the zealot Eleazar speaks of God as *despotes* in the "wars" of Josephus (7:6). Covenant grace will be victorious for God must be triumphant; He is constant and trustworthy, He cannot deny Himself in spite of the people's whoredom. But "the earlier kindergarten methods will no longer be necessary, for the nation and the individual are to become the disciples of the divine Teacher, and truth is to be imparted directly to all who seek it."[4]

We may not find in the new covenant any alteration in the terms, but we do find a profound change in the methods of its establishment, for it is to be written on the heart, not on tables of stone; nor is it to be made valid and ratified by the blood of animals, but by the virtue of the perfect sacrifice's blood. This blood makes all who have, as it were, a share in it covenanting allies. The very term used by Christ, as recorded in 1 Corinthians 11:25 and properly translated in the New English Bible with "sealed by My blood" combines the ideas of Exodus 24:8 (the blood of the covenant) and Jeremiah 31:31,34 (the new covenant of forgiveness). Through the shedding of Christ's blood the new covenant has become valid for both Jews and Gentiles,for it is poured out for many for the remission of sin.

What is new about the new covenant? Like the old covenant, it is a covenant of grace, with love coming from one side only, though there is a broad hint at the mutuality of the new knowledge and at the subjective appropriation. Through a divine act and a spiritual event the new mutuality will be established. More clearly than before, the new covenant will have the character of a deliberate injunction, a promise, rather than a legalistic agreement, or contract, or partnership. Man is neither willing nor capable to rise to any genuine compliance with the divine will, for the Ethiopian cannot change his skin, nor the leopard his spots (Jeremiah 13:23). It is the innate rejection of God's love rather than any foul deed that Jeremiah castigates, though he will not condone any unjust action either. Sin is to the prophet contempt of covenant grace. Israel and Judah have broken the covenant, made it non-existent by "not knowing God," and for that very reason the new covenant's main point will be "they shall know Me." Knowing is in both parts of the Bible by no means an intellectual process, though it includes a cognitive element, nor is it an ethical achievement or a religious possession. Knowing means having intimate experience of the other, be it friend or wife; it expresses the full realization of being loved, and hence having saving communion with God. In 31:35ff. the prophet states the everlasting character of the covenant by citing as its proof the permanency of God's cosmic order. But little as man can do about this cosmic order, as little can he do about the eternal validity of the covenant; it is all God's work, God's grace. The miracle about to happen is that Israel and Judah are to be in very truth obedient children and servants, and it is God's initiative alone that will enable them to become His partners in the new covenant. Their apostasy, guilt and dishonesty are so gigantic that nothing but a divine act can transform them into what they were meant to be from the beginning. "To write the law upon their hearts" is a phrase pregnant with the most devastating judgment, for it embodies the thought that a forsaken and betrayed Lord will, after centuries of fruitless labour, commence anew. Another of Jeremiah's favourite word pictures comes to mind: "rising up early" to instruct those rebellious children.

The God whom the prophet has come to "know" cannot be served by ritual or the magic of any sacrificial cult, but only "in spirit and in truth," though the term does not occur *expressis verbis*. His covenant has in mind a state of complete mutual possession and reciprocal intimacy that surpasses all ideas of protection, security and welfare promised by one partner and in return perhaps the rendering of service by the other. If God desires to "have" His people as a possession (we think of *segula* in Exodus 19:5), He does so for the sake of their salvation, their wholeness, which is to reflect on earth what He is, viz. purity and holiness. Here is the link to the later conception of the *malkuth Yahweh,* the kingdom of God (and cognate terms), whose realization is synonymous with the aim of the covenant in that it expresses God's final triumph in, with and through His dedicated people.

It is one thing to speak of the covenant as new, but it is quite another matter to call it better, as seems to be the case in that passage in Hebrews 8:6. The present writer feels that we ought to refrain from the expression "better" and have "more power-ful" or "more glorious" or "stronger" instead. The Greek adjective employed (*kreitton*) is not the comparative of "good" (*agathos*), but of "great," "strong," "powerful" (*megas*). The use of "better" can easily be understood to mean that God had to admit a mistake or faulty arrangement, an idea in sharp contrast to the conviction held throughout the Bible that everything God does is good. Nor should we treat as of no account what Calvin has to say in his commentary on Jeremiah 31:31ff.

"The new covenant is called new not because it is different from the first, for God does not contradict Himself, nor is He ever dissimilar to Himself. He who once made the covenant with the chosen people has not changed His plan as though He had forgotten His former promise. The first covenant was inviolable. Prior to it God had made His covenant with Abraham and the law was merely the confirmation of this covenant, the law was resting on the covenant God had made with Abraham His servant. That is why God could never make a new covenant in the sense of a different, dissimilar one. Why are we called sons of Abraham? Surely because of the common bond of faith. Why are we told that the faithful will be gathered in Abraham's bosom? Why does Christ say that many shall come from the east and west and shall sit down with Abraham, Isaac and Jacob in the kingdom of heaven?

All that is clear proof that God never made a different covenant than He did with Abraham. It is an everlasting covenant God had made from the beginning. . . . The meaning of 'new' does not refer to the substance but to the form. God does not say, 'I will give a different law,' but, 'I will put My law in their inward parts, and write it on their hearts.' "[5]

That is it. The predominant significance of the new covenant was and still is its inwardness, its being inscribed upon the heart. Thus St. Paul can speak of having inscribed the letter of Christ on the tablets of the human heart (2 Corinthians 3:3), which brings us to the New Testament references to Jeremiah 31, quite apart from the quotation in Hebrews 10:16f. C. H. Dodd sees verse 33 ("I . . . will be their God, and they shall be My People") reflected in the latter part of Romans 9:5 (theirs is the God who is over all, blessed for ever). That may or may not be the case, but St. Paul's statement in the previous verse, "theirs are the covenants," does not admit of any other interpretation but the apostle's insistence that both the old and new covenants were given to and made with Israel, and only via Israel's Messiah applicable to those who by faith in the Messiah had been grafted in among Israel. It is not without interest that some of the most important papyri as well as the Codices Vaticanus, Bezae and others have the singular "covenant," which would merely underline St. Paul's conviction and lend support to Calvin's view of the unity of both covenants. Nor can there be any reasonable doubt that the apostle's mention of the covenant in Romans 11:27 refers to the salvation of the Jews, not of the Church. In Hebrews 8:8-12, where Jeremiah 31:31ff. are quoted, the language used is not interpretable of fulfillment but only of description, as H. L. Ellison has shown in his *Ezekiel* (p. 129); "there is no suggestion that the promise has been exhausted on the Church's enjoyment of it."[6]

The new covenant, first heralded by the prophets of Judah but taking in both houses of the chosen people, entered upon the stage of its fulfillment on the night when Jesus of Nazareth was betrayed. Its completion is tied up with the eschatological conception of the end when men will make the entire, unqualified response of faith because God has taken the initiative towards their full salvation in the new covenant.

Notes

1. H. L. Ellison, *Men Spake from God* (The Paternoster Press: London, 1952), p. 86.
2. Ibid., p. 92.
3. T. H. Robinson, *Prophecy and the Prophets,* p. 140.
4. Charles F. Kent, *The Student's Old Testament.*
5. John Calvin. See his commentary on Jeremiah 31:31ff.
6. H. L. Ellison, *Ezekiel* (The Paternoster Press: London, 1956), p. 129.

42 The Unity of the Bible

David N. Freedman

The unity of the Bible is one of the most important and most significant issues confronting the Christian Church today. It is more than the academic problem of simply setting the Old and New Testaments side by side and applying certain tests, literary, historical, or theological, to see whether or not they are made of the same stuff.

The unity of the Bible, together with the authority of the Bible, is one of the two cardinal axioms from which the main propositions of the Christian religion are drawn, and from which its chief proclamation goes forth. Without these axioms, there is no Christian faith, at least not in its full classical sense.

The Church did not write the Bible, nor does it confer authority upon it, but it does acknowledge the indissoluble unity of the Old and New Testaments. In this sense, the Church created the Bible, the Bible of Old and New Testaments.

Perhaps we should put it more realistically and historically: the Church has maintained that the events and the persons described in the New Testament belong organically and dynamically with the Old Testament record.

The Church has accepted the Old Testament as given—the legacy of Moses and the prophets, the common heritage of Jews and Christians. Then, beginning with the New Testament itself, the Church has tried to show that Jesus and the apostles are the successors of Moses and the prophets, and that the New Testament so fulfils the Old that the Church can rightly claim for the New Testament the same divine authority which it accords the Old.

Judaism has consistently denied this affirmation; and from the very first the position of the Church has been to present, explain, and defend its view of the unity of the Bible: its YES in opposition to the Synagogues's NO.

At the same time, early in its history the Church rejected the view of some of its own adherents who accepted the New Testament as authoritative but ignored the Old Testament and denied its authority. Marcion, for example, the arch-heretic of the second century, dispensed with the Old Testament entirely. He asserted that the God who was the father of our Lord Jesus Christ could not possibly be the vengeful tribal deity of the Old Testament.

"The Unity of the Bible" appeared in *Western Watch* 7, no. 4 (15 December 1956):7-14, and is reprinted by permission of the author.

A similar attitude, sometimes more politely expressed, has characterized Christian thinking about the Bible in different eras and places. What is involved is an attempt to repudiate the Old Testament and supplant it by the New.

The Church has never officially accepted this position because it could never officially accept it. The New Testament is built upon the Old, and presupposes and requires the Old. Moreover, the New Testament quotes or alludes to the Old on every page, so that to drop the Old Testament entirely would mean cutting out large sections of the New.

Hence the Christian is caught inescapably in the web of both Testaments and must defend their unity as a specifically Christian idea enshrined in the millions of Bibles that exist in the world.

What do we mean when we speak of the unity of the Bible? And how do we approach the subject?

There are three qualities or aspects to be discussed in defining the unity of the Bible. The first is continuity, dynamic continuity. There must be some organic relationship between what follows and what precedes. Only that literature which carries on the revelation of God in the Old Testament can claim unity with it. The New Testament not only makes this claim, but also provides much evidence to substantiate it.

Continuity alone, however, is not enough. There must be newness, an element of originality and change. Without this, the addition would be unnecessary. It would not be part of the divine Word unless it were different from the Word already spoken.

The Old Testament itself exhibits such a pattern of continuity and change. The initial actions of God and his revelation in history form the basis for later prophetic reflection and evaluation that become part of a new revelation that in turn affects the history of the holy community. Out of all of these events arises a new situation in which a further action of God takes place. Continuity and change thus unite the two testaments.

Third, there must be finality. Unity implies totality, wholeness. With the New Testament the story of the Old Testament ends. Thus biblical unity involves not only continuity and change but completion. The New Testament is the fulfilling factor making the Bible a unity and a totality. For the Church in spite of many serious efforts has never been able to add to or subtract from this Scripture.

These, then, are the factors in the case presented by the New Testament for organic unity with the Old.

Now let us describe the framework in which the unity of the Bible, which is the unity of the Old and New Testaments, appears.

The focal point around which both Testaments revolve is the God of the Bible, and a God uniquely different from all other gods, known only in a decisive way through his revelation recorded in the Bible. There is unity between the Testaments in this God because the God of the Old Testament is the God of the New.

The Old Testament attributes to God those same qualities of justice and mercy, love and kindness, devotion and forgiveness, that are attributed to God by the New Testament (cf. Exodus 34:6,7).

Moreover, the purpose of God to establish his Kingdom on earth is the common message of both Testaments, That God has created the world good, and placed men in it so that men might fulfil the potentialities of their lives and live in harmony on the face of the earth, and further, that God has dedicated himself with all his power and all his love to the realization of this objective—these are essential parts of the message of the whole Bible.

There are differences, nevertheless, between the Testaments. Perhaps the most significant is to be found in the statement that the God who revealed himself to the patriarchs, to Moses, to the prophets, has revealed himself in the person of Jesus Christ: that is, the Word which came to the prophets became Jesus Christ. The distinctive Christian view is expressed in the doctrine of the Incarnation, or of the Trinity.

Still, there are antecedents in the Old Testament for a trinitarian position, and also for a type of incarnation. The Father, Son, and Holy Spirit of New Testament teaching correspond to the Old Testament's God, his Word, and his Spirit, the essential difference being that in the New Testament the Word of God has been sent into the world to become a man. But even in the Old Testament the Word has personal qualities and serves as the creative, active agent of God (cf. Isaiah 55:10, 11). It is an important but not inconsistent step to the personality of the Word in the New.

The Christian conviction that God became man in Christ likewise has its background in the Old Testament stories of God's self-revelation to men. When God appears to Abraham, or wrestles with Jacob, or speaks with Moses, it is as man to men (cf. Gen. 18:16-33; 32:22-30; Ex. 33:7-11). He manifests himself as his Angel, in human form. God also is bound in personal union with his servants, Moses and the prophets. Through his Word and Spirit, he speaks and acts in their lives so that these men are, in a sense, extensions of his divine personality.

In the New Testament story of the life and death of Christ and identification of God with men and his involvement in human experience are shown to be completed. There is no agony of suffering or humiliation which God is spared, not even death upon the cross. For this amazing ordeal we find no adequate parallel in the Old Testament; there are only hints in the ritual of the scapegoat (Lev. 16), and the account of the Suffering Servant (Isaiah 53). In Old and New Testaments there is the difference between partial and temporary, and total and permanent identification of God with human kind.

Belonging also to the framework of Old and New Testaments is the idea of community, the community of faith. In the Old Testament the community is called Israel—the descendants of Abraham; in the New Testament it is called the Church, and also Israel—the children of Abraham. It is the same community in organic continuity. Paul describes that continuity in terms of the grafting of a wild branch, the Church, to the trunk of the old tree, Israel.

Usually, the distinction is made between Old Israel as an essentially racial or ethnic community limited to the territory of Palestine, and the Church as neither racial nor ethnic in character but extensive throughout the world. Israel, it is said, was a nation, a political commonwealth, while the Church is a spiritual kingdom.

No one would deny that there are differences between Israel and the Church. Organic unity involves change. But major items of continuity and identity ought not to be overlooked.

The fact is that from the first Israel is a community of faith not restricted to one racial group. It is an elect community whose members are chosen and invited by God, and who enter it when they respond in faith. Abraham, the great example of faith, was the founder of this community; and they are properly his children and members of the community who make the same commitment to God.

In the Exodus and Wilderness Wanderings the community of faith consisted of those who obeyed the summons of God. Around the nucleus of the children of Jacob and Abraham many other groups gathered: Kenites, Kenizzites, Egyptians, Nubians, and others. The Bible itself calls the desert wanderers a mixed multitude and a congeries of peoples. In the light of the heterogeneous origins of Israel, any notion that the holy community was ethnically or racially pure is absurd!

Throughout its history, this community of faith has been open to those of any nation who were willing to profess the faith of Abraham, commit themselves to the God of Israel and assume the burdens of covenant obligation. The stories of pagan converts like Ruth, Naaman, and others are sufficient to establish this truth for the Old Testament.

Inevitably the exigencies of national life prevented any large-scale extension of the holy community beyond the borders of Israel. But potentially, and in ultimate expectation, the community of God embraced all the peoples of the world. The only difference between the Old and New Testaments is that what was anticipated in the Old became actual in the New.

We may conclude the discussion of the framework of biblical unity with the Covenant, the bond between God and his community.

The titles of the two major divisions of the Bible ought to be rendered, "Old Covenant," and "New Covenant," instead of Old and New Testaments, for both describe an agreement between God and his people. "Covenant" is the common word expressing the element of continuity between them, while Old and New express the difference.

The difference is not as sharp as the words Old and New imply. The words arise out of the disastrous consequences of Israel's violation of its obligation to God whereby the covenant made at Sinai was abrogated: the restoration of harmonious relations between God and his people required the ratification of a new covenant. We might better speak, therefore, of "original" and "restored" covenant, or "first" and "renewed" covenant.

Nor must the distinction commonly made between the Old Covenant as a "covenant of works" and the New as a "covenant of grace" be pressed too far.

The Old Covenant of works is described as a conditional arrangement. If the people obeyed, then all would be well; the covenant would remain in force, and material rewards would be heaped upon an obedient people. If the people failed to keep the terms of the covenant, then swift judgment would come upon them.

The New Covenant of grace, on the other hand, is described as a commitment on God's part based solely on his loyalty and love. Such a covenant involves no obligations, threatens no punishment. It is a gift to be received, not a reward to be earned.

While there is an important element of truth in equating the Old Testament with the covenant of works and the New Testament with the covenant of grace, it has had an unfortunate effect. It has made God in the Old Testament look as though he were motivated solely by considerations of strict retributive justice, and dealt out reward and punishment according to the behavior of his people, whereas in the New Testament he scraps the principles of justice in the interests of a compassionate affection for all, indifferent to moral demands.

Neither of these views, however, does justice to the profound understanding of divine-human relationships in both Old and New Testaments. The essential elements in the covenants of works and grace are present in both parts of the Bible. Love and justice are inseparable terms in describing the bond between God and his people.

Investigations in the business documents and diplomatic treaties of the ancient Near East have produced a mass of information which sheds light upon the contemporary biblical contracts. Since society in the Ancient Near East was closely stratified for the most part, the typical relationship requiring legal definition or confirmation involved parties of unequal status, that is, suzerain and vassal.

The common form of covenant reflects this inequality of status in its characteristic features. Thus the contract must be initiated by the superior. Customarily the stipulations are binding only upon the inferior, since his performance can be compelled, or his non-compliance punished. What the suzerain does is out of good will, what he gives is of grace.

Any formal agreement to which God and man are parties will necessarily be of the suzerainty type, for man is the creature, child, and servant of God. It is God who specifies the terms of the agreement, who writes in the penalties for disobedience, and who is alone able to enforce his will. It is man who must bind himself by solemn oath to obey before the contract becomes effective; and it will be his failure that breaches the contract and exposes him to dire punishment.

The covenant between God and Israel was drawn up and ratified at Mount Sinai (cf. Exodus 19-24). Through the mediation of Moses, God offered to Israel the covenant that would establish Israel as the people of God, and Yahweh as the God of Israel.

In order to enjoy this special status Israel must, however, bind itself by oath to the exclusive worship and service of God. Beyond this each Israelite is obligated to live according to fundamental rules of justice and decency with his neighbor—the Ten Commandments. The community is obligated to enforce these rules, and to punish those who disregard them. Israel swears its allegiance to the covenant in a solemn ceremony. Disobedience is punishable by death.

Israel's subsequent history is governed by the terms of the covenant. The message of the prophets is the indictment of a disobedient people. And the fall of the nation, with the destruction of Jerusalem, is the penalty for their disobedience. The covenant has been broken; the divine power sustaining national life is removed; and the nation collapses. This is the story of the Sinai covenant.

But there is another covenant of equal importance, and in fact a greater duration.

It antedates the Sinai contract by several hundred years; it was not superseded by the Mosiac contract but operated with it side by side. When the Sinai covenant was abrogated, this one remained in force. It is still in force today. It is the foundation of the Christian faith.

This is the covenant between God and Abraham described in the 15th chapter of Genesis. In a strange and solemn ritual Abraham prepares the scene for contract negotiations. According to established procedure three animals are divided in the middle. In the ratification of the contract between superior and inferior it was obligatory for inferior to stand between the severed animals. There he would take an oath of obedience, calling upon God to do to him as he had done to the animals, and even worse, should he fail to keep its terms.

At the crucial instant, however, a ball of fire passed between the pieces of the animals Abraham had severed, symbolic of the awesome truth that God had taken upon himself the obligations of the inferior, making himself the servant of Abraham his servant. Thus while God initiated the covenant with Abraham, he also obligated himself by its terms. Only God was bound by oath, not Abraham.

God's commitment to Abraham was also to his descendants, without limitations or conditions. This covenant cannot be broken, because God will not break it. Neither Abraham nor his descendants, neither Israel nor the church, can void the commitment made by God in love.

Therefore, although Israel violated the Sinai covenant and was overtaken by disaster, God's commitment remained. While the prophets could threaten punishment under the terms of the Sinai covenant, they could also promise restoration because of the unalterable word of God. However tragic the consequences of human sin, transcending all is the oath to Abraham, the permanent commitment of God to deliver his children.

There are two covenants: the covenant of grace, or self-imposed divine obligation; and the covenant of works, or man's acknowledgment of obligation to God. They are interrelated, but separate; they concern the same parties and interact, but they exist independently, each with its own terms and history. Both originate in the Old Testament. And both have their place in the New.

While the Sinai covenant was broken, the pattern of human obligation was not. The covenant between Jesus and his followers lays a heavy burden of duty upon those followers so that the obligations of the new covenant upon Christians are strongly reminiscent of the old covenant at Sinai. The two great commandments of Jesus are quotations from the law of Moses, a summary of the Ten. And the charter of Christian duty, the Sermon on the Mount, includes a penetrating commentary on several of the Ten Commandments.

The new covenant, ratified at the Last Supper, also involves God's ancient commitment to Abraham. The full cost of the divine commitment is revealed in the words of institution of the Lord's Supper. To fulfil his obligations God must surrender his own son and offer him up for the salvation of men.

As Paul tells it, Jesus Christ gave up his status of equality with God and emptied himself, becoming a human being, a slave of men, enduring suffering and death, thus giving ultimate meaning to the self-imposed obligation of God assumed two thousand years before in the presence of Abraham.

It is therefore to be seen that in both Old and New Testaments both types of covenant play their important parts in a complementary arrangement of divine commitment and human obligation. Israel was the beneficiary of God's commitment to Abraham in the deliverance from Egypt and the occupation of the Holy Land; but also Israel was obligated by the Sinai terms. The Christian Church is the beneficiary of God's commitment fulfilled in the death of Jesus Christ; but the Church is obligated by the terms of the new covenant.

From an understanding of the unity of the Bible comes an appreciation of biblical religion. Biblical religion is a religion of experiences in which we have a participating role rather than a set of doctrines or a list of rules to which we must adhere.

Just as it was with ancient Israel, so the new Israel, the Church, is the community of God bound by double covenant with Him. Consequently, by entering into the holy community, the Church, we become the heirs and legatees of the covenant given to Israel. We are thus able to participate in the divine drama; and the presence and action of God become real to us.

Thus experience of God belongs to the unity of the Bible, an experience whereby we share in the adventure of Abraham and Israel, Jesus and the Church.

The Old Testament Roots
of the Concept of the Incarnation

Therefore the Lord himself will give you a sign: Behold [the almah] will be with child and bear a son, and she will call His name Immanuel [God with us].
                                                                    Isa. 7:14 (NASB)

In the beginning was the Word, and the Word was with God, and the Word was God. . . . And the Word became flesh, and dwelt among us, and we beheld His glory, glory as of the only begotten from the Father, full of grace and truth.
                                                                    John 1:1, 14 (NASB)

The Invisibility of God and the Incarnation—*Jakob Jocz*   187
Divine Self-Disclosure in the Old Testament—
   Arthur W. Kac   195

43 The Invisibility of God and the Incarnation

Jakob Jocz

At the centre of the controversy between Church and Synagogue stands the Christological question. This is not a question whether Jesus is the Messiah, but whether the Christian understanding of the Messiah is admissible in view of the Jewish concept of God. Here lies the dividing line between Judaism and Church. On this point neither can afford to compromise. This is the reason why a Unitarian form of Christianity is a contradiction in terms; at best it can be a Gentile Synagogue, but it can never be a Church. It is important however to remember that Christology to the Church is not an abstract theological subject which can be discussed on purely theoretical lines. It is not that Christology was first formulated and then adjusted to fit the case of Jesus of Nazareth. The process was the reverse; the Church defined her Christology in view of Jesus Christ. He must remain at the centre of Christian thinking, otherwise it ceases to be Christian. For the Christian theologian the question is therefore not an academic one but a matter of faith. The Jew is in a different position. He can afford to treat the subject theoretically without involving himself in a statement of faith. This "advantage" on the part of the Jewish scholar gives an appearance of logicality which is of necessity lacking on the Christian side, where faith is already assumed in the argument.

The Christology of the Church is essentially Johannine. Without the fourth Gospel even the Pauline epistles would not have sufficed as a basis for the Trinitarian doctrine we have today. Admittedly, Colossians 2:9 [RSV] ("For in him the whole fulness of deity dwells bodily") comes very close to a Trinitarian view, but this and similar texts in the Pauline corpus could have been viewed as an exaggeration on the part of an enthusiast had they not been undergirded by the Johannine biography of the life of the Logos. We will not go far wrong when we say that the starting-point of the Church's Christology is the sentence "and the Word became flesh" (John 1:14). With this utterance we find ourselves in the heart of the fourth Gospel; all

This essay appeared in *Canadian Journal of Theology* 4, no. 3 (1958), and is used by permission of the author.

that follows is a description of how truly the Word became flesh. This means that for St. John the Gospel is not only what Jesus said or did, but also what He was—the incarnate Word of God. The words and deeds of Jesus of Nazareth derive their importance from the fact that He is the Son of God.[1] In the Johannine usage "Son of God" and "Word of God" are synonymous and refer to the historic person of Jesus the Messiah.

In this essay it is our purpose to relate the peculiar Christian doctrine of the Incarnation to the concept of the invisibility of God.

I

THE SYNAGOGUE'S POSITION

Christian theologians seldom pay any attention to the views of the Synagogue. This is a definite loss to the Church, for she understands her own position best when confronted with Judaism. Furthermore, the Synagogue is the Church's only legitimate partner in the discussion of the why of the Incarnation. She, the historic guardian of ethical monotheism, has a special right to question the Church regarding the Trinity. For the Synagogue this questioning is not a matter of curiosity but of conscience. The honour of the God of Israel is involved in it. The Synagogue therefore asks with some insistence: How does the Church hold a monotheistic faith in view of her Trinitarian position?

Judaism points to the second commandment, which follows with logical sequence upon the first, viz., that the one and only God must of necessity remain the invisible God. Judaism deduces God's invisibility from His spirituality. This is the reason why He cannot be represented by any visible form of the created order, as He is incommensurate with it.

The Synagogue's teaching regarding the invisibility of God has an interesting history. In it is revealed the distance between the God of revelation and the god of philosophy.

By way of illustration we shall start with a classical example from the Torah. In Exodus 33:11 God is represented as speaking to Moses *panim el panim* (face to face). This expression was felt by Jewish commentators to be an embarrassing anthropomorphism. Targum Onkelos therefore tries to soften the impression by using the *Hitpael* form in the rendering of the text, and this makes it appear that God spoke to Himself but in the presence of Moses. The medieval Jewish commentator Rashi follows the Targum's example in order to circumvent the difficulty.[2] But the anthropomorphism is by no means the only difficulty in this text; the real difficulty arises from the context which contradicts the statement about Moses vision of God *panim el panim*. First, God's glory which Moses asks to see is equated with God's "goodness" (Exodus 33:19); then the text tells us that Moses was placed in a position from which he could only see the "back"; again, what was meant to be a vision turns out to be an audition in which the so-called thirteen middot (attributes) are announced; and worst of all, verse 11 is flatly contradicted by verse 20, which states that no man can see God and live.

Whatever the history of the text, the complex theophany can only be understood from the characteristic Biblical concept and revelation which implies an encounter with God, but at a distance, and only by mediation. What hinders man from approaching is not His invisibility but His holiness. To the ancient Hebrew, God was not a philosophical concept but an awesome and terrifying Presence. Man cannot see God, not because He is a rarefied Spirit, but because flesh and blood cannot endure Him with immunity. That God is a real Presence could not be doubted by the Hebrew.

The ancient Synagogue still reckoned with the possibility of a concrete encounter with God by means of the Skekinah; *reot pene Shekinah*—to see the face of the Skekinah—meant to appear in the presence of God. The rabbis held to the view that every man, be he good or bad, had ultimately to meet God *panim el panim* at the hour of death. But for those who are righteous is reserved the perfect vision of God which is the consummation of all bliss.[3] It is thus obvious that to them an encounter with God was more than a mere mental realization of God; it meant a real and personal vis-a-vis meeting of God and man. Though most of the rabbis were well versed in mystical lore, their sense of God's holiness and their knowledge of man's sinfulness prevented them from seeking the unitive experience of the mystic. They regarded it as a dangerous path leading to destruction. It is said that of the four men who "entered the garden" only R. Akiba managed to return unhurt.[4]

The God of the ancient Synagogue is anything but a mental concept, nor is His invisibility a philosophical postulate. He is invisible only because the human eye cannot endure His splendour. The Talmud tells the legend of how Hadrian the emperor asked Yehoshua b. Hananya (c. A.D. 90): "I would like to see your God." Yehoshua replied: "You cannot see him." The emperor said: "Indeed I must see him." Then the rabbi took Hadrian and placed him in the full blaze of the sun and said to him: "Look into it." He answered: "I cannot." Yehoshua replied; "If of the sun you say 'I cannot look at it,' which is only one of the servants who stand in the presence of God, how much more is it true of the Skekinah?"[5]

We want to quote one more passage to illustrate our point. The Pesikta Rabbati comments on Psalm 92:5 ("How great are thy works, O LORD! Thy thoughts are very deep!" [RSV]): "Come and see the miracles of God . . . He created the world; He created men and demons (mazzikim); the demons see men, but men see them not. He created demons and servant angels, the servant angels see the demons, but the demons see not the servant angels. He created servant angels, demons and men: He sees all, but all His creatures see Him not. Say then: Thy thoughts are very deep!"[6] From this we can gauge what the invisibility of God meant to the rabbis: His blinding glory makes Him invisible to His creatures' eyes. They thus cry out: "Who is like the God of gods, who sees and cannot be seen?"[7]

In the Old Testament the awareness of God's splendour is magnificently symbolized by the behaviour of the Seraphim covering not only their faces but their bodies with their wings so as not to be seared by God's holiness (Isaiah 6:2).

It was only under Greek influence and by slow degrees that God's presence became conceptualized in the Synagogue. This led to conceiving the invisibility of God as a philosophical postulate. Before the Greek world, Biblical anthropomorphism was felt to be an embarrassing feature. It had to be explained apologetically.

Here is a typical example: "The king (i.e., Ptolomaeus Philometor) asked in what sense the Scriptures ascribe to God hands, arms, face, feet, walking. He (i.e., Aristobulus) explained it to him in keeping with the divine nature of God."[8] We can rest assured that the "explanation" was in keeping with Greek philosophical ideas more than with the "divine nature of God."

This need for "explaining" may perhaps be compared with our modern need for "demythologizing," and it is interesting to note where it led to. The greatest protagonist in explaining the Bible and Judaism to the Greek world was undoubtedly Philo of Alexandria. He may not have succeeded in working out a synthesis between Greek philosophy and Biblical faith, but towards the process of ratiocination he made a major contribution. Here is Philo's philosophical definition of God: a Being better than Good, more honourable than Unity, purer than the number One. God cannot be seen by anyone else, because he can only be comprehended by Himself.[9] It is obvious that "seeing" for Philo is a mental act, whereas for the rabbis of the ancient Synagogue, as for the Old Testament, seeing God is an encounter.

With the medieval Jewish philosophers the process of rationalizing is completed. The impact of Greek and Arab thought proved irresistible. God is now a completely spiritualized concept to be apprehended mentally. It would lead us too far to quote the evidence, but the central figure of medieval Jewish philosophy must not be passed over.

Moses Maimonides occupies a special place in Judaism. His influence extends far beyond the field of philosophy. His contribution to the general thinking of the Synagogue makes him one of the most outstanding leaders in Jewry. The "Creed" which Maimonides composed entered the liturgy and is recited daily. The third article reads: "I believe with perfect faith that the Creator, blessed be His name, is not a body and that He is free from all accidents of matter, and that He has not any form whatsoever." The meaning of this highly philosophical formula becomes clearer when read in conjunction with his other works. Here we confine ourselves solely to his *Guide for the Perplexed*.

In this book Maimonides concerns himself with a number of difficulties which arise when the Old Testament and philosophy are confronted. He spends much time explaining Biblical anthropomorphism and deals with the question of God's attributes. He stresses that these attributes must not be understood as "qualities" but as acts, because the conceptualization of God demands such an attitude. For him God exists without the attribute of existence and he is One without the attribute of unity.[10] Maimonides explains that all which is said of God in the Bible is said parabolically. He even goes so far as to contradict the notion that God "speaks"; what it really means is that God is the cause and creator of all that is said. When we read in the Scriptures that God spoke to the prophets we are meant to understand that these men attained to divine knowledge.[11]

Building on the premises of Aristotelian philosophy, Maimonides established the concept of the incorporeality of God and from thence he proceeded to prove God's unity on the supposition that incorporeal things cannot be counted. By a similar token he shows God's eternity, because motion cannot be predicated of Him, which means that He is outside the limitations of time.[12]

190

The difference between the Maimonidean God and that of the Bible is only too obvious. Maimonides' God is a philosophical postulate neatly adjusted to all the requirements of logic, but He is not alive; He is a concept. No wonder that the philosopher met with such fierce opposition on the part of the rabbis.[13] Only by slow degrees and after years of opposition did he win a place in Jewish thinking.

The Synagogue's doctrine of God is largely influenced by opposition to the Trinitarian view of the Church. In her efforts to contradict Trinitarianism she was driven to an almost numerical concept of the Unity. Thus Bahya ibn Pakuda (second half of the eleventh century) uses the numerical idea in order to show on Euclidean evidence that Unity precedes the number One.[14] For God to be God, he says, He must be an absolute, that is a non-composite Being. The Midrash already speaks with a view to the Church when it affirms that God can have neither brother nor son.[15] Yehuda Halevi (c. 1085-1142) points out the unreasonableness of the Trinitarian doctrine in his apologetic work *Alchazri*,[16] and Hasdai Crescas (c. 1340-1412) shows how it contradicts the postulate that God is a necessary existence.[17]

II

Christian Apologetics

To the Synagogue's questioning regarding the doctrine of the Trinity, the Church answered with *catenae* of proofs from the Old Testament. To establish their case Christian apologists were forced upon the slippery path of exegetical acrobatics. Some of this very dubious exegesis is still reproduced in pious tracts for the purpose of converting Jews.[18] But worse than questionable exegesis is the philosophical attempt upon the Holy Trinity. It is our conviction that an effort to establish the doctrine of the Trinity on philosophical grounds is to contradict it. It is not and was never meant to be a deduction based on human logic.

Christian writers have occasionally abandoned the method of logical deduction and adopted the argument of religious usefulness. They point out that the *Logos* concept is a necessary intermediary to bridge the gulf between God and man. Jesus Christ acts in the capacity of mediator between the invisible God and the created world. All this is based on the assumption that the Johannine *Logos* is essentially the same as that of Philo. But it seems to us that the resemblance is only in name. It is enough to place the Philonian *Logos* emanating from God side by side with the opening words of the Johannine prologue to see the difference. *In the beginning was the Word . . . and the Word was God.* Here the Church acted with unerring instinct when it formulated its creedal statement regarding the Trinity as co-eternal and co-equal, "none is greater or less than the other." This is a flat contradiction of what Philo means by the Logos. The Johannine Logos is no "middle link" between God and man, but completely God and completely man. This is the meaning of the statement *And the Word became flesh.*

We thus want to reiterate: the doctrine of the Trinity cannot be proved from the Old Testament, or from philosophy, or from logic; it is essentially a theological concept. By this we mean to say that the doctrine of the Trinity is the Church's peculiar answer to the question, Who is Jesus Christ?

III

The Christian Position

We hold to the view that there is an important connection between the concept of the invisible God and the doctrine of the Incarnation. It is our conviction that in the New Testament, exactly as in the Old Testament, God is the invisible One, not because He can be only mentally conceived, but because He is the Holy One of Israel. In other words, here as throughout the Bible, God's invisibility is founded not philosophically but religiously. He is *aoratos* (invisible) because of His tender mercy towards man; man cannot survive His visibility, for the God of Israel is a consuming fire (Deuteronomy 4:24; Hebrews 12:20). It is interesting to note that the expression *aoratos* belongs exclusively to the New Testament. Though God is referred to in several passages as the invisible One, we look upon Colossians 1:15 as the *locus classicus* because of its Christological importance. There is an obvious association of ideas between Colossians 1:15—Christ "the image of the invisible God"—and John 1:14—"The Word became flesh, and dwelt among us." In the first case God's invisibility is founded upon His love (cf. John 3:16)—and both are supplementary. He remains the hidden God not to consume us, and He becomes God incarnate to save us, from the same motive, for he is a God of love.

The crux of Christian theology is how to co-ordinate logically the contradiction implied in the Incarnation: the holy invisible God becomes visible within the limitation of a human life. The Church Fathers have wrestled with this problem from their own particular point of view. With the Greek philosophical tradition behind them they felt uncomfortable at the thought that their faith carried a hidden illogicality. The history of dogma is largely the search for a formula which would reconcile the paradox lying at the heart of the New Testament faith. The hypostatic union, *communcatio idiomatum,* the simile of soul and body, and many other devices were employed in the attempt to solve the difficulty.[19]

Every age tries to give its own answer to the perennial problem of Christian theology. In our times of humanitarian liberalism, when the distance between God and man is reduced to a minimum, the miracle of the Incarnation is neutralized by the Promethean apotheosis of man: Jesus Christ is only more fully what we already are, viz., sons of God and bearers of the divine spark. If we understood W. Norman Pittenger's article correctly, this is what he intends to say. Here are his own words: "He [i.e. Jesus Christ] is the emergence of the eternal Word in full human expression, by perfect union with the creature; of which emergence the lesser emergences of that Word in and through other men, each in its own small degree, are the adumbration and intimation. . . ."[20]

Whatever else the above quotation and the rest of the article may mean, one thing is unmistakable: this is not incarnation in the New Testament sense. For the Fourth Gospel, as for Saul of Tarsus, the Incarnation was an incomparable, unique and non-repeatable event. It had no parallel in history and was outside human anticipation. It was not founded upon logic or necessity, but solely upon the free love of God. There can be no analogy for the Incarnation if we mean what the New Testament means: *the Word became flesh.* There is only one valid explanation: the measureless love of God. This overwhelming, outrageous love made the Holy One of Israel stoop down and meet the sinner at the point of his deepest need. This is the Gospel: that God becomes visible as the Saviour of sinners. Apart from the Incarnation He remains the invisible and holy God.

IV

THE NECESSITY FOR THEOLOGICAL PRECISION

The paradox which is implied in the Gospel message is an offence to the Jew and the Greek. This is something we must acknowledge and not gloss over. The offence of the Cross is that it is the man Jesus who died for the sins of the world and that this man is the Son of God. But to acknowledge this paradox does not exonerate us from confusing our terms. We frequently use language which is not only offensive to the Jew but which is theologically unjustified. One sometimes hears theologians speak of Jesus as the Incarnate God. The Church fathers frequently offended in this respect. The author is not too sure whether the term *theotokos* was a felicitous choice, though he sympathizes with the issues involved at the Ecumenical Councils of Ephesus and Chalcedon. Though Barth defends the term it is not one which is even remotely related to Biblical terminology, and where it led to can be seen from Barth's own evidence.[21] The Poles have no other word for Christmas except *Boze Narodzenie*—the birthday of God. There is little difference between *theotokos* and the Polish word for Christmas; neither expresses the miracle of the Incarnation. In the Johannine sense *God became man; man did not become God.* The New Testament never speaks of the birth of God; such an expression would have been impossible against a Hebrew background. The fourth Gospel is very cautious; it says that *the Word became flesh* and leaves it at that. The birth of a god is a pagan possibility. We may legitimately speak of the second person of the Trinity, but then we already mean the risen and ascended Christ. That Jesus was God in disguise is something which the ancient Church vigorously opposed. But much of our devout literature and specially our hymns give that impression. Such a suggestion is foreign to the Bible. It would be wiser to curb exuberance of language and to keep strictly to New Testament terminology which operates within the Hebrew tradition. Israel Abrahams was well justified in his assumption when he said: "It is a plausible suggestion that John had the Shekinah in mind when he spoke (1:14) of the Word or glory as tabernacled (*eskenosen*) in man."[22] Language more closely related to the New Testament will greatly help us to grasp the meaning and wonder of the message that the Word became flesh. It may even happen, as it happened to the writer of the fourth Gospel, that as we ponder on the miracle of God's love in Christ and try to put it into words we will behold "his glory, the glory as of the only begotten of the Father, full of grace and truth" (John 1:14). This is exactly what St. Paul meant when he spoke of "the light of the knowledge of the glory of God in the face of Jesus Christ." This is the theme of the Incarnation, that the glory of the invisible God becomes endurable for sinners in the face of Jesus Christ. Christology is ultimately not a matter for discussion but an encounter with the invisible God in the historic person of Jesus the Messiah.

Notes

1. On this subject, see the author's essay in *Judaica,* III, 1957, entitled "The Son of God."
2. Cf. M. Rosenblum and A.M. Silberman, *Pentateuch* (1930), p. 188.
3. For the whole subject, see Hermann L. Strack and Paul Billerbeck, Kommentar Zum N. T. aus Talmud und Midrasch, I, 206ff.
4. Cf. Babylonian Talmud, Hagigah, 14*b*.
5. Ibid., Hullin, 59*b*.
6. Pesikta R. 6.
7. Deuteronomy R. 1.
8. Quoted by Eusebius, *Praeparatio Evangelica,* VIII, 10.
9. Philo, *De Praemiis et poenis,* II, 414.
10. Moses Maimonides, *The Guide for the Perplexed,* English translation by M. Friedlander, I, 54 (p. 75f).
11. Ibid., I, 65 (p. 97f).
12. Ibid., II, 1 (p. 145f).
13. Cf. M. Simon, *Jewish Religious Conflicts* (1950), chapter V.
14. Cf. *Jewish Encyclopedia* (1906), VI, 11*a*.
15. Deuteronomy R. c.2.
16. Usually referred to as Kusari: cf. ibid., I, 5.
17. *Bittul Ikre Ha-Nozrim,* p. 23.
18. Cf. Jakob Jocz, "Das exegetische Problem und die Judenmission," *Judaica,* I (1956).
19. Cf. G.D.W. Ommanney, *A Critical Dissertation on the Athanasian Creed* (1897), pp. 352ff.
20. W. N. Pittenger, "Degree or Kind?," *Canadian Journal of Theology,* October 1956.
21. Cf. Karl Barth, *Church Dogmatics,* English translation, I/2, pp. 138ff.
22. I. Abrahams, *The Glory of God* (1925), p. 52.

44 Divine Self-Disclosure in the Old Testament

Arthur W. Kac

By the term *self-disclosure* we mean the various manifestations of God's presence in the midst of His people in the Old Testament period, which manifestations culminated in the person of Messiah Jesus in whom God became flesh and dwelt in our midst.[1] In the following pages we wish to trace the gradual unfolding of that concept in the Old Testament.

I. GOD'S PRESENCE IN THE MIDST OF HIS PEOPLE

Right after the Sinai Covenant was concluded by which Israel became Jehovah's people, Moses received the following instruction.

> Speak to the people of Israel that they bring me an offering; from every man who gives it willingly you shall take an offering for me . . . And let them make me a sanctuary, that I may dwell in their midst.
> [Exod. 25:2]

In Leviticus the term "tabernacle" is used in place of "sanctuary."

> If you walk in my statutes and observe my commandments and do them. Then I will give you rain in due season, and the land shall yield its increase, and the trees of the field shall yield their fruit. . . And I will set my tabernacle among you, and my soul shall not abhor you. And I will walk among you, and will be your God, and you shall be my people.
> [Lev. 26:3-4, 11-12]

In the course of time the question arose in the minds of certain Israelites, Does God who created the whole universe really dwell on a certain spot on this earth, in a tabernacle or sanctuary made by humans hands? That was the question King Solomon posed during his dedication of the Jerusalem Temple, erected during his reign.

> But will God indeed dwell on the earth? behold, the heaven and

This article is reprinted with stylistic changes from Arthur W. Kac, *The Messianic Hope* (Grand Rapids: Baker, 1975) pp. 121-34. Copyright 1975 by Arthur W. Kac. The author's own translation is used for the Scripture quotations.

heavens cannot contain Thee; how much less this house which I have built:

[1 Kings 8:27]

But the answer to Solomon's question came even before he uttered it. When the Ark containing the two tables of stone put there by Moses in the wilderness was placed in the "inner sanctuary," the "most holy place" of the Temple, underneath the wings of the cherubim, we are told that a cloud symbolizing the Presence of God filled the sanctuary.[2] It was the same cloud, also called "the glory of Jehovah," that filled the tabernacle in the wilderness, a cloud by day and a fire by night.[3]

The belief that God did indeed dwell in the midst of His people has its source in the conviction that God is a Person, and that truth was rooted in the biblical account of the creation of man.

> Then God said, "Let us make man in our image, after our likeness. . . ." So God created man in his own image, in the image of God he created him. . . . And the Lord God formed man of the dust of the ground, and breathed into his nostrils the breath of life; and man became a living being.
>
> [Gen. 1:26a-27; 2:7]

According to the above statement man came into existence as a special creation. Since man is a person and since he was created after God's likeness, it follows that God, too, is a person, and God "breathed" into man something of His own personality. From that biblical concept man reasoned that certain characteristics of personality must be common to God and man. That does not mean that biblical man considered himself equal to God. God is the Creator, man is the creature; God is holy, man is sinful. God is self-sufficient—man is not. But the account of man's creation convinced man that man is a person, because God is a person. In a world divided between a belief in gods of stone statues and a belief in a god of pure reason, detached and far removed from the earthly sphere, biblical revelation proclaims a God who is neither the god of materialism nor the god of cold and pure reason, but a living, dynamic Divine Person, deeply involved in the welfare and destiny of the world that He created and that He sustains.

It is by virtue of the common bond of personality that God and man manifest a desire to communicate with each other. That desire underlies man's search after God, a reaching out after Him to whom man is linked by certain common bonds of personality.

> As the hart longs for the water brooks, so longs my soul for thee, O God. My soul thirsts for God, for the living God.
>
> [Psalm 42:1-2 (42:2-3, Heb.)]

It is because of certain characteristics of personality shared in common with man that God also discloses a yearning to communicate and commune with man. The program of redemption, set in motion after the Fall of man, is a divine determination to reopen the lines of communication that existed prior to man's alienation from

God. In the book of Hebrews we are told that in the biblical period God used many and various ways to communicate with man.[4] We will now consider some of those ways.

II. ANGELIC APPEARANCES

The Hebrew word "angel" means messenger. Angels are God's messengers to man. They appear in the whole biblical period, in both the Old and New Testaments. One of the remarkable features of the angelic appearances in the Old Testament is that the angel frequently speaks of Jehovah in the first person, as if he—the angel—was Jehovah Himself.

When Hagar, Sarah's maidservant, left the house of her mistress and went into the desert, we are told that an angelic messenger appeared and

> The angel of Jehovah said to her, "Return to your mistress, and submit to her." And the angel of Jehovah said to her, "I will greatly multiply your seed so that it cannot be numbered for multitude." And the angel of Jehovah said to her, "Behold, you are with child, and shall bear a son; you shall call his name Ishmael, because Jehovah has heard your affliction". . . . And she called the name of Jehovah who spake to her, "Thou God seest me"; for she said, "Have I really seen God and remained alive after seeing him?"
>
> [Gen. 16:9-11, 13]

The following is an account of the appearance of three angelic messengers to Abraham. One of the three acted as the spokesman, and he spoke and acted as if he was Jehovah Himself.

> And Jehovah appeared to him[5] by the oaks of Mamre, as he sat at the door of the tent in the heat of the day. . . . They[6] said to him, "Where is Sarah your wife?" And he said, "She is in the tent." And he[7] said, "I will certainly return to you at this time next year, and Sarah your wife shall have a son"; and Sarah heard it in the tent door which was behind him. Now Abraham and Sarah were old and advanced in years; and it had ceased to be with Sarah after the manner of women. So Sarah laughed within herself, saying, "After I have grown old, and my husband is old, shall I have pleasure?" And Jehovah said to Abraham, "Why did Sarah laugh, saying, 'Shall I indeed bear a child, now that I am old?' Is anything too hard for Jehovah?"
>
> [Gen. 18:1, 9-14]

The following three passages are taken from angelic appearances in the days of Jacob.

> Then the angel of God spoke to me in a dream, saying, "Jacob," and I said, "Here am I!" And he said . . . "I am the God of Bethel,[8] where you anointed a pillar and where you made a vow unto me; now arise, go forth from this land, and return to the land of your birth."
>
> [Gen. 31:11-13]

And Jacob was left alone; and there wrestled a man with him until the breaking of the day. When he[9] saw that he did not prevail against him, he touched the hollow of his thigh; and Jacob's thigh was put out of joint as he wrestled with him. . . . And he said unto him, "What is your name?" And he said, "Jacob." And he said, "Your name shall be called no more Jacob, but Israel: for you have striven with God and with men, and have prevailed. . . ." And Jacob called the name of the place Peniel, saying, "For I have seen God face to face, and yet my life is preserved."

[Gen. 32:24-25, 27-28, 30 (32:25-26, 28-29, 31, Heb.)]

Jacob pronounced his blessing upon his children just before he died; he uttered the following words when Joseph approached him with his two sons.

The God before whom my fathers Abraham and Isaac walked, the God who has shepherded me all life long unto this day—the angel who has redeemed me from all evil—bless the lads; and in them let my name and the name of my fathers Abraham and Isaac be perpetuated; and let them grow into a multitude in the midst of the earth.

[Gen. 48:15-16]

The following angelic appearances took place in the Exodus period of Israel's history.

And the angel of Jehovah appeared to him[10] in a flame of fire out of the midst of a bush; and he looked, and, behold, the bush burned with fire, yet it was not consumed. And Moses said, "I will turn aside and see this great sight, why the bush is not burnt. When Jehovah saw that he turned aside to see, God called to him out of the midst of the bush, and said, "Moses, Moses!" And he said, "Here am I." Then he[11] said, "Do not come near; put off your shoes from your feet, for the place on which you are standing is holy ground." And he said, "I am the God of your father, the God of Abraham, the God of Isaac, and the God of Jacob." And Moses hid his face, for he was afraid to look at God.

[Exod. 3:2-6]

In the following passage we are told that Jehovah led the Israelites through the wilderness.

And Jehovah went before them by day in a pillar of cloud to lead them along the way, and by night in a pillar of fire to give them light, that they might travel by day and night.

[Exod. 13:21]

In the passage below relating the miraculous deliverance of the Israelites from the pursuing Egyptians, Jehovah took on the form of an angel.

Then the angel of God who went before the camp of Israel moved and went behind them; and the pillar of cloud moved from before them and stood behind them. Intervening between the host of Egypt and the host of Israel; and it was a cloud of darkness to them, but it gave light by night to these; so that the one came not near the other all night. . . . And it came to pass that in the morning watch Jehovah looked upon the host of the Egyptians through the pillar of fire and of cloud and troubled the host of the Egyptians.

[Exod. 14:19-20, 24]

The same phenomenon occurs in many other situations in the Old Testament period.[12]

The following passage explains why it is that "angels" often spoke and acted as if they were Jehovah Himself.

"Behold, I send an angel before you to guard you on the way and to bring you into the place which I have prepared. Beware of him, and obey his voice, provoke him not; for he will not pardon your transgressions; for my name is in him."

[Exod. 23:20-21]

With reference to that angel, Rashi, medieval Jewish commentator, declares that rabbinic authorities identify the angel in the above passage with Metatron. Metatron is the name of the chief of the angels who, according to one Talmudic passage, sits in the inmost dwelling of God, and is the same person as the "Prince of the Presence," the angel who is the very Face of God.[13] In the Bible a person's name is identical with that person. It expresses the very essence of that person. The rabbinic statement to which Rashi refers in his exposition of the passage in Exodus 23:21 declares that "His [the angel's] name is like the name of his Master."[14] All of that means one thing: In the Bible, especially in the Old Testament, God frequently takes on the form of angels in order to communicate with man.

III. THE COVENANT

If angelic appearances were one of the ways God used to communicate with man, the Sinai covenant was a means of His identifying Himself with Israel. The ancient world was full of covenants.[15] Covenants were made between individuals, as for example, the covenant between Jonathan and David, between family clans, and between rulers. But the Sinai covenant, a covenant between God and a whole people, is something unique even in the ancient world. The covenant idea dominates the whole Bible, Old and New Testaments. The Sinai covenant brought Israel into existence as a people and a religious community. Through the Sinai covenant God entered into an extraordinary relationship with Israel.

What exactly that covenant came to mean to Israel may be seen if we realize that it was interpreted in terms of a marriage covenant. In the ancient world marriage was a covenant, and it is the only covenant institution that has come down to us from the ancient world. Israel is often spoken of as God's bride.

Fear not, for you will not be ashamed; be not confouonded, for you will not be put to shame; for you will forget the shame of your youth, and the reproach of your widowhood you will remember no more. For your Maker is your husband, the LORD of hosts is his name; and the Holy One of Israel is your Redeemer, the God of the whole earth he is called.

[Isa. 54:4-5]

The Hebrew word "Goel" ("redeemer") originally denoted the nearest of kin whose duty it was to redeem, to ransom, to purchase back, the mortgaged land and return it to the original owner who was forced to part with it through unfortunate circumstances. If an Israelite for the same reason fell into slavery, it was the duty of his nearest kin to "redeem" him, that is, to pay the ransom money necessary to set him free. The "Goel" was also obligated to avenge the death of the nearest kin. Finally the "Goel" was duty bound to marry the widow of his nearest kin who left no children in order to save the family name from extinction.[16] Through the conclusion of the Sinai covenant God became Israel's Redeemer, that is, her "Goel," her nearest kin, and He was duty bound, as it were, to "redeem" Israel when she got into trouble.

The following excerpts are additional instances in which Israel is represented as married to God.

> The word of Jehovah came to me saying, "Go and declare in the hearing of Jerusalem, thus says Jehovah, 'I remember the devotion of your youth, your love as a bride, when you followed me in the wilderness in a land that was not sown.' "

> [Jer. 2:1-2]

> Can a maiden forget her ornaments, or a bride her attire? yet my people have forgotten me days without number.

> [Jer. 2:32]

Israel had nothing to boast of as to her origin. According to the psalmist, she was of low estate,[17] of little account, few in number, wandering from country to country.[18] Ezekiel likens Israel's beginning to an exposed, castaway baby girl.

> "And as for your birth, on the day when you were born your navel string was not cut, nor were you washed with water to cleanse you, nor rubbed with salt, nor swathed with bands. No eye pitied you, to do any of these things to you, out of compassion for you; but you were cast out on the open field, for you were abhorred, on the day that you were born.

> [Ezek. 16:4-5]

It was in that state that God found her. But He picked her up, took her to Himself, nursed her to health, and cared for her until she reached puberty.

> And when I passed by you, and saw you rolling in your own blood, I said to you in your blood,[19] Live. I have caused you to multiply like the plants in the field; and you grew up and became tall and arrived at full maidenhood;[20] your breasts were formed, and your hair had grown; yet you were [still] naked and bare.[21]

> [Ezek. 16:6-7]

200

Then God took her up again, made her into his bride, lavished upon her His love, and surrounded her with all the honor and wealth at His disposal.

> When I passed by you again and looked upon you, behold, you were at the age of love; and I spread my shirt over you, and covered your nakedness;[22] yea I swore unto you,[23] and entered into a covenant with you, says the Lord God, and you became mine. Then I washed you with water, and thoroughly washed away your blood from you, and I anointed you with oil. I clothed you also with broidered work and shod you with leather, I swathed you in fine linen, and I covered you with silk. And I decked you with ornaments, and I put bracelets on your hands, and a chain on your neck. And I put a ring on your nose, and earrings in your ears, and a beautiful crown upon your head.
>
> [Ezek. 16:8-12]

Accordingly, whenever Israel goes after other gods, that is, if she chooses to follow life-goals that are inconsistent with her destiny as marked out in biblical revelation, she is called an adulteress, unfaithful to Jehovah who entered into a covenant relation with her. The speaker in the excerpt below is Jehovah and His words are addressed to Israel.

> Plead with your mother, plead, for she is not my wife, and I am not her husband; let her therefore put away her harlotry out of her sight, and her adulteries from between her breasts. Lest I strip her naked, and set her as in the day when she was born, and make her as a wilderness, and set her like a parched land, and slay her with thirst. . . . For their mother has played the harlot. . .for she said, 'I will go after my lovers, who will give me my bread and my water, my wool and my flax, my oil and my drink'. . . . And she did not know that it was I who gave her the grain, the wine, and the oil, and who lavished upon her silver and gold which they used for Baal.[24]
>
> [Hos. 2:2-3, 5, 8 (2:4-5, 7, 10, Heb.)]

IV. THE SON OF GOD

When Moses was commissioned by God to demand that Pharaoh let the Hebrews leave the country, he was given the following message to be delivered to the Egyptian king.

> Thus says Jehovah, "Israel is my son, even my first-born. And I say to you, 'Let my son go that he may serve me' ". . .
>
> [Exod. 4:22-23]

> When Israel was a child, then I loved him, and called my son out of Egypt. . . . I taught Ephraim also to walk, taking them up by their arms, but they did not know that I healed them. I drew them with cords of a man, with bands of love; and I was to them as one that eases the yoke on their jaws, and I bent down to them and fed them.[25]
>
> [Hos. 11:1, 3-4]

In the Nathan prophecy given to King David, God promised to be a father to David's immediate offspring.[26] Although that referred in the first place to Solomon, the promise was by no means limited to him. God was a father to Hezekiah and to Josiah, no less than to Solomon, who in his old age had proven unfaithful to Jehovah. By virtue of His Davidic descent, the Messianic King bears also that filial relationship to God. Not only so, but in Him the Old Testament concept of divine sonship attains its completion. He is not merely *a* son of God in the sense of the other members of the following two psalms, both of which are interpreted of the Messiah in rabbinic writings.

> He shall cry to me, 'Thou art my Father, my God, and the Rock of my salvation.' And I will make him the first-born, the highest of the kings of the earth. My mercy[27] I will keep for him for ever, and my covenant shall stand firm with him.
>
> [Psalm 89: 26-28 (89:27-29, Heb.)]

In the Midrash, verse 27 of Psalm 89 is interpreted of the Messiah.[28]

> Why do the nations rage, and the peoples plot in vain! The kings of the earth rise in rebellion, and the rulers take counsel together, against Jehovah and against His Messiah [saying], "Let us break their bands asunder, and cast away their cords from us."
>
> He who is enthroned in the heavens laughs, Jehovah mocks at them. Then he will speak to them in his wrath, and terrify them in his fury [saying], "I have established my king on Zion, my holy hill."
>
> I will declare the decree! Jehovah said to me, "You are my son, today I have begotten you. Ask of me, and I will give the nations for your inheritance, and the ends of the earth shall be your possession. You shall break them with a rod of iron, like a potter's vessel you shall dash them in pieces."
>
> And now, you kings, show yourselves wise; be admonished, you judges of the earth! Serve Jehovah with fear, and rejoice with trembling. Kiss the son,[29] lest he be angry, and you perish in the way; for his anger may easily be kindled; blessed are all they that take refuge in him.
>
> [Psalm 2:1-12]

Psalm 2 is one of the great Messianic psalms. The mission by a group of nations to the Judean kingdom in the days of Jehoshaphat may have been the historical basis of Psalm 2. The prophetic writer may have seen in that event a forerunner of a world-wide revolt of the nations against Jehovah and His Messiah taking place at the end of the age, during the period immediately preceding Messiah's coming. "The Old Testament," Delitzsch declares, "knows of no kingship to which world dominion was promised and to which sonship was ascribed (2 Samuel 7:14; Psalm 89:28) save the Davidic. The Psalm celebrates the world-dominion of a king who is a son of David and a Son of God."[30]

There are many references and comments in rabbinic writings on the Messianic significance of that psalm. The rise of the nations against Jehovah and His Messiah is applied by one source to the invasion of the land of Israel by the armies of Gog in the last days of history prior to the appearance of the Messiah as recorded in Ezekiel 38 and 39.[31]

Another source likens the rebellious uprising "against God, and His Messiah" to a robber who stands defiantly behind the palace of the king and says, "If I shall find the son of the king, I shall lay hold on him, and crucify him, and kill him in a cruel death." But the Holy Spirit mocks at him: "He that sits in the heavens shall laugh."[32]

In his introduction to Sanhedrin, chapter 10, Maimonides[33] says: "The prophets and saints have longed for the days of the Messiah, and great has been their desire towards him, for there will be with him the gathering together of the righteous and the administration of goodness, and wisdom, and royal righteousness, with the abundance of his uprightness and the spread of his wisdom, and his approach to God, as it is said: Jehovah said unto me, Thou art my son, today have I begotten thee."

Another reference states that when the hour comes, God speaks to the Messiah to make a new covenant, and He says to him: "This day have I begotten thee."[34]

With reference to the statement in Psalm 2:8 ("Ask of me, and I will give the nations for your inheritance") we have the following comment in the Talmud: "Our Rabbis have taught us in a Mishna with reference to Messiah who is about to be revealed quickly, that the Holy One, blessed be He, says to him, 'Ask of Me,' for it is said, 'I will declare the decree. Ask of me and I will give nations for thine inheritance.' "[35]

Psalm 2 is divided into four strophes, or parts, each consisting of three sentences. The first strophe is an introduction. We find ourselves in the midst of a revolt on the part of ungodly Gentile nations, aiming to eradicate the influence of biblical religion in the world.

In the second part (verses 4-6), the prophet sees how Jehovah thunders against the rebels in His hot displeasure and in defiance of the rebellious nations He proclaims the establishment of His Messianic King on David's throne in Jerusalem.

In the third portion, the Messianic King Himself speaks. He declares who He is and what He is to do by virtue of a divine decree. The Hebrew word rendered "decree" in English signifies a statute or a law. The source of the decree He refers to is Jehovah Himself; it therefore is unshakable. The decree contains a declaration that He, the Messianic King of the Davidic line, is God's Son: "Thou art my Son, this day have I begotten thee!" Delitzsch states that as far as biblical revelation is concerned that divine decree was first made known to the world in the Nathan prophecy in which God promised David that He will be a father to his seed.[36]

By virtue of His sonship, He received from Jehovah sovereignty over the nations of the earth, for the earth and all its fullness belong to Jehovah. He only needs to desire to assume sovereignty over the nations; it is His for the asking. "Ask of me, and I will give the nations for Thy inheritance, and the ends of the earth for thy possession."

The concluding portion of the psalm (verses 10-12) is recited again by the psalmist. In the first portion, the poetic seer described a rebellion of nations against

Jehovah and His Messianic King. In the last portion he gives an admonition to the rulers of the nations to serve Jehovah with reverence and to submit to His Messianic King: "Serve Jehovah with fear. . . . Kiss the son . . ." The word "kiss" signifies to pay homage. When Samuel installed Saul as king of Israel, he kissed him as an expression of his homage to the newly inaugurated king.[37] Aben Ezra,[38] one of the great Jewish commentators on the Bible, gives the following exposition of the statement "Kiss the Son": "As 'serve Jehovah' refers to God, so 'Kiss the Son' refers to His Messiah; the meaning of 'bar' (used here instead of the usual 'ben' for son) is the same here as in Proverbs 31:1 where the same word 'bar' is used for son." He goes on to say that kissing the king as a sign of homage is a custom practiced among the world's nations.

David Kimchi, another great medieval Jewish expositor of the Bible, interprets "Kiss the Son" as referring to the Messiah, and he adds the following comment: "This is the interpretation of our Rabbis of blessed memory."

Notes

1. John 1:14.
2. 1 Kings 8:10-11.
3. Exodus 40:34-38.
4. Hebrews 1:1.
5. Abraham.
6. The three angelic messengers.
7. The spokesman of the angelic messengers.
8. A reference to the divine revelation granted to Jacob at Bethel.
9. The angelic messenger.
10. Moses.
11. The angel identified as Jehovah.
12. See, e.g., Joshua 5:13-15; Judges 2:1-5; see, especially, Judges 6:11-24, and Judges 13:2-23.
13. Bab. Chagiga 15*a*.
14. Sanh. 38*b*.
15. George E. Mendenhall, *Law and Covenant in Israel and the Ancient Near East* (Pittsburgh: Biblical Colloquim, 1955).
16. See, e.g., Leviticus 25:25, 48-49; Deuteronomy 19:2-6; Ruth 3:12; 4:1-9.
17. Psalm 136:23.
18. Psalm 105:12-13.
19. The sense of the word "blood" is, probably, that had not God rescued her she would have bled to death.
20. Literally, "you came to excellent ornaments," i.e., "you acquired excellent beauty."
21. An allusion to the poverty of their state when they were yet strangers in the land of Canaan.
22. A biblical idiom for marriage (see Ruth 3:9).
23. An allusion to the marriage vow.
24. Baal—the word in Hebrew means a Canaanite god, and also a man who is his wife's lord and master.
25. The following are other references in which God is represented as Israel's Father: Deuteronomy 32:6, 18; Isaiah 63:16; 64:8; Jeremiah 3:14, 19; 31:9; Malachi 1:6.

26. See 2 Samuel 7:14.
27. The word *chesed*, translated "mercy" in the above text, is often rendered "grace," "covenant-love."
28. Exodus Rabba 19:8.
29. This has reference to the Person to whom Jehovah says in verse 7: "You are my son, today I have begotten you."
30. Franz Delitzsch, *Biblical Commentary on the Psalms* (London: Hodder and Stoughton, 1894), 1:118.
31. Berach, 7*b*; Abod. Zarah 3*b*; Midrash on Ps. 2.
32. *Yalkut*, Vol. 2, par. 620.
33. Physician and great Talmudic scholar born in Spain in 1135, whose articles of faith have been included in the Daily Prayer Book.
34. Midrash on Psalm 2:7.
35. Sukkah 52*a*.
36. 2 Samuel 7:14; also Psalm 89:27.
37. 1 Samuel 10:1.
38. Born in Toledo, Spain, in the beginning of twelfth century.

Messiah's Atoning Death

He was despised and forsaken of men,
A man of sorrows, and acquainted with grief;
And like one from whom men hide their face,
He was despised, and we did not esteem Him.
Surely our griefs He Himself bore,
And our sorrows He carried;
Yet we ourselves esteemed Him stricken,
Smitten of God, and afflicted,
But He was pierced through for our transgressions,
He was crushed for our iniquities;
The chastening for our well-being fell upon Him,
And by His scourging we are healed.

Isa. 53:3-5

The Death of Jesus—*Arthur W. Kac*   207
The Meaning of the Death of Messiah Jesus—
   Mark Malbert   208
The Mediator Element in the Messianic Hope—
   Aaron J. Kligerman   213
The Cross in Jewish Experience—*Nathan J. Stone*   221

45 The Death of Jesus

Arthur W. Kac

Was the death of Jesus a mere incident in His life? Was it something that just happened? Did He become a martyr to a righteous cause? Was His death a sacrifice of a holy life brought about by sinful men? Was it a natural climax to a struggle between good and evil? The New Testament declares that Jesus came to die, that He had known in advance that He came to die, that His death was for all mankind, that it was the instrument of accomplishing His mission.

When Jesus was placed on the cross, an inscription was nailed to the cross, containing the political aspect of the crime with which He was charged and for which He was crucified. The inscription was in Hebrew, Latin, and Greek, and it read: "Jesus of Nazareth, the King of the Jews." Latin represented the political sphere; Greek—the intellectual sphere of the Gentile world of that day; whereas Hebrew represented the Jewish people. Thus the religious leaders of the Jewish world and the political and intellectual representatives of the Gentile world joined hands in placing Jesus on the cross. But Hebrew is also the language of the Old Testament, the Hebrew Bible, in which in centuries past Jehovah of biblical revelation spelled out His redemptive purpose for the world. Back of the combined efforts of Jews and Gentiles in the crucifixion of Jesus there was the hand of God who used man's willfulness and human failure in order to save mankind from himself. For He who was nailed to the cross is none other than the Son of God, the Son of David, the Son of Abraham, the Son of Man.

> For truly in this city [of Jerusalem] there were gathered together against Thy holy servant Jesus, whom Thou didst anoint, both Herod and Pontius Pilate, along with the Gentiles and the peoples of Israel, to do whatever Thy hand and Thy purpose predestined to occur.
>
> [Acts 4:27-28]

46 The Meaning of the Death of Messiah Jesus

Mark Malbert was a first generation Hebrew Christian. A graduate of Kings College in London, he was ordained into the Anglican ministry.

As the story of Calvary is not a philosophy that appeals to the human intellect, but a revelation of the depth of human sin, and the height of God's compassion and love, I am constrained to take a passage from the inspired Apostle upon which to build my discourse. This passage you will find in First Corinthians 1 18-25. "For the preaching of the cross is to them that perish foolishness; but unto us which are saved it is the power of God. . . . For after that in the wisdom of God, the world by wisdom knew not God, it pleased God by the foolishness of preaching to save them that believe. For the Jews require a sign and the Greeks seek after wisdom. But we preach Christ crucified, unto the Jews a stumbling-block, and unto the Greeks foolishness; but unto them which are called, both Jews and Greeks, Christ the power of God and the wisdom of God. Because the foolishness of God is wiser than men; and the weakness of God is stronger than men."

Dr. James Moffatt translates it thus: "And to preach it [i.e., the Gospel] with no fine rhetoric, lest the cross of Christ should lose its power! Those who are doomed to perish find the story of the cross sheer folly, but it means the power of God for those whom He saves.

". . . Has not God stultified the wisdom of the world? For when the world with all its wisdom failed to know God in His wisdom, God resolved to save believers by the 'sheer folly' of the Christian message. Jews demand miracles and Greeks want wisdom, but our message is Christ the crucified—a stumbling-block to the Jews, 'sheer folly' to Gentiles, but for those who are called, whether Jews or Greeks, a Christ who is the power of God and the wisdom of God. For the 'foolishness' of God is wiser than men, and the 'weakness' of God is stronger than men."

The message of Calvary was never meant to convince the human intellect. Only the person who has received spiritual enlightenment, the heart that has realised the change wrought by the Holy Spirit, can understand the meaning of the Cross.

In the age in which we live the Cross is certainly regarded as foolishness. We certainly live in an age of culture, in an age of great discoveries. I, however, deny

"The Meaning of the Death of Messiah Jesus" appeared as "Calvary Made Sin for Us" in *The Hebrew Christian* 5, no. 2 (July 1932):72-76, and is reprinted by permission.

that we live in an age of greater wisdom. It is true that in our day and generation many laws which govern the powers of Nature are being discovered; but those laws have been inherent in matter since the creation of the world; and there are still millions of other laws inherent in the material universe which have not been, nor ever will be, discovered by men. But these discoveries tend towards the materialization of the mind, and breed conceit, especially in those who have no share in them. This age therefore sets up for itself a strange god, namely the human intellect, which is worshipped instead of the true God, the God of wisdom. And the worshippers of this strange god call themselves Modernists.

But materialism is not modern. It is as old as burglary. It cannot claim any originality. It may assume a different dress; it may assume a different name; but it is the same old sharp-pointed thorn. When Paul went about preaching the cross he met Modernism on all hands. His doctrine must have struck the cultured Greek and Roman as the very quintessence of absurdity. To tell them that the death of a man by crucifixion for sedition in the time of Tiberius was the means of the salvation of mankind, must have seemed to the then cultured world not only ridiculous, but sheer madness. Festus was a type of Roman intellectualism, and he certainly expressed the feelings of his class, when he declared his opinion of St. Paul's madness (Acts 26:24).

Yet if there is no meaning in the cross of Calvary, except as Modernists declare, as a mere example, the Biblical Messianic faith must disappear from the stage of the world, and leave a void in the human heart. The storms of life will never be hushed; there will be no balm to the wounds of life; no solace to the broken heart; no staff for the depressed and sad to lean upon. Nothing will remain for mankind but a desolate void; there will be no pilot to steer the ship of life, nor any hope for the future. Sin and its miseries will be gnawing in the soul, and there will be no antidote. There will be little comfort to the despairing heart with a sin-stricken conscience to tell it that in millions of years there will be no more sin, as man will then have evolved from the monkey stage. As a matter of fact, without the Cross there will be a cultured monkey-stage, something like the racketeer class of America, or Communist Russia, using all its mechanism for destruction. It will be a cultured barbarism which the world has never seen since the light of history.*

The facts of the Cross of Calvary move the world nearer and nearer to the great goal for which every child of God longs, when the knowledge of the Lord shall cover the earth as the waters cover the sea, when the kingdoms of this world shall become the kingdoms of the Lord and His Christ; when swords shall be beaten into ploughshares, and spears into pruning hooks; and nation shall not lift sword against nation any more . . . If the Death on Calvary was not an atonement and expiation, a reconciliation and a propitiation, it logically follows that the Resurrection is a fable. If that were so, what have we left? There might be an ethical teaching without the power to practise it—a beautiful motor car without the petrol within, nor any mind at the wheel to direct it. Eliminate the aim and object of the New Testament, namely, the salvation of mankind through the death and resurrection of Christ, and

*This statement was made in 1932, before the world witnessed the full scope of the horrors of Communist and Nazi totalitarianism.—EDITOR

it would be reduced either to the status of fragments of a modern novel, or quite meaningless. St. Paul is quite clear on this point—and I would rather believe St. Paul, who suffered much for the facts revealed to him by Heaven; and he was not ashamed to proclaim them and endure hardship, persecution, and death for them, because he was sure that they were facts. He is very deliberate on these fundamentals. He writes:—"If Christ hath not been raised, then is our preaching vain, your faith also, is vain . . . ye are yet in your sins" [1 Cor. 15:14, 17, RV]. According to the great Apostle of the Gentiles, if the Resurrection is not true, then Christ died in vain, and the whole fabric of the Biblical Messianic faith, therefore, must collapse.

Our Holy Faith rests not only on sentiment and emotion, but also on the firm foundation of strong evidence. The disciples of Jesus were simple, but hard-headed folk. They sacrificed everything that life was worth living for, and life itself, for this Gospel of the Cross. I, therefore, prefer to believe these unselfish and honest men, rather than the Higher Critical schools, which, as Etocles and Polynices, sons of Oesipus, are dying in their rivalry.

Now the question may be asked, how is it that an execution by which slaves and malefactors ended their lives, should become the central argument of God to mankind? That cruel and savage execution by the cross was common in the Roman Empire. Wherever man travelled he was met by the horrid and vile sight of human beings writhing on a cross. After the fall of Jerusalem thousands of Jews were crucified, yet not one of their names has come down to us as a benefactor. Let us take even Peter, the first preacher of the Atoning Death of Christ; he was like His Master crucified. Why has not the death of Peter, then, affected the world's history, religion, and civilisation even as his Master's has? No one ever died for Peter, no one ever died for Paul, whose life was the most unique life ever lived by any man. It was a life full of pathos endured for the cause of the Cross of Calvary. Eventually that life was ended by decapitation on the Appian Way. Have the sufferings of Paul stirred the hearts of mankind as those of his Lord? When we read of them in the Acts and the Epistles they only seem a matter of course.

Some years ago the great Russian painter, Vereshchagin, exhibited some paintings in three pictures hung side by side. One was of a Russian Nihilist being executed by hanging after midnight in a thick snowstorm. Another was of several wretched sepoys of the Mutiny of 1857, writhing helplessly, and in terror, as they stood chained to the muzzle of the guns, the discharge of which was to execute the sentence upon their revolt. The third was the Crucifixion of Jesus. The first two were heart-stirring, but the third picture had an inexplicable effect upon the mind. You will notice as you read the New Testament that it is never the intention of the writers to move the feelings to pity for Christ's sufferings, but rather to show in them our own degradation and God's infinite love. "He is despised and rejected of men; a man of sorrows, and acquainted with grief: and we hid as it were our faces from him; he was despised, and we esteemed him not. Surely he hath borne our griefs and carried our sorrows: yet we did esteem him stricken, smitten of God, and afflicted. But he was wounded for our transgressions, he was bruised for our iniquities: the chastisement of our peace was upon him; and with his stripes we are healed" (Isaiah 53:3-5).

If the Cross of Calvary had not been the revelation of God's love to mankind, Christianity would have perished in its infancy. For not only was the Jewish world waging war against it, but the whole Roman Empire was arrayed against it. Everything seemed to conspire to make its progress utterly impossible. Its origin was not attractive from the world's point of view. It was but a despised Jewish sect. Its advocates and followers had nothing engaging about them. They belonged for the most part to the lower and uneducated classes. Its doctrine was a "stumbling-block"; it appeared a most vexatious "foolishness." The heathen regarded the Christians as atheists, for they used no images of their God. The mysterious rites of the Holy Communion were suspected as secret orgies. The worst and most immoral conduct was attributed to the Christians. Public opinion was prejudiced against them. Philosophy assailed Christianity with its intellectual weapons, whilst the authorities opposed it with brute force. Tacitus asserted that Christianity was widely diffused as early as the reign of Nero (Ann. xv. 44). Nor did it avail to arrest its progress, that Nero, in order to divert from himself the guilt of the great conflagration of Rome, executed vast numbers of Christians not because, as Tacitus admits, they were guilty of this crime, but because they were hated of the whole human race; nevertheless, Christianity continued to spread.

An interesting letter of the younger Pliny, Governor of Bithynia, to his friend the Emperor Trajan, written about seventy years after the execution of Christ, is still extant, distinctly portraying the state of the Christian cause at the time in the place which had been the scene of St. Paul's and St. John's ministries. Pliny in his Epp. v. 97 writes:—"This superstition has spread on all sides, in towns, in villages, and in the country; the temples of our gods stand deserted, and sacrifices have now for a long time ceased to be offered. I arrested a few girls called deaconesses, and put them to the torture, and discovered nothing besides excessive and pernicious superstition." A century later, Tertullian in his Apology (c. 37) could say to the heathen,"We are but of yesterday, and yet we have taken possession of your whole country—towns, islands, the camp, the palaces, the Senate, the Forum: we have left you only the temples." Nor could the ten fierce persecutions ever hanging over the Christians arrest the triumph of their faith. Those persecutions spared neither age nor sex; all the strength of the Empire was put into requisition. Certain emperors especially considered it their duty to root out Christianity from the face of the earth, deeming that the very existence of the Empire depended on its extirpation. But the arm of the executioner failed, and Calvary triumphed. The Cross conquered scorn and hatred, because the death of Christ was the manifestation of the love of God, and all the weapons lifted up against those who reflected it failed.

Heine puts it thus:—"While the gods of Greece were assembled at the feast of the immortals, and Hebe [the goddess of youth in Greek mythology] tripped round with her goblets of pleasant nectar, the infinite laughter ran round the happy banqueting board, and the feast was in its fullest, the music at its sweetest, suddenly there came gasping towards them a pale Jew, dripping with blood, a crown of thorns on His head, bearing a great cross of wood on His shoulders; and He cast the cross on the high table of the gods, and the golden goblets trembled and fell, and the gods grew dumb and pale, and ever paler, till they melted in utter mist."

What Heine puts in poetic language we, who are Christ's, have experienced in our own soul. When the gods of pleasure, the gods of our imagination, were controlling our lives, Christ came into our hearts with His great sacrifice on the Cross by which our sins have been removed as far as the east is from the west, and they melted into mist. "His own self bare our sins in his own body on the tree." I prefer "the foolishness" of God to "the wisdom" of men. I admire the attractive philosophy of Athens, but that philosophy has no power to save my soul. The repulsive sacrifice on Calvary reveals to me the infinite beauty of God's love.

47 The Mediator Element in the Messianic Hope

Aaron Judah Kligerman was born and raised in Czarist Russia. At thirteen he entered a Talmudical school. However, stirred by the revolutionary ideas propagated by Russian university students, at seventeen he terminated his studies. He subsequently met a Hebrew Christian from whom he received a New Testament.

After emigrating to America, young Kligerman arrived at a definite decision about the Messiahship of Jesus. He spent one year at Moody Bible Institute; he then transferred to Dubuque University.

Dr. Kligerman became deeply involved in the Hebrew Christian movement both in America and abroad. He was president of the Hebrew Christian Alliance of America and president of the International Hebrew Christian Alliance. For many years he was editor of the American Hebrew Christian.

Mediation in the Bible is conceived of as referring to the "method by which God and man are reconciled through the instrumentality of some intervening process, act or person." From man's standpoint, the idea of mediation stems from "a profound human instinct or need which finds expression in some form or other in most religions."[1] That need springs from a conviction in the human heart of the impassable gulf that separates God from man and the necessity of bridging that gulf. Intercession is one aspect of mediation.

ABRAHAM

It is deeply significant that the element of mediation appears in the story of Abraham, at the very beginning of the biblical faith. Abraham was led of God to leave kin and country and settle in the land of Canaan. The reason for God's call of Abraham was to reach through him and his descendants all nations of the earth with God's redemptive message (Genesis 12:3). When Abraham started out for the land of Canaan, he took with him his nephew Lot and Lot's family. Some time after they had settled in Canaan, Lot separated himself from Abraham and took up residence

Aaron J. Kligerman's original article has been revised and expanded by Arthur W. Kac.

in Sodom, a prosperous but morally corrupt city. When Sodom's corruption had reached a point of no return, God determined to destroy it.

The biblical record informs us that shortly before the destruction of Sodom, Abraham received an advance divine communication of what was soon to happen. Abraham lived in the vicinity of Sodom, and had he not been informed beforehand, he would have accepted its destruction as an accident or a natural cataclysm. The purpose God had in mind in communicating to Abraham that advance information was to enable Abraham and his descendants, through the Sodom catastrophe, to gain a deeper insight into the need for and nature of the mission to which he was divinely appointed, as may be seen from the following statement:

> The LORD said: "Shall I hide from Abraham what I am about to do, seeing that Abraham shall become a great and mighty nation, and all nations of the earth shall be blessed through him? No, for I have chosen him that he may charge his children and his household after him to keep the way of the LORD by doing righteousness and justice: so that the LORD may bring to Abraham what he had promised him."
>
> [Genesis 18: 17-19]

"The LORD said," at the beginning of the above passage, refers to the leader among three angelic messengers, who directed the above statement to his angelic companions.

Abraham's reaction to the advance divine disclosure fully justified God's action. Undoubtedly Abraham was well acquainted with the immoral state of Sodom, and normally his response might have been: "It serves them right." But the presence of Lot and his family in the city made Abraham deeply anxious about Sodom's fate. That unquestionably prompted Abraham to intercede with God on behalf of the doomed cities. He was troubled about certain questions that have retained their relevance to the present day, namely, Can a minority of godly people save a civilization in decay? and, If an immoral society is destined for destruction, what will become of its godly remnant? Those were two of the agonizing issues with which Abraham wrestled in his intercessory prayer. Thus mediation and intercession by the godly and righteous on behalf of the ungodly and wicked were stamped on the biblical faith from the beginning.

MOSES

Moses was the first mediator between God and Israel. In Moses, the biblical concept of mediation found its greatest historical expression in the Old Testament period. Moses was the mediator of the Sinai covenant. His mediatorial function began with the promulgation of the Decalogue as seen from the following passage:

> Now when all the people perceived the thunderings and the lightnings and the sound of the trumpet and the mountain smoking, the people were afraid and troubled and said to Moses, "You speak to us, and we will hear; but let not God speak to us, lest we die."
>
> [Exodus 20:18-19]

214

The incident is recorded in greater detail in Deuteronomy on the occasion when Moses reviewed before the Israelites God's gracious dealings with them during the forty years of wanderings in the wilderness.

> These words[2] the LORD spoke to all your assembly at the mountain out of the midst of the fire, the cloud, and the thick darkness, with a loud voice; and he added no more; and he wrote them on two tables of stone, and gave them to me. And when you heard the voice out of the midst of the darkness, while the mountain was burning with fire, you came near to me, all the heads of your tribes, and your elders. And you said, "Behold, the LORD our God has shown us his glory and greatness, and we have heard his voice out of the midst of the fire; we have this day seen God speak with man and man still live. Now therefore why should we die? For this great fire shall consume us; if we hear the voice of the LORD our God any more, we shall die. For who is there of all flesh, that has heard the voice of the living God speaking out of the midst of fire, as we have, and has still lived? Go near, and hear all that the LORD our God will say; and speak to us all that the LORD our God will speak to you; and we will hear and do it."
>
> And the LORD heard your words, when you spoke to me; and the LORD said to me, "I have heard the words of this people which they have spoken to you; they have rightly said all that they have spoken. Oh, that they had such a mind as this always, to fear me and to keep all my commandments, that it might go well with them and with their children for ever!"
>
> [Deuteronomy 5:22-29]

From the above we see that in the Old Testament period man's need of a mediator was attested by God Himself.

A mediator incorporates three functions: that of king, prophet, and priest. As a king, or ruler, he dispenses justice; as a prophet, he brings God's Word to man; as a priest, he brings man near to God. In the Old Testament period man was brought to God by means of sacrifice; the general Old Testament term for sacrifice is *korban,* a term related to a Hebrew word meaning "to bring close, to come near."

Moses was an uncrowned king. He exercised more power over Israel than any king in Israel's history.

The uniqueness of Moses' position as a prophet is spelled out in the following passage:

> And he [God] said, "Hear my words: If there is a prophet among you, I the LORD make myself known to him in a vision, I speak with him in a dream. Not so with my servant Moses; he is entrusted with all my house.[3] With him I speak mouth to mouth, clearly, and not in dark speech; and he beholds the form of the LORD."
>
> [Numbers 12:6-8a, RSV]

Through this utterance on the part of Jehovah, Moses is placed above all the prophets in relation to God and also to the whole nation. The divine revelation to the prophets is thereby restricted to the two forms of inward intuition (vision and dream). The prophets were consequently simply organs through whom Jehovah made known His counsel and will at certain times, and in relation to special circumstances and features in the development of His Kingdom. It was not so with Moses. Jehovah had placed him over all His house, had called him to be the founder and organizer of the Kingdom established in Israel through his mediatorial service and had found him faithful in his service. With this servant of His, He spoke mouth to mouth without a figure or figurative cloak, with the distinctness of human interchange of thought; so that at any time he could inquire of God and wait for the divine reply. Hence, Moses was not a prophet of Jehovah, like many others, but stood above all the prophets, as the founder of the theocracy, and mediator of the Old Covenant.[4]

As the great mediator, Moses discharged also the functions of a priest. The Sinai covenant was concluded by means of a sacrifice, and it was Moses who presided over the sacrifice ritual (Exodus 24:4-8). In due time he delegated the priestly function to his brother, Aaron, and the priesthood became hereditary in the Aaronic family. But it was Moses, not Aaron, who had direct and permanent access to God. When during his long stay on Mount Sinai the Israelites committed the golden calf sin, and when God was contemplating destroying the people, it was Moses who, as their mediator and great priest, pleaded with God for forgiveness. After putting about three thousand Israelites to death, he said to the people, "You have sinned a great sin; and now I will go up to the LORD; perhaps I can make atonement for your sin" (Exodus 32:30).

In his confrontation with the Lord, Moses offered his own life as an atonement. As it happened, God had His own reason for not accepting Moses' offer, but we have here in the Old Testament the germ idea of vicarious suffering.

MOSES PREFIGURED THE FUTURE MEDIATOR

In one of his last addresses to the people of Israel at the end of their sojourn in the wilderness, Moses said to them:

> The LORD your God will raise up for you a prophet like me from among you, from your brethren; him you shall heed. Just as you desired of the LORD your God at Horeb[5] on the day of the assembly, when you said, "Let me not hear again the voice of the LORD my God, or see this great fire any more, lest I die." And the LORD said to me, "They have rightly said all they have spoken. I will raise up for them a prophet like you from among their brethren; and I will put my words in his mouth, and he shall speak to them all that I command him. And whoever will not give heed to my words which he shall speak in my name, I myself will require it of him."
>
> [Deuteronomy 18:15-19]

Although the context of the above statement obliges us to say that it had no immediate reference to the Messiah, in the foreknowledge of God, who delivered that message to Moses, no such prophet like unto Moses was to arise until the advent of the Messiah. Like Moses, Messiah was to be a ruler, a prophet, and a priest. Beginning with the Shiloh prophecy in Genesis 49:1, 10, He is represented throughout the Old Testament as a king, a descendant of the royal house of David.

In two great Messianic chapters, Isaiah 11 and 42, He appears as a prophet anointed with the Spirit of God.

> There shall come forth a twig out of the stump of Jesse, and a shoot from its roots shall bring forth fruit. And the Spirit of the LORD shall rest upon him, the spirit of wisdom and understanding, the spirit of counsel and might, the spirit of knowledge and the fear of the LORD.
>
> [Isaiah 11:1-2]

> Behold my servant, whom I uphold, mine elect in whom my soul delights; I have put my Spirit upon him; he will bring forth judgment to the nations. He will not cry nor lift up, nor cause his voice to be heard in the street. A bruised reed he will not break, and a glimmering wick he will not quench; he shall bring forth judgment according to truth. He shall not fail nor be broken, till he has established right upon earth, and the islands shall wait for his teaching.
>
> [Isaiah 42:1-4]

Like Moses, that future prophet will also be a priest, as seen from the following statement by King David.

> Jehovah said unto my Lord, "Sit thou at my right hand, until I make your enemies your footstool." . . . Jehovah has sworn and will not change his mind, "You are a priest for ever after the order of Melchizedek."
>
> [Psalm 110:1, 4]

Like Moses, the Second Moses will also be the mediator of a covenant.

> I, Jehovah, have called you in righteousness,[6] and I have taken hold of your hand, and I have kept you, and have appointed you for a covenant of the people[7] and for a light of the nations.
>
> [Isaiah 42:6]

The covenant that the Second Moses will conclude will not be another Sinai covenant; it will be a new covenant (Jeremiah 31:31-34 [Heb., 31:30-33]).

As the Sinai covenant was made by means of a sacrifice, the new covenant will also be initiated with a sacrifice. But whereas Moses in his priestly capacity presided over the sacrificial ritual, Messiah, the Second Moses, will seal the new covenant with His own blood.

> Surely our diseases he did bear, and our pains he carried; whereas we did esteem him stricken, smitten of God, and afflicted. But he was

wounded because of our transgressions, he was crushed because of our inquities; the chastisement of our welfare was upon him; and with his stripes we were healed. All we like sheep did go astray, we turned every one to his own way, and the LORD has made to light on him the iniquity of us all.

[Isaiah 53:4-6]

The book of Deuteronomy concludes with the following statement: "And there has not arisen since in Israel a prophet like Moses whom the LORD knew face to face" (Deuteronomy 34:10).

That statement might just as well have been appended to the last page of the Old Testament. No prophet like unto Moses arose during the Old Testament period.

But something happened in the upper room in Jerusalem where Jesus and the apostles had assembled to celebrate the Passover, as seen from the following:

As they were eating, Jesus took some bread, and after a blessing, he broke it and gave it to the disciples and said, "Take, eat, this is my body." And he took a cup and gave thanks, and gave it to them, saying, "Drink from it, all of you. For this is my blood of the covenant, which is to be shed on behalf of many for forgiveness of sins."

[Matthew 26:26-28]

And having taken some bread, when he had given thanks, he broke it, and gave it to them, saying, "This is my body which is given for you; do this in remembrance of me." And in the same way he took the cup after they had eaten, saying, "This cup which is poured out for you is the new covenant in my blood."

[Luke 22:19-20]

Some thirty years later the Jerusalem Temple was destroyed, and the sacrificial system of the Sinai covenant ceased.

THE MEDIATOR BELIEF IN RABBINIC JUDAISM

The belief in mediation holds a prominent place in rabbinic Judaism as reflected in the rabbinic literature and especially in the Prayer Book. Forgiveness, divine favors, and redemption are earnestly sought on the basis of the merits of the fathers, the death of the martyrs, and the death of the righteous, as seen, for example, in the following prayers:

"Our Father, our King, for the sake of our fathers who trusted in Thee and whom Thous didst teach the statutes of life, so mayest Thou be gracious unto us and teach us.[8]

"In Thee do they trust, Thou Shield of their fathers, upon whose merit they rely."[9]

"May your merits, and your perfect life assist us in our needs and protect us in times of trouble. Increase you also your prayers to the Lord our God, that He, through His infinite mercy and His abundant loving kindness and for the sake of our

218

holy fathers, and for the sake of our pious ones who have fulfilled His will, may have compassion, pity and mercy upon us."[10]

As we have seen from the preceding discussion, the mediator concept emerged at the very beginning of Israel's faith. There was a collective realization on the part of the people, standing at the foot of Mount Sinai, of man's essential inability to confront God directly. That that awareness was not a fleeting and aberrant phenomenon may be seen from the experience of the great prophet Isaiah centuries later when he saw in the Temple a vision of the holiness of God. "Woe is me! for I am undone," he cried out, "because I am a man of unclean lips, and I dwell in the midst of a people of unclean lips; for mine eyes have seen the King, the LORD of hosts" (Isaiah 6:5).

As is the case with so many Old Testament truths, it is in the New Testament that the concept of mediation receives its full elucidation. As Messiah Jesus and His disciples were seated around the table in the upper room celebrating the last Passover before He was delivered to the religious authorities, the disciples heard from the lips of their Master some of the most profound truths recorded in the New Testament. At one point during that Passover "table talk," one of his disciples, Philip, said to Him: "Lord show us the Father and we will be satisfied" (John 14:8). In utter amazement, Jesus said to him, "Have I been so long with you, and yet you have not come to know me, Philip? He who has seen me has seen the Father; how [then] do you say, 'Show us the Father?' " (John 14:9).

The apostle John, who sat next to Messiah Jesus at the table, listened attentively to what was being said, and what he saw and heard during that fateful night made an indelible impression on his heart. Years later, when he sat down to write his gospel, he remembered what Jesus had said to Philip, and John wrote: "No man has seen God at any time; the only begotten Son, who is in the bosom of the Father, he has declared him" (John 1:18).

No one has ever seen God. Jesus, the Son of God, He who is in the intimate presence of God, alone has made God known to us. The same thought is expressed in the following words recorded in the gospel of Matthew: "No one knows the Son except the Father; nor does any one know the Father except the Son and he to whom the Son wills to reveal him" (Matthew 11:27).

The above two passages summarize the reason for the biblical concept of the Mediator. On this side of heaven it is not possible to know God fully. But all we need to know about God, all that has a vital bearing on our human destiny, has been revealed to us by Messiah Jesus. That, because He is the Son of God, and because in Him God became flesh and dwelt in our midst (John 1:14).

Notes

1. D. M. Edwards, "Mediation," in *The International Standard Bible Encyclopedia*, edited by James Orr (Grand Rapids: Eerdmans, 1939), 3:2018.
2. The Ten Commandments.
3. This wording in the Revised Standard Version is a good rendering of the meaning of the Hebrew text.
4. C. F. Keil and Franz Delitzsch, *Old Testament Commentaries* (Grand Rapids: Associated Publishers and Authors, n.d.), pp. 813-14. See note on Numbers 12:6-8.
5. Mount Sinai.
6. "In righteousness" here means in accordance with God's redemptive purpose.
7. I.e., Israel.
8. One of the morning prayers, beginning with the words, "With a great love Thou didst love us."
9. From the morning prayer on the Day of Atonement, beginning with the words, "Thou didst make the tenth day . . ."
10. A prayer recited upon visiting the graves.

48 The Cross in Jewish Experience

*Nathan J. Stone was born in London and attended a
Talmud Torah school there. When he was eighteen he
emigrated to Canada, settling in Winnipeg in 1915. There,
in 1920, he became a believer in the Messiahship of Jesus.
From 1922 to 1925 he was enrolled in the Jewish studies
program at Moody Bible Institute. He later earned the
Bachelor of Divinity and Master of Theology degrees at the
Presbyterian Theological Seminary in Louisville, Kentucky.
In 1940 he assumed the professorship of the Jewish Studies
Department at Moody Bible Institute.*

A well known volume of sermons on the Cross entitled "The Cross in
Christian Experience" suggested to the writer the thought of "The Cross in Jewish
Experience" and indeed the Cross has played a large part in the experiences of the
Jewish people.

To the unbiased reader reading the Bible through for the first time, as he might
any other book, it would be obvious that the Bible is a unity, that there is one
underlying purpose running through it all. Malachi is an unfinished book. "Behold,
I will send my messenger, and he shall prepare the way before me; and the Lord,
whom ye seek, shall suddenly come to his temple, even the messenger of the
covenant, whom ye delight in: behold, he shall come, saith the LORD of hosts"
(Mal. 3:1). It is equally evident that the book of Matthew looks back, taking up
where Malachi left off. In the person of John the Immerser there is a partial
fulfillment of the messenger who was to prepare the way, as spoken of by Malachi
and other prophets of the Old Testament.

The Old Testament, therefore, is an incomplete book. A Jewish writer of note,
John Cournos, some years ago spoke of Judaism as a house without a roof and of the
New Testament as the crown and the consummation of the Old.

Dr. Stone's article is reprinted from Nathan J. Stone, The Cross in Jewish Experience," *The Hebrew
Christian Alliance Quarterly* 32, no. 1 (Spring 1946):3-8

I

The Old Testament

The highest peak of a chain of mountains is generally visible from every point of the horizon. This is true of the Cross of Jesus Christ in the Bible. It is the great peak of God's revelation of Himself to His creatures. It may be seen from any point in the Bible, as from the first pages in the book of Genesis in the Old Testament it rises gradually till it becomes a sublime and majestic peak at Calvary in the New.

When God spoke to the serpent in the Garden of Eden and said that the seed of the woman would crush his seed, and that the seed of the serpent would bruise the heel of the woman's seed, He was already beginning to point to that day of Christ of Calvary where all this was accomplished. Here the great transaction of Calvary in the Cross was already predicted from the very beginning, where from the low ground of man's sin and fall began the gradual rise toward the consummation of God's purpose in Messiah. It is common knowledge that the Targums in their paraphrase of Genesis 3:15 refer it to the day of Messiah.

Another peak in the range of God's purpose rises even more clearly as set forth in the great transaction spoken in Genesis 22, a passage familiar and dear to the Jewish heart, and repeated in the synagogue today. Of that great incident which so clearly speaks of Messiah in the person of Isaac, willing and ready to be sacrificed upon the altar, our Lord Jesus Christ said of Abraham that he saw His day and was glad. Mount Moriah means the mountain of provision, the provision of that Lamb of God which should take away the sin of the world. Abraham clearly realized that in God's dealings with him.

There is a particularly striking incident in Israel's experience in the wilderness which is also highly suggestive of this great event yet to be. Israel had sinned again in rebelling against the Lord, and the Lord had sent among them fiery serpents whose bite meant death. When Moses prayed for the people, the Lord instructed him to set up the image of a fiery serpent upon a pole or standard upon which, if the people should look, they would be healed. Was that not another peak from which Calvary could be glimpsed, where Christ became sin for us and was judged for and suffered the penalty of our sins! As in the days of old, those who looked in faith believing were saved from the death of the serpent's sting, so today we, who look in faith believing, are saved from the guilt and penalty of our sins in its eternal consequences.

Surely the twenty-second Psalm with its clear and unmistakable description of one crucified is an experience which could never have been that of the writer in his day. How minutely it fits the scene of the Cross at Calvary!

Then there is that loftiest of all peaks of Messianic prediction in the Old Testament, the fifty-third chapter of Isaiah. What a clear and remarkable picture of One who was to be a sacrifice for the sins of the people, who was to rise again in victory over death, to be an intercessor and to be a King in triumph and glory! What a pity that this portion is no longer read in the synagogue, while chapters 52 and 54 are read. Surely this is significant and indicative both of Israel's perplexity and troubled conscience over this passage.

Early in the Old Testament we are given an intimation of this mode of punishment for sin,—not in the form of crucifixion, to be sure, but, as hanging upon a tree. The mode is essentially the same; it is hanging, and particularly represents the curse of God upon sin. "If a man have committed a sin worthy of death . . . and thou hang him on a tree . . . for he that is hanged is accursed of God (margin, 'the curse of God')," Deut. 21:22-23 [RV]. So "Christ redeemed us from the curse of the law, having become a curse for us: for it is written, 'Cursed is every one that hangeth on a tree' " (Gal. 3:13, R.V.). And Galatians 3:10, quoting Deuteronomy 27:26, shows clearly that all under the law are under this curse and that, therefore, the curse must rest on some One who could bear it in our behalf to redeem us from it.

There is that well-known ceremony still practiced in connection with the Day of Atonement, in which a fowl is slaughtered and its blood shed as an atonement for sin. But why is a fowl used? It is, of course, the most convenient creature for such a purpose. But in Talmudic Hebrew the word for fowl is *gever*. A Hebrew name for man is also *gever*. Whoever sins must pay the penalty for sin. Since the man, *gever*, doesn't want to die, the fowl, *gever*, dies as substitute, so that *gever* dies after all. This is not only a striking acknowledgement of the need of atonement but also of the truth of Hebrews 10:4, that it is impossible that the blood of bulls and goats should take away sin. An infinitely more worthy sacrifice must atone for man's sins. And this was accomplished on the Cross in that hanging there of *The Man*, Christ Jesus, who in Zechariah 13:7, acknowledged by great Jewish commentators to be Messianic, is called *Gever*.

II

ISRAEL'S FAILURE TO RECOGNIZE MESSIAH JESUS

Why, then, could not Israel recognize Messiah when He came in view of all this chain of prediction which spoke so unmistakably concerning Him?

(1) It is because in the first place Israel turned its back upon God and rejected Him. Speaking through the prophet Samuel (I Samuel 8:7), He said of Israel, "They have not rejected thee, but they have rejected me, that I should not reign over them." How tragic are the words of the Psalmist (81:11), "But my people would not hearken to my voice; and Israel would have none of me." Thus He gave them up to their own hearts' lust and they walked in their own counsels till, as Hosea says, "He cast them out." "All day long," says the prophet, "have I spread out my hands to a rebellious people" (Isaiah 65:2).

Israel certainly understood God as a father. In that wonderful chapter of sorrowing reminiscence and plea on Israel's part, Isaiah 63, they say, "For thou art our father, though Abraham knoweth us not, and Israel doth not acknowledge us: thou, O LORD, art our father; our redeemer from everlasting is thy name" (v. 16 R.V.). In Malachi 1:6 we find Jehovah saying, "A son honoreth his father . . . if then I be a father, where is mine honor?" [RV]. So Israel dishonored and *rejected* the Father.

(2) But Israel also *resisted* the Holy Spirit. In that remarkable passage, Isaiah 63:8-10, which so strikingly sets forth Father, Son, and Holy Spirit, a Trinity in the Godhead, we read, "But they rebelled, and grieved his holy spirit" [RV]. So

Stephen accuses them in Acts 7:51: "Ye stiffnecked and uncircumcised in heart and ears, ye do always resist the Holy Ghost: as your fathers did, so do ye."

(3) Having, therefore, *rejected* God the Father; and having *resisted* God the Holy Spirit, it is no wonder that they failed to recognize and *refused* God the Son in spite of the many signs, increasingly fuller and clearer as time went on, of the nature of the Coming One, the Purpose of His Coming and the Manner in which He should accomplish it, even the Cross.

The stone which Jehovah laid in Zion for a foundation, that tried stone, that precious cornerstone of sure foundation (Isa. 28:16) which it was also predicted should be a stone of stumbling and a rock of offence to those who should stumble at it (Isa. 8:14), finally became the stone which the builders *rejected* (Psalm 118:22).

III

THE CHURCH AND ISRAEL

Was it not possible, however, that Israel could have seen the truth in the love of God manifested through the church? The Apostle Paul certainly hoped that such a manifestation could have provoked Israel to jealousy as he stated in Rom. 11:11. What a tragedy that the opposite was the case, and what a thing of horror the Cross came to be in Israel's history.

The first great church council of which history takes note, the Council of Nicea, in the fourth century, made a complete break with Jewry in many ways. Easter became fixed so as not to coincide with the Jewish Passover. The Roman emperor, who had merged church and state, expressed himself as desiring to have nothing in common with "the hated Jews." "We want to be free from any association with this people." Good Friday and Easter became to the Jews a time of shame and suffering at the hands of the church of those days. In the city of Toulouse, France, it was customary during that period to choose a person from the Jewish community to inflict a blow on him, the blow often resulting in death. At Beziers, in France, it became customary to have a stone throwing at the Jews on Palm Sunday to revenge Christ's shame. Permitted by the prince and blessed by the bishop, we may be sure it was very heartily performed. Jews dared not appear on the streets or outside their ghettos on those days, and such experiences have fixed themselves so indelibly on the Jewish mind in its attitude toward Christianity, that it remains with many even to this day.

A Jewish Rabbi, speaking some years ago over the radio said, "Speaking as a Jew, I ask you to believe me when I say that I know what the Cross has meant to believers through the centuries. I know that the simple and the learned, the grieving and the rejoicing, the toiling and the driven beheld in the Cross of Christ the symbol of a love that is sacrificial, the sign of a hope that is redeeming, the token of an inner peace, which the world could neither give nor take away. But I want you to know also that to a Jew the Cross of Christ represents no such sacrificial love, no such redeeming hope, no such inner token of peace. To the Jew the Cross is a symbol of persecution, opposition, discrimination, of pyre and gibbet. It is by the sign of the Cross that hundreds of Jewish communities were annihilated, thousands of Jews slaughtered, millions of Jews robbed of happiness, by those who failed to grasp the significance for Christians of that drama of which the Lenten season is the monitor and Easter Day the culmination."

IV

ISRAEL'S GLORY

Yet, in spite of all, the Cross became the glory of many Jews, even through these troublous times. To them it was, indeed, through the Christ upon it, the power of God unto salvation.

In becoming a follower of Christ and Cross, the Apostle Paul never ceased to be a Jew. In the Epistle to the Philippians, he still calls himself a Hebrew of the Hebrews, who had conformed to all its rites and practices. He had been a strict Pharisee with an unbounded zeal for the Law, but he found in Christ the fulfillment of all of which the Law spoke. In Him he found a new covenant, as foretold by the prophet Jeremiah. In Him he found a divine sacrifice of infinite merit so that the blood of bulls and of goats was no longer needed. In Him he found an eternal priest ever living to make intercession so that the priesthood after the order of Aaron was no longer necessary. In Christ he came to realize a circumcision of the heart spoken of by Ezekiel the prophet, which fulfilled that which the circumcision of the flesh represented. In the Cross he came to believe and to glory because it showed the true character of God: (1) it expressed His Holiness in His horror of sin; (2) it manifested His righteousness in His wrath over sin; (3) it revealed His love in His conquest of sin. It made him realize that the righteousness of man is not sufficient to find acceptance in the presence of God.

This had always been Israel's great error, who "being ignorant of God's righteousness, and going about to establish their own righteousness, have not submitted themselves unto the righteousness of God" (Rom. 10:3). And without Christ, who is "the end of the law for righteousness to everyone that believeth," there is no righteousness acceptable to God.

The apostle had much about which he could boast from the human standpoint, both as a zealous Pharisee and as the great apostle of the church, but he came to realize in Christ that God alone was the source and basis of religious life, and not man's efforts. It has been characteristic of Israel to boast in the self-righteousness of its merits and to trust in its own strength for its salvation. It has never yet learned the lesson of Jacob, its father, who was not permitted in the days of old to re-enter the land of Canaan in his own strength and sufficiency, because it was the land of promise and of God's gift, or Jacob would have boasted of his personal achievements as Israel has so frequently done. God must disable him first and make him realize that He would give as a gift and by grace that which man could never attain by his own strength and works. So Israel will have to come to grips with God as did Jacob, before the promises of God concerning Israel's land and Israel's restoration can come to pass.

In the Christ of the Cross Paul came to realize that God must be the object of his supreme desire. Israel today has no spiritual sustenance and strength because it has not made God the object of its supreme desire. And not having done this, it has sought the goods and the comforts of this world, the material things and the things of the flesh for its satisfaction; and how empty they have been!

It may be safely said that the example of Paul has been followed by hundreds of thousands of Jews through the ages since. Jewish authorities themselves are responsible for the statement that nearly a quarter of a million Jews became Christians during the nineteenth century. To be sure, Jewry claims that much of this was for social, and economic benefit and advantage, yet, when one realizes the imposing list of names of Jews who, as great scholars and ministers and preachers have added luster to the work of the church, one can only feel that by far the majority of those who came to be believers in our Lord Jesus Christ were genuine in their faith. Very recently Dr. Louis Finkelstein, president of the Jewish Theological Seminary of America, said that "the stream of conversion of Jews to other faiths 'has become a river' and the American Jewish community may be lost to a large extent in a generation or two."

Perhaps the day is not too far distant when Israel will say with the Apostle Paul, who in one sense is a type of Israel, "I count all things to be loss for the excellency of the knowledge of Christ Jesus my Lord: for whom I have suffered the loss of all things; and do count them but dung, that I may gain Christ" [RV]. Israel will eventually have to count all things but loss (and Israel truly lives for things in these days), but this will be gain, indeed, in comparison with knowing Jesus Christ and Him crucified upon the Cross as their Messiah and Saviour.

Life After Death

If a man die, shall he live again?
Job 14:14

In the fifteenth chapter of his first letter to the Corinthian Christians, the apostle Paul declared that if Jesus were not raised from the dead, the Christian message was worthless. How true! For if Jesus did not rise from the dead, then He was not the Son of God; and if He were not the Son of God, He may still have died for a worthy cause, but His death would not have had the redeeming value and power attributed to it in the New Testament. Moreover, if Jesus did not rise from the dead, man has no assurance of eternal life or a resurrection after death, and, consequently, human life has no purpose.

Was Jesus Raised from the Dead?—*Henry Cooper*   228
How People React to Death—*Arthur W. Kac*   234

49 Was Jesus Raised from the Dead?

Henry Cooper emigrated from Poland to England and there became a believer in the Messiahship of Jesus. An ordained Baptist clergyman, Mr. Cooper served churches in Yorkshire and the Isle of Man. He also functioned as deputation secretary for the International Hebrew Christian Alliance.

The Resurrection of Christ is the keystone in the arch of the New Testament faith. On it depends the validity of Christ's claims prior to the Crucifixion, and it alone is the adequate explanation of the rise and progress of the Christian Church. "If Christ be not risen," says Paul, "then is our preaching vain, and your faith is also vain."

Baur, the great rationalistic theologian, admits that, without the belief in Christ's resurrection of His early followers, Christianity could not have got started on its marvelous world conquering career. So he sets himself out to formulate no theory of how they came to believe in the Resurrection, but contents himself with describing very graphically the historical effects that belief had in the spreading of the faith. This attitude of Baur's is not due merely to prudential considerations. He was too daring a man to be silent for fear of offending. It was due mainly to his profound mistrust of all rational theories to account for Christ's Resurrection. To Baur those theories were dismal failures, and proved most unsatisfactory.

The difficulty of belief in Christ's Resurrection is only present in the minds of those who refuse to countenance the possibility of the miraculous altogether. They would imprison the Creator Himself within the laws of cause and effect as known to scientists so far—laws, that is, whose operation can be explained because they are capable of being tested and demonstrated by the whole gamut of the scientist's instruments. Curiously enough, the unalterable law of causation has been questioned lately, not by theologians, but by physicists, because of a further investigation into the mysterious atom. "The Universe seems to be playing ducks and drakes with us," said one of them lately.

To us, however, who believe that God transcends His creation and is free, within

"Was Jesus Raised from the Dead?" appeared as "The Power of His Resurrection" in *The Hebrew Christian 5,* no. 2 (July 1932):76-81, and is reprinted by permission of The International Hebrew Christian Alliance. The original article was not footnoted.

moral limits, there is no difficulty in believing that He can and does intervene by supernatural acts for man's highest good. Hence we hold that Christ's Resurrection was God's answer to man's treatment of the "Man of sorrows and acquainted with grief." They requited His spotless life, supreme love, matchless words, and gracious, miraculous deeds with a cross and a malefactor's death. And this same Jesus whom men put to death God raised up. That agonising cry of dereliction, "My God, My God, why hast Thou forsaken me?" was a question whose enigma lasted only from Good Friday till Easter Sunday morning. Then the solution of the enigma showed itself with mighty power. It said, in effect, "Endure as the sin-bearer, the Just for the unjust. Give thy life for the world's redemption. Let malice and wickedness do its worst, and God will demonstrate to eternity Thy conquest by bringing Thee back from the grave itself as Conqueror over death and hell." So He was "declared to be the Son of God with power, according to the spirit of holiness, by the resurrection from the dead." That declaration created the Church, completed its message of Salvation, and made it the good news of life and immortality. "If it be proved," says Dr. A. M. Fairbairn, "that no living Christ ever issued from the tomb of Joseph,* then the tomb becomes the grave not of a man, but of a religion, with all the hopes built on it, and all the splendid enthusiasm it has inspired." It is this main citadel that the enemies of the Christian faith have, with all their arts and crafts, sought to invade and destroy. With what success, if any, they have pursued their campaign, we must now briefly examine.

The earliest is recorded in Matthew xxviii. 2-15, namely, that the disciples stole the Body while the watch slept. This explanation is never now offered by men who value their reputation as honest seekers after truth. It is beset with so many pitfalls that only the ignorant street-corner man might venture to propound it. It is not in keeping with the timidity of the disciples as they are portrayed in the Gospels on the night of Christ's arrest. Even Peter was unnerved by the turn events had taken that night, and sooner than run further risks denied his Lord at the very moment when he should have stood by Him and defended Him. If that was their conduct when Christ was yet alive, how was it possible that these men should risk stealing the Body which was watched by a Roman guard? But supposing they did so. Would they not have buried the Body and escaped into hiding for fear of punishment? Instead of which, they preached the Resurrection in the very city where Christ had suffered; and defied the authorities who attempted to silence them. Here is Dr. Fairbairn's comment on this theory. "That a company of men could be confederate in evil for the purpose of good, that they could be throughout life a society of organised hypocrites without ever smiling to each other or letting the mask fall, that they could preach virtue or live virtuously with a damning lie on their consciences, that they could nurse their souls, most of all in the very face of death, in the hope of being with Christ for ever in blessedness, while aware that He was rotting in an unknown grave—are psychological impossibilities that any grave discussion on the matter would simply be absurd." I would only add that the martyrdom of Stephen and the impression it made upon Saul the Persecutor who became Paul the Apostle, would

*Joseph of Arimathea, a disciple of Jesus, a rich man, in whose new tomb Jesus laid after the crucifixion (Matt. 27:57-60).—EDITOR

be sufficient to condemn the theory of theft and false representation.

Nor does the attempt to explain Christ's Resurrection by supposing the Christians simply adopted the myth from the Phoenicians and their youthful deity Adonis, who was supposed to have been killed and raised from the dead, fare any better. It is true the Phoenicians observed days of mourning similar to our Good Friday, and joyous feasts of a resurrection similar to our Easter. But their mythological belief goes back to a vague and nebulous past, in keeping with all mythology, and cannot claim any historical basis, whereas the Christian faith is authentic history. All the elements so essential to the growth and acceptance of fables as truth are absent from the clear light of the Easter evangel. From the time of the Crucifixion to the time of the Resurrection and its proclamation on the spot, is only a matter of days and weeks, whereas it takes centuries to bring about the acceptance amongst a credulous people of a fabulous religious event. We might as well refuse to believe in aeroplanes because, long before the invention was brought about, a man wrote a book describing a trip to the moon. On the contrary, that book was only a happy anticipation of the possibility of travel by air. And the Adonis myth, too, was but the human craving for a divine proof of immortality. In due time that proof was actually given to mankind by the rising from the dead of the Son of God.

The other attempts at a rational explanation of the Resurrection are more subtle, and elaborated with a wealth of literary skill worthy of a loftier theme than the undermining of Christian faith. But, curiously enough, our task of refuting these scholarly sceptics is made comparatively light by the sceptics themselves. For each one of them who has a theory to propound adversely criticises his predecessor, and their mutual refutations work out like a cancelling in arithmetical fractions, the answer to which comes to one, and that is, Christ has risen indeed.

Take, for instance, the Apparent Death, or, as it is sometimes called, the Swoon theory advanced by Dr. Paulus, and countenanced by Schleiermacher. It runs thus:—Crucifixion, even when both hands and feet are pierced, causes little loss of blood, and kills only very slowly, by convulsions or by starvation. If, then, Jesus, believed to be dead, was taken down from the cross after some six hours, the supposed death may very well have been only a swoon, from which after lying in a cool cavern covered with healing ointments and strongly scented spices, He might readily recover. In support of this Josephus is invoked, who relates the recovery of one of three friends of his who were crucified.

But what about the piercing of His side with the unerring spear of a Roman soldier? This is not accounted for because it is in the fourth Gospel, which, according to this school, is not historical. Let this pass. Hear what Strauss has to say about this theory:—"It is impossible that a being who had been stolen half dead out of a sepulchre, who crept about weak and ill, wanting medical treatment, who required bandaging, strengthening, and indulgence, and who still at last yielded to His sufferings, could have given to His disciples the impression that He was a Conqueror over death and the grave, the Prince of Life, an impression which lay at the bottom of their future ministry." And much more in the same strain. So Strauss.

But Strauss himself has a theory. It is the same as that of Renan—the famous Vision Theory, propounded with a wealth of flowery language by Renan, a Frenchman, to the great credit of his ingenuity. "Enthusiasm and love," he says, "knows no situations without escape. They make sport of the impossible, and rather than renounce hope, they do violence to reality. Many words spoken by the Master could be interpreted in the sense that He would come forth from the tomb. Such a belief was, moreover, so natural that the faith of the disciples would have sufficed to create it. The great prophets Enoch and Elijah did not taste of death. That which happened to them must happen to Jesus. Death is so absurd when it strikes the man of genius or of a great heart, that people cannot believe in the possibility of such an error of Nature. Heroes do not die. That adored Master had filled the circle of which He was the centre with joy and hope. Could they be content to let Him rot in the tomb? To help matters, a rumour floated about concerning an empty tomb. Mary Magdalene was appropriately the first to have a vision. She stood by the Sepulchre weeping; she heard a light noise behind her. She turned; she saw a man standing, and asked Him where the Body was; she received for reply her own name, 'Mary.' It was the voice that so often made her tremble. It was the accent of Jesus. The miracle of love is accomplished. Mary has seen and heard Him; having visions will become infectious till it pass through the whole company of disciples."

Such is the Renan style of treatment—sentimental, theatrical, Parisian. The appearances of Jesus are the creation of excited nerves and ardent expectations. The slightest outward occasion, once Mary Magdalene created the miracle, acting on such susceptible subjects, will produce an apparition. During a moment of silence, some light air passes over the faces of the disciples assembled to get the surprise, and lo! He is in their midst—a current of air, a creaking window, a chance murmur, decides the belief of centuries. Nothing easier than to comprehend the hallucination of those devoted ones. Can you possibly imagine a more garbled account out of the New Testament documents?

Strauss, holding the same view, explains it somewhat differently. He starts with Paul the Apostle, who, Strauss thinks, was subject to epilepsy—that was his "thorn in the flesh"—and being disposed by his contact with the other disciples' affirmation of a living Christ, he readily had a vision during a fit on the way to Damascus. This so strengthened the impressions of the other disciples that certainty of a risen Christ hardened into positive affirmations, and crowds came forward to testify that they had seen Him alive and radiant. But they were all subjective visions, identical with that of Paul.

Men like Strauss are capable of reshaping the material on which they base their theories. This necessity for reshaping the data is the biggest condemnation of the Vision theory. He says distinctly that the belief in the Resurrection required time for the disciples to rid themselves of the depression as the result of the Crucifixion, and so he says, "The heart thinks; the hour brings." Not all at once, not so soon as the Gospels represent did the visions come. The disciples retired to Galilee, and there, brooding on the Scriptures and visiting familiar haunts, they gradually got into the state of mind required for seeing visions.

The preposterous thing about Strauss' theory is that he must needs reduce the Apostle Paul to an imbecile epileptic before he can square him into the Vision theory. Paul, mind you, whose epistles acclaim him to have possessed a cultured mind, a colossal intellect, and a wonderful fount of shrewdness which stood him in good stead in cases of emergency. About the last man in the world who could be bamboozled, we should imagine, into a state of make-believe to accept doctrines which he bitterly resented, and moreover, one who madly persecuted those who held them.

As for the other disciples—all we need do is apply common sense and rethink what impression the Crucifixion must have made on them, and we must see how impossible it would have been for them to work themselves up into an ecstasy in which they could conjure up a risen Christ. The horror of it was so great—the cruel nails, the suspension of the body, the spear thrust, the agonising cry, the falling of the head—these were the things that scorched their minds and lacerated their hearts. The Gospel narratives are strictly in accord with what we should expect would be their attitude to any rumour of Christ risen. The report of the women, St. Luke tells us, seemed to the disciples as idle tales. Thomas, who carried away from the Cross the ghastly impression of wounds, refused to believe until he saw, and wanted to touch the prints of the wounds ere he would be convinced that Christ was alive again.

But lest you become angry with Renan and Strauss for doing such violence to the truth of the Resurrection, please remain calm and let another rationalist demolish the Vision theory for you. Keim answers them adequately. He rejects the theory on three grounds:—

1. The manifestation was simple, earnest, and almost cold, which would not be the case with a subjective vision.
2. The speedy cessation of the appearances is against the Vision theory which requires at least years of hallucination—the pot must be kept boiling, so to speak, to impress generations.
3. The entire change of the disciples within a short time from visionaries to sane organisers and courageous missionaries is as contradictory and impossible as it could well be. Psychology is against it. The excitement which created the visions ought not only to have lasted a considerable time and to have cooled down gradually but terminated not in illumination and energy, but in dullness, languor, and apathy.

Very good. But does Keim accept the actual emergence of Christ from the tomb? Not he. He has a theory of his own—the Telegram theory. Jesus went to heaven and sent His disciples a telegram that He had arrived there alive and well. It is worked out, of course, with all the plausibility of a scholar who has an axe to grind; but it amounts to a divine intimation that Jesus is not lost, but safe home in His Father's house. In keeping with such a view, Keim is obliged to call in question that the grave was found empty.

Do you wonder that the fashionable thing to-day is neither to affirm nor deny the empty tomb and the actual and objective appearances of Christ, but to dwell, as does Baur, on the wonderful effects of the belief of Christ's Resurrection? The refusal to accept the miracle and the acknowledgment of its effects upon the Christian Church is as self-contradictory as to amount to a doctrine of unreality and make-believe.

We have not so learnt Christ. To us He is "the Lord who showed Himself alive after his passion by many infallible proofs, being seen of them forty days, and speaking of the things pertaining to the kingdom of God." Indeed, it is a far more reasonable thing to believe Christ rose from the dead when we realise the uniqueness of His Person, the mystery of His incarnation, the spotlessness of His life, and the supremacy of His mission. There never was such a Being as He was on this earth, and there never will be until He returns. Peter's explanation on the Day of Pentecost appeals to me far more than all the juggling of scholarly ingenuity. "Him, being delivered by the determinate counsel and foreknowledge of God, ye by the hand of lawless men [a reference to the pagan Romans—Ed.] did crucify and slay: whom God raised up, having loosed the pangs of death: because it was not possible that He should be holden of it" [RV].

Christ's Resurrection, let it never be forgotten, completed God's revelation of His love to a sinful world. If that love, as revealed by Jesus, is to be seen in its perfection, two aspects of it were necessary:—(1) Its appealing moral beauty, which culminated in the Cross as atoning love where "sorrow and love flow mingled down"; and (2) its conquering might, by overcoming the sharpness of death and opening the Kingdom of Heaven to all believers. Had it stopped short, at the first, it would have remained fragmentary and ambiguous. Man's malignity would have proved overpowering. But with the Resurrection, love divine proved itself mightier than sin. The Resurrection crowned the demonstration of God's love as the absolute power to which all reality is subservient, and which no sin of man or independent ordinance of Nature can ever defeat.

When the Risen Christ proclaimed, "All power is given unto Me," etc., He showed us the new might at the disposal of His redeemed family for their own individual lives and for their appointed mission in the world. That mysterious Resurrection Body was a proof and pattern of our Resurrection body. "Christ the first fruits; afterward they that are Christ's at his coming."

This glorious hope is the greatest power on earth, especially when the indwelling Spirit of God keeps it alive in the heart of the believer who is sanctified by Him. "If the Spirit of him that raised up Jesus from the dead dwell in you, he that raised up Christ from the dead shall also quicken your mortal bodies by his Spirit that dwelleth in you."

"And God hath both raised up the Lord, and will also raise up us by his own power." When Paul craved to know Him and the power of His Resurrection, did he not wish to be as invincible as was his Lord to be able to face the tyrant's sword and not fear?

Oh, that we might hear His mighty voice as it reverberates through the ages: "I am he that liveth, and was dead; and, behold, I am alive for evermore" (Revelation 1:18).

50 How People React to Death

Arthur W. Kac

Those who witnessed funerals among orthodox Jews in pre-World War Two in eastern Europe—until then the stronghold of Jewish orthodoxy—will recall the despair manifested by the survivors, especially those closely related to the deceased. It is true that in reciting the Maimonides Creed in his daily prayers the orthodox Jew affirms his faith in a resurrection. But that in reality his belief in resurrection is no more than skin deep becomes abundantly clear when we review some of the Talmudic laws with respect to prayers for the dead;

"Therefore the custom is [for the son of a deceased person] to recite for twelve months the Kaddish prayer, and also to read the lesson in the prophets, and to pray the evening prayer at the conclusion of the Sabbath, for that is the hour when the souls return to hell; but when the son prays and sanctifies in public, he redeems his father and his mother from hell."[1]

But that Kaddish prayer recited for twelve (or eleven) months is obviously not considered sufficient to redeem a dying Jew from hell. For an additional prayer on behalf of the dead has been instituted to be recited on the last day of the three great festivals and on the Day of Atonement;

"May God remember the soul of my revered father (or revered mother) who is gone to his (her) repose; for that I now solemnly vow charity for his (her) sake; in reward of this, may his (her) soul be bound up in the bundle of life, with the souls of Abraham, Isaac and Jacob; Sarah, Rachel and Leah, and the rest of the righteous males and females that are in Paradise; and let us say, Amen."[2]

Then there is the dying confession to be recited when a Jewish person is approaching death:

"May it be thy will to send me a perfect healing. Yet if death be fully determined by thee, I will in love accept it at thy hand. O may my death be an atonement for all the sins, iniquities and transgressions of which I have been guilty against thee."[3]

The three prayers cited above reflect the uncertainty of the Jew concerning eternal life. If the Jew went to Paradise upon his departure there would be no need of reciting the Kaddish prayer for eleven or twelve months. If the Kaddish prayer were sufficient to transfer a deceased Jew from hell to paradise, why recite the prayer for the dead on the great festival days? The petition of a dying person that his death may atone for his sins only adds to the utter Jewish uncertainty about the destiny of the dead.

Closely related to the ideas of traditional Judaism concerning death are the rigorous practices enjoined by Talmudic laws upon the mourner, especially during the first seven days following death. He may not cut his hair, wear shoes, wash his clothes, bathe, work, read Scripture, sit on a bed or couch, or give or receive greetings.[4]

Underlying those mourning laws is the Jewish belief that in death man becomes separated from God. "In the face of death," Rabbi Feldman comments, "man as a person, as an identity, as a being, as a living creature, as the image of God, ceases to exist. The rites of mourning are a physical expression of the essential facts of death. . . . The dynamic interaction with God can take place only in the context of life. . . . The mizvot [precepts] cannot be performed in a state of non-life. Death desacralizes man and estranges him from the divine."[5] The Talmudic mourning laws are "consistent with the estranging quality of death. Just as the dead are cut off from dynamic communion with God and community, so is the mourner required to behave in a similar manner since he, alone among the living, has most intimately experienced the estrangement of death."[6] The Talmudic belief that in death the Jew becomes cut off from interaction with God is a remnant from the Jews' pagan past.

The Old Testament opposed those pagan Semitic beliefs. Old Testament saints became convinced of the continuation of human life in fellowship with God beyond the grave. That truth came to them as they plumbed deep into the meaning of the new relationship established between God and man through the Abrahamic covenant. They perceived that the relationship God Himself had brought into existence was not meant to be terminated or interrupted by death. The covenant with Abraham was to be an everlasting covenant (Genesis 17:7), everlasting not merely in the sense of being transmitted from generation to generation, but also in the sense of being of everlasting validity for every individual who entered into that relationship with God.

The psalmist related how the continued prosperity of the wicked and the adversity of the righteous had been a source of much concern to him and a challenge to his faith in God.

> But as for me, my feet had almost stumbled, my steps had well nigh slipped. For I was envious of the arrogant, when I saw the prosperity of the wicked. . . . All in vain have I kept my heart clean and washed my hands in innocence. [Psalm 73:2-3, 13, RSV]

He had sought everywhere for the meaning of his problem but found none. So he repaired to God's sanctuary, and there in communion with God he found the answer.

> But when I thought how to understand this, it seemed to me a wearisome task, until I went into the sanctuary of God; then I perceived their end. [Psalm 73:16-17, RSV]

He discovered that the solution to his problem lay in man's relationship to God. The wicked were separated from God in life; they would be separated from Him eternally in death.

> For lo, those who are far from thee shall perish; thou dost put an end to those who are false to thee. [Psalm 73:27, RSV]

But the righteous are ever close to God. In that consists their felicity. Even after death their relation to God remains unchanged:

Nevertheless I am continually with thee; thou dost hold my right hand. Thou dost guide me with thy counsel, and afterward thou wilt receive me to glory. . . . My flesh and my heart may fail, but God is the strength of my heart and my portion for ever. [Psalm 73:23-24, 26, RSV]

The problem of man's final destiny is carried a step further in Psalm 49. The psalmist began by stating that he had an important message for all mankind.

Hear this, all peoples! Give ear, all inhabitants of the world. Both low and high, rich and poor together! [Psalm 49:1-2, RSV (49:2-3, Heb.)]

He was well aware that death is mankind's universal fate:

Yea, he shall see that even the wise die, the fool and the stupid alike must perish and leave their wealth to others. [Psalm 49:10, RSV (49:11, Heb.)]

But at death the separate destinies of the righteous and the wicked, the godly and the ungodly, become manifest. For those who trusted in their wealth, who lived by material values only, Sheol became their home.

Like sheep they are appointed for Sheol; Death shall be their shepherd; straight to the grave they descend, and their form shall waste away; Sheol shall be their home. [Psalm 49:14, RSV (49:15, Heb.)]

But for those whose lives were God-oriented:

God will ransom my soul from the power of Sheol, for he will receive me. [Psalm 49:15, RSV (49:16, Heb.)]

The phrase "he will receive me" or "he will take me," used in Psalm 49:15 and Psalm 73:24, takes us back to the story of Enoch in Genesis:

Enoch walked with God; and he was not; for God took him. [Gen. 5:24]

Enoch and Elijah are the two persons in the Old Testament period who, having bypassed death, were received by God.

The ideas set forth in Psalms 49 and 73 constitute an important milestone in the unfolding of the biblical doctrine of human immortality. They express the conviction that human destiny beyond the grave is determined entirely by one's relation to God.

As the future of the world at large is linked with the coming of Messiah and His establishment of God's visible and universal rule on earth, so also the final destiny of the individual, the question of life and death, is bound up with Messiah's advent. It is no wonder then that the greatest statements about the resurrection are found in Isaiah and Daniel, the two Old Testament books in which the Messianic hope is dealt with most fully. In Daniel—whose first prophetic utterance concerns events of the "latter days" period (i.e., events taking place in the end-time of history) and who in the seventh chapter sees a vision of the Messianic Son of Man—the passage concerning the resurrection is found in the last chapter.

And at that time shall Michael stand up, the great prince which standeth for the children of thy people: and there shall be a time of trouble, such as never was since there was a nation even to that same time; and at that time thy people shall be delivered, every one that shall be found written in the book. And many of them that sleep in the dust of the earth shall awake, some to everlasting life, and some to shame and everlasting contempt. [Daniel 12:1-2]

In Isaiah the statement about the resurrection is recorded in chapter 25, right after chapter 24's description of the general catastrophe that will overtake the whole earth as part of God's judgment upon a wicked world.

> On this mountain the LORD [Jehovah] of hosts will make for all peoples a feast of fat things, a feast of wine on the lees, of fat things full of marrow, of wine on the lees well refined. And he will destroy on this mountain the covering that is cast over all peoples, the veil that is spread over all nations. He will swallow up death for ever, and the Lord GOD will wipe away tears from all faces, and the reproach of his people he will take away from all the earth; we have waited for him, that he might save us. This is the LORD [Jehovah]; we have waited for him; let us be glad and rejoice in his salvation. [Isaiah 25:6-9, RSV]

The feast referred to in chapter 25 is a spiritual feast, and all nations will participate in it. The cause for the world-wide rejoicing is that God has removed the veil that was spread over the nations of the earth; death has been abolished, and sorrow and suffering have ceased. "He will swallow up death for ever, and the Lord GOD will wipe away tears from all faces." The above passage in Isaiah 25 has been Messianically interpreted in several rabbinic passages.

In the remainder of this article I shall cite thoughts about and reactions to death on the part of those who represent three groups of people: (1) those who stand outside the biblical faith; (2) those who embrace Talmudic Judaism; and (3) those who are grounded in the biblical faith.

THOSE WHO STAND OUTSIDE THE BIBLICAL FAITH, ANCIENT AND MODERN

Aristotle, who lived in the fourth century B.C., was one of the world's greatest philosophers. The following words are attributed to him when he was facing death: "A wailing babe came I into the world. In trouble and sorrow have I passed through it. And now I go I know not whither: O, cause of all causes, have pity on me."[7]

The following, an epigram attributed to Palladas, a Greek writer of the fifth century A.D.: "Weeping I was born and having wept I die, and I found all living amid many tears; O tearful, weak, pitiable race of men, dragged under earth and mouldering away."[8]

The late Madame Marie Curie was described as the "greatest of all women scientist." With her physicist husband, Pierre, she was the codiscoverer of radium. Twice she received the Nobel prize. Her husband's untimely death through an accident was a shock from which she found it difficult to recover. Her diary reflects the despondency she experienced on the day of her husband's funeral. Addressing her dead husband, she wrote: "We took you to Sceaux, and we saw you go down into a big deep hole. . . . Everything is over; Pierre is sleeping his last sleep beneath the earth; it is the end of everything, everything, everything."[9]

Bertrand Russell was an outstanding British mathematician and thinker. He was also an outspoken atheist. The following is an excerpt from his writings: "The life of Man is a long march through the night, surrounded by invisible foes, tortured by weariness and pain, towards a goal that few can hope to reach, and where none may tarry long. One by one, as they march, our comrades vanish from our sight, seized by the silent order of omnipotent Death."[10]

THOSE WHO EMBRACE TALMUDIC JUDAISM

Rabbi Yochanan ben Zakkai was the founder and first president of the rabbinical academy at Yabneh (Yamnia), which he established soon after the destruction of the second Temple. In his day he was the greatest representative of rabbinic Judaism. When he was about to die, his disciples visited him at his home, and the rabbi began to weep. "Rabbi," exclaimed his astonished visitors, "do you weep, you, the light of Israel, the right-hand pillar of Judaism, and the mighty interpreter of the Law!" To that the dying rabbi replied,

> Ah, my children, should I not weep if I were at this moment led before an earthly king, who may be in his grave tomorrow; whose anger, therefore, and the punishment he might inflict upon one could not last forever, and who moreover, might be moved to pity by words of entreaty, or be pacified with a gift? And you ask me why I weep, when I am being led into the presence of the Supreme King of kings, who lives throughout the countless ages of eternity; whose anger, therefore, and the punishment He may inflict upon me must last forever; who will not be moved by words of entreaty nor by the offer of a gift. Here are two ways before me, one leading to Paradise and the other to Gehenna [hell], and I know not whither I am going.[11]

Emmanuel Deutsch, sublibrarian of the British Museum, wrote a dissertation "What Is the Talmud?" In it he sang the glories of traditional Judaism and sought to downgrade the person and mission of Jesus. Soon afterwards he became ill and went to Egypt in the hope of regaining his shattered health. When he perceived the end was approaching, he penned the following lines to the editor of the *Quarterly Review*:

"I cannot take comfort in the thought of death. I want to live—there is so much life, hot, full life, within me, that it shrinks from darkness and deadness. I envy those who can fly on the mind's wing to that harbor of refuge—I cannot follow, but keep tossing outside in my broken craft, amid foam, rock and mist."[12]

THOSE WHO ARE GROUNDED IN THE BIBLICAL FAITH

The following is from a letter to Timothy by Saul of Tarsus (the apostle Paul). It was written in prison while the apostle was waiting to be executed on account of his faith:

"Remember [Messiah Jesus], risen from the dead. . . . For I am already on the point of being sacrificed; the time of my departure has come. I have fought the good fight, I have finished the race, I have kept the faith. Henceforth there is laid up for me the crown of righteousness, which the Lord, the righteous judge, will award to me on thàt Day, and not only to me but also to all who have loved his appearing" (2 Timothy 2:8; 4:6-8, RSV).

Dr. Samuel M. Shoemaker, a prominent Episcopal clergyman who touched many lives, was a great and worthy representative of biblical Christianity. Several months before his death he wrote the following lines to his wife, Helen, to be read on the occasion of his death. I am indebted to Mrs. Shoemaker for permission to reprint them.

> As I sit in the study on a beautiful, cool August afternoon, I look back with many thanks. It has been a great run. I wouldn't have missed it for anything. Much could and should have been better, and I have, by no means, done what I should have done with all that I have been given. But the overall experience of being alive has been a thrilling experience. I believe that death is a doorway to more of it; clearer, cleaner, better, with more of the secret opened than unlocked. I do not feel much confidence in myself as regards all this, for very few have ever "deserved" eternal life. But with Christ's atonement and Him gone on before, I have neither doubt nor fear whether I am left here a brief time or long one. I believe that I shall see Him and know Him, and that eternity will be an endless opportunity to consort with the great souls and the lesser ones who have entered into the freedom of the heavenly city. It is His forgiveness and grace that gives confidence and not merits of our own. But again I say, it's been a great run. I'm thankful for it and for all the people who have helped to make it so, and especially those closest and dearest to me.

Dr. Edward Wilson was a member of Captain Robert Falcon Scott's fateful Antarctic expedition. Dr. Wilson was the medical officer, and he was among the picked band that reached the South Pole. It was on the return journey that members of the advance party were overwhelmed with disaster.

They were caught in a fearful blizzard that raged without intermission day after day. One by one they succumbed to the appalling rigors of frostbite and cold. Only Captain Scott and Edward Wilson were left alive. Isolated from their supplies, snowbound within their tent, they knew there was no possibility of survival. Wilson's farewell letter to his wife was found months later on his frozen body, together with his Bible and his prayer book. This is what he had written:

> To my beloved wife. Don't be unhappy—all is for the best. We are playing a good part in a great scheme arranged by God Himself, and all is well. . . . We will all meet after death and death has no terrors. . . . All is for the best to those that love God, and oh, my Ory, we have both loved Him with all our lives. All is well. . . . My beloved wife . . . life itself is a small thing to me now, but my love for you is forever and a part of our love for God. I do not cease to pray for you and to desire that you may be filled with the knowledge of His will. . . .
>
> All the things I had hoped to do with you after the Expedition are as nothing now, but there are greater things for us to do in the world to

come. . . . Your little testament and prayer book will be in my hand or in my breast pocket when the end comes. All is well . . .[13]

"These deeply poignant and moving words reveal something of the simple and sincere faith which animated and sustained Dr. Edward Wilson. He was a man of transparent sincerity and earnest faith. He was a man who trusted God and who sought to serve Him, and as a consequence, he was able to face death calm and unafraid. His last words breathe a spirit of quiet serenity and confident trust.[13]

" 'Death,' Aristotle confessed, 'is a dreadful thing, for it is the end.' Thomas Hobbes complained, 'I am about to take my last voyage, a great leap in the dark.' 'He who pretends to face death without fear,' Rousseau bluntly affirmed, 'is a liar.' 'No rational man,' Dr. Johnson insisted, 'can die without uneasy apprehension.' T.S. Eliot likens the way men die to the whimpering of a dying dog. . . .[14]

"For the Christian man, however, the last word is not with the grave but with God; that is why there is no whimpering and no whining, no repining and no complaining. That is why the Christian man is able to say, with the Shepherd psalmist: 'Even though I walk through the valley of the shadow of death, I will fear no evil: for thou art with me' [Psalm 23:1], and that is why the Apostle Paul is able to say: 'For I am sure that neither death, nor life . . . will be able to separate us from the love of God in Christ Jesus our Lord' "[Romans 8:38-39, RSV].[15]

Notes

1. Tur Yoreh Deah, section 376.
2. See "Memorial Service for the Dead" in *The Prayer Book*.
3. See "Confession on a Death Bed," *The Authorized Daily Prayer Book*, ed. Joseph H. Hertz, Chief Rabbi of the British Empire, p. 1064.
4. Hilchoth Avel., c. V.
5. Emanuel Feldman, "Death as Estrangement: The Halakhah of Mourning," *Judaism*, Winter 1972, p. 63.
6. Ibid., p. 66.
7. Quoted by M. Wolkenberg in *Judaism and Christianity on the Threshold of Eternity* (London: London Society House, 1904), p. 7.
8. J. W. Mackail, *Select Epigrams from the Greek Anthology,* (Mount Vernon, N.Y.: Peter Pauper, 1940), p. 123.
9. Eve Curie, *Madame Curie* (Garden City, N.Y.: Doubleday, 1937) p. 249.
10. Bertrand Russell, "A Free Man's Worship," in *Mysticism and Logic* (New York: Barnes & Noble, 1970) p. 46.
11. Berachoth 28*b*.
12. *Deutsch's Literary Remains*, p. 12; quoted by M. Wolkenberg, ibid. pp. 16-17.
13. Stuart Barton Babbage, "Death of Death," *The Church Herald*, 10 April 1965. Used by permission.
14. Ibid.
15. Ibid.

The Mission and Message of Jesus

And it came about soon afterwards, that He went to a city called Nain; and his disciples were going along with Him, accompanied by a large multitude. Now as He approached the gate of the city, behold, a dead man was being carried out, the only son of his mother, and she was a widow; and a sizeable crowd from the city was with her. And when the Lord saw her, He felt compassion for her, and said to her, "Do not weep." And He came up and touched the coffin; and the bearers came to a halt. And He said, "Young man, I say to you, arise!" And the dead man sat up, and began to speak. And Jesus gave him back to his mother. And fear gripped them all, and they began glorifying God, saying, "A great prophet has arisen among us!" and, God has visited His people!" And this report concerning him went out all over Judea, and in all the surrounding district.

And the disciples of John reported to him about all of these things. And summoning two of his disciples, John sent them to the Lord, saying, "Are You the One who is coming, or do we look for someone else?" " And when the men had come to Him, they said, "John the Baptist has sent us to You, saying, 'Are You the One who is coming, or do we look for someone else?" At that very time He cured many people of diseases and afflictions and evil spirits; and He granted sight to many who were blind. And He answered and said to them, "Go and report to John what you have seen and heard: THE BLIND RECEIVE SIGHT, the lame walk, the lepers are cleansed, and the deaf hear, the dead are raised up, the POOR HAVE THE GOSPEL PREACHED TO THEM. And blessed is he who keeps from stumbling over Me."

Luke 7:11-23 (NASB) (see also Matt. 11:2-6)

Jesus the Prophet: A Critique—*Emmanuel M. Gitlin*   243

Was Jesus the Messiah?—*Nahum Levison*   245

Gaal G'ullah—*T. H. Bendor Samuel*   252

Bethlehem: Born Under the Law—*Harcourt Samuel*   256

Fundamentals of Our Holy Faith—
  Joseph Immanuel Landsman   260

Fulfillment in the Messiah—*Bernard B. Gair*   264

Jesus of Nazareth . . . the Eternal Glory of the
  Jewish Race—*Benjamin Disraeli*   268

51 Jesus the Prophet: A Critique

*Emmanuel M. Gitlin is a third generation Hebrew
Christian. His father brought his family to the United States
ten days before Hitler invaded Poland, thus escaping the
Holocaust. Dr. Gitlin earned the M. Div. and Ph.D.
degrees from Duke University. He has taught at the
University of North Carolina, at the Perkins School of
Theology of Southern Methodist University, and at the
University of Florida. He collaborated with his father in the
translation of the Bible into the White Russian language.
Dr. Gitlin is presently professor of religion at Lenoir-Rhyne
College in North Carolina.*

In the December 1949 issue of the *Journal of Biblical Literature* Professor
Franklin W. Young, of Yale University, has a paper which deserves a permanent
place in Hebrew Christian apologetics. It is entitled "Jesus the Prophet: A Re-
examination."

Contemporary Jewish religious and literary leaders show increasingly less reserve
in referring to Jesus as a prophet, or at least as one conscious of His prophetic
calling. At the same time the possibility of Jesus' Messianic self-consciousness is
dismissed as a fabrication of His followers. This situation bears out Professor
Young's point of departure: "Scholars who have violently disagreed over whether
Jesus claimed to be the Messiah have found no difficulty in acknowledging His
prophetic role. The title, prophet, has in a sense served as a least common denominator for studies in Christology. All could start with the assumption that Jesus
was 'at least' a prophet. Beyond that the battle waxed warm whether or not he was
'more than a prophet!' "

Professor Young's thesis is that Jesus could not have thought of Himself as a
prophet without at the same time thinking of Himself as the Messiah. To have done
so would have been a contradiction of the well-established thought patterns of His
day.

For the Jew of Jesus' day the term "prophet" was a technical term. Neither
prognostication, nor railing against the "system" in the manner of Amos, nor even
passionate pleas for holiness as those of Isaiah, were sufficient to label a person a

Dr. Gitlin's article is reprinted from Emmanuel M. Gitlin, "Jesus the Prophet: A Critique," *The Hebrew
Christian* 25, no. 2 (Summer 1952):62-63, by permission of The International Hebrew Christian Alliance.

prophet. Only in the writings of Philo do we find a Jew suggesting that his contemporaries could through their own religious experience attain to the prophetic office and be called prophets. On this assumption he was ranging far from his Jewish base. The hellenization of the Jewish concept of prophecy in Philo's writings is generally overlooked but it certainly represents a radical departure from the attitude reflected in other extant Jewish literature of this period. This is the fundamental point in the argument. If Jesus thought of Himself as a Prophet it was not because of the nature of His teachings but because He thought that God had called Him to be a prophet.

Having established this point, Professor Young draws upon numerous biblical and extra-biblical sources to make it quite clear that there was in the Judaism of Jesus' day a very clear conviction that prophecy had ceased and that there were to be no more prophets until the Messianic era. Young writes: ". . . in Jesus' day there were no Jewish prophets. For the Jew the return of the prophetic spirit was inextricably related to Messianic times. No Jew could use the phrase 'just another prophet' as so many modern scholars do. The next prophet would be one of two individuals: Elijah (the forerunner of the Messiah) or the Messiah Himself. In each case the claimant would of necessity be involved in the advent of the Messianic age and the return of the prophetic spirit. Only in the case of the Messiah would the fullness of the Spirit be known." The implication is that if Jesus claimed to have been a prophet, and if the tradition of His disavowal of being the new Elijah is correct, then He must surely have been laying claim to being the Messiah Himself.

The one apparent difficulty is a reference to John Hyrcanus as a prophet. However, Young concurs with Professor R. H. Charles in the opinion that John Hyrcanus was, in fact, for a time widely regarded as the fulfillment of the Messianic hope. Just as in the case of Jesus, his contemporaries' reference to him as a prophet was tantamount to their recognition of him as the Messiah.

Further supporting evidence is gained from the study of the records of the two roughly contemporary individuals whom Josephus portrays as attempting to make the claims of being prophets. In each case the "prophet" tries to demonstrate his claim by his attempts to "redeem Israel" (that is, deliver Israel from the bondage of Rome). Thus is obtained the triangular formula: to be a prophet, is to redeem Israel, is to be the Messiah.

An interesting point is Professor Young's reference to a sentiment, expressed in the intertestamental books, that "the true prophet sealed his mission by his death." This, Young feels, is not so much an echo of the Servant passages of the book of Isaiah as it is a reflection of the tradition that the great prophets of the past not only lived for and spoke to their people, but also died for them, and that "both of these phases characterized the office of the prophet." It is a pity that more space is not devoted to this phase of the argument. However, enough is said to enable Professor Young to conclude forcefully that "Jesus' consideration of the possibility (rather the probability) of death cannot be easily postponed until some late date in His ministry. We cannot think of Him facing His death for the first time in the shadow of the cross on Calvary. If one insists that He went to the cross 'bewildered' it cannot be because the idea of death had never entered His head."

52 Was Jesus the Messiah?

Nahum Levison

I

Much has been said on this subject from the time of the ministry of Jesus to this day. We have evidence that neither the term itself, the function, nor the Scriptural implications were understood in His day, and the question must be raised today, What does the term mean, imply, and sum up?

It will be agreed that so far as the term Mashiach is concerned the verb Mashach means to smear or anoint; the Arabic is Masacha, to wipe or stroke with the hand; and the Aramaic also is to anoint. Thus we have a root well established in the Semitic languages, for we find it also in the other Semitic dialects and languages. In the Old Testament we come into contact with it first in connection with the priestly office, then with the office of kingship, and then in the case of the prophet Elisha (I Kings xix, 16). In the same passage it should be noted that Chazael, a Gentile of Syria, was also to be anointed by Elijah. The anointing was always done with oil, and the oil was often of a sacred nature (Psalm lxxxix, 21). Again, it should be noted that the only time the term is used in the Old Testament, apart from the Psalms, is in connection with a person not in the above-mentioned categories—Cyrus, a Gentile (Isaiah xlv, 1). (In the Psalms, as we shall see, the term is used in a broader sense and with various implications.) It is used in a way that might with perfect justice be assumed to point to a person who does not belong to the priestly, kingly, or prophetic schools of the general Old Testament application. Yet the one exception is very significant: "The Spirit of the Lord Yahweh (is) upon me because Yahweh anointed me to proclaim to the lowly, he sent me to bind up the broken hearted, to call freedom to the prisoners, and to captives the opening of new avenues of strength!" (Isaiah 61:1). It is open to argument that this is meant to convey the message that the prophet was directed to preach. I shall deal with that later; all I wish to point out now is that at least as it stands the passage does not point to any person directly, nor does it apply to the other personalities with which the Old Testament generally associates the term.

"Was Jesus the Messiah?" has been adapted from Nahum Levison, "Was Jesus the Messiah?" Part 1, *The Hebrew Christian* 22, no. 1 (April 1949):10-13; Part 2, *The Hebrew Christian* 22, no. 2 (July 1949):38-40, and is reprinted by permission of The International Hebrew Christian Alliance.

In the Psalms the term becomes more impersonal, as in Psalm ii, 2. Whether we take the term "bar" as the Aramaic word for son, or the Hebrew derivative of "Bar-rar," to purify, select, or as having the meaning of the Arabic "Barhah," pious, virtuous, honest, depends on the placing of the psalm historically. In early Hebrew the word is not used with the meaning of son, but in late Hebrew it is so used. When the whole psalm is considered the impression is left on the mind of the careful reader that it does not cover the categories generally applied in the Old Testament. But we must examine the passages in the Psalms as a whole before we come to any appraisal of the subject. In Psalm xviii, 50, it is clearly applied to the king. Again in Psalm xx, 6, that the king is in view is clearly indicated in the last verse. Psalm xxviii belongs to the group which begin "L'David," which may either mean David's or to David, which would bear the interpretation dedicated to David, so we must simply content ourselves with the bare reference. Psalm lxxxiv, 9, we have to place on the border line; it is not clear enough either way. In Psalm lxxxix, 39-52, the king would seem to be the subject. In Psalm cv, 15, Messiah and prophet are coupled, so we must assume that it is used in the ordinary way. In Psalm cxxxii, 10-17, again David is mentioned and again we must assume that it is used in the ordinary way. But here we must ask the question, In these passages is David meant personally or is the ideal person or king of the Davidic stamp intended? I think the test of the passages quoted makes it clear beyond any shadow of doubt that the term "David" stands for a person who will be of the Davidic type but much greater than David. The best picture of this person is given us in Isaiah ix, 5, 6 [Heb.], and xi, 1-11. It can be ascertained positively that this picture of the Messiah dominated the doctrine right through Jewish history, though it did not hold the file by itself. There was the prophetic conception of "Yom Yahweh"—the Day of the Lord—which kept the field alongside the Davidic conception, and often merged with it. I have no intention to enter upon chronological problems, for it matters very little for our purpose whether Daniel was written before the fifth century, or after the middle of the second, or whether Joel was written in the second century and Isaiah xl-lxvi, in the fourth. We are here merely concerned with an investigation if Jesus was the Messiah envisaged in the Old Testament, and in pre-Christian Jewish literature, and what He Himself and His earliest followers believed and taught. That the Psalms are not the only source that set forth the ideal of the future in a Davidic cast the two passages from Isaiah amply prove, but there is hardly a book in the Old Testament which deals with the future of Israel that does not do so. I will cite just a few passages from these other books to demonstrate the doctrine.

"In that day I will raise up the Tabernacle of David which is fallen, I will fence about their breaches, and the destroyed I will rebuild, and establish her as in the days of yore!" (Amos ix, 11 [Heb. text]). Jewish commentators find three other passages with Messianic meaning in this book (Amos iv, 7; v, 18 and viii, 11).

In Hosea iii, 5, we have this passage: "Then shall Israel turn and seek Yahweh their God, and David their king, they shall come in fear to Yahweh, and to his benificence in the end of the days" [Heb. text] But Jewish commentators also find the following passages to have a Messianic content: Hosea ii, 2, 13, 18; iii; 5; vi, 2; xiii, 14.

In Isaiah i-xxxix, the Jewish commentators find forty-four passages which they look upon as Messianic. Whatever the case may be in regards to the "Servant poems," whether these are interpreted of Israel, or "the Servant," whom some scholars identify with one prophet or another, and whom others identify with the Messiah, there are twenty-four passages which Jewish commentators identify as Messianic, including chapters lii, 13 and liii, 1-12. For the rest of Isaiah there are another twenty-nine passages.

Isaiah's younger contemporary, Micah, contains some famous passages, especially the one in chapter v, 1 (Hebrew text): "And thou Bethlehem Ephratha, young to be [counted] chiefs of Judah, from thee there will come forth to me a Ruler to be Governor in Israel, and His coming forth is from aforetimes, from days of eternity." The theology of Micah is theocratic; Yahweh is to reign in Zion, He is to establish the covenant with Abraham.

In Jeremiah we have fifteen passages which Jewish commentators have considered as Messianic. So we can go through each book of the Old Testament. Edersheim (*Life and Times of Jesus the Messiah,* Vol II, pp. 710-743) has cited all the 456 passages in which the Jewish commentators have seen Messianic references. These passages when examined very carefully suggest three outstanding views: (1) that Messiah is to be a son of David, physically and spiritually; (2) that he is to bring in a new age, an age of salvation, materially and spiritually; (3) that he is to suffer and be humiliated, also that though a son of David yet he exists "from the days of eternity" and the time of his appearance will be decided by Yahweh.

Scholars have raised the question as to whether Jewry borrowed its concepts of the Messiah from Zoroastrianism. To form judgment on this point a very brief outline of the Zoroastrian doctrine will now be given. But before I do this I must draw attention to a very important factor relative to revelation. Some of our Jewish Christian brethren contend that only that of which Israel was the mediator is true revelation, and it follows from that that the Gentiles were left in absolute darkness concerning the Being, Will and purpose of God. Apart from the statement of St. Paul at Lystra (Acts xiv, 17) the justice which is inherent in the being of God demands that this should not be so. And as we have seen, when we considered the meaning of the term Messiah, the king of Syria was to be anointed by Elijah, and Cyrus was designated "His anointed." While, of course, it must be maintained that the supreme channel of revelation was Israel, and the ultimate and fullest revelation is Christ, it must yet be conceded that light, however dim, was vouchsafed the Gentiles. Balaam, Zarathustra of Iran, Socrates, Plato, Aristotle and Epictetus, to name only a few, bear witness to this.

There is considerable difference of opinion among scholars about the person and parentage of Zarathustra, the age in which he lived, and even the country in which he worked. The Greeks called him Zoroaster, but the Iranian form and spelling of the name is Zarathustra. The date of his activities is somewhere about 1000 B.C. Claims are made by scholars for a near approach to monotheism in Babylonia with Marduk as the supreme deity, in Egypt with Atan, and in Assyria with Ashur. While in these deities we have an approach to unity, the unity is only that of gathering up the functions of the lesser deities into the one paramount deity of the state. Zoroaster (to give him his Greek name) is the first of the non-Biblical religious leaders or reformers to come near to what we would accept as monotheistic, though his monotheism is vitiated by his treatment of the problem of good and evil. He confuses the issues with the person of God, and thus arrives at two gods, Ahura Mazda, the good God, and the God of light, and Ahriman, the evil God, the God of darkness. It is in the ultimate triumph of the God of Light and goodness that his theology develops round a personality. This personality he calls Shasoiant, who will come forth from the good God and bring salvation to enlightened and good men. The priests of his system are known as Magi. So that when we read the story in Matthew of the coming of the Magi, we contact the religious system of Zarathustra at its fundamentals. But in order to make plain the system I will quote from Professor G. F. Moore (*History of Religions,* volume I, page 358):

"The monotheism of the Gathas is much more advanced than that of the loftiest Vedic hymns to Varuna. Ahura Mazda [footnote: "No other god is even mentioned in the Gathas"] has no partner nor rival. He is the creator of the world and all that therein is. He knows all that men do; his eyes behold the secret deeds as well as those done in open day; he knows all that is and is to be. He requites for their deeds in this world and the other."

With this approach to monotheism we must surely give him a place among the great. But it is not so much with the philosophy or theology of Zarathustra that I am concerned as with his dim vision of the coming of the Messiah which ultimately led his Magi followers to follow the star that led them to Bethlehem. His Messianic doctrines are worth studying, though I shall not go into that here. All I am anxious to establish here is the Messianic doctrine in the Old Testament, in the intertestamental era, and in the Gentile world, and to demonstrate how these point to Jesus of Nazareth.

II.

Let us now look at the broad outline of Biblical teaching. In the Old Testament Scriptures we have three distinct lines. The most prominent is a monarchy of the Davidic type, that is to say a monarchy in which the king is a devoted follower and worshipper of the God of Israel, and while he is His anointed, he also is His servant.

Secondly, we have "the day of the Lord" concept, on which day God will judge mankind, a day that will come in power.

Thirdly, we have the Suffering Servant concept. And though in Israel this was not generally interpreted Messianically, there can be no doubt that in the supreme passage, Isaiah xl-lv, the prophet sees both a suffering nation, and a suffering individual, who suffers for the nation.

It is not quite clear whether we should add to these three the individual whom Daniel describes as "like unto the Son of God." The literature between the Testaments, while it helps us to realize how varied were the theories and beliefs of the people and the writers, does not clear up the point as to whether the "day of the Lord," the Davidic king, and the Suffering Servant are complementary, or exclude each other.

It is clear from the prophets Haggai and Zechariah that they expected the scion of the house of David (Zerubbabel) to assume the office of king. But nothing came of this hope, and the nation passed under the leadership of the priesthood; the high priests were accepted both as spiritual leaders and political representatives. There were of course good and bad high priests.

We are therefore not surprised when we read in the book of "The Testament of the Twelve Patriarchs" the following: "And draw ye near to Levi in humbleness of heart that ye may receive a blessing from his mouth. For he shall bless Israel and Judah, because him hath the Lord chosen to be king over all the nations. And bow down before his seed, for on our behalf it will die in wars visible and invisible, and will be among you an eternal king" (Reuben vi, 19-12). And again: "But they shall not be able to withstand Levi; for he shall wage the war of the Lord, and shall conquer all the hosts" (Simeon, verse 5). Thus we have here a Messiah no longer of the Davidic line, but that of Levi, and a combination of "The day of the Lord" and kingship. The book belongs to the beginning of the last century B.C.

During the early part of this century there came to light a document known as "the Zadokite Fragments." These fragments tell of a Jewish community, settled near Damascus, who called themselves "Zadokites," and in fragment ix, 10, we read of the hopes of these people that God would raise unto them a Messiah from the house of Aaron. In the so-called "Odes and Psalms of Solomon" also, we read: "Behold, O Lord, and raise up to them their king, the Son of David, according to the time which thou seest, O God: and let Him reign over Israel thy servant, and strengthen Him with power that He may humble the sinful rulers" (Psalm xvii, 23-26 [Apocrypha]).

We shall examine in detail the party or sect concepts, but before doing so we must consider one of the most important books of the period between the Testaments, the book, or rather the collection of manuscripts which are gathered under the title, "The Book of Enoch": It should be noted that from this collection we have a quotation in the New Testament (Jude 14). It would serve no useful purpose to enter into the literary criticism of this collection, nor yet to concern ourselves here with the possible dates of the various parts. Suffice it to say that it is beyond reasonable doubt that the passages we shall be dealing with are pre-Christian.

The importance of the teaching of the book is (1) the eternal pre-existence of the Messiah; (2) while the name "The Elect One" is most often applied to the Messiah, the name "Son of Man" occurs frequently. And now let us examine some passages.

"And there I saw One, who had a head of days,
And His head white like wool,
And with Him was another being whose countenance had the appearance
    of a man,
And His face was full of graciousness, like one of the holy angels.
And I asked the angel who went with me and he showed me all the
    hidden things, concerning that Son of Man, who he was, and
    whence he was, and why he went with the Head of Days?
And he answered and said unto me:
This is the Son of man who hath righteousness.
With whom dwelleth righteousness,

And who revealeth all the treasures that are hidden,
Because the Lord of Spirits hath chosen him,
And whose lot hath the pre-eminence before the Lord of Spirits in
    uprightness for ever.
And this Son of man whom thou hast seen,
Shall raise up the kings and the mighty from their seats
And shall loosen the reign of the strong,
And break the teeth of the sinner;
And shall put down the kings from their thrones and kingdoms.
Because they do not extol and praise Him,
Nor humbly acknowledge whence the kingdom was bestowed upon
    them" (xlvi, 1-6).

One other quotation which will confirm and emphasize what has already been said:

"And in that place I saw the fountain of righteousness,
Which was inexhaustible,
And around it were many fountains of wisdom,
And all the thirsty drank from them,
And were filled with wisdom,
And their dwellings were with the righteous and the holy elect.
And at that hour the Son of man was named
In the presence of the Lord of Spirits,
And his name before the Head of Days.
Yea, before the sun and signs were created,
Before the stars of the heavens were made,
His name was named before the Lord of Spirits.
He shall be a staff to the righteous whereon to stay themselves and
    not fall,
And he shall be the light of the Gentiles,
And the hope of those who are troubled of heart" (xlviii, 1-4).

Many other passages might be quoted amplifying what has been cited, but only by reading the whole section can one get the full import of the concept.

For those who ask why Jesus did not use the title "Messiah," and why He used the title "Son of man," there may be a simple answer in the foregoing passages, yet the answer is not so simple.

We have seen something of the diversity of opinions or doctrines of individuals and a whole community, and when we come to consider the parties in Jewry in our Lord's time we find things even more difficult. The Sadducees did not believe in the coming of Messiah; for them the Temple and its services comprised the beginning and end of all things. Nor had the Essenes a Messianic doctrine (as far as we know). What there was of Messianic doctrine at the time was that held and taught by the Pharisees.

Of recent date some scholars have maintained that our Lord did not accept the title "Messiah," indeed He forbade people calling Him by that title; though He

Himself considered Himself the Messiah, He wanted it kept a secret. The position in which our Lord was placed, with all the different beliefs and unbeliefs about the Messiah, was a very, very difficult one. To have proclaimed Himself Messiah He would have had to identify Himself with one of the sects or parties; moreover, the concept of the Suffering Servant had altogether disappeared from the Messianic teaching of the time.

It was in the light of His teaching, life, death and resurrection that He desired man to know and acknowledge Him. No prophet, priest, seer, or school of thought could envisage the whole. He did not hide His Messiahship, but He would not allow that He could be claimed by any sect or under any of the individual theories or theological doctrines of the prophetic schools. He was not only to be the glory of His people Israel, but also a light to lighten the Gentiles. That the Jews at the time of His ministry could not understand or accept Him should be obvious from the doctrines between the Testaments, and if the tomb had not been empty, and His resurrection not been beyond any doubt at least as far as His disciples were concerned, we should have known as little about Him as any of the pretenders to the Messianic office through Jewish history. Of course, all that Moses and the prophets said concerning Him was true, and all that the Psalms and the rest of the Scriptures said was amply justified by the events, and much that the writers between the Testaments speculated upon in relation to the Messiah was a shadow of things to come. But a Messiah that was these things and these things only would never have opened the gates of mercy to the Gentiles. If we get to know all that the Old Testament said, and all that the sages of the Gentiles, men like Zoroaster and others, taught, and all that has been said since His glorious resurrection, and all that is being said now, our knowledge of Him will still fall very short of what He was and is. So let us be done with the "know-all" folk, whose knowledge only leads them to give to Jesus of Nazareth a large place in their little sectarian and partisan theories. He is too great for the greatest that have ever lived. Knowledge of all that had been said about Him does not reveal Him. Only as He comes to one's innermost life, bringing salvation and reconciliation, does one pray. "Oh, that I might know Him (in) the power of His resurrection, and the fellowship of His suffering." And then the heart cries out, "And now I live by faith in the Son of God, who loved me and gave Himself for me."

53 Gaal G'ullah

Born in England. **T. H. Bendor-Samuel** *is a second generation Hebrew Christian and an ordained Baptist clergyman. Currently director of the Messianic Testimony, London, he served as president of the Fellowship of Independent Evangelical Churches, 1967-68 and 1977-78.*

Basic to the Biblical revelation of God are the related concepts of human need and divine aid. God does for us that which we are unable to do for ourselves. He is the God whom we worship and serve, not initially because we are able to meet His requirements and obey His laws, but because, when we were helpless, He intervened to become our Saviour. Among the Bible terms used to describe this are the words, *Gaal,* "to redeem," and *G'ullah,* "redemption." "The word 'redeem' and its related terms appear in the Bible some 130 times" (Jewish Encyclopaedia).

Girdlestone suggests that the original meaning of "Gaal" is to demand back and hence to extricate. It is used in connection with family law in order to preserve the solidarity of the clan. Where the members themselves were unable to act, a relative had the right, and even the obligation, to act for the family. Later, society took over this responsibility. Leviticus 25:25 imposes upon the next of kin the duty to buy back property that had been forfeited and otherwise would have been lost to the family. Leviticus 25:47-49 gives the next of kin the right to redeem a member of the family who had been sold into bondage. In both cases the right and obligation follows the inability of the member to help himself. Numbers 35:16-19 refers to the duty of the kinsman to avenge the death of a member of the family suffering wrong that could only be righted by another. He was the "avenger of blood." The beautiful little book of Ruth is concerned with the position of two helpless women with no prospect of security and prosperity who are raised out of destitution by the action of the *Goel.* Boaz, the nearest kinsman who would accept the responsibility, both preserves the line of the dead husband through the levirate marriage and purchases and property that else would have passed out of the family of Elimelech. In a case of the death of the husband when childless it was the *Goel* who had the obligation of marrying the widow and ensuring that the line did not end. Gesenius suggests that these actions of purchasing, redeeming, avenging and marrying belonging to the near relative resulted in transferring the verb to this office and so to the use of the

"Gaal G'ullah" was published under the title "Great Words of the Old Testament: Gaal G'ullah" in *The Hebrew Christian* 49, no.3 (Autumn 1976):114-18, and is reprinted by permission of The International Hebrew Christian Alliance.

term "Goel," kinsman-redeemer. This practice of family law is found in Israel's early history but there is an interesting example of its survival to a later period in the story in Jeremiah 32. The prophet, who had so faithfully warned Jerusalem of the imminent fall and captivity of the city and who indeed was in prison on account of his predictions, is commanded to demonstrate his confidence in a future restoration by exercising his right as a kinsman to purchase a field that would otherwise have been lost to the family. The right of redemption was his and his use of it recorded in such troublous times was an expression of faith that the exile would end.

NATIONAL REDEMPTION AT THE EXODUS

This term, taken from human and family relationships and practice, is used in Exodus 6:6 and 15:13 of God's action in bringing His people out of their helpless condition of bondage. Moses was told to tell the children of Israel, "I will rid you out of [the Egyptians'] bondage, and I will redeem you with a stretched out arm, and with great judgments." The promise was given to those who were totally unable to save themselves. Israel was to become God's special property on account of what He was about to do for her and He would avenge her of the wrong she had suffered. After the exodus Moses' song of thanksgiving in chapter 15 says, "Thou in thy mercy hast led forth the people which thou hast redeemed." This is an important reminder that God revealed Himself to Israel by what He did. Emil Brunner contrasts the "Redeemer-gods" of mythology with the Biblical religion. He says, "In mythology even the mystery of redemption remains an idea, a possibility, a longing. In the Biblical religion it is attested as 'Factum est,' as something which has taken place at the nadir of human history." This is the sense in which God has done for a helpless people in becoming their redeemer and showing Himself to be the living God.

On God's side, His people are seen as belonging to Him just as the property or persons of those who are redeemed in family law belong to the clan. Their loss deprived the group and had to be made good. So Israel belonged to the Lord. Her slavery deprived Him of His people and something had to be done about it. He could not disregard the position, and national redemption was the assertion of His rights. On her side, God's people had a claim upon Him. Their inability to save themselves constituted a claim upon Him. In a very real sense, whether she was aware of it or not, the promise and covenant with Abraham placed the Lord Who made it under the obligation of redeeming her. The very covenant relationship guaranteed His intervention, and the use of the term Gaal suggests this. Exodus 4:22 "Israel is my son" expresses this relationship.

"REDEMPTION" IN THE PROPHETS

Israel's need and the Lord's power to meet it did not end with the birth of the nation. Succeeding generations brought repeated manifestations of both. This was especially so at the Captivity, and the prophets use the term for their national hope and for the triumph of God over evil. Hosea, Micah and Jeremiah all use the word when speaking of their hope for the future. But it is in Isaiah that this use is found the most, so much so that A. R. Johnson writes that "Yahweh's role as the Redeemer, 'Goel,' of His people is a conception which dominates the thought of Deutero-Isaiah from end to end.'' The relationship between the Lord and the nation is seen as continuing despite adversity and captivity and this is the guarantee of her ultimate restoration. He is her Redeemer Who will restore her to her lost position and her Avenger Who will redress the wrong that she has suffered. He is "the LORD, the Redeemer of Israel" 49:7. "Thou, O LORD, art our father, our redeemer" Isaiah 63:16.

"Redemption" as a Personal Faith

Side by side with this national hope for the future is the use of the term for a personal relationship with God. What He is to the nation He is also to the individual. Klausner attributes the growth of a personal faith in the Messiah to Israel's experience of oppression and captivity. "The prophets were the first in Israel who began to feel that there is in the world a greater evil than [political wrong]: *Personal evil,* the wrong which man does to his fellow man. It is no wonder, then, that for the most part the prophets thought of the redemption from personal evil as a personal redemption. Thus the man who will bring this redemption, the Messiah, had to be the embodiment of the highest righteousness which tolerates no evil."[1] Apart from the title "Redeemer" as applied to the Messiah it is frequently used for a personal relationship with God. Jacob does so in Genesis 48:16, "The Angel which redeemed me from all evil." Many of Psalms do so: "O Lord, my strength and my redeemer" 19:14; "Who redeemeth thy life from destruction" 103:4. The best-known instance of this is Job's remarkable cry of faith in a personal "Goel" in spite of all that he was suffering and even in spite of death itself. "I know that my redeemer liveth" 19:25. We must leave on one side the dispute as to whether Job says he will see God in this or in a future life and any reference to a bodily resurrection. He had faith in a God-given vindication. H. L. Ellison says, "He knew that God must vindicate him" and describes his words as "the leap of faith." What the "Goel" was to the family when in need and under oppression God will be to him in spite of his suffering and rejection. It was the duty of the avenger of blood to vindicate the honour of the family. This is what Job so passionately claimed. The very fact that his words come out of the twilight of revelation and without the clearer knowledge that we possess through the New Testament revelation of a risen Christ makes his faith the more remarkable. This warm personal use of the term "Goel" is something more than a legal function or even a national hope. "Redeemer" has become one of the most precious titles that needy men employ for a gracious and omnipotent God.

The Function of the Messiah

In Christian thought the title Redeemer is used most frequently of the Messiah, the Lord Jesus. The functions of the "Goel" in liberating the slave, redeeming the lost property, giving life to the dying family and vindicating the oppressed and dishonoured, are often said to be fulfilled in a spiritual sense by Him. Actually, the term is not used directly and specifically of the Messiah in the Old Testament. Redemption is spoken of as the work of God Himself. Isaiah's use of the title is, however, in a Messianic setting. The Lord Himself redeems and delivers but the passages which tell of this also show that it is to be accomplished through the Messiah, His chosen Servant. Isaiah 59:20, ''And the Redeemer shall come to Zion, and unto them that turn from transgression in Jacob,'' is applied by St. Paul to the returning Messiah in Romans 11:26. Klausner traces the origin of the idea of a Messiah back to the figure of Moses. ''The exalted picture of Moses impressed itself upon the spirit of the nation and became the symbol of the redeemer in general.'' ''The Talmud and Midrash name Moses 'the first redeemer' in contrast to the Messiah, who is 'the last redeemer.' '' ''Gaal'' is sometimes used in the Old Testament in the simple sense of deliverance apart from the function of the kinsman. It is the natural tendency of language to lose its specific aspect and to be used in a more general way. The New Testament words for purchase and liberation by purchase are frequently used of the Lord Jesus Who ''redeemed us by His blood.'' It would be difficult to say that the office of the kinsman-redeemer does not find its highest expression in the person and work of the Messiah but the title is not directly used of Him in the Old Testament. The anointed One, Messiah, is the agent of the Lord. The Goel is God Who used Him. Christian identification of the ''Goel'' with the Lord Jesus is beautifully expressed in Jean Ingelow's line, ''O God, O Kinsman loved but not enough.'' God's relationship to His people as ''Goel'' is ultimately discharged through Him Who in the Incarnation became one with us in our humanity, and Who paid redemption's price by His great sacrifice.

Notes

1. Joseph Klausner, *The Messianic Idea in Israel,* trans. W. F. F. Stinespring (New York: Macmillan, 1955), p. 23. Reprinted with permission of Macmillan Publishing Co., Inc. from *The Messianic Idea in Israel* by Joseph Klausner, trans. W. F. F. Stinespring. Copyright 1955 by Macmillan Publishing Co., Inc.

54 Bethlehem: Born Under the Law

Harcourt Samuel is a second generation Hebrew Christian.
He was born in England and held the office of mayor of
Ramsgate 1944-45 and 1955-58. Harcourt Samuel is
currently treasurer of the International Hebrew Christian
Alliance and an officer of the Order of the British Empire.

"But when the fulness of the time was come, God sent forth His Son, made of a woman, made under the law, to redeem them that were under the law, that we might receive the adoption of sons"—Galatians iv. 4, 5.

At Bethlehem, the Son of God was born a man that in Him all men might become sons of God. He was born subject to the Law that those subject to the Law might be rescued from bondage.

In the Galatian passage cited above we have brought before us the great *fact of His coming*; we have also the *time of His coming*; then we get the *manner of His coming*, and lastly, the *purpose of His coming*. The *fact* is stated thus: God sent forth His Son; the *time* is given to us—it was "when the fulness of the time was come"; the *manner* of His coming is shown to us—He was made of a woman, made under the Law. The *purpose* for which He came was that He might redeem them that were under the law, and that we might receive the adoption of sons.

First, we get the *fact of His coming*, simply and concisely stated: "God sent forth His Son." There are implications in that very simple statement which we must not overlook, the first of which most surely is that God sent Him—"God sent forth"—Christ therefore existed before He came into the world. Surely of no other son could it be said that on his coming into the world he was sent forth by his father. Yet the fact is that long before Bethlehem, Christ was. He was in the beginning with God, and was sent forth by His Father. Another of the implications of this statement is that in the sublime mystery of the Trinity there are at least two distinct Persons— three, of course, but at the moment we are only concerned with two—existing side by side. The very fact that God sent forth His Son declares to us, then, that there were two persons, each existing side by side, in one, yet they were separate—one God, the other His Son.

And the last of the implications is bound up in that word "sent" —God " 'sent'

"Bethlehem: Born Under the Law" is reprinted from *The Hebrew Christian 5*, no.2 (July 1932):69-72, by permission of The International Hebrew Christian Alliance.

forth His Son." He came with a commission to fulfil and a task to accomplish, obedient to the commands of His Father, to carry out His will. Thus the simple fact of His coming is that God sent forth His Son.

Second, we have here also the *time of His coming*—it was "when the fulness of the time was come," that is the time fixed in the counsels of God. The world had waited long for His coming; through long weary years the Deliverer who had been promised was constantly expected. We are told that every mother in Israel secretly hoped that hers might be the privilege of giving birth to the coming Deliverer. Certainly Eve expected that privilege, for when her first son was born she called him Cain, and said, "I have gotten The Man"—not "a man," mind you, but "The Man." But she was unhappily mistaken; and soon she was to find that out . . .

So we might pass through the long centuries, and how the hearts of the people must have been heavy; how they must have cried out and longed for the coming of their Messiah; and all the time wickedness and oppression increased. In God's own time He came—"When the fulness of His time was come"—the time fixed in the counsels of Eternity. He came, too, just when the world was ripe for His coming. God makes no mistakes, and the fulness of His time proved to be that when the time was best suited for the spreading of the Gospel. True, it seemed a weary and a sin-worn world that met the coming of the Redeemer, but now, looking back, we notice how carefully the world had been prepared for His advent, and that the conditions then existing were those best suited for the spreading of the Gospel.

There were three great peoples at that time; first there were the Romans, the masters of the world; secondly, the Greeks, now decadent, but not without influence; and thirdly, the Jews, most despised of all, yet playing a wonderful part in spreading the Gospel.

The Roman Empire meant a world at peace—it was peace at the point of the sword, we know, but nevertheless, peace; a peace which existed because the rest of the world was crushed into submission. But still, it was peace. In every part of the then civilised world it was possible for men to travel from country to country without any disturbance. The Roman power had constructed many great roads— some of the roads they built in this little island of ours [British Isles—Ed.] still remain. In Asia Minor, Europe, North Africa, Palestine and Syria they made their roads—the Roman roads that were used by the first heralds of the Cross. Even pagan Rome had its part to play in the preparation for the coming of Christ.

Then there were the Greeks. It was not their philosophy, but their language which God used. They possessed one of the most beautiful and flexible of all tongues, and their language was spoken well-nigh universally; all over the Roman Empire, in Athens and Alexandria, even in Palestine and throughout Asia Minor, in all these places Greek was spoken. Just a little while before, the Old Testament had been translated into Greek, the version we now call the Septuagint. This language was destined to be the vehicle for the transmission of the New Testament. Had the Scriptures been written in Hebrew only, they would have been very limited in their circulation. But all knew Greek, and in Greek the Scriptures were written and passed from country to country, and, in all those countries, they were understood.

Then there were the Jews, dispersed throughout the world. The majority of the

Jewish people had not lived in Palestine since the Babylonian captivity, there were far more Jews outside Palestine than in. Trade took them far and wide into the furthest outposts of the Empire, and everywhere they went they talked of their faith in Jehovah, in their one God, Jehovah; and everywhere they went they built a Synagogue or proseuche, a little house of prayer by the waterside, and gradually they gathered around them those who were dissatisfied with their heathen rites. Thus there grew up a company of proselytes, and devout men who knew the one true God.

The Romans made the spread of the Gospel possible by the peace that prevailed; the Greeks gave their language, and the Jews spread abroad, even in their dispersion, the knowledge of the one God. The time had fully come—prepared by the Hand of God Himself.

Then, we have the *manner of His coming*. This is stated to us quite clearly— "God sent forth his Son, made of a woman, made under the law." "Made of a woman"; by this we understand that He entered into relationship with all mankind. "Made under the law." That means to say He took upon Himself the obligations imposed by the Law of Moses and entered into a special relationship with the Jewish people. Born of a Jewish mother, at the age of eight days He was circumcised; and when one month old He was presented in the Temple. We read of His presence at the different feasts as they recurred; that He willingly paid the Temple Tax, although He pointed out that He was free therefrom—the law was made for God's servants, and not for His Divine Son. But willingly He became as others, and paid the tax . . .

He lived but to fulfil the will of His Father. He Himself said, "I come not to destroy, but to fulfi ," and perfectly He fulfilled the Law, both as to precept and penalty, not for His own sins, but for ours.

So we come to the climax of the whole argument—the great *purpose of His coming*. This is two-fold, even as the manner of His coming—"To redeem them that were under the law, that we might receive the adoption of sons."

"To redeem them that were under the law." Let us take that first. There are three Greek words that are translated "Redeem." First, *"lutroo,"* which means to ransom; then *"agorazo,"* which means to buy in the market place—a figure of speech taken from the prevailing slavery; and thirdly, *"exagorazo,"* which means to buy out of the market place, never again to be exposed for sale. The last is the word that is used in our text. He redeemed them that were under the Law—He bought out those that were under the Law. The word itself gives us a hint of the bondage in which the Law held those who were born under it and those who took its yoke upon them. From that bondage Christ has set us free, never again to be entangled with its yoke. The yoke of the Law was indeed a heavy one. Peter's testimony was that it was a yoke that neither he nor his fathers had ever been able to bear. Christ took that yoke upon Himself that it might be lifted from our shoulders; He redeemed us from the curse of the Law, Himself being made a curse for us. On those who failed beneath its burden the Law pronounced a curse—Christ took that curse and bore it—nay, He did more than that. Look at Galatians Chapter iii, verse 13, and let every word sink in:—"Christ hath redeemed us from the curse of the law, being made a curse for us." . . . Free from the curse Himself, He not only passed under it, but was actually made a curse Himself that we might be bought out and set free for ever.

The second purpose of His coming was that we might receive the adoption of sons. Adoption is the giving of legal sonship to those who do not possess it by nature. We are not by nature the children of God, but are children of wrath (Eph. ii.3); but in Christ we receive the adoption of sons. We who were not His by nature become His because He receives us into His family. A beautiful example of this is given us in Onesimus, a slave, who ran away from his master, Philemon, and we may safely assume that he did not go empty-handed. He fled to Rome, and whilst there he came under the influence of the Gospel. He became useful to Paul, but Paul was too much of a Christian gentleman to profit at another man's expense, so he sent the slave back to his master, and asked him to overlook his misdeed, to forgive him and set him free. The Roman law dealt harshly with slaves and decreed that slaves who deserted their masters should be put to death or else set free; so Paul writes to Philemon and says, "Receive him no longer as a slave, but as a brother;—set him free." And then he goes yet farther, and says, "Receive him as myself." Can you picture that? If Paul had been set free from his prison chamber and come to the house of Philemon, how gladly he would have been welcomed, and given of their very best. And Paul tells them, "The welcome you would give to me, give to him.

And this is what Christ has done for us. We were in bondage but He has set us free; and He has not only set us free, but brought us the adoption of sons. "In Him the tribes of Adam boast more blessings than their father lost"; we have passed into the family of God; we have received the adoption of sons.

So we see that Bethlehem is the story of how the Son of God was born of a woman, that the sons of the woman might, through union with Him, become the sons of God.

55 Fundamentals of Our Holy Faith

*Joseph Immanuel Landsman was the son of pious and
well-to-do Jewish parents who lived in Lithuania. He
studied at the famous Yeshivahs of Vilno and Volozhin,
where he received an excellent knowledge of Hebrew and
rabbinics. At about eighteen he gained a conviction of the
Messiahship of Jesus and as a result was obliged to leave
his parents' home. He enrolled at the University of
Stockholm, where he studied theology, philosophy, and
Oriental languages. He also studied under Franz Delitzsch,
the great scholar of Semitics, at the Judaic Institute in
Leipzig. For about twenty-five years he was associated with
the Hebrew Christian testimony to Israel in London. In 1926
he founded in Warsaw a school for biblical and Judaistic
studies for young Hebrew Christians. He wrote numerous
pamphlets, a* Life of Jesus the Messiah, *and edited* Der
Weg, *a bimonthly in Yiddish and Hebrew.*

    The religion of Jesus the Messiah is neither a heathenish nor a new fangled
religion. It is the old religion of Moses, the prophets and their true and upright
followers, but with this difference: while the prophets and their followers longed
and waited for the redemption Messiah would bring to Israel and the world, we
Hebrew Christians, together with all true Christians, believe that Messiah has come,
and that Jesus of Nazareth is the true Messiah of Israel, and that he has brought us
and the whole world the salvation of which all the prophets from Moses to Malachi
prophesied. The religion of the New Testament, therefore, is the old and pure
religion of our nation with the promises He made through the prophets.
    We, as well as all true Christians, believe in the God of Israel, in God Who
created Heaven and earth, who revealed Himself to our people first through Moses
and the prophets and last through our Messiah Jesus, Blessed be His Name! How
marvelous is God's creation above, under and around us! In creation God's greatness, His infinite power, His unsearchable wisdom and goodness are revealed to our
intellect. Yet creation is silent about the deepest things in God, His thoughts, His
will, His attributes and His plan for man. The highest in His being God reveals to us
through His holy word spoken through the prophets. The Holy Scriptures of our

This essay, written originally in Yiddish, is adapted from J. I. Landsman, *Fundamentals of Our Holy
Faith,* E. S. Greenbaum (Newark, N.J.: Lightbearers, 1927).

people are also precious and holy to all true Christians, but we consider as holy not only the Old Testament, but also the New Testament, which narrates to us the story of God sending "Messiah our Righteousness" into the world. It tells how He lived, what He did, how our people rejected Him, how He suffered and sacrificed His own body. The New Testament also contains books which explain to us the *meaning* of the life, suffering, death and resurrection of the Messiah. The New Testament, therefore, must have for us the same authority as the Old Testament, for they both are the words of the living God.

On the following pages the reader will find our messianic "*I believe.*" It contains the fundamentals of our faith. This is not the place for a commentary on our articles of faith. That would form a book by itself. We must be content by merely saying that the greater part of our "*I believe*" deals with God's Salvation who appeared in the world for Israel and all the human race. It also shows the way sinful man can be saved and become His true child, and how man can be enabled to live according to God's good and perfect will, as it is revealed in the life and teaching of the Lord Jesus.

When we say, "I believe," we do not wish merely to state that we hold as truth that which is contained in the article of faith, but first and foremost that we believe in God with a living and personal faith, trust Him fully, love Him with our whole heart, our whole soul and with all the powers of our body and intellect. Also when we say, "We believe in Jesus the Messiah," we do not merely mean that we hold as truth His claim to be the Messiah and Son of God, but that we long to live in full communion with Him, continually to be kept under His influence, to learn of Him and be guided by Him all the days of our life, so that He may rule and govern our lives. As soon as our faith becomes a living faith, a continual looking up to Him, we realize that we have a living God Who saves, redeems and sanctifies us through the Righteous Redeemer. Such a faith makes us new creatures, gives us strength and helps us to overcome the world and all its evils.

> "Who is he that overcometh the world, but he that believeth that Jesus is the Son of God? . . . This is the victory that overcometh the world, even our faith." 1 John 5:5, 4.

1. I believe with a perfect faith* in Jehovah the Eternal God of Israel, the God of Love and Salvation, the Creator of heaven and earth, and of all things visible and invisible. He is the One God and Father. Of Him, and through Him, and to Him are all things, and He is over all and with all and in all. He is the glory for ever. Amen.

> 1 John 4:7-15; John 3:16; Romans 5:8; Genesis 1:1; Psalm 33:6; 1 Corinthians 8:6; Ephesians 4:6; Romans 11:36; Mark 12:28-34; John 17:23.

2. I believe with a perfect faith that God—blessed be His name!—is Spirit, and that the true worshippers must worship their Father in heaven in spirit and in truth, for with such worshippers the Father is well pleased.

> John 4:21-24; Romans 12:1; Hebrews 12:15; James 1:27.

3. I believe with a perfect faith in Messiah Jesus our Lord, the only begotten and

---

*I retain the idiom in the Hebrew formula used by Mr. Landsman, which is the same as that with which the Thirteen Articles of the Jewish Creed commence. What is meant is, "I believe firmly," or, "with all my heart."—TRANSLATOR

well-beloved of His Father in heaven, whom God raised up to be the Redeemer of Israel, according to the promise which He made to our Fathers through His holy prophets—Who for us men and our salvation descended from heaven and became man.

He was conceived of the Holy Spirit, born of the Virgin Mary, of the seed of David, and was anointed of God with the Holy Spirit and with power. He was in all points tempted as we are, but without sin. He glorified His father in heaven, and made known His Name and His holy will to the children of men. He walked about on earth doing good to the people of Israel.

He bore the reproach of sinners, and was afflicted and humbled Himself unto death; yea, the death of the cross—the Righteous One for the unrighteous.

He was bruised for our iniquities; the chastisement of our peace was upon Him! and with His stripes we are healed.

Wherefore also God has highly exalted Him and raised Him up again from the dead on the third day after His death and burial. He showed Himself openly to His disciples after His resurrection, and ascended into heaven, where He now sits at the right hand of God; but thence He shall come again a second time in glory to set up His Kingdom, restore all things, and to judge the living and the dead.

He shall reign over the house of Jacob for ever, and of His Kingdom there shall be no end.

> Matthew 3:17, 17:5; Luke 2:10-11; John 3:13; Philippians 2:5-11; Matthew 1:1, 18-23; Romans 1:3, 4; Matthew 3:13-17; Acts 10:38; Hebrews 1:13-14, 2:17, 18; 1 Peter 3:18; Isaiah 9:6-7; Matthew 20:28, 26:26, 27; Acts 2:22-36, 3:12-26, 4:8-12, 5:30-31; Romans 8:34; Acts 1:9-11; Timothy 4:1; Luke 1:30-35.

4. I believe with a perfect faith that Messiah Jesus our Lord is the image of the invisible God, the effulgence of His glory, the very image of His being, and the pre-existing cause of all things. He is the power of God and the wisdom of God. In Him dwells the fulness of the Godhead bodily, and in Him are hid all the treasures of wisdom and knowledge. He that sees Him sees our Father in heaven. He is the Way, the Truth and the Life, and no one comes unto the Father but by Him.

> Matthew 11:26-30; Colossians 1:16-17; Hebrews 1:1-4; 1 Corinthians 1:23-24; Colossians 2:3-9; John 14:1-14.

5. I believe with a perfect faith that for us first God did raise up Messiah Jesus, and sent Him to bless and to save His people from all their sins, and although our fathers rebelled and sinned against Him, God did not cast off His people, but exalted Jesus to be a Prince and a Saviour, to give repentance unto Israel and the forgiveness of sins—even to as many as believe on the Name of Messiah Jesus with a true and perfect heart.

> Acts 3:25-26, 13:26, 5:31, 3:19-20.

6. I believe with a perfect faith that by the determinate counsel and foreknowledge of God our fathers rejected Messiah Jesus, the King of Israel, but through their fall the door of salvation was flung wide open to the Gentiles, that they might be brought near to God and to His salvation in the Messiah. But when the mission of making the message of the Gospel known to all the nations will be completed, the

end-time will come; Messiah Jesus will return; Israel will be redeemed spiritually and fully restored nationally, and God's rule will be established in the whole earth.

> Hosea 3:1-5; Isaiah 11:1-12; Matthew 24:14; Acts 2:23; 3:17-18; 15:1-18; Romans 11:11-32.

7. I believe with a perfect faith that when Messiah Jesus offered Himself on the Cross as an atonement for the sins of the whole world, He fulfilled the substance and aim of the Law; He broke down the wall of partition between Jews and Gentiles. He reconciled both to God, and one to another, and made of both a new creature. And now there is neither slave nor free, neither Jew nor Gentile, neither male nor female; but all are one in Messiah Jesus.

> Ephesians 2:14-22; Galatians 3:26-29; Colossians 3:10-11.

8. I believe with a perfect faith that the Messiah is the fulfillment of the law unto righteousness to all them that believe on Him, and that it is by faith in Him apart from the works of the law that men are justified before God; for by the works of the law no human being can either be justified or perfected.

> Romans 3:21-30; 4:5; Galatians 2:15-17; 3:10-11; Hebrews 7:18-19.

9. I believe with a perfect faith that in Messiah Jesus neither circumcision availeth anything nor uncircumcision, but a new creation, and faith which works by love; for love out of a pure heart is the aim of the whole law and its true fulfilment, and whoever is in the Messiah is a new creation, created unto good works.

> Galatians 5:5; 6:15; 1 Timothy 1:5; Romans 13:8-10; 2 Corinthians 5:17; Ephesians 2:10.

10. I believe with a perfect faith in the Holy Spirit, the Blessed Comforter, who dwells for ever with them that believe, to sanctify them and to lead them into all truth.

> John 14:16-17, 26; 16:7-14.

11. I believe with a perfect faith that God, Who spoke unto our fathers through the prophets, has in the last days spoken unto us by His Son Jesus the Messiah, and that both alike are the words of the living God.

> Hebrews 1:1; 2 Peter 1:21; John 6:63, 68; 7:16-18; 12:44-50.

12. I believe with a perfect faith that the Holy Scriptures which we now possess were written under the perfect inspiration of the Holy Spirit, and are able to make us wise unto Salvation through faith in the Messiah Jesus, and to lead us in the ways of righteousness so that we may be . . . completely furnished unto all good works.

> 2 Timothy 3:15-17; Hebrews 4:12-13.

13. I believe with a perfect faith in one holy Messianic body, consisting of all true believers, and built on the foundation of the Apostles and Prophets, Jesus the Messiah Himself being the chief Cornerstone. I believe in one baptism; in the forgiveness of sins; in the resurrection of the dead, and in the life everlasting. Amen.

> Ephesians 2:19-22; Romans 12:4-5; 1 Corinthians 12:12-13; Colossians 1:18; 1 Corinthians 1:2; 2 Corinthians 1:1; Ephesians 1:1; Philippians 1:1; Ephesians 4:5; Acts 2:38; Ephesians 1:7-8; Colossians 1:14; 1 John 1:8-9; 1 Corinthians 15; John 5:24-29; 6:32-55.

56 Fulfillment in the Messiah

Bernard B. Gair received the M.A. degree from New York University and taught history in New York City high schools. A past president of the Hebrew Christian Alliance of America, he is currently an associate editor of The Interpreter.

The Bible, basic source of moral and spiritual teachings for Jew and Christian alike, was a closed book to me until I reached my thirties. I was able to get through college and well advanced in my graduate studies before I was confronted with the dynamism of its spiritual message.

In my childhood, up to the age of Bar Mitzvah (when the Jewish boy is ceremoniously admitted into the membership of the community of Israel), I had attended the Talmud Torah (Jewish schools) and was introduced in a superficial way to the books of Moses (the Pentateuch). I was instructed by my rabbis in traditional Jewish teachings and observances. But I was ignorant of the relationship between the Bible and God's plan for the Jew and how that plan linked the Jew with the spiritual destiny of other people.

Was the Bible to be taken seriously? Were not its contents and teachings out of tune with enlightened man and modern scientific knowledge? Could its teachings help man solve the deep personal, moral, and social problems of the twentieth century? In short, was the Bible a live option and a serious competitor of the widespread dogmas of Communism, secularism, and materialism?

I began a detailed study of the Bible—Old and New Testament. And what I discovered changed my life. A new vision of what life was meant to be came to me and a new power to deal with my own human nature was imparted to me. God became a personal and firsthand reality.

"Come now, and let us reason together, saith the LORD" (Isa. 1:18). Thus spoke the Old Testament prophet to the people of Israel. His inspired words were directed to the minds and consciences of God's chosen people, and they are directed towards us.

About what shall we reason? What is more profitable to man, more suited to his dignity as a spiritual being made in the image of God, than to reflect on his divine origin, his spiritual destiny, and his relationship to his Creator? "For what shall it profit a man, if he shall gain the whole world, and lose his own soul?" (Mark 8:36).

Is man only an animal, that he should confine his intellectual and moral powers to the satisfaction of his physical and natural appetites and to the acquisition of knowledge related only to the world of nature? Is human life purely a matter of biology and physics? Are man's supreme values confined within the parentheses of birth and death?

Human philosophy has exhausted itself in seeking answers to questions like those. But is man capable of peering into the ultimates and finding solutions to his deepest spiritual and moral problems? The Bible comes to us with unparalleled authority and speaks in no uncertain tones. Can we afford to reject words that purport to come from God Himself? We do so at the peril of deepest loss.

The authority for our knowledge of man as he came from the hands of God is the Tanach (the Old Testament). Although a creature of flesh and blood, man was endowed with an intimate and wondrous comradeship with the Creator. He was on talking terms with God and was to exercise authority over the lesser creatures of the earth. But through the sin of the first human, Adam, in the Garden of Eden that perfect fellowship was broken.

Tragic consequences for Adam and all mankind were set in motion. The tree of the knowledge of good and evil has borne bitter fruit: pride, lust, fear, envy, greed, injustice. The Bible calls that evil assortment by the short but ugly name of sin. The facts of history and biology cooperate to demonstrate that the ultimate consequence of sin is death: death in the body and death in the spirit. And the Bible teaches that spiritual death is separation from God, alienation of the human spirit from the Holy Spirit. When the human spirit at death sheds its physical body without having recovered its true spiritual relation to God, the separation from God is forever: eternal death.

Apparently the fate of man and mankind is sealed. Is there no way out of this awful situation? Has man no future filled with promise and hope? The answer would be no, except for God. God, whose very nature is love, is moved with infinite compassion by the tragic plight of man. Love and mercy set into motion a divine plan to rescue man hopelessly caught in his web of self-centered strivings and to restore him to acceptance with God.

From man's side, obviously such a spiritual restoration is impossible. Man's essential nature has been utterly corrupted by his act of high treason against God. The tragic gap between man's sinfulness and God's utter holiness is unbridgeable. Only the Lord by an act of free and sovereign mercy can reestablish communication.

In His infinite wisdom God chose from among all the peoples of the earth a people insignificant from the standpoint of political, economic, cultural, and military power. He chose Israel to be the instrument for human redemption. Why did He select Israel for His program? "Thou art an holy people unto the Lord thy God: the Lord thy God hath chosen thee to be a special people unto himself, above all people that are upon the face of the earth. The Lord did not set his love upon you, nor choose you, because ye were more in number than any people . . . but because the Lord loved you, and because he would keep the oath which he had sworn unto your fathers" (Deut. 7:6-8).

Israel as a people would prepare the way for the coming of a Deliverer, or Messiah. He would be God's way of healing the tragic rift that Adam had caused by his disobedience. The Messiah would provide atonement, reconciliation, and restoration.

The world was not yet ready to receive Him. Israel would have to pave the way by preparing the minds and consciences of people to accept Him when He came as Messiah and Savior. How was that to be done? Israel would be educated and prepared for a coming Redeemer by law and sacrifice. Israel was to be provided with a set of moral principles and ceremonial observances by means of which she would witness to God as a holy, altogether righteous Sovereign. That meant Israel would have to become a separated and dedicated people. The moral law would permit man no excuse for ignorance. God had spoken; it was for man to obey.

Cleansings, offerings, sacrifices, specific acts of worship, and ritualistic observances—all were planned by God to teach moral and spiritual lessons. What was the heart of the sacrificial system? Always the sacrifices pointed to the time when God would provide a permanent and spiritual atonement, a divine sacrifice who would do for man what no moral effort or sacrificial ritual could do. And what was that atonement to do? To make man wholly acceptable to God, forgiven, restored, and made righteous in His sight.

The intrusion of God into the stream of human history would be the most revolutionary event of man's life upon earth. How could the people of Israel recognize the Redeemer when He came? God revealed in the Old Testament in utmost detail how, where, and under what circumstances the God-Man would come. Some biblical references are presented here for earnest study:

His manner of birth (Isa. 7:14); His place of birth (Mic. 5:2); when He was to come (Gen. 49:10); what His mission would be (Deut. 18:15; Isa. 53; 61:1-3); how He would be received (Isa. 53:3); how He would respond to mistreatment (Isa. 53:7-9); what would happen to Him (Psalm 16:10; Isa. 53:10; Jer. 23:5; Dan. 7:14); various aspects of His character (Isa. 32:1-2; Num. 24:7; Jer. 23:5-6; Mic. 5:2-4; Isa. 9:6-7).

The Old Testament vividly sets forth man's need for a redeemer who would bring salvation to Israel and to all men. The New Testament is the fulfillment of the Old. The old covenant with its priesthood, its Temple, and its sacrificial system is no more. It has been superseded by the Messiah who became our sacrifice, is now our High Priest, and is to be worshiped in spirit and in truth in our hearts.

Jeremiah had prophesied that the old covenant with its absolute moral principles was not adequate to change the heart of man. God was soon to establish a new covenant that would bring spiritual regeneration and an inner righteousness to Israel that would indeed be acceptable to Almighty God. "Behold, the days come, saith the LORD, that I will make a new covenant with the house of Israel, and with the house of Judah; not according to the covenant that I made with their fathers . . . which my covenant they brake . . . but this shall be the covenant that I will make with the house of Israel; After those days, saith the LORD, I will put my law in their inward parts, and write it in their hearts; and will be their God, and they shall be my people" (Jer. 31:31-33).

That new and radical relationship to God became a reality with the coming of Jesus of Nazareth, of the house of David, tribe of Judah, and His crucifixion at

Calvary. The Messiah, Jesus, was rejected by His own people just as Isaiah had predicted (chapter 53). The apostle John recounted: "He came unto his own, and his own received him not" (John 1:11). Isaiah, commenting on the mission of the coming Messiah, wrote: "He was wounded for our transgressions, he was bruised for our iniquities: the chastisement of our peace was upon him; and with his stripes we are healed. All we like sheep have gone astray; we have turned every one to his own way; and the LORD hath laid on him the iniquity of us all" (Isa. 53:5-6).

Jesus bore the full penalty for man's sin and disobedience. His identification with our human nature was complete to the point of being crushed by the weight of man's moral failure and guilt. For one awful moment Jesus endured separation from God. God's judgment on our sin fell on Him. "My God, my God," He uttered, "why hast thou forsaken me?" (Matt. 27:46).

But death could not hold the sinless One. "It is finished" (John 19:30), He cried—words filled with infinite significance for all the ages to come. Man's sins were paid for—in full. God's Messiah had purchased man's complete liberation. The enemy, Satan, had been conquered. The divine sacrifice had been made. Full pardon to all men was now available to any who would receive God's gift of reconciliation. By receiving Jesus in an act of faith, men can now enter into the very Holy of Holies—God—not because we have merited such divine forgiveness and intimacy but solely because of His mercy and grace. Isaiah's prophecy seven centuries earlier was consummated. "With his stripes we are healed" (Isa. 53:5).

The sacrifice of the Messiah, Jesus, on the cross is only the prologue to God's further merciful dealings with man. What do we learn as we search the Scriptures? (1) The mighty Spirit of God raised Jesus from the dead, (2) He walked the earth and continued teaching His disciples for forty days, (3) He ascended to heaven and was restored to His position at the right hand of God the Father, (4) He poured out His Holy Spirit on assembled believers, thus forming the church, (5) He is now seated in the heavenlies, hearing our prayers and opening up the resources of heaven to those who trust Him, and (6) He will return again to the earth, at that time to judge those who have rejected God's offer of mercy and salvation. There will be no appeal from His judgment. Eternal separation awaits the unbeliever who refused to accept God as the Sovereign of his life and instead chose self. That is the major offense: rejection of God and His love.

For those who have admitted Jesus Christ into their lives as Savior and Lord He will one day perform the miracle of resurrection; He will raise their bodies and transform them into glorious, incorruptible bodies. They shall indeed reign with Christ.

When a Jew accepts the Messiah, Jesus, he is not less a Jew, but rather becomes a "completed" Jew, for he has found in his life and spirit the fulfillment of the promises made by God to our fathers. He becomes, together with all believers—Jew and Gentile—a redeemed son of God, a spiritual Israelite.

57 Jesus of Nazareth . . . The Eternal Glory of the Jewish Race

*The following is an excerpt from a statement by **Benjamin Disraeli**, otherwise known as Lord Beaconsfield, one of Queen Victoria's prime ministers.**

Perhaps, too, in this enlightened age, as his mind expands, and he takes a comprehensive view of this period of progress, the pupil of Moses may ask himself, whether all the princes of the house of David have done so much for the Jews as that prince who was crucified on Calvary. Had it not been for Him, the Jews would have been comparatively unknown, or known only as a high Oriental caste which had lost its country. Has not He made their history the most famous in the world? Has not He hung up their laws in every temple? Has He not vindicated all their wrongs? Has not He avenged the victory of Titus and conquered the Caesars? What success did they anticipate from their Messiah? The wildest dreams of their Rabbis have been far exceeded. Has not Jesus conquered Europe and changed its name into Christendom? . . . The whole of the new world is devoted to the Semitic principle and its most glorious offspring, the Jewish faith, and the time will come when the vast communities and countless myriads of America and Australia, looking upon Greece, and wondering how so small a space could have achieved such great deeds, will still find music in the songs of Zion and still seek solace in the parables of Galilee.

These may be dreams, but there is one fact which none can contest. Christians may continue to persecute Jews, and Jews may persist in disbelieving Christians, but who can deny that Jesus of Nazareth, the Incarnate Son of the Most High God, is the eternal glory of the Jewish race?

*Benjamin Disraeli, *Lord George Bentinck: A Political Biography* (London: Colburn, 1852), pp. 363-64.

The Return of Jesus

And so when they had come together, they were asking Him, saying, "Lord, is it at this time You are restoring the kingdom to Israel?" He said to them, "It is not for you to know times or epochs which the Father has fixed by His own authority; but you shall receive power when the Holy Spirit has come upon you; and you shall be My witnesses both in Jerusalem, and in all Judea and Samaria, and even to the remotest part of the earth." And after He had said these things, He was lifted up while they were looking on, and a cloud received Him out of their sight. And as they were gazing intently into the sky while He was departing, behold, two men in white clothing stood beside them; and they also said, "Men of Galilee, why do you stand looking into the sky? This Jesus, who has been taken up from you into heaven, will come in just the same way as you have watched Him go into heaven."

Acts 1:6-11 (NASB)

58 The Coming Again of Jesus the Messiah: Why a Second Coming?

Arthur W. Kac

THE TWOFOLD CHARACTER OF MESSIAH'S MISSION
IN THE OLD TESTAMENT

The student of the Messianic idea in the Old Testament soon becomes aware of the twofold character of Messiah's mission: the political and the spiritual, or the mission of the Messianic King and that of the Suffering Servant. As Messianic King, He will restore the Davidic dynasty.[1] Israel will be regathered in the Land of Israel (Isa. 11:11-12; Jer. 23:5-6). As Suffering Servant, He is the chosen One of God, in whom God delights. He is meek and humble and unostentatious. He is appointed of God to be the mediator of a new covenant for Israel and a light to the nations, who wait expectantly for His instruction (Isa. 42:1-7; 49:6; 54:10; 61:8; Jer. 31:31-34 [31:30-33, Heb.]). He does not draw back from ill-treatment (Isa. 50:6). He is a man of sorrows, and acquainted with grief. Freely and willingly He gives His life as a ransom for the sins of His people. Because He pours out His soul unto death, He will see the fruit of the travail of His soul and will be satisfied. Though sinless Himself, He identifies Himself with the transgressors, and, bearing the sins of the many, He makes intercession for transgressors (Isa. 53:1-12).

A careful analysis of the Messianic portions of the Old Testament will show that we do not have two different Messianic personalities but rather two aspects of the Messianic mission of one and the same Person.

The link between the personality of the Messianic King and the Suffering Servant may be found in the Immanuel passage in Isaiah. By refusing to heed Isaiah's advice against appealing to Assyria for help, King Ahaz laid the foundation for the destruction of the Davidic dynasty. Through that action of Ahaz, the coming Messianic Prince will have become disinherited. His mother will wear no queen's crown on her head. She will be a simple, unnamed, and unknown maiden (Isa. 7:14); His birthplace will not be the proud royal city of Jerusalem but the insignificant hamlet of Bethlehem (Mic. 5:2 [5:1, Heb.]). Before He reaches maturity, the Messianic Prince will experience poverty and want (Isa. 7:15).

It is as the Suffering Servant, whose earthly career ends in death, that the Messianic Person encounters resistance and rejection (Isa. 49:7a; 53:1-4). It is as the risen and ever-living Messianic King that He meets with universal acceptance (Gen. 49:10; Isa. 11:10; Zech. 12:10).

THE DAY OF THE LORD

In the Old Testament, the day of the LORD is a day of divine manifestation for judgment, for salvation, or for both.

JUDGMENT ON ISRAEL

> Woe unto you that desire the day of the LORD! to what end is it for you? the day of the LORD is darkness, and not light. [Amos 5:18]

> Be silent before the Lord GOD! For the day of the LORD is at hand; the LORD has prepared a sacrifice, and consecrated his guests. [Zeph. 1:7, RSV]

Verses 8-11 clearly show that the people of Israel are the sacrifice, and the "guests" are the nations that carry out God's visitation upon Israel.

> And it shall come to pass at that time, that I will search Jerusalem with candles, and punish the men that are settled on their lees[2]: that say in their heart, The LORD will not do good, neither will he do evil. [Zeph. 1:12]

JUDGMENT UPON THE NATIONS

> For the day of the LORD is near upon all the nations. As you have done,[3] it shall be done to you, your deeds shall return on your own head. [Obad. 1:15, RSV]

SALVATION UPON THE RIGHTEOUS IN ISRAEL

> And I will show wonders in the heavens and in the earth, blood, and fire, and pillars of smoke. The sun shall be turned into darkness, and the moon into blood, before the great and terrible day of the LORD comes. And it shall come to pass, that whosoever shall call on the name of the LORD shall be delivered; for in Mount Zion and in Jerusalem there shall be those who escape, as the LORD has said, and among the survivors shall be those whom the LORD calls. [Joel 2:30-32, author's trans. (3:3-5, Heb.)]

UNIVERSAL JUDGMENT AND SALVATION

> Say among the nations, "The LORD reigns; yea, the world is established, it shall never be moved; he will judge the peoples with equity." Let the heavens be glad, and let the earth rejoice; let the sea roar, and all that fills it. Let the fields be joyful, and everything in it; then shall all the trees of the wood sing for joy before the LORD for he comes, for he comes to judge the earth; he shall judge the world with righteousness, and the peoples with his truth. [Psalm 96:10-13, author's trans.]

THE MESSIAH TO BE JUDGE OF ALL MANKIND

Scarcely has there been any time in history that has not experienced God's judgment. But those judgments were limited to a particular part of the world. The universal Day of Judgment is reserved for the end-time of history, and it will encompass the whole earth and all mankind, Jews and Gentiles. In the Old Testament, the universal Day of Judgment and the coming of King Messiah to establish the universal Kingdom of God both take place in the "latter days," or end-time of history. And it is King Messiah who acts as Judge of all mankind.

The eleventh chapter of Isaiah is considered by both Jews and Christians as one of the great Messianic chapters of the Bible. At the very beginning of that chapter we are told that the Messianic King is well equipped for his mission as the Judge of the world.

> And the Spirit of the LORD shall rest upon him, the spirit of wisdom and understanding, the spirit of counsel and might, the spirit of knowledge and of the fear of the LORD. [Isa. 11:2]

That concise introductory statement is followed immediately by a description of Messiah's judicial functions.

> He shall not judge by what his eyes see, neither shall he pass sentence by what his ears hear. But with righteousness he shall judge the poor, and shall decide with equity for the humble of the earth; and he shall smite the earth with the rod of his mouth, and with the breath of his lips he shall slay the wicked. Righteousness shall be the girdle of his waist, and faithfulness the girdle of his hips. [Isa. 11:3-5, author's trans.]

That the Messianic King and Suffering Servant are identical may be seen from the following passage, which introduces the Suffering Servant in Isaiah and which assigns to that Suffering Servant a judicial function, a function that properly belongs to the Messianic King.

> Behold my servant, whom I uphold, my chosen, in whom my soul delights; I have put my spirit upon him, he will bring forth justice to the nations. . . . He will not fail or be discouraged till he has established justice in the earth; and the [isles] wait for his [instruction]. [Isa. 42:1, 4, RSV]

The same truth is taught in the New Testament. The following are the words of Jesus:

> When the Son of man[5] comes in his glory,[6] and all the angels with him, then he will sit on his glorious throne. Before Him will be gathered all the nations, and he will separate them one from another as a shepherd separates the sheep from the goats, and he will place the sheep at his right hand, but the goats at the left. Then the King will say to those at his right hand, "Come, O blessed of my Father, inherit the kingdom prepared for you from the foundation of the world; for I was hungry and you gave me food, I was thirsty and you gave me drink, I was a stranger and you welcomed me, I was naked and you clothed me, I was sick and you visited me, I was in prison and you came to me." Then the righteous will answer him, "Lord, when did we see thee hungry and feed thee, or thirsty and give thee drink? And when did we see thee a stranger and welcome thee, or naked and clothe thee? And when did we

see thee sick or in prison and visit thee?'' And the King will answer them, ''Truly, I say to you, as you did it to one of the least of these my brethren, you did it to me.'' Then he will say to those at his left hand, ''Depart from me, you cursed, into the eternal fire prepared for the devil and his angels; for I was hungry and you gave me no food, I was thirsty and you gave me no drink, I was a stranger and you did not welcome me, naked and you did not clothe me, sick and in prison and you did not visit me.'' Then they also will answer, ''Lord, when did we see thee hungry or thirsty or a stranger or naked or sick or in prison, and did not minister to thee?'' Then he will answer them, ''Truly, I say to you, as you did it not to one of the least of these, you did it not to me.'' And they will go away into eternal punishment, but the righteous into eternal life. [Matt. 25:31-46]

Because the Messianic King is to be the judge of all nations, including Israel, had the universal Day of Judgment taken place prior to the destruction of the second Temple, and prior to the first coming of Jesus, by what moral and legal standards would the Messianic Judge have been guided? Obviously, with relation to the Jewish people His standards would have had to be the Mosaic code of the Sinai covenant. How would the Jews have fared if they had been judged by the Mosaic Law?

What about the Gentiles who have always formed the bulk of the world's population? By what divine standard would they have been judged? Until the last two centuries B.C., the Hebrew Bible was unknown in the Gentile world. Even after the Hebrew Bible had been translated into Greek and thus became accessible to the Greek-speaking Gentile peoples, could the Mosaic Law have served as the divine standard for the Gentile world?

The Mosaic Law, or the Sinai covenant, consists of three parts: The Decalogue (Ten Commandments); the Levitical code; and the civil code. The civil code was designed for a people engaged in agriculture and living in a certain geographical area at a certain stage of history. The Levitical code with its sacrificial system was bound up with the existence of the Jerusalem Temple. And in the days of the second Temple, when Jews lived all over the Mediterranean world, distance alone made it impossible for most Jews to comply with the requirements of the Levitical code.

The Decalogue alone has a universal character and is capable of serving as a religious and moral standard for the peoples of the world, irrespective of time and place. However, a close look at the introductory portion of the Ten Commandments will show that even the Decalogue has a strong Israelite, or particularist, connotation. It reads like this:

And God spoke all these words, saying, ''I am [Jehovah] your God, who brought you out of the land of Egypt, out of the house of bondage.'' [Exod. 20:1-2, RSV]

That Scripture declares that Israel owes its national existence to having been liberated by God from Egyptian bondage. The reason God brought Israel into existence is that Israel may serve God's purpose (see Exod. 9:13). To serve God's purpose, Israel must first become the people of God (Exod. 19:3-6), and in order to become the people of God, Israel must shape its relation to God and to one another in accordance with the principles laid down in the Decalogue.

Thus, although the Decalogue taken by itself could possibly have served as a universal religious and moral standard, no non-Israelite people would have had the same motivation to live by its principles as Israel had or should have had; for the mighty acts that God did for Israel mentioned in the preface to the Decalogue were not experienced by any other people.

But let us assume that the Gentiles *were* to be judged on the basis of the Decalogue or the Noachian laws, would they have fared better than the Jewish people who have failed under the Sinai Covenant? That the Jews would fail under Mosaic Law was revealed to Moses by God Himself, just before Moses died (see Deut. 31:16-29). That failure was written in large letters by all the prophets, it is acknowledged by the Talmud, and the admission of that failure has been incorporated into the Prayer Book.[7]

It is obvious, therefore, that if the universal Day of Judgment had taken place at any time in the world's history prior to the first coming of Jesus, all mankind—Jews and Gentiles—would have stood condemned in the sight of God. That thought may have been in Malachi's mind when he wrote the following passage in connection with Messiah's coming:

> Behold, I send my messenger to prepare the way before me, and the Lord whom you seek will suddenly come to his temple; the messenger of the covenant in whom you delight, behold, he is coming, says the LORD of hosts. But who can endure the day of his coming, and who can stand when he appears? [Mal. 3:1-2]

That Malachi's words do not represent an isolated opinion may be seen from the following passages in the Psalms:

> If thou, O LORD, shouldst mark iniquities, Lord, who could stand? [Psalm 130:3, RSV]

> And enter not into judgment with thy servant: for in thy sight shall no man living be justified. [Psalm 143:2]

The death and resurrection of Jesus were God's solution to man's terrible dilemma. Through His identification with Messiah's death on the cross, God took upon Himself the penalty due mankind and mankind was pronounced "not guilty!" That was God's gift to man, His mighty act, not only on behalf of Israel, but for the whole human race.

> "Behold, the Lamb of God, who takes away the sin of the world!" [John 1:29, RSV]

> "For God so loved the world that he gave his only Son, that whoever believes in him should not perish but have eternal life. For God sent the Son into the world, not to condemn the world, but that the world might be saved through him." [John 3:16-17, RSV]

THE RETURN OF JESUS THE MESSIAH

Jesus must have received the news of John (Yochanan) the Immerser's baptismal activities as heaven's signal for Him to enter upon His Messianic ministry, and He went from Galilee to the Jordan River to be baptized by John. The baptism ritual that John performed was a baptism of repentance, that is, those who submitted to it expressed a desire to repent of their sins. When Jesus presented Himself to John, John at first declined to baptize Him. "I need to be baptized by you," John said to Jesus, "and do you come to me?" (Matt. 3:14, RSV). Possibly baptism was to Jesus His first act of identification with sinful men and women. As he was about to begin His Messianic ministry, Jesus "was numbered with transgressors," even as on the cross the process of being "numbered with transgressors" became complete.

The statement "This is my beloved Son, in whom I am well pleased," which was heard as Jesus emerged from the Jordan waters, consists of two parts. The first takes us back to the second psalm where God says to the Messianic King: "You are my Son" (Psalm 2:7). The second part refers us to the opening sentence of Isaiah 42 in which God introduces the Messiah as His servant: "Behold my servant, whom I uphold, my chosen, in whom my soul delights" (RSV).[8] Thus at the very inception of His Messianic career, mention is made of the twofold character of His Messiaship, that of the Messianic King and of the Suffering Servant.

From the beginning of His ministry, Jesus manifested a prescience that He must die in order to accomplish His Messianic mission. To Nicodemus who interviewed Jesus when He was in Judea in the first few months of His ministry, Jesus said that before donning the Messianic crown, He will be mounted upon a cross.

> As Moses lifted up the serpent in the wilderness, even so must the Son of man be lifted up. [John 3:14]

To the disciples of John the Immerser who one day asked Jesus why His followers did not observe fast days, He said:

> Can the wedding guests mourn as long as the bridegroom is with them? The days will come, when the bridegroom is taken away from them, and then they will fast. [Matt. 9:15]

Here was another early indirect disclosure about His death.

In the first half, or two-thirds, of His public ministry, before His disciples gained any real insight into the nature of His Messiahship, the references to His death were few and somewhat cryptic. But they furnish incontrovertible evidence that at least from the beginning of His Messianic career Jesus had been conscious of His full identification with the destiny of the Suffering Servant of the Lord as delineated in Isaiah and therefore that His Messianic task would be accomplished in two stages.

> And all the multitude kept silent, and they were listening to Barnabas and Paul as they were relating what signs and wonders God had done through them among the Gentiles. And after they had stopped speaking, James[9] answered, saying, "Brethren, listen to me. Simeon[10] has related how God first concerned himself about taking from among the Gentiles a people for his name. And with this the words of the Prophets agree, just as it is written, 'AFTER THESE THINGS I WILL RETURN, AND I WILL REBUILD THE TABERNACLE OF DAVID WHICH HAS FALLEN, AND I WILL REBUILD ITS RUINS, AND I WILL RESTORE IT, IN ORDER THAT THE REST OF MANKIND MAY SEEK THE LORD, AND ALL THE GENTILES WHO ARE CALLED BY MY NAME.' " [Acts 15:12-17, NASB]

The above statement was made by James, one of the leaders of the Jerusalem church, at a meeting that had been convened to consider a weighty problem. Large numbers of Gentiles were converted as a result of the labors of Paul and Barnabas, Paul did not insist that the Gentile converts adhere to the Mosaic Law. The essence of his message, the "good news," was that man's salvation is secured by the atoning death and resurrection of Messiah Jesus and by that alone. Certain Hebrew Christians took exception to that position. They believed Gentile converts should be asked to submit to circumcision and to observe the Mosaic Law. The Jerusalem church met to consider that important issue. Present at the meeting were the apostles and many members of the Jerusalem church. Most, if not all, those who attended the meeting were Jews. After due deliberations the conference approved the position of Paul and Barnabas, namely, that Gentile converts should not be required to accept the Mosaic Law.

But approval did not come until James, who appears to have presided at the meeting, made the statement recorded in Acts 15:13-17. The full significance of what he said can only be understood if we realize what lay behind the controversy. As increasing numbers of Gentiles continued to flock into the church, it was not difficult to foresee the day was not far off when the Messianic movement would become a predominantly Gentile movement. Such an anticipation must have appeared quite distressing to Hebrew Christians, who felt deep attachment to their Jewish heritage. One wonders whether the demand to have Gentile converts adhere to the Mosaic Law may not have been motivated, in part at least, by a desire to slow down the flow of Gentile converts into the church.

James, who undoubtedly had been aware of those Hebrew Christian anxieties, was led of the Spirit of God to make the remarks cited above with a view to settling the question at issue and also to calming Hebrew Christian fears. Brief as his statement was—only six sentences—it contains nothing less than an outline of the whole Messianic program during the interval between the resurrection of Jesus and His return.

According to James in Acts 15:14 and Acts 15:15-16, the Messianic mission of Jesus will be accomplished in two stages. First,

> Simeon has related how God first concerned Himself about taking from among the Gentiles a people for His name. [Acts 15:14, NASB]

The reference to Simon Peter had to do with a statement he had made at that Jerusalem conference, relating how God had used him to bring the first Gentile family into the Messianic fold. From the words of James we are led to believe that the *whole* Gentile world was not expected to be converted to the Messianic faith of Jesus in the first stage of the Messianic mission. During that initial phase, God has been calling out[11] a certain number of Gentiles to become His people. When that process will have been completed, the first stage of the Messianic mission will be terminated. Second,

> And with this the words of the Prophets agree, just as it is written,
> "AFTER THESE THINGS I WILL RETURN, AND I WILL REBUILD THE [dwelling] OF DAVID WHICH HAS FALLEN, AND I WILL REBUILD ITS RUINS, AND I WILL RESTORE IT." [Acts 15:15-16]

The above words are quoted by James from the opening lines of a Messianic passage from the prophet Amos (9:11-15). In that Scripture it is God who restores the Davidic dynasty; in the James passage that restoration is accomplished by God through the agency of the Messiah, a descendant of the Davidic line, in the second stage of the Messianic mission of Jesus. James was pointing out that "after these things," that is, after the process of a partial ingathering of the Gentiles had been completed, Jesus will return ("I will return"), and He will restore the Davidic dynasty.

The restoration of the Davidic dynasty implies a national restoration of Israel. The question immediately arises, For what purpose would the returning Messiah accomplish the restoration of the Davidic dynasty and the national rebirth of Israel? James answers this question in the following words.

> In order that the rest of mankind may seek the Lord and all the Gentiles upon whom my name has been invoked. [Acts 15:17, NASB and Amp.]

That portion of the James passage also cites the Amos prophecy (9:12). As applied to the return of Jesus, James declares that the purpose of His return and the national restoration of Israel is that *Messiah's salvation may reach the entire Gentile world.*

The above statement focuses our attention on what the Bible conceives to be the destiny of the Jewish people. In the first divine message delivered to the Egyptian king, Moses was bidden to say:

> Thus says the LORD, Israel is my first-born son. And I say to you, Let my son go that he may serve me. [Exod. 4:22-23, RSV]

Israel was called out of Egypt in order to serve God. How Israel was to serve God was spelled out soon after the departure from Egypt and just as the people of Israel had reached Mount Sinai.

> You have seen what I did to the Egyptians, and how I bore you on eagles' wings[12] and brought you to myself. Now therefore, if you will obey my voice and keep my covenant, you shall be my own possession among all peoples; for all the earth is mine. And[13] you shall be to me a kingdom of priests and a holy nation. [Exod. 19:4-6, RSV]

Israel is God's "peculiar treasure" because she is an instrument for a certain purpose, and "the purpose is greater than the instrument."[14] "Israel's call has not been to privilege and rulership, but to martyrdom and service."[15] Israel was called out of Egypt as God's first-born son. Her divinely appointed mission was to be a kingdom of priests, that is, to bring God's redemption to the other nations of the earth. "As the priest is a mediator between God and man, so Israel was called to be the vehicle of the knowledge and salvation of God to the nations of the earth."[16]

As a matter of fact, the purpose of Israel's existence was made known to the patriarchs centuries before the exodus from Egypt. In the following words we have the reason for the divine summons of Abraham to leave his kin and country and to proceed to the Promised Land.

> And I will make of you a great nation, and I will bless you, and make your name great, so that you will be a blessing. I will bless those who bless you, and him who curses you I will curse; and by you all the families of the earth [will be blessed]. [Gen. 12:2-3, RSV]

278

In summary, the return of Jesus the Messiah will enable Israel to fulfill the mission for which she was called into existence, that is, to bring the nations of the earth to a saving knowledge of God,

> In order that the rest of mankind may seek the Lord, and all the Gentiles upon whom my name has been invoked. [Acts 15:17]

It should be noted that the apostle Paul was in full agreement with the James statement. Writing to the Christians in Rome, Paul said:

> For I do not want you, brethren, to be uninformed of this mystery, lest you be wise in your own estimation, that a partial hardening has happened to Israel until the fulness of the Gentiles has come in. [Rom. 11:25, NASB]

By "the fulness of the Gentiles" Paul understands the completion of the process of the partial ingathering of the Gentiles taking place in the first stage of the Messianic mission. The reference to the "partial hardening" of Israel means by implication that in the first stage of the Messianic mission there will be a partial ingathering of Jews as well as a partial ingathering of Gentiles. That prophecy by Paul has been fulfilling itself throughout the past nineteen centuries. There are today many thousands of Jewish followers of Messiah Jesus all over the world, including the state of Israel. The full ingathering of the Jewish people will be accomplished in the second stage of the Messianic mission, with the return of Messiah Jesus.

> And thus all Israel will be saved. [Rom. 11:26, NASB]

As the partial ingathering of Jews took place before the partial ingathering of Gentiles in the first stage of the Messianic mission, so will the full ingathering of Jews precede the full ingathering of Gentiles in the second stage of the Messianic mission.

THE PREPARATION OF THE WORLD
FOR THE RETURN OF JESUS

The coming of King Messiah in the Old Testament and the coming again of Messiah Jesus in the New Testament, coincide with the "latter days" period, the end-time, or consummation of history as we know it. In his letter to the Christian converts in the Roman province of Galatia, the apostle Paul remarked that Jesus came in the fullness of time (Gal. 4:4). By that he meant that the world into which Jesus came had been prepared historically for His coming. That process of preparation was of a negative and a positive character. On the negative side were the rise and fall of the first three world civilizations—Mesopotamia, Persia, and Greece— and the failings of Rome, presaging the eventual fall of the last world empire of the ancient world, were already much in evidence in the first century of our era. On the other hand, the undermining of ancient paganism wrought by Greek philosophy, and the unification of the ancient world by the Greek language and Roman military power and administrative skill, were positive elements in the preparation of the Gentile world for the first advent of Messiah Jesus.

A process of preparation was also taking place among the Jews. The miserable internal history of the first Jewish commonwealth; its eventual collapse at the beginning of the sixth century B.C., which all Old Testament writers attribute to

Israel's transgressions; the equally sorry record of the short-lived Maccabean state, marked by dissension, turmoil, and bloodshed—these were negative factors in the preparation of the Jewish people for Messiah's coming. On the positive side may be mentioned an increasing knowledge of the Old Testament writings, the growth of an apocalyptic literature in the centuries following the return from the Babylonian exile, and a deepened understanding by the Jewish people of their destiny as the people of God and of their mission in the world.

But that "fullness of time," that preparation of the world for the first coming of Jesus, affected only the Mediterranean portion of the ancient world of the first century. Beyond the frontiers of that Mediterranean world lay the vast stretches of the continents of Asia, Africa, and Europe, teeming with millions of Mongolian, Hindu, Black, Germanic, and Slavic peoples—most of them in a semicivilized state. Of the existence of that larger world, including the American continent, the nations of the Mediterranean world knew little or nothing. The peoples of that larger outlying world had not been historically prepared for His coming and for the gospel.

We must never lose sight of the fact that biblical revelation aims to reach *all* mankind. Abraham was called that in him *all* the families of the earth should be blessed (Gen. 12:1-3). When the people of Israel were liberated from Egyptian rule they were informed that they had a mission to *all* the nations of the earth (Exod. 19:4-6). Likewise, the commission given to the followers of Jesus was to take the Gospel to *all* nations (Matt. 28:19; Luke 24:47). That larger world must be historically prepared for the *second* coming of Jesus, even as the small Mediterranean world of the first century had been prepared for His *first* coming.

Many signs indicate that the process of preparation of the whole world for the second coming of Jesus is rapidly approaching completion.

WESTERN CIVILIZATION

Prior to World War One, the industrialized West clung to a firm belief in the perfectibility of man through education and the inevitability of progress through science. Man was assumed to be essentially good. He was expected to derive from science all the power he requires, from education all the knowledge he needs, and from democracy all the freedom he wants. The golden era of human history was to be brought about by human effort alone. Events since World War One have combined to shatter all those expectations. "Since 1914 one tragic experience has followed after another, as if history had been designed to refute and confound the vain delusions of modern man."[17] Had Jesus returned prior to World War One, Western civilization could have asserted that it would have brought in the Millennium even had Jesus not returned.

THE DEVELOPING NATIONS

Most of the nations in Asia and Africa that were ruled by colonial powers have gained political independence since the end of World War Two. Internally, and in relations with other developing nations in their areas, their problems have not changed much for the better. In some respects they are worse off than they were under colonial rule. The comparative ineffectiveness of the United Nations is attributed to the fact that the developing nations form a majority of that world organization. Had Jesus returned before World War Two, the developing nations could have claimed that they would have solved all their problems had they been freed of colonial rule.

THE COMMUNIST WORLD

This discussion of the communist world will be confined to Soviet Russia, the mother of world Communism and the first of the totalitarian systems that have sprung up since the end of World War One. In 1917 the numerically small Bolshevik group overthrew the democratic government of Kerensky and set up the Soviet system of government in Russia. The ideology of Russian Communism is supposed to be Marxism as modified by Lenin, the father of Soviet Russia. The Marxist creed has several primary doctrines:

1. The doctrine of communist economy, which requires the abolition of capitalist private initiative and its replacement by a collective economy with the ultimate implementation of the principle "from each according to his abilities, to each according to his needs"
2. The doctrine of democracy according to which all authority springs from the people's will
3. The doctrine of the "withering state," which looked forward to a time when the role of the state would vanish, and its place would be taken by the classless society
4. The doctrine of equality, which would deny all privilege on the basis of class, race, *or* religion.[18]

It was on this "infallible" creed of Marxism that Russian communists were to erect the Soviet system.

It is now sixty-three years (1980) since the Bolsheviks seized power in Russia. In place of Marxism's "temporary dictatorship of the proletariat,"[19] Russia has a dictatorship not of the working class but of a small group and their subordinates. It is a dictatorship over the workers, not of the workers. The state is the employer, all others are employees. Strikes are forbidden. Instead of enjoying democracy based on the will of the people expressed in free elections, the country is ruled by the communist party, which is guided and controlled by a governing clique. It is a system in which all the public media are in the hands of the government and are maintained by various means available to a modern dictatorship, including secret police, spies, and slave labor camps.

Under Communism all political power and all economic power are vested in the hands of the government. When private enterprise is made illegal, every person is an employee of the government. His whole economic existence, his chance for advancement, his seniority—all depend on some government functionary. He cannot quit his job or look for another job without permission from the government. He is at the mercy of the government in a way that is unthinkable and intolerable in a true democracy.[20]

What became of the Marxist doctrine of equality and the classless society is best told by one who knew the system from inside. One of the most important documents on the social system under Communism is a book written by Milovan Djilas, formerly vice president of communist Yugoslavia. For writing that book he was put in prison. The following excerpt from his work concerns the new ruling class in communist countries.

> Property is legally considered social and national property. But, in actuality, a single group manages it in its own interest. . . . In communism, power and ownership are almost always in the same hands but this fact is concealed under a legal guise. . . . The formal owner is the nation. In reality, because of monopolistic administration, only the narrowest stratum of administrators enjoys the rights of ownership. . . . While promising to abolish social difference, [the new class] must always increase them by acquiring the products of the nation's workshops and granting privileges to its adherents. . . . This is a class whose power over men is the most complete known to history. . . . Having achieved industrialization, the new class can now do nothing more than strengthen its brute force and pillage the people.[21]

In the process of evolving the communist type of "classless" society, communist Russia destroyed the upper class of czarist Russia and eliminated the Kulak peasants. Originally, a "kulak" denoted a peasant of some means. Under dictator Stalin, the term *Kulak* included every peasant who owned more than two cows and any peasant who was seeking to retain his own parcel of land.[22]

In his determination to collectivize Russian agriculture, Stalin ordered in December 1929 the liquidation of the Kulaks as a class. No less than a million families numbering about five million people were deprived of their property, herded into cattle cars and unloaded in the deserts of Central Asia or the lumber region of the frozen North. Thousands never reached their destination, having succumbed on the way from starvation, disease, and exposure. Many others died in the wilderness of their dispersion.[23]

But the peasants did not take these things lying down. The Red Army had to be called out frequently to put down peasant uprisings. Hundreds of government officials charged with enforcing collectivization were murdered. The slaughtering of animals became a serious form of sabotage. In 1932 the peasants embarked on another kind of sabotage: they planted just enough to take care of their needs. In retaliation Stalin sent army trucks into the country in the fall of that year and the soldiers removed all grain, fruit, eggs, and vegetables, leaving the peasants to starve. The effect of those measures was a famine that caused the death of countless thousands in Russia. Cannibalism was resorted to in many of the stricken areas.[24]

Following are several excerpts from an article by Hal Piper, the Baltimore *Sun* correspondent stationed in Moscow. Under the title "An Unrealized Dream," Mr. Piper writes: "Measured by its dream, the Soviet Union after 60 years is cast-ridden, not egalitarian; insular, not internationalist; authoritarian, not participatory; intellectually stagnant, not dynamic, and timid, not confident of its proclaimed historical inevitability."[25]

Referring to the Soviet boast that in sixty years it has transformed Russia from a primitive to a scientific and literate nation, Piper and other Western students of the

Russian Revolution rightly state that during the same period many other backward countries also made great strides. For the scientific advancement that Soviet Russia achieved in those sixty years, she has paid "unimaginable social costs, including the wholesale resettlement of entire ethnic populations and execution by firing squad, forced labor, famine or neglect of nearly 20 million of their fellow country-men by Soviet leaders.

The Russian aristocracy and the landlord and "bourgeois" classes are gone, but their place as the privileged stratum in a hierarchical society has been taken by Communist party and government leaders who enjoy through "closed" stores, hospitals, restaurants and resorts—access to luxury goods and services that are not made available to ordinary people. . . .

Officially, the social conditions that breed crime do not exist in the Soviet Union, but more than a million prisoners strain the prison sys-tem. Official corruption is widespread, judging from Soviet newspapers exposing embezzlers, speculators and those who divert government property to their own uses—or who simply neglect to care properly for it. . . .[26]

Despite tight policing, Soviet jails hold more than twice as many prisoners as American jails—common criminals, not political ones. Alcoholism is pandemic, so are job absenteeism and divorce. . . . The Soviet Union does not send its ideas, fads, life-styles, pop music, cultural trends into the world. Its major contribution to world civiliza-tion is the steady stream of talented but unhappy emigrés and defectors—Rostropovich, Nurfzo and Baryshnikov, a whole colony of writers and artists in Paris, even the chess grandmaster Victor Korchnoi. Most of these people had security and status in their homeland, yet they left.[27]

Soviet Russia has made the term Communism and, to a degree slightly less, the term Socialism utterly putrid. Marxism stinks in the nostrils of history. From its materialistic assumptions about history and man it has rotted and festered into a bloody tyranny, into a cynical a-moralism, into the corruption of conscience.[28]

Had Jesus returned prior to 1917, the Communists and their fellow-travelers could have claimed that Communism was the best ideology yet devised by man and, had it been given a chance, Communism would have produced an earthly paradise; it could have evolved a system under which people would have lived happily ever after. History has given Communism a chance, and we can now judge it by its fruits.

THE STATE OF ISRAEL

The restoration of Jewish nationhood in the land of Israel has been one of the cardinal tenets of Jewish Messianic expectations. The ease with which the many false Messiahs were able, in every period of Jewish history, to win multitudes of Jewish adherents to their cause, can be accounted for by their promises of a speedy Jewish restoration in the land of Israel. The reemergence of the present state of

Israel in 1948 posed a vexing question to the religious Jew: Is it possible that Israel is being restored without the Messiah?

In its efforts to reconstruct Judaism and make it adaptable to the needs of the modern Jew, the Liberal Synagogue, which sprang up in the nineteenth century in Western Europe, gave up the ancient Jewish belief in a Messianic Person and substituted belief in a Messianic age. By "Messianic age," Liberal Judaism meant that justice, peace, and happiness in the world can be accomplished by man without a Messianic Person. In essence, that position was a Jewish version of the secularist philosophy of Western civilization about the perfectibility of the individual and the inevitability of human progress to be realized by education, science, and democracy. By and large, the pioneers of political Zionism, which came into existence towards the end of the nineteenth century, were secularist Jews.

The rebuilding of the devasted land of Israel by the Zionist pioneers, both prior to and since 1948, in the face of intense and bitter Arab hostility, is a phenomenon bordering on the miraculous and has excited the admiration of the civilized world. However, the Yom Kippur War in October 1973 and events since then have made painfully clear that Israel's redemption, apart from the Messiah, is not yet complete. Internationally, the Yom Kippur War demonstrated that in time of her greatest need, Israel was politically isolated from the whole world, with the exception of the United States. Economically, since the Yom Kippur War Israel has been plagued with the highest inflation rate in the world. She is forced to peddle her manufactured war hardware in the world's markets to bolster her sagging economy. What a contrast to the prophetic forecast of an Israel under Messiah's rule that would inspire the nations of the earth to transform their armaments into tools of peace (Isa. 2:2-4)!

In 1975 Israel was second world-wide in the number of strikes in the public sector of the country, ninety percent of which were unauthorized.[29] Because a cabinet minister cited the case of a Israeli doctor who refused treatment to a patient, the doctors in retaliation closed down that particular government hospital. Whole sections of the public sector were paralyzed by labor action committees in open breach of signed contracts.[30]

A prominent American Jew who settled in Israel charged that money sent to Israel by the Diaspora[31] for housing for new immigrants and social services was being used to subsidize the activities of political parties and give office jobs to "do-nothing clerks." He accused the middle class of allowing the Histadrut[32] and the political parties to take over the management of the country. That is a disaster, he said, and the people of Israel should rebel against a political system responsible for that state of affairs.[33]

A Russian immigrant, a professor of mechanical engineering, declared that the Zionist pioneer aimed to build "a country like all other countries and a people like all other peoples," in consequence of which Israel is beset with many of the problems peculiar to secular societies. Israel, he said, has now "its thieves, its murderers, and its prostitutes."[34]

In an address at the Technion graduating exercises, Supreme Court Justice Moshe Landau criticized the drive among Israelis for costly cars, for luxury apartments filled with conspicuous furniture, paid more and more from the labor of others. He cited the danger of perpetuating the country's social and economic problems by means of excessive consumption. "True democracy cannot be fostered by lack of inner discipline or lack of responsibility of citizens as individuals or as groups."[35]

In his assessment of the factors behind Likud's victory in the Israeli elections in May 1977, an Israeli observer attributed the election results to a resentment of the voters of the way the Labor Government was running the affairs of the country. The Government, he charged, had no authority over the Histadrut, the Histadrut no authority over the unions, and the unions exercised no control over the workers' committees. "We endlessly argue, and never decide. It is true in labor relations, in the educational field, in the handling of social problems, in the management of the economy—and in foreign affairs."[36]

Religion in Israel is mixed up with party politics as perhaps in no other modern country, certainly not in any Western country. During national elections the religious parties present to the voting public a list of their own candidates for the Israeli Parliament. The country has two Orthodox chief rabbis, one for the Oriental Jewish community (Sephardim), the other for the Jews of European origin (Ashkenazim). The two rabbis are state functionaries. The state has entrusted to those representatives of Orthodox Judaism jurisdiction over personal status, birth, divorce, and the right to decide who is a Jew. No religious representatives other than the Orthodox have this jurisdiction in Israel.

The representatives of Orthodox Judaism are striving hard to transform Israel into an Orthodox Jewish state, notwithstanding the fact that Orthodox Judaism is a product of life in the Diaspora, totally unsuitable for a modern state. A Jewish intellectual from Britain, whom we quoted previously in this work, revealed that there is now in Israel a revival of certain half-forgotten ancient religious practices, such as mass pilgrimages to holy places and a renewal of the practice of ancestor worship, using magical forms of prayers, addressed to certain holy ancestors who are requested to act as intercessors in heaven. On anniversaries of the death of certain holy men and on certain religious festivals, old burial places are visited by devotees who place there little notes and candles. Those pilgrimages to holy places are encouraged, often being arranged or sponsored by the Ministry of Religious Affairs, which is always in the hand of a representative of the religious parties.[37] The tragedy of Israel is that the old religion, practiced only by the Orthodox, is ritualistic, petrified and ossified," and to the large mass of Israeli Jews it seems "uninspiring and uninspired."[38]

In his book *The Jewish State* published in 1896 in Vienna, Dr. Theodor Herzl, the father of modern political Zionism, made the following concluding statement: "I believe that [in the Jewish State] a wondrous generation of Jews will spring into existence. . . . We shall live at last as free men on our own soil, and die peacefully in our own homes. The world will be freed by our liberty, enriched by our wealth, magnified by our greatness."[39] The present state of Israel, brought into existence by the Jewish people after a lapse of almost nineteen centuries, serves to prove that the aspirations of Zionism as expressed by Dr. Herzl cannot be fully realized, and Israel's redemption cannot be completed, apart from the Messiah.

The first advent of Jesus proclaimed to the *whole* world *a single* divine standard for *all* mankind, Jews and Gentiles. Unlike the Mosaic code, the universal Messianic standard of Jesus is suitable for all human needs and all human situations, irrespective of race, time, or geographic area.

In the interval between the first and second comings of Jesus, two historical movements were destined to exist alongside each other. One of these is the spiritual movement planted by God with the call of Abraham; the other is the man-made world system that began with the Tower of Babel event, or history as we know it, proceeding in ignorance of, disregard of, or active opposition to the redemptive purpose of the biblical faith. In the parable of the wheat and tares, those world movements are depicted as growing side by side until they will have reached their fullest development at the approach of the "end-time" or "latter days" period of history (Matt. 13:24-30). The Bible declares that in the end-time that man-made world system will be swept away by divine intervention and a new world order—the universal Kingdom of God—will come into being (Dan. 2:25-45; Zech. 14:1-9; Rev. 11:15).

During the great interval between the first and second comings of Jesus, the gospel was to be made known among all nations. The completion of the task of propagating the gospel is to coincide with the return of Jesus.

> "And this gospel of the kingdom[40] shall be preached in the whole world for a witness unto all nations; and then shall the end[41] come." [Matt. 24:14]

During the interval between the first and second comings, the gospel offers its message of salvation to individuals in every nation. Those who willfully reject the divine gift of salvation will appear in all their guilt before the judgment seat of Messiah Jesus. Those who accept the gift of salvation wrought on Calvary's cross experience a new birth. They are born spiritually, just as once they were born physically. Their lives become transformed through the indwelling presence of the Spirit of God. It is no more they who live, but Jesus, the Son of God, lives in them. Over that life, death and the grave have no power. Their lives are invested with new meaning and purpose, and they receive strength and courage to face life's daily tasks. The risen and everliving Messiah identifies Himself with their joys and sorrows. He abides with them until the end of the age.

> Lo, I am with you always, even to the end of the age. [Matt. 28:20]

That is the "good tidings" (the "gospel") that Isaiah spoke of (Isa. 40:9; 52:7). That is the "new covenant" that Jeremiah promised, a covenant, as he said, unlike the Sinai Covenant, a religious code of do's and don't's, written on stone or parchment, but a covenant engraved on human hearts and regenerated human nature (Jer. 31:31-34 [31:30-33, Heb.]).

Notes

1. Isaiah 9:6-7; Amos 9:11—Rabbinic writings apply Amos 9:11 to the Messiah.
2. "Who sit contented in their sins."
3. To Israel.
4. I.e., by outward appearance.
5. A Messianic title by which Jesus frequently identified Himself.
6. Referring to His return as the Messianic King.
7. "Because of our sins we were exiled from our land and were far removed from our soil."
8. Targum Jonathan interprets this passage of King Messiah.
9. In the Greek original he is identified by his Hebrew name Jacob.
10. Simon Peter.
11. *Ecclesia* (Church)—a calling out of people.
12. An allusion to the miraculous crossing of the Red Sea.
13. Or, "But."
14. C. G. Montefiore, quoted in the 1938 edition of *The Pentateuch,* ed. J. H. Hertz (London: Soncino, 1938), p. 291.
15. Ibid.
16. C. F. Keil and Franz Delitzsch, *Old Testament Commentaries,* 6 vols. (Grand Rapids: Assoc. Pub. and Authors, n.d.), 1:453.
17. Reinhold Niebuhr, *Faith and History* (New York: Scribner's 1949), pp. 6-7.
18. Robert M. MacIver and R. R. Palmer, "Totalitarian Life and Politics," in *Chapters in Western Civilization,* 2 vols. (New York: Columbia U. Press, 1960), 2:448.
19. "Proletariat"—industrial working class.
20. Ibid., p. 453.
21. Milovan Djilas, *The New Class* (New York: Holt, Rinehart and Winston, Praeger Publns, 1957), pp. 65-66, 69.
22. Eugene Lyons, *Workers Paradise Lost* (New York: Paperback, n.d.), p. 219. This work was previously published as *Workers Paradise Lost: Fifty Years of Soviet Communism, a Balance Sheet* (New York: Funk & Wagnalls, 1967).
23. Ibid, p. 220.
24. Ibid, p. 222.
25. Hal Piper, "An Unrealized Dream—I: After 60 Years, Soviet Goal Is Not in Sight," *The Sun* (Baltimore), 7 November 1977. Used by permission of the Sunpapers.
26. Ibid. Used by permission of the Sunpapers.
27. Hal Piper, "An Unrealized Dream—II: Soviet Is a Land of Wood Plows," *The Sun* (Baltimore), 8 November 1977. Used by permission of the Sunpapers.
28. D. R. Davies, *The Sin of Our Age* (New York: Macmillan, 1947), p. 122.
29. *The Jewish Post,* 15 October 1976.
30. David Krivine, "Something Gave," *The Jerusalem Post Weekly,* 16 November 1976.
31. "Diaspora"—countries of Jewish residence outside of Israel.
32. The Israel labor federation.
33. Louis Rapoport, "Tackling the Bureaucrats," *The Jerusalem Post Weekly,* 18 May 1976.
34. Herman Branover, "The Dropouts," *The Jerusalem Post Weekly,* 26 October 1976.

35. Ya'acov Friedler, "Self-discipline Is the Cure to Israel's Ills," *The Jerusalem Post Weekly,* 25 May 1976.
36. David Krivine, "Back to Basics with the Likud," *The Jerusalem Post Weekly,* 24 May 1977.
37. Ferdynand Zweig, *Israel, the Sword and the Harp* (Cranbury, N.J.: Associated U. Presses, 1969), p. 85.
38. Ibid., pp. 228-29.
39. Theodor Herzl, *The Jewish State* (New York: Amer. Zionist Emergency Council, 1946), pp. 156-57.
40. I.e., the Kingdom of God.
41. The end-time of history as we know it and the return of Jesus.

The Return of the Jews
to the Land of Israel

*Then Jehovah appeared to Abram, and said, "To your descendants I will
give this land. . . . And I will give to you, and to your descendants after you,
the land of your sojournings, all the land of Canaan, for an everlasting
possession; and I will be their God."*

Gen. 12:7; 17:8 (author's trans.)

*And Jehovah appeared to him [Isaac] and said, "Do not go down to Egypt;
dwell in the land of which I shall tell you. Sojourn in this land, and I will be
with you, and will bless you; for to you and to your descendants I will give all
these lands, and I will fulfil the oath which I swore to Abraham your father."*

Gen. 26:2-3 (author's trans.)

The promise of the land made to Abraham and confirmed to Isaac was reaffirmed
by God in His dealings with Jacob.

*I am Jehovah, the God of Abraham your father and the God of Isaac; the
land on which you lie I will give to you and to your descendants.*

Gen. 28:13 (author's trans.)

*Then Jehovah said [to Moses], "I have seen the affliction of my people who
are in Egypt, and have heard their cry because of their taskmasters, because I
know their sufferings. And I have come down to deliver them out of the hand of
the Egyptians, and to bring them up out of that land to a good and broad land,
a land flowing with milk and honey, to the place of the Canaanites, the
Hittites, the Amorites, the Perizzites, the Hivites, and the Jebusites."*

Exod. 3:7-8 (author's trans.)

*Thus says Jehovah, who gives the sun for light by day and the fixed order of
the moon and the stars for light by night, who stirs up the sea so that its waves
roar—Jehovah of hosts is his name: "If this fixed order departs from before
me, says Jehovah, then shall the descendants of Israel cease from being a
nation before me for ever."*

Jer. 31:35-36 (author's trans.; 31:34-35, Heb.)

Non-Jewish Pioneers of Zionism—*Elias Newman*   291

Zionism and the State of Israel—*Jakob Jocz*   303

The Eschatological Significance of the Return
  of Israel to the Land—*Stephen B. Levinson*   309

The Rebuilding of Zion—*Max I. Reich*   314

59 Non-Jewish Pioneers of Zionism

Elias Newman was born in czarist Russia of orthodox Jewish parents. His parents soon moved to England, where he attended the public schools and also took courses in Judaism in a Jewish religious school. At fifteen he became exposed to the gospel through the efforts of a saintly Christian, and after many soul struggles arrived at a decision concerning the Messiahship of Jesus.

For a while he engaged in business, but the youth longed to devote himself to religious work. Accordingly he studied one year in a Bible school in Germany. He also studied German, philosophy, and theology at the Royal University of Berlin. In 1912 he came to America and after further training at Southern Baptist Seminary was ordained to the ministry. In 1924 he was asked by the Presbyterian Church of Ireland to head up two schools in Damascus, which numbered some six hundred Jewish children among their students.

Mr. Newman was also one of the founders of the Hebrew Christian Alliance of America.

One of the earliest writers in the English language to espouse the Zionist cause was the Reverend Paul Knell, who published a book on the subject in 1648.

The name "Israel" was used by writers of his age with so much laxity that it was often impossible to define the sense which it was generally intended to convey. Knell used the word in its plain meaning: for him "Israel" meant simply the people in the land of Israel.

The influence of the Hebrew spirit so abundantly manifest in the work of Knell is also clearly visible in some of the works of John Milton. Milton knew Hebrew, and his poetry is throughout inspired by the genius of that language. Milton believed that the whole twelve tribes would return to Zion.

In the negotiations between Rabbi Menasseh ben Israel and Cromwell there was a biblical and Messianic idea at the very root of that great event. In effect, Zionism

Mr. Newman's essay has been adapted, by permission, from Elias Newman, "Christian Pioneers of Zionism," *The Hebrew Christian Alliance Quarterly* 35, no. 2 (Summer 1949) and Elias Newman, "Non-Jewish Pioneers of Zionism," *The Israel Messenger,* September-December, 1957, pp. 8-9, 11.

stood at the cradle of the resettlement of the Jews in England. Both men wished for the "assembling of God's people" in their ancestral home and were inclined to help and promote it.

John Sadler, town clerk of London and friend of Cromwell, also wrote expressing belief in the restoration of Israel.

Edmund Bunny, Isaac de La Peyrere, Thomas Draxe, Isaac Vossius, Hugo Grotius, Gerhard John Vossius, David Bondel, and Paulus Felgenhauer, all living at the beginning of the seventeenth century, supported similar ideas pertaining to the restoration of Israel.

Thomas Brightman, a Puritan Bible exegete, in his comment on Revelation 16:12, published in 1641, gives reasons why those "kings of the east" must mean the Jews, and then he says: "What! Shall they return to Jerusalem again? There is nothing more certain: the prophets do everywhere confirm it."

James Durham (1622-1658) expounds with abundant delight the Scriptures pertaining to the subject. He upholds Zionist principles and gives solid reasons for his belief in the restoration of Israel.

Vasover Powel (1617-1660) writes in a similar vein and enumerates a long list of Scripture references on the return and re-establishment of the Jews as a nation.

Roger Williams (1604-1683), the great pioneer of religious liberty and the founder of the Rhode Island colony, was an ardent supporter of Israel and believed tenaciously in her restoration.

Thomas Newton, who in 1761 was Bishop of Bristol, defended the idea of the restoration in words that no Jewish national enthusiast could excel. The Jews, he believed, would be restored to their own country, and he vigorously condemned all anti-Jewish prejudice.

Edward King (1725-1807), an essayist, was the zealous champion of the return of the Jews as Jews to the Holy Land.

In that connection special mention should be made of a great American who was undoubtedly inspired by English Puritanism and displayed the same spirit as the Puritans in relation to the Jewish problem. He was John Adams (1735-1826), the second president of the United States (1797-1801) and one of the most distinguished patriots of the Revolution. He was one of the most enthusiastic supporters of the Zionist idea. In a letter to Major Mordecai Manuel he says: "I really wish the Jews again in Judea, an independent nation, for, as I believe, the most enlightened men of it have participated in the amelioration of the philosophy of the ages; once restored to an independent government, and no longer persecuted, they would soon wear away some of the asperities and peculiarities of their character."

Thomas Witherby (1790-1820), a London solicitor of repute, wrote *An Attempt to Remove Prejudices Concerning the Jewish Nation*. According to him the just demand for equality of rights for the Jews does not conflict with the claim of the Jewish nation to a land of its own. He recognized both the right of the Jews to decide for themselves in matters affecting the preservation of the nation, and the independent validity of the considerations that led to the recognition of Jewish rights in all countries. It was his opinion that although humanity and justice must refuse to recognize anything in the laws of any country that was at variance with the principle of equality, they should be the more ready to admit the higher claim of the Jewish nation to a home of its own.

Witherby stood for the restoration of Israel as for Jewish emancipation in all countries of the diaspora. There can be no stronger and more convincing protest against the fallacious assumption of the irreconcilability of Zionism and emancipation than Witherby's interesting and instructive pamphlet. His ideal was to do justice to those Jews who lived in any country and accordingly formed an integral part of the organism of the state, working like others for the prosperity and safety of the country of which they were the citizens. Equally, he considered it a sacred duty of humanity to enable that ancient and disinherited nation to rebuild a central home for those of its members who saw the necessity of such a home, and had the inclination to go there.

William Whiston (1667-1752), Bishop Robert Lowth of London (1710-1787), and Dr. Philip Doddridge (1702-1751) supported the idea of a speedy restoration of the Jews. That expectation was also looked forward to by John Gill (1697-1770), Dr. Henry Porter (1741-1802), and John Scott (1777-1834).

Speaking of the preservation of the Jews, the Reverend John Scott says in his book *The Destiny of Israel*, published in 1813, pages 17-18: "But wherefore are the Jews thus preserved? Is it only as monuments of Divine vengeance, and to bear testimony to others of blessings which they shall never taste themselves? 'Hath God' for ever 'cast off His people?' 'Have they stumbled that they might fall' to rise no more? God forbid! All the facts before, and particularly their preservation, might well raise hopes in our minds that mercy was still in reserve for Israel."

In England the Zionist idea not only has a long and unbroken history, at least until the time of Ernest Bevin, but it links together periods and men of the most widely different convictions and emotions. That is well illustrated by the fact that at the very moment that the Jewish leader Sir Moses Montefiore was endeavoring to find a suitable place in Palestine in which to found a Jewish commonwealth, another famous man, one of the greatest Christians of his time, was working in his way and according to his light, with similar enthusiasm and strength of conviction, for precisely the same cause. He was the seventh Earl of Shaftesbury (1801-1885), one of the most interesting personalities of the age, a man of the soundest intellect and the keenest perceptions, sagacious, far-seeing, of great honesty of purpose, modest and averse to notoriety, and ardent, earnest, devoted Christian and broadminded philanthropist.

In 1838 and 1839 Lord Shaftesbury was most prolific in his public appeals for Israel and her right to independent status as a nation. Those were addressed to Victoria, Queen of England, and to the London *Times*, in which they were published. Accompanying his statements were memoranda and petitions, signed by other leading Christians.

The propaganda started by Lord Shaftesbury made considerable progress. In 1852 the Reverend A. G. H. Hollingsworth came out for the Zionist cause as also did Dr. Thomas Clarke in 1861.

James Finn (1806-1872), British Consul in Jerusalem, was an ardent Zionist and took an active part in colonization schemes.

Edward Cazalet (1827-1883) and Laurence Oliphant (1829-1888) should both receive a place of honor for their adherance to the plans and Zionist program of Lord Shaftesbury.

In the realm of English literature we must at least refer to two outstanding names: Lord Byron (1788-1824)—who was conversant with every phase of human life and touched every string of the musical lyre of life from its faintest to its most powerful and heartstirring tones—rivals Milton in his own sphere, in his noble and powerful biblical drama, *Cain*. Byron had seen much in his wanderings in Palestine and the Middle East. Zionist poetry owes much more to Byron than any other Gentile poet. His *Hebrew Melodies*, which are among the most beautiful of his productions, have been translated several times into Hebrew, and there were no lines more popular and more often quoted than:

> The wild dove hath her nest, the fox his cave,
> Mankind their country, Israel but the grave—

which might well have been a Zionist motto. Byron was a poet and a hero; the keynote of his character is to be found in the word *revolt*. This "Pilgrim of Eternity," as Shelley called him, died as a martyr to his zeal in the cause of the freedom of Greece and might perhaps have been equally able to sacrifice his life for the political freedom of Israel, had the deliverance of Israel offered scope for a similar struggle in his time.

Among English writers who have understood the idea of Zionism in all its depth and breadth, a distinguished place belongs unquestionably to George Eliot (Mary Ann Evans, 1819-1880). She chose the Zionist idea for the theme of an imaginative creation, wherein she displayed unequalled depth of comprehension and breadth of conception. In *Daniel Deronda* the Jew demands the rights pertaining to his race and claims admittance into the community of nations as one of its legitimate members. He demands real emancipation, real equality. The blood of the prophets surges in his veins, the voice of God calls to him, and he becomes conscious, and emphatically declares, that he has a distinct nationality. It is a memorable book, written by an author devoted to humanity. Its atmosphere is far removed from the conception of a materialistic world. The Jewish nationality is represented as it actually is: not an artificial combination. The book is practical in the highest sense. It preaches a great idea. It is indeed a great Zionist message. *Daniel Deronda* will take its place in the halls of fame as the proudest testimony to English recognition of the Zionist claim.

On March 5, 1891, William E. Blackstone, of Chicago, presented a memorial to President Harrison on behalf of Israel's restoration to the Holy Land. This was signed by over five hundred of America's leading Protestant clergymen, civic leaders, editors, and publishers. In 1917 Mr. Blackstone repeated his effort, reintroduced his memorial, and that time sent it to President Wilson. Part of the memorial reads as follows: "Why not give Palestine back to them [the Jews] again? According to God's distribution of nations it is their home—an inalienable possession from which they were expelled by force. Under their cultivation it was a remarkably fruitful land, sustaining millions of Israelites, who industriously tilled its hillsides and valleys. They were agriculturists and producers as well as a nation of great commercial importance—the centre of civilization and religion.

"Why shall not the powers which under the treaty of Berlin, in 1878, gave Bulgaria to Bulgarians and Servia to Servians now give Palestine back to the Jews? These provinces, as well as Rumania, Montenegro, and Greece were wrested from the Turks and given to their natural owners. Does not Palestine as rightfully belong to the Jews?''

The last name we shall mention is that of Mr. A. J. (afterwards Lord) Balfour, the British foreign secretary during the First World War. It was he who issued the now famous document called the Balfour Declaration, in 1917.

Mr. Balfour was always interested in the Jews. In the beginning of the twentieth century he supported Joseph Chamberlain's efforts for the mitigation of the effects of Russian anti-Semitism under the rule of the Czar. He believed that it was evident that "Zionism will mitigate the lot and elevate the status of no negligible fraction of the Jewish race. Those who go to Palestine will not be like those who now migrate to London or New York. They will not be animated merely by the desire to lead in happier surroundings the kind of life they formerly led in Eastern Europe. They will go in order to join a civil community which completely harmonizes with historical and religious sentiments.''

In his endeavors Lord Balfour was supported by Prime Minister David Lloyd George, Sir Winston Churchill, General Jan Christian Smuts of South Africa, and President Woodrow Wilson.

William H. Hechler, chaplain to the British Embassy in Vienna 1896, and author of *The Restoration of the Jews to Palestine according to the Prophets,* was an ardent supporter of Theodore Herzl and an enthusiastic Zionist.[1]

The Dane Oliger Pauli Holger in 1695 submitted to William III of England a plan for the establishment of a Jewish kingdom in Palestine.

The founder of the Red Cross, Jean Henry Dunant (1828-1910), was an advocate of the Zionist idea.

The people of the Scandinavian countries today are interested in the new state of Israel. That is largely due to two men who were not strictly Zionists, but who nevertheless prepared the way: Henrik Wergeland of Norway (1818-1845) appealed from an ethical and humanitarian standpoint for removal of discrimination against Jews. Hans Christian Andersen of Denmark (1805-1875), in all his writings and throughout his entire life, had a deep appreciation of the poverty, persecution, and underestimation that the Jews had frequently experienced.

In the twentieth century a number of Czech writers showed an interest in the developments of the Jewish homeland in Palestine. Especially significant is the diary of the geologist Petribok and the writings of Viktor Musik. Thomas Garrigue Masaryk, first president of the Czechoslovak republic (1918-1935), his own son, Jan Masaryk, foreign minister, and Edward Benes, second president of Czechoslovakia, took an active part in the defense of Jewish rights and the reconstruction of the Jewish national home.

Major General Orde C. Wingate, who took an active part in the Second World War in Palestine and the Near East, was a passionate and ardent Zionist as well as an earnest Christian.

Pierre Van Paassen, a Canadian journalist, wrote of the Jewish settlements in

Palestine and advocated the establishment of Jewish state. His most notable work is *The Forgotten Ally,* published in 1943.

Dr. Daniel A. Poling, editor of the Christian Herald, [and] Theodore R. McKeldin, governor of Maryland, were both advocates of the Zionist cause.

Walter Clay Loudermilk, an American, wrote *Palestine Land of Promise,* which was published in 1944.

Bartley C. Crum, a California lawyer and ardent Zionist is the author of *Behind the Silken Curtain*, published in 1947.

Richard Crossman, a labor member of the British House of Commons, wrote *Palestine Mission,* published in 1947, and Jorge Garcia Granados of Guatemala in 1948 wrote *The Rebirth of Israel.*

Dr. Herman Maas, pastor in Heidelberg, Germany, was a life-long proponent of Zionism after he attended the second Zionist Congress at Basle, Switzerland in 1898. His consistent fight against the Nazis, and his valiant effort in behalf of the Jews in Germany's darkest days of shame, have made him a well-known figure throughout the civilized world. It was partly through his efforts that the Bonn government decided to make some restitution to Israel for the Nazi barbarities of the Hitler regime.

For over three centuries Zionism was a religious as well as a political idea, which great men, Christians as well as Jews, handed down to posterity. History shows that the Zionist idea and the continual effort at the resuscitation of Jewish nationalism have been a tradition with the English people for a long time. English Christians taught the undying principle of Jewish nationality. In spite of the setback the cause has received at the hands of Ernest Bevin and his followers, we must not forget that the Zionist cause has always appealed to the Christian feelings of Englishmen and touched the heart of the British nation. The facts of history give ample and convincing proof of the high moral dignity and practical value of the Zionist cause as championed by prominent Christian thinkers, theologians, men of letters, and distinguished writers throughout many generations.

Notes

1. The remarkable story of William H. Hechler's Zionist activities is recounted in *The Prince and Prophet* by Claude Duvernoy, translated from the French by Jack Joffe, and published by Christian Action for Israel, Box 3367, Jerusalem. Hechler, a British clergyman, was born to missionary parents in India in 1845. The Grand Duke Frederick of Baden, Germany, appointed him as his private chaplain and tutor to his two sons. During his chaplaincy at the British Embassy in Vienna, Hechler met Herzl, the father of modern Zionism, whom he introduced to many leading political and ecclesiastical persons, including the grand duke, who subsequently became Kaiser Wilhelm II. For nine years Hechler played a most significant role in Herzl's preoccupation with Zionism. In times of despondency and disillusionment Herzl was spurred on by this dedicated evangelical Christian. "God chose you," he would say to Herzl. "Your people will get its promised land. God is with you." Based on his studies in the book of Daniel, Hechler predicted in 1895 that 1897 would be a fateful year in Jewish history. As we know, the First Zionist Congress was convened in 1897. To the German-Jewish philospher Martin Buber, Hechler said in 1913: "Your fatherland will soon be given back to you. For a serious crisis will occur, whose deep meaning is the liberation of your Messianic Jerusalem from the yoke of the nations . . . We are moving towards a world war . . ." Shortly before his death, he said this to the family of the Zionist leader Nahum Sokolov: "Part of European Jewry is going to be sacrificed for the resurrection of your biblical fatherland."

Addendum

Arthur W. Kac

Beginning with America's bicentennial celebration, three declarations of support for Israel have been published by evangelical Christians in America. The first was a proclamation issued by a group of Christians called "Evangelicals United for Zion," July 3, 1976, at the "Salute to America Bicentennial Congress on Prophecy" in Philadelphia. The proclamation was signed by eleven world-renowned evangelical Christians. October 28, 1976, at a luncheon meeting of Jewish and evangelical leaders in Washington, D.C., the proclamation was presented to Israel's ambassador Simcha Dimitz. The proclamation was accompanied by 7,000 individual letters of support for Israel. The president of Evangelicals United for Zion stated that there are many thousands of evangelical Christians, other than the 7,000, who are ready to lend their support to Israel. It was mentioned that evangelical Christians supporting Israel number some forty million people. The following is a reprint of that proclamation.

We, the undersigned evangelical Christians attending a "Salute to America Bicentennial Congress on Prophecy," July third, in the year of our Lord, Nineteen Hundred and Seventy Six, at Philadelphia, Pennsylvania, attest to the following . . .

Whereas

We believe the Bible, including the Old and New Testament, is the inspired Word of God and that . . .

God has established an everlasting covenant relationship between Himself, the Jewish people and the land of Israel and . . .

Whereas

The holocaust, a racist act, is part of Israel's sacred history, and although detractors of the nation claim this to be a break in the covenant of God with the Jewish people . . .

We believe that the perpetrators of the holocaust were in essence the enemies of God, working against God and the eternal message of Israel, and that the establishment of the nation of Israel following the holocaust is in fact proof that the covenant of God with his people had not been broken and . . .

Whereas

Believing the Jewish people to be God's chosen people of prophecy, they are the people of the land and . . .

Further

In the Bible God vigorously proclaims His love for the nation of Israel and the Jewish people and . . .

Whereas

Through the nation of Israel came the promised Messiah, and according to Scripture, the Messiah will return to Jerusalem to reign as King and . . .

Therefore

Be it resolved that we protest the recent action of the United Nations which equated Zionism with racism, as being contrary to the Word of God and, as throughout history, self-condemning to any body or individual nation voting against Israel's right to exist and . . .

Further

We, knowing Him who made the promise, totally support the people and land of Israel in their God given, God promised, God ordained right to exist and . . .

Further

That any nation who bitterly assails Israel and the right of the state to exist can be seen, not only as the enemies of the Jewish people, but also the enemies of God.

We have therefore affixed our signatures this July third, Nineteen Hundred and Seventy Six, at Philadelphia, Pennsylvania.

On November 1, 1977, a full-page statement of support for Israel was published in the *New York Times* and *Washington Post*. The full text of that statement follows. It was signed by ministers of prominent evangelical churches, a Protestant bishop, presidents of theological schools, educators, editors, and other evangelical leaders.

Evangelicals' Concern for Israel

We the undersigned Evangelical Christians affirm our belief in the right of Israel to exist as a free and independent nation and in this light we voice our grave apprehension concerning the recent direction of American foreign policy vis a vis the Middle East.

We are particularly troubled by the erosion of American governmental support for Israel evident in the joint U.S.-U.S.S.R. statement.

While we are sympathetic to the human needs of all the peoples of the Middle East, mindful that promises were made to the other descendants of Abraham and concerned about the welfare of Christians in all the countries of the Middle East, we affirm as Evangelicals our belief in the promise of the land to the Jewish people—a promise first made to Abraham and repeated throughout Scripture, a promise which has never been abrogated.

We believe the rebirth of Israel as a nation and the return of her people to the land is clearly foretold in the Bible and this fulfillment in our time is one of the most momentous events in all human history.

While the exact boundaries of the land of promise are open to discussion, we, along with most evangelicals, understand the Jewish homeland generally to include the territory west of the Jordan River.

It should be remembered that from the time of Joshua, this land mass has been the exclusive homeland for the Jewish nation. Jerusalem has never been the capital for any other people since the time of David.

We pray for peace in the Middle East and we pledge ourselves to work for justice for all of the peoples involved, yet we also declare our belief that lasting peace cannot be achieved until the international community accepts the inalienable right of the Jewish people to live and create a nation within the boundaries of their ancient homeland.

Further, from the perspective of Israel's security requirements as well as from our understanding of her legacy, we would view with grave concern any effort to carve out of the historic Jewish homeland another nation or political entity, particularly one which would be governed by terrorists whose stated goal is the destruction of the Jewish state.

As Evangelicals we are convinced that Israel's future should not and will not be determined by political intrigue, fluctuating world opinion or the imposition of world powers. Rather, we put our trust in the eternality of the covenant God made with Abraham and we find comfort in the words of the prophet Amos—

"And I will plant them upon their land, and they
shall no more be pulled up out of their land which
I have given them, saith the LORD, thy God."—Amos 9:15

The time has come for Evangelical Christians to affirm their belief in biblical prophecy and Israel's Divine Right to the land by speaking out now.

On November 15, 1977, a full-page statement signed by fifteen evangelical leaders was printed in the *New York Times*. The following are several excerpts from the statement.

The United Nations, on October 28, 1977 voted 131-1 to censure Israel. The United States abstained. Israel voted for herself and stood all alone. This spectacle has stirred the hearts of Bible-believing Christians all over the world.

We the undersigned arise to announce that we vote with Israel. . . .

The Old Testament belongs to Jews and Christians alike. Here we learn that the Holy Land is the "Land of Promise" for Israel and the Messiah. We are called Fundamentalists because we believe the Bible to be the very Word of God and that it is to be taken literally on its every representation. . . .

Christians owe the Jews a debt that can never be repaid. The Prophets, the Apostles are Jews. Jesus Christ, the Savior, is of the seed of David, the seed of Abraham. The Holy Land is sacred. The establishment of the State of Israel, May 14, 1948, recognized immediately by President Truman, the coming of Jewish refugees to their land from Hitler's persecution, and the opening up of all sacred shrines, to all people and all religions, we believe is a service to all mankind. . . .

The Christian is accounted close to the Jews. Just before the Six-Day War, the radios from the Arab lands were announcing that on Saturday the Jews would be driven into the sea, the Mediterranean, and on Sunday the Christians would also be dealt with.

The Palestine Liberation Organization (PLO) with its terror and determination to destroy Israel, a program of genocide and slaughter, simply cannot be dealt with either by Israel or the United States. . . .

The fear of the loss of Arab oil cannot replace the fear of God. Nor can it be used against the prophecies and purposes of God.

60 Zionism and the State of Israel

Jakob Jocz

It is an odd fact of the human predicament that every solution creates new problems. Zionism was meant to solve the aggravated problem of the Jewish exile. It was born at a time when Jewish life in the Diaspora had almost reached breaking point. Anti-Semitic agitation spread all over Europe, chiefly in France and Germany. In Eastern Europe, Jew-baiting was so endemic to daily experience that it was almost taken for granted. In the "Dreyfus case," when Captain Alfred Dreyfus on the general staff of the French army was falsely charged with spying for the Germans (1894), the cruelty of anti-Semitic agitation was revealed to the world. At that time Theodor Herzl (1860-1904) conceived the vision of an Israel gathered in her homeland.

In a sense Zionism is as old as the Jewish exile. Since the destruction of Jerusalem by the Romans in A.D. 70, Jews have longed, prayed, and hoped for their return. That hope is deeply embedded in the Jewish liturgy and in folk-tradition. *Erets* (country; land) for Jews always meant Erets Yisrael (the Land of Israel). The sentiment of Jewry is expressed in the Psalmist's cry: "If I forget thee, O Jerusalem, let my right hand forget her cunning" (Psalm 137:5). The traditional greeting through the ages was: "Next year in Jerusalem." That Zionism was inspired by religious and Messianic conviction that God will gather in His people at His appointed time.

The new Zionism initiated by Herzl was founded not upon religion but upon nationhood. Herzl rejected the idea that Jews are essentially a religious community: "We are a nation, a nation," he declared to the world. A nation needs a home to call its own. The political aspirations of modern Zionism were laid down in Herzl's tract *The Jewish State* (1896). The First Zionist Congress met a year later. The characteristic of political Zionism is active exertion towards the goal in counter-distinction to the age-old passivity of the Jewish people.

The years between the publication of Herzl's tract and the establishment of the Jewish state in Israel (1948) were years of mounting nightmare that reached its climax with the Nazi holocaust of European Jewry.

The rest of the story since 1948 is well known. Israel has endured four wars, each time emerging victorious by a sheer miracle. The Yom Kippur War in 1973, when the Israelis were taken by surprise, brought the newly-formed state almost to the precipice. The precariousness of Israeli statehood is still a political fact, and peace is yet far off.

The tragedy of the situation lies in the fact that both warring parties can claim justice. It would seem that force is the only solution, though one is loathe to accept the validity of Tamerlane's motto, *"Rasti rousti"* —might is in the right. Jews have suffered too much to be content with purely military solution to the dilemma. They are sensitive to the fact that the situation in Israel raises profound moral problems that lie beyond politics. Jewish leaders both in Israel and the Diaspora agonize over the problem of how to safeguard the rights of the Jewish people and at the same time do justice to the Arabs. That is Israel's most burning problem.

But there are also internal ideological problems, which occupy Jewish leaders and which find expression in the Jewish press. To two of those we will now turn.

THE UNIQUENESS OF THE JEWISH STATE

In view of the religious and spiritual past, what is the ultimate objective of Zionism? Is Israel just a state among other states, or is it meant to be different? The question is an important one even for non-religious Jews. There are two possible answers: Zionism aims only at securing the continuity of the Jewish people; or, Zionism seeks to turn Israel into a spiritual center for the good of mankind. For Jews, both answers have Messianic overtones.

Even Jews estranged from Judaism are not content with regarding Zionism as a purely political movement. "The State of Israel must not be like any other state. What we seek in Israel is not a society of greater affluence, but a framework in which to create and grow spiritually and morally."[1] The antecedents of Zionism intrude strongly enough to press for more than a physical geographical solution. That raises the question, What is a spiritual center?

The question has already exercised the mind of Ahad Ha-am (pen name of Asher Ginsberg, 1856-1927). Secularized Jews understand it in terms of culture: there is cultural difference between Isarel and the other states.

An article by Robert Alter, contributing editor to *Commentary* and professor at the University of California at Berkeley, entitled "Israeli Culture and the Jews,"[2] attaches special importance to the Hebrew language as the vehicle of culture. That of course applies primarily to Jews, who are urged to acquire proficiency in Hebrew. Israel is understood to be a bastion of the Hebrew tongue. But does language guarantee specific cultural values?

Professor Alter's admission is that it does not. He cites an Israeli poet, whom he describes as "a post-ideological Israeli, a self-avowed cosmopolitan," who shies away from Israeli particularism and who "rejects all grandiose national and rational perspectives." That "fictitious Hebrew poet," Gaby Daniel, is admittedly not the only one to take such a stance. Alter explains: "Certainly all of the Hebrew writers I have known personally have seen their language as one of the tongues of men" without attaching to it special importance. The exception, according to Alter, is Uri Zwi Greenberg "who still preserves unambiguously a sense of Hebrew as the instrument of *yehud,* of a grand unique destiny."

Apparently language as such is no guarantor of culture unless there are values lying behind the language. That raises the basic question, What are the specific Jewish values? Are there values that radically distinguish Jews as a special people?

In the past the answer given would have been in the affirmative, and without hesitation: Judaism was the distinctive mark of Jewry. Jews knew themselves as different. The *havdalah* blessing at the end of the Shabat gives ample expression to that fact: "Blessed art thou . . . who makest a distinction between Israel and nations." It is not man who makes the distinction; it is God. But for the secularized, Westernized Jew, both in Israel and in the Diaspora, that is no longer an acceptable truth, hence the problem.

The modern Jew knows himself as part of a larger entity. He is steeped in "universal culture" and is unwilling to surrender it. Professor Nathan Rotenstreich of Hebrew University, Jerusalem, makes this important admission: "The Jews all over the world, including those who live in Israel, try to find their place within the universal culture, both highbrow and popular, and thus expose themselves to the unavoidable pressures which go along with any style of existence."

The Jew, like everyone else in the contemporary world, is torn between particularism and universalism. Rotenstreich explains: "It is only natural that Jews adhere to their surroundings not only because they have to be there but because they value the distinctive feature of their environment. Hence the Jews of the Western world live within a complexity to maintain pockets of Jewish collective existence within the framework of universal culture."

But unless there are specific Jewish values to counterbalance the drag in the opposite direction, the struggle for distinctiveness is futile. Rotenstreich sees the only solution in the concept of Jewish solidarity. "The strength of Zionism," he writes, "can depend only on the attempt to build Jewish collective existence which will be imbued with the sense of service for the sake of collectivity."[3]

But, we venture to ask, is "collectivity" an adequate substitute for Jewish values? Somewhere on the way, "Jewish culture" has been lost. For once we hang our distinctiveness on the peg of culture we have surrendered to universalism. Rotenstreich knows about that, for in the end he is forced to reduce the "Jewish horizon" to "human meanings" that continue to shape Jewish attitudes and convictions.

Can there be an answer to the problem outside biblical revelation?

Jewish Christian believers hold that in Yeshua the Messiah particularism and universalism find the perfect solution. In Him, Jews express their distinctiveness as messengers to the Gentiles, so that both become the new man, the new humanity. That is the Messianic vision for Israel and the world. The prophetic hope transcends Jewish particularism and embraces mankind. To lose that hope is to betray our heritage.

THE PROBLEM OF "DOUBLE LOYALTY"

Before the founding of the Israeli state, the fact of Jewish diversity was taken for granted. Not only was Judaism divided but the people were also divided in respect to culture and language. Jewishness was interpreted in various ways. Some understood their Jewishness in purely religious terms; others preferred to interpret their Jewishness as an ethnic tradition. In lands of toleration Jews regarded themselves as loyal citizens of their respective countries of birth or residence.

Against the background of American pluralistic society, Jewish diversity constituted no problem. While Zionism was only an ideological aspiration and, in the United States, a form of philanthropy, no real problem existed. But with the creation of a Jewish state the question of divided loyalties arose.

For Ahad Ha-am, the classical figure of cultural Zionism, political issues seemed still remote. Israel, in his vision, was destined to serve as the spiritual and moral center for world Jewry. But the situation changed with the concrete fact of a Jewish state. The promulgation of the Law of Return suddenly made every Jew the world over a political citizen of Israel by virtue of birth.

During the Arab-Jewish wars, many Jews from different countries enlisted in the Israeli army. The late Ben Gurion challenged world Jewry to participate actively in the fight for independence. He poked fun at Zionists who stayed at home and expected others to do the fighting. What angered American Zionists most was his insistence that true Zionism implies emigration to Israel. That has become a contentious issue.

Israelis argued that since the creation of the Israeli state, Zionism as an ideology has become redundant. Now, the political fact of Israeli existence required total commitment to the Jewish state. They were critical of Western Jews to whom being a Zionist came to mean a remote notion of support for Israel. "Calling oneself a 'Zionist' was, in the dominant Israeli point of view, a way of expressing a certain lack of commitment, an unwillingness to commit oneself wholly to the real sacrifices and trials of Israeli life." That is the way Professor Warran Bargard of Hebrew Union College, Cincinnati, describes the Israeli attitude towards Diaspora Zionism. He quotes David Ben-Gurion as saying that a Zionist is "only one who was preparing himself and his family. . .for aliyah."

Professor Bargad, however, sees a radical change in the Israeli attitude towards Zionism since the 1967 war. The "Israeli animosity or negative attitude towards Zionism" disappeared when Israel discovered the solidarity on the part of the world Jewry at a time of crisis: "There was a tremendous outpouring of support from world Jewry, and the Israelis responded in kind by reaffirming Israel-Diaspora ties."[4]

What has become known as the Jerusalem Program, adopted by the Twenty-seventh Zionist Congress in 1968, lays down as the first rule of Zionism: "The unity of the Jewish people and the centrality of Israel in Jewish life." It is that all-inclusiveness that raises problems for Jews in the Diaspora. To start with, Israel cannot survive as a state without the support, both material and moral, from world Jewry. One therefore can be a dedicated Zionist, seeking the peace of Jerusalem, without emigration.

The more difficult problem is that of divided loyalties. Some have argued that there is no problem. It is argued that Jews can participate in their countries' cultures and at the same time remain loyal to their own people's destiny and aspiration. Others take the view that it is a peculiar feature of Jewish life to bear the strain of double loyalty whatever that may imply. Non-Jews have to accept that as a fact and come to terms with it. Thus Robert Alter writes: "The last twenty years have made it increasingly clear both to Jews and other Americans that the Jews are in many respects a stubborn anomaly in the American denominational arrangement. To put it bluntly, the so-called 'dual loyalty' that made non-Zionists so uneasy seems to have become, for both Gentiles and Jews in America, a quietly acknowledged fact."[5]

In ordinary times and under American conditions such division of loyalties appears to be inoffensive. But it is questionable whether under different conditions, say under the stress of war, Jewish commitment to a foreign state would be equally tolerated.

A case in point is Ben Dunkelman's command of the armored Seventh Brigade, which captured most of Galilee. Dunkelman is an officer of the Queen's Own Regiment of Canada who distinguished himself in World War II and was decorated with the Distinguished Service Order for bravery. His autobiography, *Dual Allegiance* (1976), is written in the spirit of non-conflict between two loyalties.

Dunkelman's reviewer asks: "How does he cope with what he calls, in his title, Dual Allegiance to Canada and to Israel?" "Apparently," writes Kildate Dobbs, "by not thinking much about it. As a Canadian he shows himself ready to die for his country; as a Jew, for the State of Israel. A conflict between Canada and Israel, if that ever came about, might cause him sleepless nights. But Dunkelman is not a man to brood over remote possibilities."[6] At present it is a non-issue, but who can foretell the strange and unexpected exigencies of history?

Professor Rotenstreich prefers a more restricted concept of loyalty. In the case of Diaspora Jews, he suggests loyalty to Israel need not mean political loyalty: "Other attachment of a broadly human character should not immediately be translated into political language," except for the Israeli Jew.

But the whole tenor of Zionism contradicts a restriction that limits itself to "broadly human" concerns. Zionism is concerned with practical issues and the concept of loyalty is another term for "faithful allegiance." Whether one can serve two masters at the same time is a disputed question. Some Jewish intellectuals feel uneasy with that unresolved problem.

In the sphere of practical issues, the tension between the double loyalties surfaces from time to time on the question of mutual understanding between Israel and the Diaspora, especially in the United States. Martin Ballonoff suggests extended dialogue facilitated by better knowledge of both Hebrew and English as a remedy to misunderstanding.

Ballonoff explains that American Jewry "is just beginning to awaken to the fact that it has until now subjugated itself (by its own free will) in many areas to the policies of the State of Israel." As a result of such awakening, he continues, "there are now leaders in the American Jewish community who question whether subjugation to Israel was or is a proper policy for American Jewry, which has interests of its own not included among those of the State of Israel." Those leaders object to "the tendency on the part of Israeli representatives to ignore differences of opinion," which unfortunately leads to frustration and tension resulting in "resentment and antagonism."[7]

Being misunderstood is a common human experience. Wherever people work for a common goal there is always difference of opinion regarding ways, means, and methods. But the question of divided loyalties goes deeper than lack of communication.

What is needed is a common denominator that transcends goals in history. Such a denominator was Israel's faith. In the past, Jews had only *one* loyalty, namely to the God of Israel. Jewish loyalty to God was the unifying principle that gave purpose to Jewish life. There can be no doubt that for the majority of Jews today, Eretz Yisrael has become a substitute for religious faith. Rabbi Stuart E. Rosenberg isolated the malaise by pointing to the subtle shift from *Judaism* to *Jewishness*. This is what he says many times over: "A 'religious consensus' permeates all three Jewish 'denominations' in America, a consensus based upon the survivalist motivations of *Jewishness* rather than on fundamental religious commitments of *Judaism*."[8] What Jews are experiencing both in Israel and in the Diaspora is a profound spiritual crisis. Ferdynand Zweig has already drawn attention to the fact that " the spread of the new secularized version of the Jewish religion where Land itself becomes the main object of religious worship" is a prevailing attitude, especially in Israel. The close association of state and religion as now constituted "has a distorting influence on religious life in Israel," according to Zweig.[9]

Whether secularized Judaism, which centers upon survival, can serve as a substitute for man's need of God is a question that confronts and challenges us at this juncture of our long history. Jewish Christians believe that what Jesus did for the Gentiles He can do for our people today: bring us back to the God of Israel and thus help us to transcend our divided loyalties. "No one can serve two masters" (Matt. 6:24, NASB) and retain his integrity. To serve God is man's only freedom. No man is truly free *for* God.

Notes

1. Abraham Schenker, *Forum* 24, no. 1, 1976.
2. Robert Alter, "Israeli Culture and the Jews," *Commentary,* November 1976, pp. 59-65.
3. Nathan Rotenstreich, *The American Zionist,* December 1976, p. 14.
4. Warran Bargad, *The American Zionist*, October 1976, pp. 17ff.
5. Alter, ibid.
6. Review of Ben Dunkelman, *Dual Allegiance, Toronto Globe and Mail,* October 23, 1976.
7. Martin Ballonoff, "Dialogue: The Israeli and the American Jew" *Conservative Judaism,* Spring 1976, pp. 72-75.
8. Stuart E. Rosenberg, *American Is Different* (Toronto, Nelson: 1964), p. 192.
9. Ferdynand Zweig, *Israel: The Sword and the Harp* (Cranbury, N.J.: Associated U. Presses, 1969), p. 82.

61 The Eschatalogical Significance of the Return of Israel to the Land

Steven B. Levinson grew up in London, having confessed his faith in Jesus at age eleven. At sixteen he enlisted in the British Merchant Navy and served in it during World II. Following his discharge he committed his life anew to the cause of Messiah Jesus. To prepare himself, he enrolled at All Nations Bible College in London and later studied at Tyndale Hall, Bristol University. In 1962 he was ordained in the Anglican ministry and became curate of St. James, Carlisle, from 1961 to 1964. He then was vicar in Jerusalem from 1964-1967. At the same time he served as Secretary in Israel for the International Hebrew Christian Alliance. In the last years before his death, he was director of the Christian Witness to Israel and was closely associated with the work of the British and International Hebrew Christian Alliances.*

What I want to discuss in this paper is whether or not we can see any eschatological significance in the return of Israel to their land. I will seek to show this from the Jewish point of view, bearing in mind that what Christians call the "Second Advent" is in the eyes of Jews the Coming of the Messiah for whom they wait.

Definition of Terms

(1) *Eschatology.* In general this term designates the doctrine concerning the "last things." The word "last" can be understood either absolutely as referring to the ultimate destiny of mankind in general or of each individual man, or relatively as referring to the end of a certain period in the history of mankind or of a nation, that

*Stephen B. Levinson's article is reprinted from *The Hebrew Christian* 48, no. 3 (Autumn 1973):114-19, by permission of the International Hebrew Christian Alliance.

is followed by another, entirely different, historical period. A worthy eschatology, says Dr. [Lewis Sperry] Chafer, must embrace all prediction, whether fulfilled or unfulfilled at a given time. In other words, a true eschatology attempts to account for all that is foretold in the Bible. The end in the Bible is always the beginning of something more glorious, and the end of this present age will usher in a period of blessedness such as the world has never seen. "For the earth shall be full of the knowledge of [God] as the waters cover the sea" (Isa. 11:9).

(2) *Israel.* This name was given to Jacob after his mysterious conflict with the angel (Gen. 32:28-29). It came to designate all Jacob's descendants and is used to denote the nation as early as Gen. 49:7. Although after the division of the kingdom after Solomon's death it was used to denote the Northern Kingdom, the name is used of the people of God. Today, since the formation of the State, we should note that the term Israeli applies to all citizens of the state irrespective of religion.

(3) *The Land* (of Israel). *Erets Yisrael* designates the whole area which, according to the Bible, was promised as an inheritance to the Israelite tribes. There are three different borders of land according to the Bible and Talmudic sources.

> (i) The boundary of the Patriarchs—Gen. 15:18-21, "from the river of Egypt unto the great river Euphrates," though this may mean no more than the boundaries under (ii).
>
> (ii) The boundary of those coming out of Egypt based on Deut. 1:7, 8; 11:24; Joshua 1:4 and 13:2-5 which was interpreted as extending from Mt. Amanus to the brook of Egypt (Wadi el-Arish).
>
> (iii) The boundary of those returning from Babylonia, this is the actual area of Jewish settlement in Talmudic times. Excluding the Gentile coastal towns, it extended from Galilee to Ijon, to the Hauran in the East and Petra back to the coast. The Biblical expression "from Dan to Beersheba" designates the area from Mount Hermon to the valley of the Arnon (Josh. 12:1). N.B.—The boundary of the land given in Ezekiel 47 includes the Hauran but omits Gilead, nor does it stretch to the Euphrates.

When the expression ["the land"] is used in this paper, the first definition is meant, i.e. the boundary of the Patriarchs.

Old Testament Significance

There is no O.T. word for the abstract idea of eschatology. It does however have a term *aharit ha-yammim* which means "the end of time." The idea of doctrine for the last days is not found in the pre-prophetic period and there is little to be found in the Torah. Yet the basis for later Israelite eschatology was laid down from a very early time. From the call of Abraham, those who descended from him venerated their God as a "living God," i.e. One Who took an active part in the history of His people. They were conscious of the fact that He had made them His "chosen people." Since He was not only the special God of Israel but also the sole Lord of the entire world, they combined a particularism as the "chosen people" with a universalism which looked forward to their just God's reign over the entire world. Because of His covenant with them, He proved Himself to be faithful and loyal to

His promises, thus showing His frequently praised emunah (faithfulness) and chesed (steadfast love), thus sending to them in time of need saviours such as Moses, Joshua, the Judges and especially David. The hope and expectation that this relationship between the God of Israel and His people would continue in the future, led to an explicit eschatology found in the writing prophets. The essential origin of this lay in Israel's belief in its election by God as the means by which He would establish His universal reign over all mankind, combined with His promise to Israel of its own land, the "Promised Land," the "land of Canaan," as His pledge guaranteeing this promise.

The concept that the return of the people to the land would be an inevitable part of the events accompanying the "Day of the Lord" is often referred to by the Prophets. Among the pre-exilic, Amos stands out. He was the first recorded as designating the events of the last days as the "Day of the Lord" (Amos 5:18). Although he did not invent the term, by this time the common people were using it to describe the time when their God would bring them complete victory over their enemies and thus lead them into the light of lasting peace and prosperity in their land (Amos 9:13-15). Hosea writes of a renewal of God's love for and covenant with Israel as in the days following the Exodus from Egypt (2:14, 15; 11:1). He sees a future in which Israel will not only never again be attacked by human enemies from without, but will live in peaceful harmony with all living creatures within the borders of the land. In Isaiah 24:1-23 the theme is of Mount Zion as the religious centre of the world in the last days with the people firmly established. Jeremiah also foresaw that Israel's re-establishment in the land would entail a renewal of the ancient Sinaitic covenant in such a way that it would bring about a true change of heart, a new inner spirituality. Most of the prophets both before and after the exile affirm that in the "latter days" Israel will return to their land and this will usher in the Messianic age (Micah 5:1-3; Zeph. 3:12, 13, 20; Haggai 2:6-7). Isaiah speaks of the restoration of Israel as a "new creation" for all mankind as well as for the Jews (Is. 11:6; 41:17-20; 42:5-7). In Joel 3:2 the Prophet used the term "the valley of Jehoshaphat" which has no geographical significance, meaning "the place where the Lord judges." Later tradition identified it with the Kidron Valley in the east of Jerusalem and consequently it and the slope of the Mount of Olives to the east became a favourite burial place, where the dead would be at hand at the resurrection for the general judgment of the last day. Zechariah sees the coming of the Messiah as a time when the people will be in the land and the King will ride up to Jerusalem (Zech. 9:9-10). In mysterious imagery Daniel sees Israel back in their land as a sure sign of the ushering in of the Messianic era. As the Lord had come to rescue Daniel, so He would intervene by putting an end to pagan empires and establishing His reign over the whole earth by means of His chosen people (Dan. 2:44).

From the earliest beginnings in God's promises to the Patriarchs until the dispersion of the Jewish nation after the destruction of the Second Temple, Israel always kept alive its eschatological hope and expectation based on a belief in God's justice and on an optimism that, with God's help, good would ultimately triumph over evil and they would be called from the four corners of the earth to resettle in their land and then Messiah would come.

Nothing in the New Testament weakens the concept of Israel's continuing as a nation and not just as a race. Not all the promises made to the nation in the Old Testament can be taken over by the Church without violence to their obvious meaning. Israel is addressed as a nation in such passages as Acts 15:16-17. A most significant illustration is Paul's prayer for Israel that they might be saved (Romans 10:1) which is a clear reference to the use of Israel as a nation outside the Church (see also Romans 9:3-5). Paul's argument in Romans 9 is certainly built on the idea of Israel as a separate nation. Not only are they regarded as a separate nation, but Gentiles are expressely excluded; this is clearly affirmed in Eph. 2:12. In the verses that follow it is important to note that the Apostle does not indicate the Gentiles come into these promises given to Israel, but rather pictures both Jew and Gentile being joined together in an entirely new entity, namely, the Body of Christ. The fact therefore that in the New Testament Israel and the Gentiles are contrasted with each other, is strong evidence that the term *Israel* continues to mean what it meant in the Old Testament, namely, the descendants of Jacob. In this connection it is important to note Paul's argument in Romans 11. After asking the question, "Did God cast off His people?" he answers it first of all with an absolute negative by asserting that there has always been a remnant of Israel and that there will be a remnant in the future. The hope set before them is not that given to the Church, which already is in the place of blessing in this present age and makes no claim to promises given to Israel of possession of the land.

One of the more familiar arguments against the continuance of Israel as a nation is the idea that in their rejection of Christ they were rejected as God's people and the promise of the land was cancelled. According to this argument the only promises available to a Jew today are those given to the Church. While the value of national contributions to the Church are stressed, many would deny that any could be given by the Jew. This assertion is answered by the presentation of their future hope as a nation in Romans 11. It is also implicit in the words of Jesus in Matt. 21:43. New Testament teaching on this subject stresses that the promises made to Abraham are everlasting and the land is promised to Israel as an everlasting possession.

The question remains, when will Israel re-possess the land? In the Olivet Discourse (Matt. 24-25), Jesus outlined some of the events which will precede His return. His aim was to prevent those of His followers who were to witness the destruction of Jerusalem by Rome from identifying that catastrophe with the end of the age. He spoke of some of the trends, movements and developments which would occur at the time of the end and which would forewarn those who were watching for His return. Now, while He refused to fix any definite date He intimated that a period which might be long would intervene prior to His return. Just as the budding of the fig tree is a sign of summer (Luke 21:29) so in the coming into existence of the State of Israel may be seen the beginning of the fulfilment of Jesus' words. We have witnessed a wonderful recovery of an ancient people regaining their land, a land to which they have always laid claim. Has not this regathering of the people an eschatological significance? Nearly all the other signs mentioned in Matt. 24:1-11 have been fulfilled time and again. The reason why I believe the set time is come is that the return of the people of God to their land is an unique event. The arguments for the fulfilment of the promise hang on the certainty of the Word of God. Just as prophecy concerning Israel has always had its fulfilment in the past, so will it also in the future. Israel's promise of the land is just as sure as the Christian hope of heaven.

62 The Rebuilding of Zion

All his enemies surprising,
From the dust the Jew is rising;
See him rising from the grave,
Keen, alert, for conflict brave;
A new spirit now has come
That will gather Israel home.

In their land in deserts thorny,
Hands unused to toil, made horny;
Build and plant with sacred joy;
Busy at their loved employ.

In the valleys long neglected,
By disease germs long infected;
Many die, but others come,
Eager to reclaim their home.

While the latter rain from heaven
To the land once more is given,
Land that looked like stoned to death;
Feeling now God's quickening breath.

Mother Zion, they are coming,
From their ghettos, from their roaming;
From their tossings on the sea
Of the Gentiles, back to thee!

What though Ishmael opposing
God's sure plan and settled choosing!
Not a word our God has spoken
Shall be canceled, shall be broken.

The above poem is reprinted from Max I. Reich, *The Jubilee* (Grand Rapids: Eerdmans, 1943), pp. 21-22. Used by permission.

And the covenant will stand,
Signed and sealed by God's own hand,
To a thousand generations,
Midst the rise and fall of nations.

Like the stars on Mamre's plain,
Israel will still remain;
And the promised land be theirs,
Through the everlasting years.

—MAX I. REICH

Why Jews Become
Followers of Jesus

And Jesus went out, along with His disciples, to the villages of Caesarea Philippi; and on the way He questioned His disciples, saying to them, "Who do people say that I am?" And they answered and said, "John the Baptist*; but others say, Elijah; and others, that one of the prophets of old has risen again." He said to them, "But who do you say that I am?" And Simon Peter answered and said, "Thou art the [Messiah], the Son of the living God."

Mark 8:27; Luke 9:19; Matt. 16: 15-16 (NASB)

When the Brother Daniel case was being discussed in the Israeli press, *The Jerusalem Post* printed the stories of three Jewish Christians residing in Israel. They spoke of their Hebrew Christian faith and of their love for their Jewish people and for the land of Israel. We often hear Jewish spokesmen state that the young Jewish people who now become followers of Jesus hail from homes in which they did not receive a proper Jewish upbringing and who are ignorant of their Jewish heritage. The Jewish Christians whose stories are related in the following pages all came from Orthodox homes and were steeped in Jewish religious life and lore.

A Polish Talmudical Scholar—*Emmanuel S. Greenbaum*   317
A Great-Grandson of a German Rabbi—
   Karl Jakob Hirsch   321
A Hungarian Jewess—*Serena Rosengarten Kiss*   325
A Hungarian Rabbi—*Isaac Lichtenstein*   328
A British Jewess—*Lydia Montefiore*   333
An American Rabbi—*Max Wertheimer*   336

*John the Baptist (or Baptizer) had already been beheaded.

63 A Polish Talmudical Scholar

Dr. Emmanuel S. Greenbaum was born in 1888 in the Russian part of Poland.* At the age of thirteen he was thoroughly saturated with the best there was in the wisdom and learning of rabbinical Judaism. About this time he began to experience dissatisfaction with the religion of his fathers. Soon there began the restless period of 1903-1905. While the Russian government was embroiled in a war with Japan, the Russian people made an attempt to overthrow the feudal and despotic regime. Slogans of political and civil freedom stirred the younger generation all over the Russian empire. Jewish youth contributed its share in that momentous struggle for liberty. Thousands of young Jews left their religious schools and threw themselves, heart and soul, into the revolutionary movement. The war with Japan ended in Russia's defeat, but the Russian government resolved to turn this defeat into a slaughter of its own defenseless citizens. A life and death struggle ensued between the reactionary and dark clique that ruled Russia and its enslaved but awakening people. The revolutionaries formed fighting squads in the various communities in order to meet violence with violence.

The young Greenbaum, who was then about fifteen years old, joined one such fighting squad, which operated in the district in which he resided. Having become convinced of the justice of the revolutionary cause, he threw himself headlong into the thick of the struggle. One day the mounted police invaded the radical neighborhood in his town in their search for the trouble-making ringleaders. One of these "mounties" was especially generous with his whip and club. Young Greenbaum, desiring to teach this "gentle" fellow a lesson, deposited a large dose of pepper in his horse's nostrils, which caused the infuriated animal to give its rider a good shake-up.

Finally the revolution was bloodily and brutally suppressed. Many of its active participants had to flee the country in order to save their lives, and the Greenbaum boy joined the exodus. He was about seventeen years old when he crossed the Russian-Austrian border and, with a group of his fellow exiles, found temporary refuge in a Jewish home. That Jewish family in Austria had a son who had embraced the Christian faith. It appears that the Lord began at that time to work in the heart of the young revolutionary.

While yet in Jewish theological school, Greenbaum at age twelve had become interested in the "boy Jesus" of whose "unfortunate fate" he used to hear the rabbi talk on Christmas Eve. He had felt sorry for the smart Jewish boy who used his

*This account of Dr. Greenbaum's life is reprinted, with changes, from Arthur W. Kac, "Dr. E. S. Greenbaum As I Knew Him." *The Hebrew Christian Alliance Quarterly* 24, no. 2 (Summer 1939):18-22.

cleverness in the wrong direction. The revolution changed his opinions on the question of Jesus. As he meditated now upon the real significance of that stormy period in Russia he had just left behind, he began to believe that Jesus was in reality a socialist in disguise who had fought to deliver His people from their oppressors, the rich and the high priests. His sympathy for the "boy Jesus" of his synagogue days ripened now into an admiration for Jesus the "great revolutionary."

One day he received from a friend a package wrapped in a page from a Yiddish tract. He became interested in the wrapping and read it through. Finding that it emanated from a Jewish mission in Crakow (then in Austria), he wrote to the Reverend L. Zeckhausen, then head of that mission, requesting more literature.

The Greenbaum lad became deeply interested in the subject of Christianity. In 1907 he went to London where he studied the New Testament and gained a new and deep appreciation of the Old Testament. The Lord, who to the twelve-year-old boy had been the unfortunate "boy Jesus," and to the seventeen-year-old socialist in exile was the first great revolutionary, now revealed Himself to Greenbaum as his Savior and his Lord. In 1908 he was baptized at St. Jude's Church in London. He worked in a printing shop during the day, studied at night, and used his free time to witness of Christ to his Jewish people.

When World War I broke out, he came to America. He enrolled at McCormick Seminary and was ordained to the ministry. In 1918 he was called to head the Bethany Community Center in Newark, New Jersey. In 1930 he was called to a similar work in Montreal.

A few days after my arrival in the United States (1927), Dr. Greenbaum took me for a walk through the Jewish district in Newark. I was impressed by the friendly greetings on the part of the Jews we met. I soon learned that Dr. Greenbaum possessed the God-given gift of making friends everywhere. There was something about him that drew people to him. His natural cheerfulness was contagious. He used to say, "Christianity must be caught as well as taught."

One does not often meet men who combine in themselves several qualities. As a rule, the scholarly individual keeps himself aloof from the menial tasks of everyday life. Dr. Greenbaum was not that type of scholar. In Bethany Camp at Roseland, New Jersey, one could see him dig the ground, scrub the floor, cut the bread, dish out the food—and wash the dishes, if necessary; a few minutes later he could be heard delivering in the chapel an inspiring message from the Scriptures, or discoursing on theological problems with Jews at the table. Yes, he was all things to all men, in the sense in which Paul, whom he so closely resembled in spirit, used those words.

That Dr. Greenbaum exerted a powerful influence on certain types of Jews can be seen from the following incident. When he became forty years old, some of his Jewish friends decided to give him a surprise birthday party and enlisted Mrs. Greenbaum's assistance. When the Greenbaums returned home that evening from the Center, we were all gathered there. The birthday gift consisted of a set of the Mishnah (the Talmudic interpretation of the Law).

Present in the group was a certain Jew, originally from Poland, a man who knew the Talmud well and hailed from the same Orthodox group from which Dr.

Greenbaum sprang. That man arose and this is what he said: "I value Dr. Greenbaum because of his fine Jewish background; he and I understand each other; to me he is the bridge between the Jewish people and Christ." I know that Dr. Greenbaum was deeply moved by that spontaneous expression of appreciation and especially by the last remark, because, ever since he had become a child of God, his great longing was that he be a bridge leading his people to Christ his Savior.

In those days when practically all Jews were Orthodox, the Hebrew Christian presented Christ to them as the One of whom "Moses and the prophets spoke." Today the great majority of Jews do not believe in, or do not know, Moses and the prophets; nor do they care whether or not Jesus is the fulfillment of the Old Testament prophecies. Still, many today continue to approach the Jew in the same old fashion. Dr. Greenbaum was one of the pioneers of the present day method of approaching the Jew with the gospel of Jesus Christ. At the Second General Conference of the Hebrew Christian Alliance held in Philadelphia, May 2 to 5, 1916, Dr. Greenbaum delivered an address on the subject "Literature for Jews." This is part of what he said, and much still holds true today:

> While we have more than enough literature dealing with the Orthodox or Talmudic Jew, we have very little, or rather no literature, dealing with the other classes of our nation. We have four different classes of Jews, the Orthodox, the Reformed, the Zionist or nationalistic Jew, and the Atheistic Jew. Is it because we have no message for the last three classes that we have not taken the trouble to write tracts presenting our Lord and His claims in a way which would be attractive to them? Can we not show our brethren of the Reformed stock, that while they are talking so much about Israel's mission and are so ready to claim the good fruits of Christianity as their own, they must not reject the root and stem. For unless the root is conveying life to the branches, the branches will wither and there will be no fruit. Can we not show our Zionist brother, that while he is striving to make Israel like unto all the nations around them, what a poor ideal it is to have before one's eyes! In Christ we have the ideal of our nation becoming "A priestly kingdom and a holy nation." Can we not show the atheistic Jew, that while he threw off religion because he was taught to consider as religion so many things which have no place in it, there is One who is "The Way, the Truth, and the Life"? Need I remind you that there is no real atheist among our people? How many times did you converse with one who claimed to be a strong, red-hot radical atheist, and when you appealed to his religious instinct there was a warm response? The reason why we have so many Jewish atheists is well known to us. There are here quite a few who once belonged to their ranks. I was one, but what drove me away from the religion of my Fathers? The heap of rubbish, hiding the precious gem of truth, besmearing and bemuddling it and claiming for itself to be the precious gem. I, as thousands—yes, tens of thousands—of the young generation, kicked away the heap, little realizing that in the midst of it all there was something worthwhile possess-

ing. How many of these wandering sheep could be brought back to the true Shepherd by presenting Him in a way which would appeal to them? Brethren, the Gospel of Christ is for us all. He is the Saviour of the whole world. We have a message of salvation for all the Jews, no matter whether they be Reformed, nationalistic, or atheistic.[1]

I might add that, acting upon his suggestions, the Hebrew Christians assembled at that time decided to begin the publication of the *Hebrew Christian Quarterly.*

Dr. Greenbaum's life was a continuous service for others. He was always in the forefront of the battle. He chose socialism at an early age and became devoted to it. When, however, Jesus crossed his path, he forsook everything else and followed Him. To Dr. Greenbaum, Jesus Christ was not merely a theological creed or a certain ideal to talk about at leisure. To him He was Life. In Him he lived, moved, and had his being. He preached Him, he exemplified Him, and he breathed His very Spirit.

Notes

1. Emmanuel S. Greenbaum, "Literature for Jews," in *Papers, Addresses and Proceedings of the Second General Conference of the Hebrew Christian Alliance of America* (Philadelphia: Heb. Christian Alliance, 1916). pp. 55-57.

64 A Great-Grandson of a German Rabbi

Karl Jakob Hirsh was a great-grandchild of Samson Raphael Hirsch, probably the most famous rabbi of the last century, whose name will always be connected with the revival of Jewish orthodoxy in Europe. But the young man received an overdose of orthodox religion in his early life, which made him turn from all religion and join the ranks of the atheists. In the fields both of art and literature Karl Jakob Hirsch had great success: one of his books was a best seller just prior to the beginning of the Hitler regime which drove him, like so many others, into exile. He reached the United States where he earned his living as an ordinary worker, at the same time continuing his literary activity, which alone could not support him and his family. A serious illness gave him time and cause to ponder upon the meaning of life and brought him face to face with the Bible and thus with Jesus. In his book *The Return to God* he gives a most moving account of the various phases through which he passed: utter loneliness and despair; the ever-growing conviction that he was a creature of God, who had made him for some purpose; the realization that his illness and suffering were a vehicle of conveying God's mercy and grace to him; and eventually the dawning of light when he discovered the Savior's hand reaching out for him. When he publicly confessed his faith in the Lord Jesus on Good Friday 1945, he remarked that he believed that he had never been a better Jew than today.

After the war he returned to Germany, only to meet much misunderstanding. The last years of his life were spent on a sick bed. He kept his faith under circumstances that might have unnerved many a man stronger than he was, and he died a loyal follower of the Messiah a few months before his sixtieth birthday. He passed away in the summer of 1952 after a prolonged illness that reduced him to a state of utter physical helplessness. Outstanding men of letters, among them Thomas Mann, have paid high tribute to his courage of conviction and his great gift as a writer. Articles in the Jewish press claimed him as a great son of the Jewish people. But he was above all a true follower of Jesus the Messiah.

In the following article, Karl Jakob Hirsch relates something of his religious experience.

The above material is reprinted from H. D. Leuner, "Letter from Europe," *The Hebrew Christian* 25, no. 3 (Autumn 1952):93; and from Karl Jakob Hirsch, "How I Found God," *The Hebrew Christian* 26, no. 3 (Autumn 1953):79-81. Both articles are used by permission.

How I Found God

My way to God I described in a book which appeared in 1946. Its title was *The Return to God* and it was read by many. As the great-grandson of a famous rabbi, Samson Raphael Hirsch, of Frankfort-on-the-Main, my childhood was a circumscribed one in which the Mosaic law ruled all. But I do not wish to speak of this, but rather of the way—a way difficult and, it seems to me, stony—which led me to God, to Christ who redeemed me.

There is in me a strong sense of living in this world: an urge to fulfill the commitments of terrestrial duty, which I would not disobey. Let us not deceive ourselves: it is no simple change which one makes when one confesses Christ, but it is an earnest obligation. This is appreciated by but a few. I described in my book how a serious illness was the spiritual and physical occasion by which I found a staff and a comfort in a foreign land. At that time I was abroad and far from the country which I loved and which I called home. I understood only too well that the Sermon on the Mount was to all men, and not only to the chosen Jews who were scorned, and, indeed, done to death by the Pharisees. It is necessary to appreciate that a conversion to the Messianism of Jesus is not merely an isolated action which one performs with good intent and to the best of one's knowledge, but an action that has a variety of results and the implications of which one has to understand thoroughly.

Concerning this I wrote some time ago, in *The Return to God,* how the childhood I described would end in nothingness, for I had lost God completely. I am not afraid to say that I believed in nothing, in absolutely nothing, during the years in which I both achieved fame and experienced calamity; when men concurred with me and condemned me; when fate was both kind and cruel. But the purpose of my existence was hidden from me until I found Christ, who revealed purpose in my life through His death.

So via atheism (and not, as many believed, from Judaism) did I attain Christianity. Judaism is difficult, toilsome. Its purpose may have been understood by my great-grandfather and my grandfather, but I myself never grasped it. I knew how to set aside the harsh duties which the Jewish faith imposes. I remember, for instance, how I desecrated that most sacred feast, Yom Kippur, by ignoring the law of the fast. I knew that this was a mortal sin, but I did not believe in the wrath of God, nor that the Jewish law was according to the will of God. As far as he himself was concerned, the Jew in Germany at the turn of the century was lax and superficial in his religion. I felt this particularly strongly as a child and consequently the importance of the law lost all meaning for me.

In those lost years I never read the Bible. I wrote books, learnt to understand people, felt happy among them and seldom thought to ask anybody, "What is your relationship with God?"

This took place between the years 1920 and 1933. During this period I led an active, successful life, I was to realize later that this was vouchsafed me of the grace of God. In those days, like a playful child or pleasure-seeking adolescent, I tasted tidbits of the fame that was dear to me.

Then came the bitterness of the exile. I, with my people, the Jews, was driven out. I managed to reach the great land where freedom reigns and where every man is allowed to live in freedom. But I had lost my *raison d'être* for the freedom which I could enjoy had no value, since I could not speak out, dared not acknowledge that I was a lost man.

I was lost, but now I am saved. Salvation, however, carries its obligations. It is not as if a drowning man clutches a plank until a ship picks him up. It is something entirely different. Life had no purpose, for I had lost the tongue of my motherland. Here I dared only whisper it, while around me all spoke loudly. It needed the shock of illness (as I realized during the nights that I lay sick) to convince me that the purpose of life was not eating and drinking. There had to be something else. I saw the shadows of my folk around me: how they professed to be Jews but were nothing but the members of a faith few believed in. My meeting with myself, when I understood myself, took place in the night that death was near. I saw my life clearly and distinctly; saw that if I died now I should become a corpse, nothing more. But I got up again. I wandered about. By chance (does chance exist?) I found a Bible. I turned its pages and found that by upbringing and tradition I had always finished at Malachi, without ever reading the New Testament of our Lord and Saviour. I read it then, and when in the third chapter of St. John's Gospel I found the words, "Except a man be born again, he cannot see the kingdom of God," I understood that the responsibility of the new birth lay with me, and that it would leave me no peace until I had acknowledged it aloud.

I tried at the time to overcome what had tortured me during the years of my exile. It was my own fault, nobody else's. I could say of myself, "The good that I would, that I do not, but the evil which I would not, that I do." I had to escape from this prison of malevolence. It was not made easy for me, for I may admit that the convert is not welcomed with open arms by Judaism; he is rather like a probationer who has to pass certain examinations. But (although I was only just over fifty) I had my life behind me and I wanted to live the rest of it with God's help.

I sat down and wrote my life story: it became my book *The Return to God*. From my Jewish friends it brought me nothing but scorn and contempt, for I had taken upon me the cross of Christ, and to them it seemed ridiculous. This cross I carried, and although my strength was insufficient and I sometimes stumbled, although I became often tired and helpless, I never doubted. And let it be clear to everyone before he attempts the stony path up to the Lord and Saviour, that he can earn nothing but adversity and scorn, as Jesus of Nazareth Himself did. For in all things He must be our example, not only in suffering adversity, but in standing upright under the weight of the cross. That is the crux of the matter.

I was not frightened of death any more. I learned from the New Testament that ". . . our light affliction, which is but for a moment, worketh for us a far more exceeding and eternal weight of glory" (2 Corinthians 4:17).

It was a winding and thorny path that I had to follow, and I almost gave up. But something kept me going: not the desire for death, but the will to live: the will to live for Jesus Christ and the teaching of the Sermon on the Mount, which set the poorest on a par with the others. I felt at that time more than ever that the Lord had always preferred the poor, never the rich. And "the rich" meant those, as I found out, who pretended to sanctity, so much so that the poor were relegated to the background, where they were lost to view.

It seems obvious to me (as I hope it is obvious to many) that I had to speak out aloud: not only "to believe in my heart . . . but . . . with my mouth to make confessions . . ." And that also is very important.

It was necessary, as long as one had a tongue, to speak out and to confess Christ. The Christian faith demands such confession. And it demands action to mitigate injustice until there are neither rich nor poor on earth.

I understand today, as I suspected then, that there is no standing still in the discipleship of Jesus Christ, but that one has to go on, and that Golgotha, which stands at every destination, is no more than the way to redemption and resurrection.

Thus my conversion to the Messianism of Jesus has strengthened and settled me; I have lost everything I once thought I possessed, but I have gained much: my faith, and myself. And I have gained the strength to alter things, even though it may mean to be misunderstood and to be crucified, like Jesus Christ. And that is, of all things, most wonderful.

65 A Hungarian Jewess

Serena Rosengarten Kiss

I was born in Hungary into a family with a strong religious tradition. My father's parents emigrated to Hungary from Wilno, Luthuania, which for many years had been a center of Jewish learning. He entered a Talmudical school at an early age, where he took up rabbinic subjects, and also studies in synagogue music. When his training was over, he was engaged in teaching religion in three schools. In the course of his teaching functions he made the acquaintance of Catholic and Protestant clergymen with whom he enjoyed frequent discussions on biblical subjects.

My parents had ten children, seven boys and three girls. We were brought up in the firm belief that the Hebrew Scriptures embody God's Word entrusted to Israel, and we were taught to hope for the coming of the Messiah. We prayed, sang, and dreamed about Messiah's coming, when the Jewish people would be restored to the land of Israel, the world would enjoy an era of peace and prosperity, and the Messiah, the Son of David, would rule in righteousness.

I was especially fond of the Hebrew hymn "L'cho Dodi," which welcomes the arrival of the Sabbath and is sung on Sabbath eve. That hymn was composed some four centuries ago by one of the medieval Cabalists in Safed, Israel. The hymn strikes a Messianic note in the following words taken from Isaiah: "Shake thyself from the dust of the earth, my people, put on thy garments of glory; through the Son of Jesse the Bethlehemite redemption draws nigh to my soul."

In the course of time I married, and the Lord favored us with a beautiful baby girl. As I needed someone to help me with my house duties, we engaged the services of a young and lovely girl. I later learned that she was a recent convert to the evangelical Christian faith and was affiliated with the Baptist denomination. When accepting the job she asked to be off one evening a week in order to attend the midweek hour for Bible study and prayer, and Sunday mornings for chapel service.

That girl was the first genuine Christian we had met, and she represented a Christianity of which I had known nothing before. I learned from her that the Christian faith has nothing to do with birth, race, or nationality, that a Christian is one who at a certain point in life decides to follow Jesus Christ, and that Christian conversion involves a complete transformation of one's world view and way of life. This Christian girl was singing hymns while she scrubbed the floor, she was praying while ironing our clothes. She spent evenings in her room studying the Bible.

One day, when the proper opportunity arose, she told us that her Lord Jesus is our Messiah. I was rather upset and resented such a statement. But to every objection I could summon to prove that she was in error she had a ready answer. I soon came to realize how little I knew my own Bible in comparison with that Gentile Christian girl. She once brought me a book entitled *The Prince of the House of David.* I placed it on my night table. But for a whole month I did not even touch it; I was held back by centuries of prejudice and resistance to the person of Jesus.

Once the girl told me that certain guest speakers were coming to our town, and she wondered whether they would be permitted to pay us a visit one evening. After talking the matter over with the members of my family, I granted her request. About nine o'clock in the evening on the appointed day they arrived bringing Bibles with them.

We all sat down around the table and beginning with Genesis 3:15 they expounded a large number of Messianic passages from the Old Testament. It was about two o'clock in the morning when we reached the book of Daniel where, in chapter nine, we read that the Messiah shall be "cut off," that the Temple shall be destroyed, and so on. To me that was a night of nights. We heard much and we learned much. We were conscious of the presence of the Holy Spirit, the Spirit of God, in our midst as never before in our lives. I was deeply moved and became convinced that the things we read and heard were true.

I could not fall asleep that night, and I pondered what the next step would be. For the first time in my life I silently prayed, and that without a Prayer Book, for God's guidance and help. "O God of Abraham, Isaac, and Jacob," I whispered within me, "do not let me go wrong; if this Jesus is the Messiah, if all these prophecies we read refer to Him, please stand by us and lead us safely by Thy Light."

At the first opportunity I discussed the whole matter with my husband. To my pleasant surprise he confessed to me that at the age of six he had been exposed for the first time to the Christian faith when the Gentile maid in his grandparents' home took him with her to church one day. His second visit to a Christian church was during the First World War when he joined the men in his outfit in a chapel service.

After the visit of the above-mentioned gentlemen, my husband secured a Bible, and our servant girl let me read her New Testament. Words fail me to express my reaction when reading the New Testament. I was struck by its Jewishness, and its very title—The New Covenant—took me back to Jeremiah 31 with its promise that God will some day make with Israel a new covenant. As a result of my extensive reading of the Bible—Old and New Testaments—I became convinced that the Old and New Testament complete each other and that in Jesus we have the fullness of God's revealed truth.

My next problem was how to break to my father the news of my newly-gained conviction concerning the Messiahship of Jesus. At first I sought to conceal it from him, but he himself sensed that something had happened to me. At last he approached my husband one day, and in the course of a heated conversation he challenged him, saying: "If you are the man of the house you ought to stop all this foolishness!" My husband's gentle reply was: "Father, you have given to your daughter a solid foundation; she cannot build anything false upon it.''

There were many pleadings and tears, many arguments and much travail of soul. Before my husband, our daughter, and I emigrated to the United States, I bought a Hebrew New Testament and left it with my father.

In spite of a perverted Christendom of past centuries and in spite of all the tragic experiences of my people during the Nazi period, I found in Jesus my Redeemer, and I committed my life to Him. He enabled me to ''see the invisible, believe the incredible, expect the impossible.'' He graciously clothed me with the garment of salvation (Psalm 149:4; Isaiah 61:10). He is the Logos, God's Word, the Memra, the Metatron, the Malach Ha'Panim (the Angel of God's Face). He is the Lamb of God who took upon Himself the sin of the world.

I praise my Lord and give Him thanks that in His appointed time He sent His messenger in the person of a humble, young, faithful servant-girl, and in His pity and love He saved and redeemed many members of my family, even my dear parents in their seventies, before all of them were consumed in the fiery furnace of Nazi brutality.

66 A Hungarian Rabbi

He was not yet twenty when he became a rabbi, and after officiating for several years in various communities in northern Hungary, *Isaac Lichtenstein* finally settled as District Rabbi in Tapio Szele. There he remained for nearly forty years, laboring ceaselessly and unselfishly for the good of his people.

One day a teacher in one of his district schools showed him a German Bible. Turning the pages, Rabbi Lichtenstein's eyes fell on the name "Jesu Christi." He became furiously angry and sharply reproved the teacher for having such a book in his possession. In his rage he flung it across the room, where it fell behind others on a shelf, and lay dusty and forgotten for some thirty-odd years.

During a fierce wave of anti-Semitism in the picturesque little Hungarian town of Tisza Eslar, situated on the Theiss, twelve Jews and a Jewess were thrown into prison, accused of having killed a Christian girl in order to use her blood for ritual purposes. As in every other case in which such a diabolical charge was brought against Jews, the blood accusation in Tisza Eslar was ultimately proven to be false and baseless.

It occurred to Rabbi Lichtenstein that there must be something in the teachings of the New Testament which excited enmity against the Jews, and while browsing among his books he came upon the German Bible which thirty years before he had thrown away in a rage. He picked it up and examined it carefully. The state of his mind at this time is best revealed in his publication, *Judenspiegel, A Jewish Mirror*, in which he wrote:

" 'Much have they afflicted me from my youth up, let Israel now say' (Psalm 129:1). No long explanation is needed to show that in these few words the Psalmist sums up the bitter experiences and sorrows which we, at least of the older generation, have suffered from our youth at the hands of the Gentile populations surrounding us.

"As impressions of early life take deep hold, and as in my later years I still had no cause to modify these impressions, it is no wonder that I came to think that Christ himself was the plague and curse of the Jews—the cause of our sorrows and persecutions.

"In this conviction I grew to manhood, and still cherishing it I became old. I knew no difference between true and nominal Christianity; of the fountainhead of Christianity itself, I knew nothing.

"An Hungarian Rabbi" is reprinted from Henry Einspruch, ed., *Would I? Would You?* (Baltimore: Lederer Found., n.d.). pp. 62-69, and is used by permission of the Lewis and Harriet Lederer Foundation, Inc.

"Strangely enough, it was the horrible Tisza Eslar blood accusation which first drew me to read the New Testament. This trial brought from their lurking-places all our enemies, and once again, as in olden time, the cry re-echoed, 'Death to the Jew!' The frenzy was excessive, and among the ringleaders were many who used the name of Christ as a cloak to cover their abominable doings.

"These wicked practices of men wearing the name of Christ only to further their evil designs, aroused the indignation of some true Christians, notably Professor Franz Delitzsch of the Leipzig University, who, with pens on fire and warning voices, denounced the lying rage of the anti-Semites. In articles written by the latter in defence of the Jews, I often met with passages where Christ was spoken of as he who brings joy to man, the Prince of Peace, and the Redeemer; and his Gospel was extolled as a message of love and life to all people.

"I was surprised and scarcely trusted my eyes when I found, in a hidden corner, the book which some thirty years before I had taken in anger from a Jewish teacher. I opened the book, turned over its pages and read. How can I express the impression which I received?

"Not the half had been told me of the greatness, power, and glory of this Book, formerly a sealed book to me. All seemed so new, and yet it did me good, like the sight of an old friend who has laid aside his dusty, travel-worn garments, and appears in festive attire, like a bridegroom in wedding robes or a bride adorned with her jewels."

For two or three years Rabbi Lichtenstein kept these convictions locked in his own breast. He began, however, to preach strange and new ideas in his synagogue, which both interested and astonished his hearers. At last he could contain himself no longer. Preaching one Saturday from the "Parable of the whited sepulchre," he openly admitted that his subject was taken from the New Testament, and he spoke of Jesus as the Messiah, the Redeemer of Israel.

He embodied his ideas in three publications, appearing in rapid succession, which created a sensation among Jews, not only in Hungary, but throughout the continent of Europe. And no wonder! For here was an old and respected Rabbi, still in office, calling upon his people to range themselves under the banner of Jesus of Nazareth, and hail him as their true Messiah.

As was inevitable, as soon as official Jewry realized the significance of Rabbi Lichtenstein's position, a storm of persecution broke loose upon him. And he, who but a few weeks before was classed among their noblest of leaders and teachers, was now described as a disgrace and a reproach.

The charge was made that he had sold himself to missionaries. Some even asserted that he had never written the pamphlets himself, but had only been bribed to sign his name to them. He was cited to appear before the assembled Rabbinate in Budapest. He obeyed. On entering the hall he was greeted with the cry, "Retract! Retract!"

"Gentlemen," he replied, "I shall most willingly retract if you can convince me that I am wrong."

Chief Rabbi Kohn proposed a compromise: Rabbi Lichtenstein might believe whatever he liked, if he would only refrain from preaching Christ. And as to those dreadful pamphlets which he had already written, the mischief could be undone by a very simple process: the Conference of Rabbis would draw up a document to the effect that Rabbi Lichtenstein wrote what he did in a fit of temporary insanity!

Rabbi Lichtenstein answered calmly but indignantly that this was a strange proposal to make, seeing that he had only now come to his right mind. They then demanded that he resign his position as Rabbi and be formally baptized. He replied that he had no intention of joining any church; that he had found in the New Testament the *true Judaism*; and that he would remain as before, with his congregation.

He did so, and this in spite of many persecutions and reproaches which were heaped upon him. From his official position as District Rabbi he continued to teach and preach from the New Testament. This was a touching testimony to the strong attachment of his own community, which alone had the power to make request for his dismissal. As a matter of fact, much pressure was brought to bear, and some members of the congregation and relatives of his wife were completely ruined by loss of trade, but still they clung to him.

By this time Rabbi Lichtenstein and his writings had become widely known, and various church and missionary organizations sought his services. The Papacy, too, learned of the existence and significance of the man, and a special emissary from the Pope visited Tapio Szele with tempting offers if the Rabbi would enter the service of Rome.

To all he had one reply: "I will remain among my own people. I love Jesus my Messiah; I believe in the New Testament; but I am not drawn to join Christendom. Just as the prophet Jeremiah, after the destruction of Jerusalem, chose rather to remain and lament among the ruins of the Holy City with the remnant of his brethren, so will I remain among my own brethren as a watchman from within, to warn them and to plead with them to behold in Jesus the true glory of Israel."

At last, however, with his health much impaired by the many trials and sorrows which fell to his lot, he voluntarily resigned his office as District Rabbi. He settled in Budapest where he found ample scope for his talents, but opposition to him was relentless.

He was shadowed and even physically attacked on the street. His barber was bribed to disfigure his beautiful beard. His landlord kept a close watch on everyone who visited him, and reported to the Rabbinical authorities. But, as a stream stemmed in its course forces for itself new channels, so he was continually interviewed and drawn into discussion with Jews from every walk of life.

"Wisdom cries without and causes her voice to be heard in the street," he wrote to his friend in London, David Baron. "Doctors, professors and officials come to my house. Many families of position also visit us and condemn the harsh conduct of the Rabbinate here in relation to me. I often have grave and important discussions with Talmudists and Rabbis who wish to bring me to a compromise, and it is worthy of note that many who formerly had no knowledge of the New Testament have afterwards asked me for a copy."

For over twenty years Rabbi Lichtenstein witnessed in many parts of the Continent to the truth as he saw it in Christ. At last the storms of controversy, misunderstanding and antagonism began to tell on him. His spirit, however, remained undaunted.

About this time he wrote: "Dear Jewish brethren: I have been young, and now am old. I have attained the age of eighty years, which the Psalmist speaks of as the utmost period of human life on earth. When others my age are reaping with joy the fruits of their labors, I am alone, almost forsaken, because I have lifted up my voice in warning: 'Return, O Israel, return unto the Lord thy God; for thou hast stumbled in thine iniquity. Take with you words, and return unto the Lord' (Hosea 14:2-3).

"I, an honored Rabbi for nearly forty years, am now in my old age treated by my friends as one possessed by an evil spirit, and by my enemies as an outcast. I am become the butt of mockers who point the finger at me. But while I live I will stand on my watchtower, though I may stand there alone. I will listen to the words of God, and look for the time when he will return to Zion in mercy, and Israel shall fill the world with his joyous cry: 'Hosannah to the Son of David! Blessed is he that cometh in the name of the Lord! Hosannah in the highest!'"

Quite unexpectedly he was taken ill and lingered only a short time. As he realized that his end was approaching, he said, in the presence of his wife and the nurse:

"Give my warmest thanks and greetings to my brethren and friends; good night, my children; good night, my enemies, you can injure me no more. We have one God and one Father of us all in heaven and on earth, and one Messiah Jesus who gave his life for the salvation of men. Into thy hands I commend my spirit."

The day was dismal; it was eight o'clock in the morning of Friday, October 16, 1909, when the aged Rabbi entered into the presence of his Lord.

How different was his beautiful spirit of love and forgiveness from the bitter spirit of his enemies! On the day after his burial there appeared an editorial in the *Allgemeine Jüdische Zeitung,* the organ of the Jewish Orthodox party in Budapest, and it is here reproduced to show the relentless hatred and persecution which a Jewish Christian, however blameless his life, has to endure for having the courage of his convictions and for speaking out for the truth as he sees it.

Of course, the editorial contains many falsehoods and slanders, and was another attempt to discredit Rabbi Lichtenstein's testimony in the eyes of Jewry. Yet in its way it bears witness to the unique character of the man who, in his official capacity, proclaimed the basic doctrines of Christianity.

A literal translation of the Yiddish editorial reads as follows:

Death of a Missionary

Yesterday the former Reform Rabbi of Tapio Szele, I. Lichtenstein—may his name be blotted out!—was buried here. While still Rabbi he was in the service of the soul-entrapping mission. From the Jewish pulpit he proclaimed the foundation doctrines of Christianity, and wrote a pamphlet in which he invited Jews to recognize the Founder of the Christian religion. Not until the scandal had lasted quite a while did the Reform Rabbinate of Budapest succeed in inducing the representatives of the community of Tapio Szele, composed for the most part of relatives or friends of Lichtenstein, to demand his dismissal, in order that he should withdraw from the Rabbinate.

Since that time the old apostate has lived in Budapest on money supplied him by English missionary societies, because he lent his name to missionary purposes. He was not, however, formally baptized, and thus this "deceiver and misleader" was buried in the cemetery of the Reform Synagogue of Budapest. "The name of the wicked shall rot."

67 A British Jewess

"You will find her an out-and-out Jewess and a great bigot," said a Christian lady of *Miss Lydia Montefiore*.* Her early training and background was that of a strictly orthodox Jewess. She rigorously observed the Sabbath as a sacred day, as well as the feasts and fasts and other ceremonies prescribed by the Law of Moses. In later life Miss Montefiore took up her residence on the Riviera, settling in Marseilles, for she was a member of the wealthy English Jewish family of that name, and an aunt of the famous Sir Moses Montefiore, friend of Queen Victoria.

When she was well over eighty, an English lady introduced to her a Hebrew Christian couple, Mr. and Mrs. J. P. Cohen, who were laboring among the Jews under the auspices of the British Society. On entering her home, the lady said, "I have brought an Israelite, Mr. Cohen and his wife, to see you." Observing a Bible on the small table, Mr. Cohen remarked to Miss Montefiore, "You read the Bible, I see." "Yes," she replied, "it is my greatest comfort."

He took the sacred volume and, turning to the 53rd of Isaiah, read to her:

> But he was wounded for our transgressions, he was bruised for our iniquities; the chastisement of our peace was upon him, and with his stripes we are healed . . . for he was cut off, out of the land of the living: for the transgression of my people was he stricken.

Finishing the chapter, Mr. Cohen asked her what she thought of it. "I should like to hear your opinion of it," replied Miss Montefiore. Mr. Cohen unhesitatingly declared that it referred to the life and death of the Messiah, and that it was literally accomplished in the person of Jesus, who must therefore be the promised Messiah. "Then you are a Christian," Miss Montefiore asked, and turning angrily to the lady who had introduced them, said: "I thought you told me they were Israelites." "So they are,—true Israelites," replied the lady. A short pause ensued, then Miss Montefiore, with flushed cheeks and quivering lips, retorted: "I think it is most insulting to call on people, and try to convert them from the faith of their fathers. Why not let everyone remain in the religion in which they were born? I must tell you, I am a thorough Jewess: I was born a Jewess, and I have lived eighty-three years as a Jewess, and hope I shall die a Jewess."

Quickly recovering her composure, however, she went on, "I repeatedly hear Christians say that they love the God of Abraham. I cannot conceive how they can do that and not keep the law which He gave to His servant Moses. If Christ has done away with the Law of Moses, how can he be the Messiah?" Mr. Cohen replied, "This is one of the many erroneous ideas the Jews have of Christ, for He did not

*The above account is adapted from A. Bernstein, ed., *Some Jewish Witnesses for Christ* (London: Operative Jewish Converts Institution, 1909), pp. 371-81.

come to destroy the Law or the Prophets, as they seem to think, but to fulfill all that the Law and the Prophets wrote concerning Him. It was He who made known the true meaning of all the Mosaic ordinances and institutions which the traditions of the scribes and Pharisees had rendered of none effect." "Besides," he went on to tell her, "God had promised to make a new covenant with Israel, and to write His Law in our hearts."

At this point, she interrupted him rather abruptly, insisting: "It is not in my Bible," Mr. Cohen then turned to Jeremiah 31:31-34, and Miss Montefiore, with evident surprise, read the words of the prophet:

> Behold, the days come, saith the LORD, that I will make a new covenant with the house of Israel and with the house of Judah: not according to the covenant that I made with their fathers . . . but this shall be the covenant that I will make with the house of Israel; after those days, saith the LORD, I will put my law in their inward parts and write it in their hearts; and will be their God, and they shall be my people.

In parting, Miss Montefiore pleasantly remarked: "I cannot understand how a Jew who believes in Jesus can still be an Israelite." Mr. Cohen told her not to think he had ceased to be a Jew because of his faith in Jesus—far from it. Jesus Himself was a Jew and all His first disciples were Jews, and it was not until Jewish opposition grew that they were sent to preach to the Gentiles. She seemed much pleased with his explanation, and invited Mr. Cohen to visit her again.

On the second visit, Miss Montefiore turned the conversation to the need for repentance. To this Mr. Cohen replied, "What we need most is to have our sins forgiven; not always to be repenting of them but to forsake them altogether. God did not say to our fathers in the land of Egypt, 'When I hear you repenting, I will save you,' but, 'When I see the blood I will pass over you.' The blood was Israel's security then, and it is the blood now that makes atonement for the soul. And without shedding of blood is no remission."

After a little hesitation, Miss Montefiore said, "We have no priest, no temple; the place appointed where alone it was lawful to offer sacrifice is inaccessible to us Jews. Surely the Almighty will not require of us that which we cannot perform; He will mercifully accept our prayers, our fastings, our observance of the Sabbath, and the reading of the Law, as I do daily, as a substitute for performing the Law." "Dear Madam," Mr. Cohen said, "let me beg of you not to rely on such bruised reeds, nor build your soul's salvation on such sinking sand; they are but vain excuses; they may quiet your conscience, calm your fears, and lull you into a false security, which you may only discover when too late."

A few days before Yom Kippur, she said, "The more I read my Bible, the more I am beginning to feel my being born a Jewess could never save me; I must have something better than my fastings and prayers." Gradually she came to see her need of the Saviour, the One who had shed His blood to make atonement. One day she said to Mr. Cohen, with clasped hands and uplifted eyes, "I'll tell you what I say to the Anointed One, Jesus, I mean, 'If I have done or said anything against Thee, pardon, Oh pardon me, for I did it in ignorance.' "

After receiving a New Testament, she wrote to her niece in England, saying: "I

334

have studied it closely during many evenings, which has sorely pained my eyes; but oh, how plainly and typically the Bible shows the coming of Messiah. I read it with much interest, and I pray ardently it may bring the whole world to believe as I now do, that Jesus Christ, God's 'only begotten Son was ordained to be crucified, to take away all our sins; and that by believing in Him, we shall be saved.' "

At first, Miss Montefiore wanted her new faith to be kept a secret, and said: "I should not even like my servant to know of it." Mr. Cohen reminded her that "the fear of man bringeth a snare," and that Jesus Christ warned us, saying: "Whosoever shall deny me before men, him will I also deny before my Father which is in heaven." Finally, Miss Montefiore came to the place where she could say, "How thankful do I feel I have not only told my intentions to my servant, but told her to tell others of it; in fact, I wish all my relations to know it, and I pray God they may be brought to the knowledge of the truth ere they die."

Thus a most bigoted Jewess became a child-like, trusting child of God, a follower of Jesus the Messiah in her old age.

68 An American Rabbi

Max Wertheimer was born in an orthodox Jewish environment at Kippenheim, in Baden, Germany. He attended Gymnasium at Ettenheim, worked for a brief period at Strassburg, Alsace, and came to the United States while still in his teens. He lived first in Buffalo, New York. He attended the Hebrew Temple there, where the late Rabbi Dr. Falk was the spiritual leader. In the autumn of 1882 Wertheimer left for the Hebrew Union College in Cincinnati to study for the rabbinate. The late Dr. Isaac M. Wise was very kind to him and helped with his financial struggles during the seven-year course. He chose him as the tutor of his children and had him stay with him at his country home at College Hill, Ohio.

In 1887 Wertheimer graduated from the University of Cincinnati, and in 1889 he received his degree and rabbinical diploma. Dr. Wertheimer received a call from Temple B'nai Yeshurun in Dayton, Ohio, where he spent a number of years and was revered by both Jews and Gentiles.

Dr. Wertheimer married Hannah Affelder, daughter of Mr. and Mrs. Louis Affelder of Peru, Indiana. Three months following the birth of their second child Mrs. Wertheimer died, leaving her husband with their two-and-one-half-year-old boy and three-months-old girl. The following is Dr. Wertheimer's story as told by himself.

> Born of orthodox Jewish parents, my earliest childhood impression was of my parents rising in the morning very early in order to spend a long time reading the Hebrew prayers.

> From the age of five to fifteen my training was in orthodox Judaism. At the age of 16 my parents decided to send me to America to pursue my classical education at the Hebrew Union College in Cincinnati, Ohio. After seven years, I graduated from it, having meanwhile also taken my degrees in letters and Hebrew literature, and four years later, my Master's degree.

> I finished the rabbinical course, and was publicly ordained and inducted into the Rabbinical office. My first call was to Dayton, Ohio, where I officiated as rabbi for ten years. In my Friday evening lectures I spoke on social, industrial and economic questions, monotheism, ethical culture, the moral systems of the Jews, etc. On Saturday morning I explained the weekly sections of the Pentateuch. On Sunday I taught Sunday School from eight in the morning until five in the evening, with one hour intermission for the mid-day meal.

Some of the information about Rabbi Wertheimer is derived from Dr. Dan B. Bravin in *The Dawn*. Rabbi Max Wertheimer's own account appeared in the article "These Found the Way" in *The American Hebrew Christian* 41, no. 1 (Summer 1955):6-10.

In 1895 a series of meetings was held in the Christian Church at Dayton. I stood proudly before that audience of professing Christians and told them why I was a Jew, and would not believe in their Christ as my Messiah and Saviour. I gloried in Reformed Judaism that acknowledged no need of an atoning sacrifice for sin. In the audience sat a humble aged woman, a devout Christian, who was deeply stirred as she listened. "O God," she prayed, "bring Dr. Wertheimer to realize his utter need of that Saviour he so boastingly rejects." No doubt, others also prayed the same prayer.

What unforeseen forces were brought into action, as a result of that unknown woman's heartcry! I was perfectly satisfied with life that day, was rabbi of the B'nai Yeshurun Synagogue, had a beautiful home, a comfortable income, a place of prominence in the community, had become an honorary member of the Ministerial Association. Had you visited my library at that time you would have found a wide range of reading. We had a large home, two servants, and a beautiful baby boy and a daughter, Rose.

But suddenly there came a change! My wife was taken seriously ill, and in spite of many physicians and specialists, she died, leaving me a distraught widower with two little children. My dreams of a successful career and serene domestic life were all shattered. Where was comfort to be found? . . . Heaven seemed as brass when I called on the God of my fathers! How could I speak, as a rabbi, words of comfort to others when my own sorrow had brought me to despair? The tenth year of my rabbinical office drew to its close. I decided not to accept re-election, and resigned. I wanted to think things over! I would study! I turned to my Bible!

I also began reading the New Testament and comparing it with the Old. One chapter in the Prophet Isaiah, the 53rd, made a definite impression on me, especially the eleventh verse, last clause of that verse: "By his knowledge shall my righteous servant justify many, for he shall bear their iniquities." Here was the only mention in the whole Bible of that phrase, "My righteous servant." It is found nowhere else in the Word of God in either Testament. We have "David, my servant," but here it is "My *righteous* servant." I said to myself: "Who is that righteous servant? To whom does the prophet refer?"

I argued: "Whoever that 'righteous servant' of Jehovah is, of one thing I am sure: he is not Israel, because the same prophet, in an earlier chapter, declares Israel to be a sinful nation, a people laden with iniquity, a leprous nation. The righteous servant of Jehovah must be One Who is holy. If it is not Israel, who could it be?" I decided it must be Isaiah. But in Isaiah 6 I found it could never be the prophet for he confesses himself to be a guilty sinner and a man of unclean lips in God's sight. "My righteous servant." Who could it be? Then I began to study the context of the fifty-third chapter and in Isaiah 50:6 I found, "I gave my back to the smiters.'' I pondered: Who gave his back to the smiters? In the beginning of the chapter it says: "Thus saith Jehovah." Jehovah is the only speaker in the chapter. Jehovah, then, gave His back to the smiters? Had God a back? When and why was it smitten? Who smote it? Further I read: "I gave my cheeks to them that plucked off the hair." And still further: "I hid not my face from shame and spitting." What did all this mean? Who had been so abused? When? Why? Did Jehovah have all these human characteristics? I studied more and more various prophetic utterances. In Psalm 110:1 it is written: "The Lord said to my Lord, Sit thou at my right hand, until I make thine enemies thy footstool." Here was David himself, speaking of his own seed and calling Him "Lord." How did He get up there?

In confusion I decided to begin at the first chapter of Isaiah and read the book through. I was stopped at the ninth: "For unto us a child is born, unto us a son is given: and the government shall be upon his shoulders; and his name shall be called Wonderful, Counsellor, The mighty God, The everlasting Father, The Prince of Peace." Here was a most incomprehensible thing! How can a "child" born of a woman, a "son" be called the "Mighty God," the "Everlasting Father?"

I was then faced with the doctrine of the Trinity. We Jews have a popular monotheistic slogan: "Sh'ma Yisrael, Adonai, Elohaynu, Adonai, Echad." The word "echad" means one. Taught by the Rabbis for ages, that word "echad" meant absolute unity. I began to study the word, and I discovered it meant, not *absolute* unity, but *composite* unity. Let me illustrate: Adam and Eve became one flesh; the Hebrew for one flesh is *basar echad,* a composite unity. Moses sent twelve spies into Canaan, and they returned bearing a gigantic bunch of grapes. That cluster of grapes is called in Hebrew *Eshcol Echad.* With hundreds of grapes on the stem it could not have been an absolute unity; they are called in Hebrew "one cluster." These and other Scriptures showed conclusively that *Echad* does not signify an absolute unity.

Another problem succeeded it: "Why is the name Jesus never mentioned in the Hebrew Scriptures?" I studied this question. Imagine my surprise when I found that 275 years before Christ, King Ptolemy Philadelphus summoned men from Israel, and bade them translate the Hebrew Scriptures into the Greek vernacular. They took the Pentateuch first and when they came to the name "Yeshua" they translated it as "Yesous," written with a circumflex over it to show there had been a suppression of a Hebrew letter that could not be expressed in Greek. When Yeshua went into Canaan with the other eleven spies, he was called "Yehoshua" (Jehovah is the Saviour). That is exactly what the word "Jesus" means.

I could hold out no longer; I was convinced of the truth that God was revealed in Messiah Jesus. I cried: "Lord, I believe that Thou as Yeshua hast made the atonement for me. I believe that Yeshua died for me!

From henceforth I will publicly confess Yeshua as my Saviour and Lord!'' Thus after months of searching I was convinced that Jesus was the righteous servant of Jehovah (Jehovah-tsidkenu), ''The Lord our righteousness!''

As a rabbi I had yearned to give the bereaved some hope on which to lean but how could I give that which I did not possess myself? I gave sympathy, but in times of heart-aching grief and tragedy, sympathy is of little comfort. But to the heart-broken how satisfying and glorious are the words of our Lord Jesus Christ: ''I am the resurrection and the life: he that believeth in me, though he were dead, yet shall he live; and whosoever liveth and believeth in me shall never die.'' And again, ''Verily, verily, I say unto you; he that heareth My Word, and believeth on him that sent Me, hath [possesses now] everlasting life and shall not come into condemnation, but *is* passed from death unto life'' [emphasis added].

There is but one eternal life. There is but one source of eternal life; that is God's Son, the Messiah of Israel. What a great and glorious message we, His redeemed ones, are commissioned to deliver today!

Conclusion
AWAKE, MY PEOPLE!

Emmanuel S. Greenbaum

Back, back in the far distant past you were awake! Your eyes were open and penetrating! Your children could see not only the present, but also pierce through the far distant future and with their prophetic eyes lighten the darkness, unravel mysteries, and reveal the hidden things! Your Isaiahs, your Jeremiahs, your Ezekiels penetrated the deepest darkness and in the brightest colors painted the glorious time of your joy and your peace! You, you alone, out of all the nations were chosen and appointed to bring into reality the golden age of which so many sons of men dreamed! You have given the world the "Book" above all books! Your singers make millions of hearts to rejoice and awaken the soul to religious ecstasy! You have given to the world Him who is the "Light of the world," the "Crown of humanity"! You have given to the world Him who opened the way for all men to God, and many fallen, slain, and fainting souls, through Him, are uplifted, healed and refreshed! All this you have done for others! But for yourself? Alas! You have fallen into a heavy lethargic sleep and for two millennia your heavenly pulse ceased to beat! Your prophetic eyes are closed! From Jesus, "the fairest of the children of men," you have turned away as from a leper! Him, your "Crown of Glory," you would not know! How long, how long will you sleep? Arise! Shine! for your light is come! Jesus, your Jesus, is your only salvation.*

*The source of this appeal is unknown.

Subject Index

Abraham
as a mediator, 213-14
importance of the call of, 79
relationship with God, 169
Abrahamic Covenant, foundation of the
New Testament, 182-83
Adam, sin of, 265
Adonis, Phoenician myth compared to
resurrection, 230
American Christian Palestine Committee,
93
American-Israel Society, 93
Angelic appearances, relationship to divine
self-disclosure, 197-99
The Anguish of the Jews, 81
Anthropomorphism of God, Jewish
philosophical explanations of, 189-91
Anti-Semitism
cure for, 113-14, 118
history of, 116-18
of pagans, 109-11
practiced by pagans, 82
results of, 38-39

Babylonian exile, purifying effect on Jews,
173-74
Balfour Declaration, 295
Bible
authority of, 265
church's relationship to, 178
importance of to man, 264
modern Jewish attitudes toward, 85
unity of defined, 179
unity of Old and New Testaments,
178-84, 221
Birkat Ha-Minim, prayer of hate, 137
"Brother Daniel Case," Jewish
disapproval of court decision, 138-39

Canon, preservation of linked to Judaism,
101

Christian, definition of, 98
Christianity
as a check on barbarism, 32
is complementary to Judaism, 56, 60-61
is a fulfillment of Judaism, 260
Greek and Roman influence on, 37-38
relationship to Judaism, 77-79, 87
similarities and differences from
Judaism, 143
sympathy with Judaism and Zionism,
140
unity with Judaism, 22, 34, 55
and Zionism, 67
Christians
contrasted with Muslims, 22
differentiated from pseudo-Christians,
80-82
sided with Jews during Holocaust, 82
Christocentricity of Christianity is not
recognized by Jews, 90-91
Christology, basis of controversy between
Christianity and Judaism, 187
Church
relationship to the Bible, 178
relationship to Israel, 181, 312
Communism, failure of, 282-83
Communist world, and the second coming
of Jesus, 281-83
Coexistence of Jews and Christians, 131-32
Council of Nicea, Christianity broke from
Judaism, 224
Covenant
as a means of divine self-disclosure,
199-200
basis of New, 266-67
distinctions between the Old and New,
181-83
grace and works in the Old and New,
183-84
inadequacy of Old, 266
Old contrasted with New, 175-77

Cross of Jesus, Jewish disdain of, 224-25
Crucifixion of Jesus, 36
  importance of, 209-10
  not a cause of anti-Semitism, 111
  significance of, 207
  supposed cause of anti-Semitism, 109

Day of Atonement, a Messianic type, 223
Davidic dynasty, restoration of, 278
"Day of the Lord"
  eschatalogical significance of, 311
  Messianic significance of, 272
Death
  Christian view of, 238-40
  Jewish reaction toward, 234-35
  Old Testament view of, 235
  pagan beliefs, 237-38
  Talmudic Jewish views of, 238
Decalogue, universal character and
  limitations of, 274-75
Developing nations, and the second coming
  of Jesus, 280-81
Dialogue
  basis of, 133-34
  between Jews and Christians, 84
  a challenge to Hebrew Christians, 134
  difficulties of, 86-91
  obstacles to, 100
The Disputation, an attack on Christianity,
  147-48
Divine self-disclosure, 195-204
Doctrines of Christianity, Jewish
  misunderstanding of, 100
"Dreyfus Case," 303
Dual loyalty of Jews, 307
Dualism in rabbinical teaching, 165

Erets Yisrael, defined, 310
Eschatology
  defined, 309-10
  in the New Testament, 312-13
  in the Old Testament, 310-11
"Ethical Monotheism," 143
Evangelicals and Jews in Conversation on
  Scripture, Theology, and History, 12
Evangelism, and world politics, 94
Evangelism of Jews, 82-83, 92-97
  Christian attitude toward, 96
  Hebrew Christian position, 95-97

Jewish opposition to, 93-95, 132-33
Exodus
  and national redemption, 253
  God's purpose in, 278

Fatalism in rabbinical teachings, 165
First Zionist Congress, 303
Freedom of religion in Israel, 140-41
Freedom of conscience, violated by
  "Brother Daniel" case, 138-39

Gaal, defined, 252
Gentiles, importance of their attitude to
  Jews, 114
God
  Fatherhood of, 53
  love of, 53-54
  nature of, 162
  tri-unity of, 163
Golden Rule, in Jesus' teachings, 43
Gospel, applicability to Jews as well as
  Gentiles, 78-79
Grace, fulfilled in Jesus only, 170-71
Grace and Law in the Old Testament,
  167-71
Grace versus Law, 167-71
Greek language at the time of the
  Incarnation, 257
G'ullah, defined, 252

Habba, 103
Hebrew Christians
  have accepted persecution along with
    other Jews, 141
  Jewish attitude toward, 137-38
  Jewishness of, 140-41
Holocaust, 303
  affected Christians as well as Jews, 81
  Christian aid to Jews during, 92-93
  Christians' attitude toward Jews during,
    40
  Christians protected Jews during, 22
  historical and spiritual importance of, 71

"I believe," 261-63
Incarnation
  differentiated from pagan "birth of
    god," 193
  fact of, 256

intimated in the Old Testament, 180
manner of, 258
necessary for salvation, 192-93
of Messiah, 256-59
purpose of, 258-59
relationship to the invisibility of God,
187-93
time of, 257
Invisibility of God, practical application
of, 189
Isaac, as a type of Christ, 222
Islam, relationship to Judaism, 139
Israel
as the "bride of God," 199-201
Christian attitude toward, 93
defined, 310
economic problems in, 284-85
ethnic interpretation of, 90
preparation for the second coming of
Jesus, 283-85
reasons for persecution of, 83-84
relationship to the church, 180-81, 312
secularization of, 172-73
selection of for service, 265-66
spiritual and historical significance of
creation of, 71
a spiritual vacuum, 70
uniqueness of, 304

Jehovah, personality of, 196
Jeremiah, his high view of God, 174
Jerusalem counsel, 276-77
Jesus
as a Galilean, 35-36
as the greatest Jew, 268
as Messiah, 104, 245-51
as a paraclete, 168
as a prophet, 68, 104, 243-44
as "Super-Jew," 30
baptism of, 275-76
cannot be detached from Christianity,
123
claimed divinity for Himself, 126-27
connected morality with politics, 154
death and resurrection of, 267, 275
deity of, 122, 164-65
His influence in Israel, 66
His message is inseparable from His
person, 149-50

His ministry pointed to His Messiahship,
128
His teachings were similar to those of
other rabbis, 62
humility of, 62
impact on modern Israel, 148-49
in Israeli literature, 11
Jewish attitude toward, 137
Jewish derision of, 146
Jewishness of, 24-25, 31, 32-33, 34-39,
49-50, 64-65
Jewishness of His teachings, 153
love commandment of, 155-56
ministry of, 276
preparation of the world for His return,
279-85
reasons for Jewish hostility toward,
146-47
resurrection of, 44
return of, 275-79
role as a prophet is acceptable to Jews,
243
second coming of, 271-86
significance of the death of, 207-8
superiority over other prophets, 149
teachings of, claims that His followers
changed them, 152
transfiguration of, 44
universal influence of, 42, 46-47, 67
universality of, 51, 63
Jew, definition of, 98, 137-38
Jewish Christians, only persons qualified to
interpret both Jewish and Christian
faiths, 14
Jewish converts to Christianity, 96
Jewish culture at the time of the
Incarnation, 257-58
Jewish interest in Jesus, 70
Jewishness of Jesus
Jewish preoccupation with, 148
various Jewish author's views, 147-48
Jews
dual loyalty of, 306-7
what happens when a Jew converts to
Christianity, 99
Johannine influence on Christian
Christology, 187-88
Judah, historical significance of tribe of,
173

344

Judaism
Christology of, 188-91
compatability with Christianity, 99
failure of orthodoxy, 149
miraculous survival of, 101-2
relationship to Christianity, 77-79
similarities and differences from
Christianity, 143-44
Judgment
on Israel, 272
on the nations, 272
universal, 272
Justification through Jesus, 165

Kaddish prayer, 234
Kenosis, Jewish reaction to, 13
Kinsman-redeemer, 253

Law
fulfilled in Jesus only, 173
purpose of, 266
Law versus Grace, 167-71
Law of Return, 136

Maimonides Creed, 138
Man, fate of, 265
Marxism
creeds of, 281
effects of, 281-82
Messiah
claim that Jesus would not accept the
title for Himself, 250-51
etymology and usage of term, 245-48
in "Book of Enoch," 249-50
incarnation of, 256-59
Jewish concept of contrasted with
Christian concept, 48-50
Jewish fulfillment in, 267
Jewish understanding of His person, 247
judicial functions prophecied, 273
king and suffering servant in one person,
273
Levitical concepts of, 249
pagan concepts of, 247-48
redemptive function of, 254-55
"Messianic Age," defined, 284
Messianic mission, stages of, 277
Messianic prophecies, 222-23, 271-286
Mediation

defined, 213
importance to Messianic hope, 213-14
Mediator
belief in rabbinic Judaism, 218-19
biblical concept summarized, 219
concept in the New Testament, 219
functions of, 215-16
Modernism, is actually old materialism,
209
Monotheism, 161-66
as expressed by Zarathrustra, 247-48
Mosaic convenant, distinguished from
Messianic covenant, 217-18
Mosaic Law, and the preservation of
Jewish identity, 68
Moses
as a mediator, 214-16
as a type of the future Mediator, 216-18
Moslems, alliance with Hitler, 22

National Conference of Christians and
Jews, 12
Nazis
persecuted Christians as well as Jews, 81
were not true Christians, 87
New Testament
Jewishness of, 35, 70
Jewish understanding of, 58-59
Nicean Council, brought pseudo-Christians
into Christendom, 81
"No Religion Is an Island," 77-79

Old Testament, universality of, 36
Olivet Discourse, and eschatology, 312

Paul
Jewishness of, 225-26
said to be founder of Christianity, 88,
121, 124
Persecution
of Christians by Jews, 111
of Hebrew Christians by Jews, 329-32
of Jews by "Christians," 100, 224
of Jews by non-Christians, 109-11
of pagans by Jews, 110-11
Personality of God, 196-97
Philo of Alexandria, supposedly an
influence on John's writing, 125
"Post-Christian Era," a misnomer, 80

Prayers regarding death, 234
Prejudices, of Jews, 134

Rabbinical Judaism
functioned to perserve Jewish identity,
102
problems of, 85
Redemption, in the prophets, 253-54
Rejection of Messiah, reasons for, 223-24
Resurrection
Jewish hope for closely tied to Messiah,
236-37
of Christians, 267
Resurrection of Jesus, 44, 228-33
attempts by critics to discredit, 229-33
importance to Christianity, 229
qualities of, 233
"Swoon theory," 230
"Telegram theory," 232
"Vision theory," 230-31
Return of Jews to Israel, eschatalogical
significance, 309-13
Ritual Law, 68
Roman rule at the time of the incarnation,
257

Salvation
for the righteous in Israel, 272
universal, 272
Seed of the woman (Gen. 3:15), 222
Separation of church and state, 155
Serpents in the wilderness, 222
Servant passage (Isaiah 53), 222
Son of God, in the Old Testament, 201-4
"Son of Man," Jesus' use of, 127
"Swoon theory." See Resurrection of
Jesus

"Tabernacling," related to Divine
self-disclosure, 195
Tannaitic rabbis, Jesus' teachings are found
in the writings of, 128
"Telegram theory." See Resurrection of
Jesus
Toledoth Yeshu, 25
Transfiguration of Jesus, 44
Transubstantiation, Jewish
misunderstanding of, 100
Trinity, 143
cannot be deduced philosophically, 191
intimated in the Old Testament, 183
proven only by revelation, 191
roles in the incarnation, 256-57

"Vision theory." See Resurrection of
Jesus

Western civilization, and the second
coming of Jesus, 280

"Yeshu," 146
Yom Kippur War, 304

Zadokites, Messianic hope of, 249
Zionism
and the state of Israel, 303-6
Christian assistance to, 67
Christians who were Zionists, 93
objectives of, 304
non-Jewish supporters of, 291-97
roots of, 303
supported by Evangelical Christians,
299-302
Zoroastrianism, influence on Jewish
Messianic concepts, 247

Index of Persons

Abrahams, Israel, on the Incarnation, 193
Adams, John, supported Zionism, 292
Alter, Roberts, "Israeli Culture and the
Jews," 304
Andersen, Hans Christian, supported
Zionism, 295
Aristotle, view of death, 237, 240

Asch, Sholem, The Apostle
biographical data, 21
Mary, 21, 147
on Jewishness of Paul, 21, 88, 125, 147
The Nazarene, 21, 147
rejected by Jews for his view of Jesus, 96
Augustine, teaching regarding Jews, 83

Baeck, Leo
biographical data, 24
critical of Christianity, 89
The Essence of Judaism, 24
"The Scope and Limitations of
Co-operation between Christians
and Jews," 133
Balfour, Arthur James
efforts in support of Zionism, 295
was a Christian Zionist, 93
Ballonoff, Martin, on American Jewish
misunderstanding of Israel, 307
Bargard, Warran, on Zionism, 306
Baur, F. C., said Paul was founder of
Christianity, 124
Ben-Chorin, Shalom
biographical data, 25
Bruder Jesus, 25
Jewishness of Jesus, 147
Mutter Mirjam, 25
Paulus, 25
Bendor-Samuel, T. H., 252
Benes, Edward, supported Zionism, 295
Ben-Gurion, David, called for Jews of all
countries to join Israeli army, 306
Berkovits, Eliezer, "Judaism in the
Post-Christian Era," 80-85
Bevin, Ernest, opponent of Zionism, 293
Bialik, Chaim Nachman, on mission and
miracle of Israel, 69
Birnbaum, Solomon, biographical data,
112
Blackstone, William E.
a Christian Zionist, 93
efforts in support of Zionism, 294-95
Bondel, David, supported Zionism, 292
Brainin, Reuben
biographical data, 27
"I seek Him," 27
Bravin, Dan, biographical data, 121
Brenner, Y. C. H., on Jewishness of the
New Testament, 70
Brightman, Thomas, Puritan supporter of
Zionism, 292
Brod, Max, attitude toward Paul, 88
Brother Daniel. *See* Rufeisen, Oswald
Brunner, Constantin
biographical data, 30
Der Judenhass und Die Juden, 30

Buber, Martin
biographical data, 31
collaborated with Franz Rosenzweig on
Hebrew Bible, 56
interpreted Paul's theology in terms of
mystery religions in *Two Types of
Faith,* 125
on Jewishness of Jesus, 147
on Judeo-Christian dialogue, 86-87
on "resist no evil," 68-69
Bunny, Edmund, supported Zionism, 292
Byron, Lord, *Cain* and *Hebrew Melodies*
supported Zionism, 294

Calvin, John, on contrast between Old and
New covenants, 176-78
Caspari, Karl Paul, convert to Christianity,
96
Cazalet, Edward, supported Zionism, 294
Charles, R. H., on John Hyrcanus as a
prophet, 244
Chesterton, G. K., *Francis of Assisi,* 121
Churchill, Winston, was a Christian
Zionist, 93
Chwolson, Daniel, convert to Christianity,
96
Clarke, Thomas, supported Zionism, 293
Cooper, Henry, biographical data, 228
Cournos, John, biographical data, 32
Cousins, Norman
biographical data, 34
"The Jewishness of Jesus," 152-56
Criswell, Dr. W. A., support of
evangelicals for Israel, 93
Cromwell, Oliver, supported Zionism, 291
Crossman, Richard, *Palestine Mission,*
296
Crum, Bartley C., *Behind the Silken
Curtain,* 296
Curie, Pierre and Marie, view of death,
237

Davies, W. D., on Jewishness of Paul, 126
Delitzsch, Franz
on Davidic covenant, 202
on "son of man," 127
teacher of J. I. Landsman, 260
Deutsch, Emmanuel, view of death, 238
Dewitz, Ludwig R., biographical data, 77

Dhu Nowar, persecuted Christians, 111
Disraeli, Benjamin
  biographical data, 268
  convert to Christianity, 96
Djilas, Milovan, on effects of communism, 282
Dobbs, Kildate, on dual allegiance of Jews, 307
Doddridge, Philip, supported Zionism, 293
Draxe, Thomas, supported Zionism, 292
Dreyfus, Alfred, trial of, 303
Dunant, Jean Henry, supported Zionism, 295
Dunkelman, Ben, *Dual Allegiance*, 307
Durham, James, supported Zionism, 292
Durkheim, Emil, on importance of the holocaust and the creation of Israel, 71

Edersheim, Alfred
  converted to Christianity, 96
  Life and Times of Jesus the Messiah, 96, 247
  on Messiah's personality, 247
Eigeles, Marion, on Jewishness of Hebrew Christians, 142
Einstein, Albert
  biographical data, 40
  view of Christianity, 40-41
Eisen, Max, *Christian Missions to Jews in North America and Great Britain*, 133
Eliot, George, (Mary Ann Evans), supported Zionism, 294
Ellison, H. L., biographical data, 124
Enelow, Hyman G., biographical data, 42
Ezra, Aben, on "kiss the Son," 204

Feldman, Emanual, on death, 235
Felgenhauer, Paulus, supported Zionism, 292
Fin, James, supported Zionism, 293
Finkelstein, Louis, on Israel and redemption, 69
Flannery, Edward H., *The Anguish of the Jews*, 81
Flusser, David
  biographical data, 43
  Jesus, 43
  on Jewish converts to Christianity, 138
Freedman, David N., biographical data, 98

Freehof, Solomon B.
  biographical data, 46
  on uniqueness of Jesus, 122
Freuder, Samuel, spoke against evangelism of Jews, 133

Gair, Bernard B., biographical data, 264
George, David Lloyd, was a Christian Zionist, 93
Gill, John, supported Zionism, 293
Gitlin, Emmanuel M., biographical data, 243
Gittelsohn, Roland B., article "Not so Simple, Mr. Cousins" rebuked, 152-56
Goldberg, Louis, biographical data, 80
Granados, Jorge Garcia, *The Rebirth of Israel*, 296
Greenbaum, Emmanuel S., testimony of, 317-20
Grotius, Hugo, supported Zionism, 292

Ha-am, Ahad, political issues of Zionism, 306
Halevi, Judah, ethnic interpretation of Judaism, 90
Halevi, Yehuda, *Alchazri*, 191
Harnack, Adolf, *The Essence of Christianity*, 24
Hechler, William H., *The Restoration of the Jews to Palestine According to the Prophets*, 295
Herberg, Will, *Protestant, Catholic, Jew*, 132
Hertzberg, Arthur, on evangelism of Jews, 92
Herzl, Theodor, *The Jewish State*, 285, 303
Heschel, Abraham Joshua, "No Religion Is an Island," 77-79
Hirsh, Karl Jakob, testimony of, 321-24
Hobbs, Thomas, view of death, 240
Holger, Oliger Pauli, supported Zionism, 295
Hollingsworth, A. G. H., supported Zionism, 293
House, Francis H., on differences between Judaism and Christianity, 132

Isaac of Troki, on Jewishness of Jesus, 147

Jacob, Walter
 attitude toward Paul, 88
 on ethnic interpretation of Judaism, 90
 on Judeo-Christian dialogue, 87-88
Jocz, Jakob, biographical data, 86
Johnson, A. R., on Yahweh as redeemer, 253-54

Kac, Arthur W., biographical data, 92
Kimchi, David, on messianic interpretation of "kiss the Son," 204
King, Edward, supported Zionism, 292
Kiss, Serena Rosengarten, testimony of, 325-27
Klausner, Joseph G.
 biographical data, 48
 Jesus of Nazareth, 68
 Life of Jesus, on "Yeshu," 146
 The Messianic Idea in Israel, 48
Kligerman, Aaron Judah, biographical data, 213
Knell, Paul, supported Zionism, 291
Kohler, Kaufmann
 biographical data, 51
 doctrine of God, 144
Kung, Hans
 dialogue with Pinchas E. Lapide, 12-13
 Signposts for the Future, 12

Landau, Moshe, on economic problems in Israel, 284-85
Landsman, Joseph Immanuel
 biographical data, 260
 Life of Jesus the Messiah, 260
Lapide, Pinchas E.
 dialogue with Hans Kung, 12-13
 Is This Not Joseph's Son? 13
 on David Flusser, 44-45
 Signposts for the Future, 12
Laubach, Frank, on effects of evangelism, 94
Leuner, Heinz David
 biographical data, 172
 When Compassion Was a Crime, 172
Levin, Tereska, in defense of Jewishness of Hebrew Christians, 140-41
Levinson, Steven B., biographical data, 309
Levison, Nahum, biographical data, 161

Lichtenstein, Isaac, testimony of, 328-32
Loudermilk, Walter Clay, *Palestine: Land of Promise,* 296
Lowth, Robert, supported Zionism, 293

Maas, Herman, efforts in behalf of Zionism, 296
McKelldin, Theodore R., supported Zionism, 296
Maimonides, Moses
 creed of, 138
 Guide for the Perplexed, 190-91
 on the Messianic hope, 203
 on person of Jesus, 26
 said Jesus was a forerunner of Messiah, 104
 Thirteen Principles of Faith, 125
Malbert, Mark, biographical data, 208
Marcion, rejected the Old Testament, 178
Marty, Martin E., *The New Shape of American Religion,* 132
Masaryk, Jan, supported Zionism, 295
Masaryk, Thomas Garrigue, supported Zionism, 295
Matt, Hershel, "How Shall a Believing Jew View Christianity?" 88
Mendelssohn, Moses
 effect of his philosphy on Jewish theology, 144
 pioneer in Judeo-Christian dialogue, 87
Mendelssohn-Bartholdy, Felix, converted to Christianity, 96
Milner, Alfred, was a Christian Zionist, 93
Milton, John, supported Zionism, 291
Montefiore, Claude G.
 biographical data, 53
 "father of liberalism," 89
 said Paul misunderstood Judaism, 125
Montefiore, Lydia, testimony of, 333-35
Montefiore, Moses, Jewish Zionist pioneer, 293
Musik, Viktor, supported Zionism, 295

Neander, Johann, Jewish convert to Christianity, 96
Neibuhr, Reinhold, opposed evangelism of Jews, 132
Newman, Elias, biographical data, 291
Newton, Thomas, supported Zionism, 292

Oliphant, Laurence, supported Zionism, 294

Paassen, Pierre Van, *The Forgotten Ally,* 296
Peyrere, Isaac de la, supported Zionism, 292
Philo
on the prophetic office, 244
philosophical definition of God, 190
Piper, Hal, "An Unrealized Dream," failure of Communism, 282
Pittenger, W. Norman, on the Incarnation, 192
Pliny, on the spread of Christianity, 211
Poling, Daniel A., supported Zionism, 296
Polish, David, on Jewish interest in Jesus, 70
Porter, Henry, supported Zionism, 293
Powell, Vasover, supported Zionism, 292
Poysner, Isaac Joseph
biographical data, 55
The Kingdom of the Messiah, 55

Reich, Max, biographical data, 116
Robinson, J. A. T., on the dating of John's gospel, 126
Rosenberg, Stuart E., on the shift to ethnic interpretation of Jewishness, 308
Rosenzweig, Franz
biographical data, 56
collaborated with Dr. Martin Buber on Hebrew Bible, 56
ethnic interpretation of Israel, 90
The Star of Redemption, 56
view of Christianity, 88
Rotenstreich, Nathan, on Jewish culture, 305
Roth, Philip, on problems of dialogue, 134
Rubinstein, Richard, attitude toward Paul, 88
Rufeisen, Oswald, refused citizenship in Israel, 136-42
Russell, Bertrand, pagan view of death, 237-38

Sadler, John, supported Zionism, 292
Safrai, S., *The Jewish People in the First Century,* 126

Samuel, Harcourt, biographical data, 256
Sandmel, Samuel
attitude toward Paul, 88
biographical data, 58
Schereschevsky, Bishop, convert to Christianity, 96
Schoeps, Hans Joachim
attitude toward Paul, 88
biographical data, 60
on Jewishness of Jesus, 147
on revelation outside Judaism, 88
Schonfield, Hugh J., *The Passover Plot,* 147
Scott, John, *The Destiny of Israel,* 293
Shaftesbury, Earl of, supported Zionism, 293
Shoemaker, Dr. Samuel M., view of death, 239
Simpson, W. W., *The Church and the Jewish People,* 132
Singer, Dr. Isidore, on changing Jewish attitude toward Jesus (*Jewish Encyclopedia*), 11
Smuts, General Jan Christaan, was a Christian Zionist, 93
Spinoza, effect of his philosophy on Jewish theology, 144
Stone, Nathan J., biographical data, 221
Sweazy, Dr. George E., on evangelism of Jews, 96

Talmadge, Frank Ephraim, *Disputation and Dialogue,* 12
Tillich, Paul, opposed active evangelism of Jews, 132-33

Vermes, Geza
biographical data, 62
Jesus the Jew, 62
Vossius, Gerhard John, supported Zionism, 292
Vossius, Isaac, supported Zionism, 292

Weinstock, Harris, biographical data, 63
Weizmann, Chaim, on Christian Zionists, 93
Werblowsky, Zwi, on evangelism of Jews, 134

Wergeland, Henrik, supported Zionism, 295

Wertheimer, Max, testimony of, 336-39

Whiston, William, supported Zionism, 293

Williams, Roger, supported Zionism, 292

Wilson, Dr. Edward, view of death, 239

Wingate, Orde C., supported Zionism, 93, 295

Wise, Stephen S., biographical data, 64

Witherby, Thomas, *An Attempt to Remove Prejudices Concerning the Jewish Nation,* 292

Wreschner, Lilly, on Jewishness of Hebrew Christians, 141-42

Young, Franklin W., "Jesus the Prophet: a Re-examination," 243

Zakkai, Yochanan ben, view of death, 238

Zarathrustra, background of, 248

Zeidman, Morris, biographical data, 109

Zweig, Ferdynand
  biographical data, 66
  "The Figure of Jesus on the Israeli Horizon" in *Israel: the Sword and the Harp,* 148
  on the impact of Jesus on modern Israel, 148-50
  on secularization of Judaism, 308